ENDURING RUIN

ENDURING RUIN

Environmental Destruction during the Irish Revolution

by

JUSTIN DOLAN STOVER

UNIVERSITY COLLEGE DUBLIN PRESS
PREAS CHOLÁISTE OLLSCOILE BHAILE ÁTHA CLIATH
2022

First published 2022
by University College Dublin Press
UCD Humanities Institute, Room H103,
Belfield,
Dublin 4

www.ucdpress.ie

Text and notes © Justin Dolan Stover, 2022

ISBN 978-19-1-08208-34

All rights reserved. No part of this publication may be reproduced, stored in a retrieval system, or transmitted in any form or by any means, electronic, photocopying, recording or otherwise without the prior permission of the publisher.

CIP data available from the British Library

The right of the author to be identified as the author of this work has been asserted by him

Typeset in Dublin by Gough Typesetting Limited
Text design by Lyn Davies
Printed in the UK on acid-free paper by CPI Antony Rowe, Chippenham, Wiltshire

For my parents

Russ and Colleen

Contents

	Acknowledgements	ix
	List of Illustrations	xi
	Introduction	xiii
1	The Destruction of Dublin: Easter 1916	1
2	Contested Spaces & Militarised Landscapes	29
3	Ireland's Fifth Column: Environment & Landscape in the War of Independence	53
4	'The Curse of Ananias Greenwood': Crown Force Reprisals & Displacement	85
5	Cultivating Environmental Victimhood in Ireland and Abroad	112
6	Destruction in the Fog of War	135
	Conclusion	152
	Bibliography	154
	Index	167

Acknowledgements

I am happy to acknowledge the immeasurable debt I owe to those who inspired, guided and supported this project, and whose encouragement ensured its completion. Ryan Jones, Kevin Marsh and Richard Tucker sparked my interest in environmental history, and I am grateful for their encouragement. Many others were generous with their time, opened their homes to me on research trips and were reassuring. They include Marie Coleman, Anne Dolan, Hal Hodson, James Marron, Tim and Kara Bearpark, Simon and Liz Connor, James and Susie Murphy-O'Connor, Daniel Jordan, Kevin O'Sullivan, William Murphy, Malcolm Sen, Kevin Whelan, Oliver P. Rafferty, Brian Ó Conchubhair, Tim McMahon, Anna Teekell, Nicholas Wolf, Kelly Sullivan and Kate Costello-Sullivan.

I am grateful to the various sponsors, institutions and funding bodies that supported this project, including the Idaho State University College of Arts & Letters; the Idaho Humanities Council; Mike Cronin, Mark Duncan, Thea Gilien, Claire McGowan and Boston College Ireland; James H. Murphy, Joan Reilly and the Boston College Irish Studies program; Nessa Cronin and the Moore Institute at NUI Galway; and Linda Connolly, Jennifer Redmond, John Paul Newman, Terence Dooley and the Maynooth University Social Science Institute. Ciara Meehan, Sarah Campbell, Kristopher Phillips, Jaime Campbell, Eamon Darcy, Ryan Keating, Hannah Cutting-Jones, Denise and Greg McReynolds, and Zack Heern deserve special recognition as they carried me through a particularly difficult 2020. Jason Myers read drafts of the text, offered much-needed direction and clarity, and was immensely supportive. A special recognition and thank you go to my children, Liam and Catherine, who patiently endured my absences and distraction while writing this book.

Finally, my thanks to the readers who gave their time and expertise to the manuscript, and to University College Dublin Press and its Executive Editor, Noelle Moran, whose steady reassurance brought this project to completion. It's serendipitous that this book should be published with UCD Press as the Belfield campus was my first stop in Ireland nearly 20 years ago. It feels good to be home.

Justin Dolan Stover
Pocatello
November 2022

List of Illustrations

Preliminary image

1. 'Their Way', *Freeman's Journal*, 4 August 1922. With thanks to Irish Newspaper Archive and the *Freeman's Journal*.

Plate Section

2. Mounted photograph, possibly taken from Henry Street, of the rear of the GPO showing extensive structural damage; many of the buildings on Moore Street and Henry Street have been totally demolished. Nelson's Pillar is silhouetted against the skyline. Reproduced by kind permission of UCD Archives, Desmond FitzGerald Photographs P80/PH/1.

3. Mounted photograph of a soldier on duty outside a ruined building, possibly near the Munster and Leinster Bank on Sackville Street; the gables of other badly damaged buildings are visible in the background. Reproduced by kind permission of UCD Archives, Desmond FitzGerald Photographs P80/PH/3.

4. Two mounted photographs (with some differences of detail) of very badly damaged buildings, possibly on Sackville Street; the foreground contains twisted metal including the remains of a tram and a sign advertising Nestle's. Reproduced by kind permission of UCD Archives, Desmond FitzGerald Photographs P80/PH/10.

5. Photograph of a burned-out building, possibly the creamery in Ballymacelligott, County Kerry; the roof has collapsed at one end and the interior has been gutted; a water tank is lying on the grass outside; a sign on the side of the building which is partially fire-damaged reads, 'The Ballymacelligott Cooperative Agricultural...'. Reproduced by kind permission of UCD Archives, Desmond FitzGerald Photographs P80/PH/15.

6. Destruction in Cork after the official reprisal of the city. Reproduced by kind permission of the Imperial War Museum, Major General Peter Strickland Collection, Q107757.

7. Photograph of a group of men viewing the gutted interior of an imposing entrance hall surrounded by debris. The caption reads: 'Labour Commission and Cork LCC, Town Hall, Cork.' Reproduced by kind permission of UCD Archives, Desmond FitzGerald Photographs P80/PH/18.

8. British Army road cleaning operations. Reproduced by kind permission of the Imperial War Museum, Major General Peter Strickland Collection, Q107765.

9. British Army road cleaning operations. Reproduced by kind permission of the Imperial War Museum, Major General Peter Strickland Collection, Q107766.

10. British Army road cleaning operations at Carrignovac, 10 June 1921. Reproduced by kind permission of the Imperial War Museum, Major General Peter Strickland Collection, Q107762.

11. British Army troops at the bridge near Kinsale blown up by the IRA. Reproduced by kind permission of the Imperial War Museum, Major General Peter Strickland Collection, Q071704.

12. British troops standing on the remains of a bridge in Clydagh Valley, Reproduced by kind permission of the Imperial War Museum, Major General Peter Strickland Collection, Q107769.

13. Remains of Dripsey Bridge, County Cork after IRA action, showing an Intelligence car, Reproduced by kind permission of the Imperial War Museum, Major General Peter Strickland Collection, Q107760.

14. British Army officers inspecting damage to a bridge on the Ballinspittle road (inflicted by the IRA), whilst local labourers are employed in repairs. Reproduced by kind permission of the Imperial War Museum, Major General Peter Strickland Collection, Q071706.

15. Photograph by W. D. Hogan of the ruined interior of the Four Courts. Debris and broken pillars lie around. The imposing statue of a judge has been badly damaged. Reproduced by kind permission of UCD Archives, Desmond FitzGerald Photographs P80/PH/32.

16. Photograph by W. D. Hogan of a gentleman standing in the ruins of part of the Four Courts surrounded by debris and broken pillars. He is holding what is possibly the remnant of a document from the explosion in the treasury of the PRO. Reproduced by kind permission of UCD Archives, Desmond FitzGerald Photographs P80/PH/33.

17. Photograph by W. D. Hogan of the gutted interior of a building; the interior consists of a mass of twisted metal; through the breached walls a more imposing building, also damaged, is visible [possibly the mezzanine storage treasury of the Public Record Office although the window apertures are church-like]. Reproduced by kind permission of UCD Archives, Desmond FitzGerald Photographs P80/PH/97.

Introduction

To get the fruit—cut down the tree.

In early August 1922, amongst columns that highlighted the Provisional Government's advance on republican positions throughout Ireland, the *Freeman's Journal* printed a political cartoon entitled 'Their Way'.[1] The accusatory image depicted 'Irregulars' – an incumbent pro-government term meant to delegitimise the anti-Treaty republican faction – attempting to haul down a tree marked 'Ireland'.[2] The caption, 'To get the fruit – cut down the tree', was as much a critique of republicans' imprudent military strategy during the Irish Civil War as it was a condemnation of their destructive methods that constituted that strategy. The cartoon seems appropriate in the context of summer 1922. Stand-offs in Dublin and throughout the country between former comrades, factions entrenched behind respective ideological positions on the Anglo-Irish Treaty and the degree of freedom it provided for a 26-county Irish Free State, destroyed a significant portion of the Capital and wore a trail of destruction behind republicans' withdrawal towards the south and west of the country. 'Their Way' struck a superior moral tone above what were alleged to be illegitimate guerrilla methods, one that circumvented the fact that Ireland's recent conflict against British forces had been fought in the same destructive manner.[3]

In her study of French landscapes destroyed as a result of the Great War, Emmanuelle Danchin states: 'Ruins are the first direct and visible consequence of a conflict.'[4] This is true of Ireland's experience of revolution between the years 1916 and 1923, when rebellion, guerrilla warfare, counter-insurgency efforts and civil war caused damage that ranged from broken window panes to the wholesale destruction of towns. Conflict changed the composition of many urban and rural landscapes, and transformed people's association with their surroundings. Bullet-chipped columns showed that a post office was once a rebel headquarters; a home, business or social club, raided for arms, intelligence or as an act of terror, never again provided the same degree of comfort, security or leisure; the low rumble of a lorry truck, the smell of paraffin or the sound of a pronounced English accent modified and militarised many civilian spaces.

Conflict also proceeded outside direct confrontation and material destruction and could often be found throughout the country in the tension surrounding environmental change. Altered landscapes often provided subtle indications that conflict was present. Something as simple as a tri-colour flag wafting above a municipal building showcased defiance; its removal and replacement with a Union Jack attempted to restore order and counter sedition. Station platforms crammed with Sinn Féin organisers and a curious public eager to get a glimpse of discharged prisoners transformed train depots into political rallying points, while to chance upon road barricades, such as fallen trees or trenches, exhibited a rebel presence in an area. Environmental manipulation was an almost unremitting process that took various forms to alter both landscapes and people's places within them. Enduring ruin meant attesting to the violent events that damaged Irish environments throughout the revolution, while also confronting the spaces transformed by that violence in the years that followed.

This book is a story of the nature, scope and embodiment of destruction in Ireland during the revolutionary period. It shows how Irish environments – rural, urban, natural and built-up – were understood, altered and damaged throughout this formative time. It explores the devastating effects of the 1916 Easter Rising, including sensory responses to war and destruction. It is about the widespread, often banal landscape manipulation from which the Irish Republican Army's guerrilla war proceeded. It observes the social displacement that resulted from the Crown forces' destruction of homes and businesses, and how the Irish newspaper media and international bodies sympathetic to the Irish cause aligned this destruction to existing Great War atrocity narratives. This book is not a fundamental environmental history per se, nor is it a definitive study of damage that occurred during the period or efforts to compensate or repair it. Rather, it examines aspects of the political revolution and military conflict through an environmental lens and attempts to centre the historical narrative on the landscapes that hosted violence. In a sense, it is as focused on the tree as the person pulling it down.

Methods

The county-centric methodology emerged to present intimate experiences of political change and violence against broader narratives that were previously unable to illustrate local nuances. It is a logical approach given the imbalanced geography of revolutionary activity in Ireland, and the archive's conventional organisation hierarchy.[5] Most appropriately, work produced on this model has highlighted how some activities within a particular region did not represent the movement as whole, revising interpretations of guerrilla behaviour and challenging conventional wisdom on the movement's romantic insinuations and parochial support.[6] Environmental damage can be observed within a similar context. The types, locations and pace of environmental damage reflected the ecology, topography and human development of a specific place, *as well as* the initiative of individuals who operated in it. But prioritising environmental studies in our own time does not retroactively activate their prominence in the record, and much must be read against the grain. Damage was often underreported or generalised. Criminal Injury Claims for malicious damage, Witness Statements and Brigade Activity Reports help to localise affected landscapes, but some instances were simply too numerous, and damage too compounded, to report in detail. A tree was a tool, a barrack an obstacle. Their destruction served greater ends, and details of the method of their destruction were often discounted, reduced to general descriptions or overlooked entirely. For these reasons, a complete picture of environmental damage in Ireland is problematic.

Rather than pursuing a quantitative tally of each road trenched, tree felled or building destroyed, landscapes, built features and refined or spoiled natural elements should be understood collectively as enduring a war of material attrition. Sites often experienced repeated attacks before being completely destroyed, and their surrounding territory was repeatedly blockaded and cleared throughout the period. Concentrations and patterns of damage, widespread and unique phenomena, and categorical destruction (of trees, roads, barracks, from IRA activity and Crown force reprisals) proceed here in an effort to analyse environmental damage in Ireland on a national scale throughout the Irish Revolution.

Damage to the built environment might be more narrowly categorised to better understand its types and frequency, and as a way to navigate its social and political impacts. Environmental destruction complemented the IRA's overall strategy to erode British rule in Ireland by isolating and eliminating its security installations. Such low-level destruction was often transregionally coordinated to great effect, as the 1920 Easter arson campaign demonstrates. The permeating republican intimidation campaign lent itself to this work but was more immediately apparent in local communities, where the impacts of wrecked shops and creameries, and boycotted goods and businesses, affected individual and collective behaviour. Military supply and transportation logistics comprise a pervading category of destruction in environmental and military contexts. The IRA targeted, commandeered, burned or sank lorry trucks and cars, and procured oil and petrol stores to reduce enemy mobility and capacity. Conversely, the Royal Irish Constabulary (RIC) and British Army conducted raids that dislocated individuals from their homes and eroded, through destruction or repeated raids, the security and valuable cover they provided. Damage to windows, furniture and doors is frequently cited, and theft was a common occurrence, while reprisals against property were levelled as deterrents to local rebel activity.

Because of this variety and the very large scale and spectrum of ruin it represents, environmental damage has been documented categorically against the revolution's familiar phases. While intending a holistic approach, oversights are inevitable due to the sheer volume of recorded incidents, in addition to the fact that many individual claims were revised or embellished to ensure legal hearing and maximum compensation. Also, it should not be taken that urban damage was divorced from a rural catalyst or logistical support. Quite the opposite: operations were fluid and interdependent. Ambushes staged on country roads sparked punitive attacks on urban centres, while rural sabotage, such as felling trees and trenching, supported attacks on isolated barracks and prevented pursuit or withdrawal.

Outline

The book begins with the 1916 Easter Rising, which damaged and destroyed a number of public and commercial buildings in and around Dublin. Much of this destruction followed from nationalist rebels' use of civic buildings as defensive positions and British efforts to dislodge them. Rebel strongholds, which were concentrated on and adjacent to Dublin's main thoroughfare of Sackville Street (now O'Connell Street), claimed numerous homes and businesses, which succumbed to fire, looting and artillery shelling. But broken glass, toppled stone and charred tenements represent but one aspect of the damage. The fires that ravaged the General Post Office (GPO) and surrounding buildings released immeasurable levels of smoke into the atmosphere over several days. At times, fire consumed more than timber and plaster, compounding its imprint; large stocks of oil and chemicals consumed by fire exploded and filled the air with thick smoke. The weather, too, underscored the week's larger impact. An unseasonably warm spring, for example, emphasised dead bodies throughout the city. This chapter presents the multifaceted experiences of landscape manipulation and contamination through sabotage, barricading, looting, urban destruction and pollution, and the resulting threats to public health during and after the 1916 Easter Rising. Each complement a more holistic understanding of the Rising and its broader interpretive scope. It shows the rebels' destructive foresight and capabilities in acquiring and refining explosives and their application throughout the Rising. Sensory history is also present here, explored through Easter Week's various toxic and sonic environments and their impact on combatants and witnesses. The immediate post-rebellion period presented additional environmental challenges. Coffin shortages, temporary internments and a gravedigger strike taxed Dublin's ability to receive, process and bury the dead. The city itself resisted an ultimate capitulation. Smoking debris, rubble and shattered glass remained in the streets in the months and years that followed, to be repurposed for rebuilding efforts and weaponised by riotous crowds.

Ireland's cultural revolution preceded its political revolution, present in the foundation and growth of the Gaelic League and Gaelic Athletic Association decades prior to that of Sinn Féin. However, a simultaneous cultural and political maturity may be seen in the development of nationalist spatial character after 1916. Chapter Two shows how demonstrations, protests and receiving parties for political prisoners politicised civic space as spontaneous platforms for dissent. Nationalist symbolism also challenged colonialised spaces. Republican tri-colours were hoisted onto buildings and trees – a low-risk act of defiance and national reclamation. Police and military often struggled to remove these markers, and their methods regularly showcased reactionary violence that damaged landscapes and the built environment. Landscapes were effectively militarised in this manner, but Crown forces cannot be wholly blamed. Republicans effectively militarised numerous civilian and commercial spaces in their raids for arms, theft and transport of explosive material, and training exercises. This chapter moves beyond the narrative around republican Ireland's ostracism of the RIC and their families by exploring the intentional manipulation of their social and professional environments. Serving, lodging or even acknowledging policemen carried penalties that either threatened physical violence or, more commonly, preyed upon the offender's property and business. Rather than focusing on the relationship between the two groupings, as has traditionally been done, this chapter shifts the focus to the sites of interactions and considers how they shaped engagement.

The Easter Rising inaugurated what would be a series of large-scale and concentrated episodes of urban destruction during the War of Independence, 1919–1921. However, the Irish Republican Army's program of widespread, steady, low-intensity landscape manipulation and damage throws these intensely destructive events into stark relief. Chapter Three explores how the IRA and its supporters enlisted the land as a native fifth column in their guerrilla war against Crown forces. In doing so, it sabotaged bridges and roads through demolition and trenching to prevent pursuit, and felled thousands of trees and scattered stonewalls upon roads to herd enemy convoys into ambush zones or prevent their retreat or reinforcement. The land was also implicated in aligning Irish society to the republican program. Pre-emptive graves dug outside the homes of non-compliant civilians and State officials curbed revolutionary dissent. These types of landscape manipulation represent the sort of consistent, low-intensity engagement that characterised the Irish Revolution much more than the sensationalised exploits of ambush and assassination. As such, this chapter delivers important insight on the relationship between collective violence and environmental destruction, on the weather's influence on the pace and scale of guerrilla activity, and on advantageous or favourably prepared landscapes as geographic indicators of conflict.

The British Army and the RIC and its Auxiliary forces targeted a variety of private and commercial spaces in their pursuit and harassment of rebels. These included private homes, meeting halls, farms, markets and co-operative dairy creameries, as well as public spaces such as parks, sporting fields and entire commercial districts. Chapter Four examines Britain's counter-insurrection policies and tactics, which were environmentally punitive and extended the militarisation of public space. Raids on homes where only women and children were present further eroded conventional military boundaries. Attacks on Ireland's co-operative creameries disrupted the rural economy and left a trail of destruction. Overall, counter-insurgency left a damning legacy of physical destruction and terror in Ireland.

Irish nationalists, foreign observers and journalists cultivated this narrative in the light of the German Army's occupation of Belgium and northern France during the Great War, the subject of Chapter Five. Public memory of the Great War in Europe helped nationalist Ireland articulate its political and environmental victimhood to international audiences. It also spurred the formation and funding of Irish relief societies abroad. Though often dramatised to ensure impact, centres of Irish support in North America and Europe emphatically echoed Ireland's suffering. New York's 'Friends of Irish Freedom' reprinted reports from the Irish White Cross and *Irish Bulletin*, which described episodes of arson terror, while a variety of French news outlets and Irish ex-patriot societies in Paris and throughout the Francophone world empathised and identified with Ireland's war-torn landscapes. This chapter explores how environmental damage mobilised public opinion in Europe and beyond to internationalise the Irish Revolution and align its cause to the moral questions on which the Great War was fought.

The Irish landscape experienced a unique form of collateral damage throughout the revolution, one often suffered outside the pretence of militarism. The ebb and flow of security and control, exercised by the IRA and Crown forces, presented opportunities for pre-revolution grievances to re-emerge in the fog of war. Agrarian sabotage occurred in connection to local rivalries, land jealousy and unresolved land transfers, and included the destruction of fences, walls and earthen boundaries, cattle maiming, and the burning of fields, crops, ricks of turf and farming implements. Each of the revolution's preceding categories of environmental destruction featured during the Irish Civil War. However, their direct and indirect impacts on both active combatants and civilians amplified the destruction. Many endured ruined landscapes and infrastructure that impeded their livelihoods and complicated independent Ireland's emergence into statehood. Overall, the final chapter reinforces many of the book's themes and demonstrates the complexities and opportunities an environmental approach to the Irish Revolution provides.

NOTES

1. *Freeman's Journal*, 4 Aug. 1922, p. 4.
2. On morally divisive terminology between civil war opponents, see Stathis N. Kalyvas, *The Logic of Violence in Civil War* (Cambridge, 2006; 2013 edn), p. 17.
3. Asymmetric warfare, loosely defined by Keith Jeffery, is where 'apparently weak insurgent forces use imagination, improvisation and technical expertise to challenge materially better-resourced, and ostensibly more powerful, orthodox military formations.' Keith Jeffery, 'Forward', in W. H. Kautt, *Ambushes and Armour: The Irish Rebellion, 1919–1921* (Dublin: Irish Academic Press, 2010), p. xv.
4. Emmanuelle Danchin, *Les Temps des Ruines 1914–1921* (Presses Universitaires de Rennes, 2015), p. 19.
5. Peter Hart writes 'The county is the primary unit of analysis in this and previous studies for a number of reasons. As it was the standard administrative unit, using it allows easy comparison with census and (some) electoral figures.' Peter Hart, 'The geography of revolution in Ireland 1917–1923', in *Past & Present* 155 (May 1997), p. 146.
6. Michael Hopkinson dismissed 'single-cause explanations' for revolutionary activity, and downplayed activism at the local or regional level as indicative of the county or province to which it belonged. 'Too many conclusions have been drawn from work on limited regions and too many generalisations made about the contributions of whole counties. The more important question is how such part-time, untrained, under-resourced force could succeed to the extent it did. The answer to that lies in the nature of guerrilla warfare and the weakness of British policy.' Michael Hopkinson, *The Irish War of Independence* (Dublin, 2004 edn), p. 201.

CHAPTER ONE

THE DESTRUCTION OF DUBLIN: EASTER 1916

INTRODUCTION

The Leinster hurling final between Dublin and Laois was played on 19 March 1916 in Tullamore, with proceeds benefitting the local Wolfe Tone memorial fund.[1] Dublin succumbed to the reigning All-Ireland champions 5–2 to 3–4 on a wet field that slowed play. Two separate teams vying for supremacy reflected the prevailing social and political milieu. Tensions between moderate and advanced nationalists were high at this time, particularly in places like Tullamore where the population of approximately 5,000 maintained a significant pro-war stance behind the 452 men it had sent to the front.[2] Clear differences had emerged within nationalist opinion at this time. On one side, the Irish Volunteers, an advanced nationalist paramilitary association under the leadership of Eoin MacNeill, rejected Ireland's role in the war. On the other, the Irish Parliamentary Party, the more moderate brand of Irish political opinion, and its leader John Redmond supported the war effort. More than 22,000 Irish National Volunteers, those who had maintained their support for the war under Redmond's leadership, enlisted or were called up from reserves by March 1916.[3] The day after the Leinster hurling final, these divergent attitudes turned violent.

It is unknown whether 'Sinn Féiners' waving republican flags at Sunday's match incited confrontation, but on the following evening a crowd of over 100 young men – perhaps friends, relatives or sympathisers of the 21 Tullamore men who had died on various fronts since the war's commencement – descended on the Irish Volunteers and Cumann na mBan meeting hall, waving Union Jacks and jeering 'down with the Sinn Féiners.'[4] Peadar Bracken and Joe Wrafter escorted Cumann na mBan women home under a hail of stones and other projectiles.[5] Members of the RIC arrived on the scene but allowed the mob to operate; ultimately, they entered the hall and attempted to search those present, but were met with resistance. A stand-off ensued, during which Sergeant Aherne was shot in the arm and chest. County Inspector Crane, District-Inspector Fitzgerald and Head-Constable Stuard were also wounded during a hand-to-hand struggle that resulted in one policeman receiving a hurley blow to the head. In the end, four Irish Volunteers – Thomas Byrne, Joseph Morris, Henry McNally and Joe Wrafter – were arrested and three revolvers confiscated.[6] Another nine men were detained during the week and charged under the Defence of the Realm Regulations (a broad set of wartime legislation meant to ensure security) with 'attempting to cause disaffection among the civilian population'.[7] What was reported as the attempted murder of RIC officers featured in several regional and national newspapers and was passed up the chain of command to Dublin Castle.[8]

As much as prevailing social and political divisions had stoked violence, so did they yield alternative interpretation. Patrick Pearse, a Romantic nationalist poet, teacher, and emerging figure within the underground revolutionary Irish Republican Brotherhood

(IRB), presented the event in a different light. A student at his school, St Enda's, later recalled how Pearse claimed that the Tullamore incident represented 'the first blood spilled and first blow struck in defence of the Volunteers' right to carry arms'.[9] Other protests, violence and even deaths connected to the nationalist movement had occurred prior to the 1916 Easter Rising, but the Tullamore scuffle foreshadowed a different type of violence that would be experienced throughout Ireland's revolutionary period – the destruction of built-up spaces and natural environments. After the police withdrew, the hostile crowd resumed its assault on the Sinn Féin meeting hall. Its windows were shattered, along with the large glass display pane in Malachy Scally's drapery shop on the opposite side of the street. The mob also allegedly made a 'complete wreck' of the hall and its furniture.[10] Irish Volunteers observed a self-imposed house arrest throughout the week; the influence of police and priests prevented attacks on their homes and persons.[11]

The destruction of the Sinn Féin hall in Tullamore represented a growing overlap between radical nationalism's physical and ideological influence on Irish politics and the consequential violence against individuals and destruction of physical spaces and property it often provoked.[12] It is an often overlooked but significant episode that foreshadowed the nature of revolutionary violence to come – one that recognised landscapes, buildings and infrastructure as platforms for resistance as well as legitimate targets. In many ways, the 1916 Easter Rising initiated this process on a grand scale.

Preparing the Field

Ireland's political and social conversion from moderate nationalism to populist republicanism occurred in the foreground of concentrated material loss, landscape manipulation and resulting waste and pollution. This damage and degradation occurred in varying waves of intensity, perpetrated directly and indirectly through the activities of, and support for, the Irish Volunteers, Irish Citizen Army, Cumann na mBan, the RIC and the British Army. The 1916 Easter Rising demonstrates a concentrated episode of this impact and was the most significant spike in urban destruction throughout the broader revolutionary period. The rebellion, positions established to enact it, attempts to contain and quell it, and looted shops and businesses resulted in significant damage to both commercial and private property, transportation infrastructure and municipal services, and contaminated the air, water and soil to varying degrees. Though incomparable to the lives lost and affected through insurrectionary violence, the immediate and consequential damage to Dublin's city centre, suburbs and outlying posts demonstrates how the rebellion altered more than ideological or political outlooks and left a lasting impact on the streets of Dublin.

In other ways, what Dublin Castle termed 'seditious' activities, such as recruiting for the Volunteers, drilling, attending lectures on guerrilla warfare and preparing war materials – particularly bomb making – strengthened and extended a social and spatial framework around which the revolutionary movement became embedded. Landscape intimacy – one's familiarity with local landscapes and recognition of their application in war – was a key element in this regard, both during the 1916 rebellion and throughout the revolutionary period. Much of the Easter Rising's potential success relied on preparation and participants' knowledge of the city, its friendly quarters, its reinforcement routes and its potential weapons caches. This was particularly true when requisitioning materials for explosives and establishing reliable safe-houses and arms dumps. For instance, gelignite, an explosive jelly used in mining, was collected from diverse sources and stored in various unassuming spaces. Acquisition sites included the De Selby Quarries at Jobstown, the Roundwood Reservoir Works at Stillorgan, Dolphin's Barn Brick Works and various storehouses under police protection. This practice continued throughout the revolutionary period and sources extended beyond Ireland.[13] From Glasgow, IRB member Seamus Reader directed raids on the Hamilton Coal Mines Magazine,[14] while Michael O'Flanagan and others spent the better part of 1915 obtaining 'from any and every source explosive material', which he stockpiled in his house before escorting it, concealed in furniture, to Constance Markiewicz and Fianna Éireann boy scouts in Dublin.[15]

Gelignite significantly expanded the republican movement's destructive capacity. It is a versatile material that can be moulded at will or stored and concealed in damp conditions. This flexibility proved vital to numerous operations, but it also carried health risks. Beyond unintended detonations, intimate exposure could be hazardous. Andrew McDonnell explained how in 1917, attempts to defrost gelignite, which had been 'packed in biscuit tins' and buried in south Dublin, produced fumes that caused 'a sort of flu feeling – headache, lightness, etc.'.[16] Catherine Byrne experienced similar side effects after smuggling 'the stuff' from Belfast to Dublin following its delivery from Glasgow in 1918. She, too, carried the gelignite close to her person, which inadvertently transferred poison into her body. 'It was also on that account,' she recalled 34 years later, 'that I had to get my first pair of glasses; my sight was affected and I have had to wear glasses ever since.'[17] The Daly brothers, Francis and Seamus, also worked closely with gelignite and established a bomb and grenade factory in the back kitchen of a rented house in Clontarf. The IRB ordered production to increase throughout February and March 1916. Additional facilities were established in Kimmage and at Liberty Hall to meet demands. Bomb making and gelignite collection continued up until Easter Sunday, undertaken by a spectrum of individuals at various locations with a view towards building an arsenal and extending rebellion beyond Easter Week.[18]

Gelignite's potential to affect the peace was not lost on the Irish police, and foiled attempts to procure it were sensationalised in the national press as evidence of premeditated sedition on the part of would-be revolutionaries.[19] Contemporary RIC reports linked together stolen explosives, heightened anti-war agitation amongst known Sinn Féin members, distribution of seditious pamphlets and the growth of the Irish Volunteer movement. Concerns peaked in early February 1916 when 60 lbs of explosives were discovered in a Kildare field culvert.[20] The same week, the High Court acquitted Alex McCabe, a schoolteacher and Irish Volunteer from Sligo, who had been arrested the previous November for possession of, amongst other things, gelignite, detonators and fuses.[21] McCabe's was a highly visible attempt to secure and potentially distribute weapons and explosives; other efforts were hidden in plain sight. In mid-February, the 'Our Magazine' column within the *Anglo-Celt* produced an ostensibly innocent shopping list of chemicals and other compounds required to produce a range of high explosives – all of which excluded cotton, the subject of the article's misleading title.[22] But potential threats to national defence failed to appreciably alarm other government authorities.[23] On the whole, the Defence of the Realm Act legislation countered overt activism (several Volunteer organisers were deported to Britain prior to the Rising), while pro-war antagonism curtailed other localised efforts. Charles

Townshend described the Volunteers' rebuilding process in the years before the Easter Rising as 'painfully slow', with the country exhibiting a 'persistent public hostility' towards the movement.[24] Castle perceptions of the Irish Volunteers and Sinn Féin, which were often taken as one and the same, downplayed their significance.[25] RIC Inspector General Neville Chamberlain considered the Irish Volunteers to be 'numerically insignificant' (September 1915), and not led by men of position or influence (October and November 1915).[26] By March 1916, his position changed. Coupled with growing anti-conscription sentiment, Chamberlain believed that permitting free reign to such seditious elements would have disastrous results, an opinion he communicated to the Under Secretary, Sir Matthew Nathan:

> If the speeches of the Irish Volunteer leaders and articles in Sinn Féin journals have any meaning at all it must be that the force is being organized with a view to insurrection, and in the event of the enemy being able to effect [sic] a landing in Ireland, the Volunteers could no doubt delay the dispatch of troops to the scene [of insurrection] by blowing up the railway and bridges, provided the organizers were at liberty to plan and direct the operations.[27]

Despite its membership growth (the RIC set Irish Volunteer membership at approximately 8,000 at this time),[28] authorities viewed its weapons to be archaic, improvised and undersupplied, and its leadership disorganised. While this was correct to varying degrees, Chamberlain's foresight acknowledged a sequence of notable factors that might lead to rebellion in Ireland. He recognised the Great War as fulfilling the Fenian idiom of his youth; that 'England's difficulty is Ireland's opportunity'; that the French had exploited Ireland's position on Britain's vulnerable flank in the eighteenth century and Germany could very well do the same; and finally, that a rebellion did not require the Irish Volunteers to field a large or well-equipped force. Despite mixed views, fears of a nationalist backlash gave pause towards actively suppressing the Volunteers. The arrest of Roger Casement on Good Friday 1916, and confiscation of his escorted cargo of 20,000 German rifles aboard the *Aud*, calmed anxieties regarding an imminent revolt.[29]

Eoin MacNeill publicly rescinded mobilisation orders for Easter Sunday following Casement's capture, which the IRB-dominated military council privately overturned, making for a confusing weekend. The rebellion proceeded on 24 April 1916, a day later than originally planned, and was executed on the whole through sabotage, preparatory fortification and adaptable resistance – tactics that sustained the Irish Republic over six days.[30] Measures taken to prepare and defend various rebellion garrisons and to dislodge their guardians, as well as the palpable heat of fires, thickness of smoke, smell of the dead and the unnavigable ruin of central Dublin, convey intimate and transformative impressions of Easter Week and its unique place in the liturgy of Irish rebellion. Beyond the internment of participants and suspected sympathisers and the execution of those identified as its principal leaders, the scale, extent and cost of the damage it produced greatly informed the popular memory of the Rising. This destruction varied by location and was compounded as the Rising progressed throughout late April, but its initial imprint was felt through the rebels' efforts to establish and fortify their defences.

Rebel efforts to occupy positions, disrupt transport routes and erect barricades produced minor damage that initially resembled vandalism rather than revolution. After ejecting clerks and clients from the GPO on Easter Monday, 24 April, Volunteers smashed its windows and barricaded them with mailbags filled with sand, coal and, it was reported, 'all the available books'.[31] From the roof, Volunteers bored through slate to establish communication with the floors below. 'Loop-holing' between adjacent buildings prevailed at various locations and created mobility between otherwise static positions. Several units made quick progress. Oscar Traynor and Seán Russell burrowed between several buildings in order to navigate the area, establishing routes between Easons and the Metropole Hotel by Wednesday afternoon.[32] West of the GPO, other early movements saw Fianna Éireann boy scouts and Irish Volunteers attempt to ignite the British Army high explosive and ammunition reserve in the Phoenix Park, an improvised initiative indicative of what some referred to as the Rising's 'chaotic' planning and intentionally destructive execution.[33] But charges failed to detonate any explosives stores, which, it was believed, had been transferred to England for the war effort.[34] Fires set in another portion of the fort consumed some small arms and ammunition, which produced a 'dull boom' as the saboteurs departed – an impromptu signal to the rebellion's start.[35]

Other preparations prevented troop movement and secured routes for a potential retreat along the River Liffey. The Four Courts was occupied to provide both a commanding view of the area and to act as a bulwark against British reinforcements.[36] Its windows were also smashed and barricades constructed from its Law Library holdings – an ironic gesture that utilised edicts of British law in order to defy it.[37] It was, however, the honeycomb of streets and alleys behind the Four Courts that truly entrenched the rebels and ensured that the Rising's collateral damage would extend to homes and businesses. Dublin Volunteers under the command of Edward 'Ned' Daly established various positions along Church Street, its branching side streets and their intersections, preparing barricades and smashing glass bottles on the streets to deter trespass.[38] The barricades' composition in the Four Courts area and other rebel strongholds reflected the immediacy of their locality as well as the rebels' unapologetic practicality. Extracted paving stones and carts and other vehicles gave the impression that the street extended up into the barriers. Pubs were raided for furniture and barrels and at times occupied, such as Reilly's Pub ('fort') on North King Street; private homes, too, were stripped of their furniture and goods to congest the area and prevent movement.[39] Items ranging from bicycles to motorcars to scrap from building yards built up barriers throughout the inner city.[40] Large drums of paper taken from the *Irish Times* office supplemented a barricade in Lower Abbey Street, which 'a young man of the student type' doused with petrol and ignited as troops advanced.[41] These experiences were not unique to any one area, as the *Kerry Weekly Reporter* conveyed to its eager readers:

> The rebels were not particular how they got barricades. At Sackville St. and East-street corner one is made of cushions, chairs, furniture, etc., seized from Tyler's shop nearby, which is a wreck. The barricade in Sackville-place is made from old packing cases raided from White's shop. In Lower Abbey-street there is a barricade made of new bicycles, cycle accessories of all kinds, and barbed wire taken from neighbouring shops, and near Jacob's biscuit works there is a barricade of flour and sugar sacks.[42]

In this, rebels successfully transformed Dublin's congested streets and immediate materials into platforms and tools for rebellion; actions that, in the case of commerce, extended the Rising's economic impact beyond a brief interruption of operating hours. Many individuals and businesses filing property loss claims as a result of the Rising cited consequential loss, such as destruction of inventory that would have been sold and loss of potential business, due to the rebels' initial movements. Claims as diverse as those registered by Miss Kathleen Gregg, proprietor of the Antient Concert Rooms of Great Brunswick Street, who claimed a loss of bookings as a result of the rebellion that amounted to over £82, and Devine & Sons Fruit Sellers of Corporation Market, who sought recompense for 358 cases of apples that spoiled awaiting collection at the North Wall, populate the record. As consequential losses were not permitted within the scheme, neither were compensated.[43]

South of the river, Volunteers prepared defences to impede Dublin's reinforcement by British troops and to disrupt their communication. The Grand Canal and docklands provided natural barriers, while the bridges that crossed the Grand Canal and rail lines linking central Dublin to Kingstown (now Dún Laoghaire) or Kingsbridge Station (now Heuston) experienced some of the week's first action. On Monday morning, Volunteers destroyed communication lines and began to occupy and barricade key positions along the canal and surrounding streets and buildings.[44] They neutralised the area, removing bolted rail joints ('fish plates') to disconnect rails, trenched the lines between Beggars Bush and Westland Row, and barricaded railway workshops intermittently stationed alongside the track. Volunteer Joseph O'Connor explained that uprooting and trenching the line would 'prevent an armoured train or the like from passing through'.[45] The measures permitted the 3rd Battalion operating at Boland's Mill and in the Moore Street area to reform the landscape to their preferred pace of engagement. On Wednesday, Seán O'Keeffe and others reinforced barricades at the railway timber yard, destroyed telephone installations, continued trenching train lines, and erected barbed wire that was eventually extended to cover positions between Erne Street and South Lotts Road, a distance of nearly a mile.[46] As the national terminus, Dublin's railway and tram systems were explicitly targeted. Attacks on Barrow Bridge, Rogerstown Bridge, a bridge linking Cabra and North Circular Road, Blanchardstown Bridge, and the east line between Fairview and Wharf Road occurred with varied success and cost.[47] Occupation and destruction of Dublin and South Eastern Railway property, for instance, required £2,000 to repair.[48]

In some commands, trenching and cutting communications proceeded on Easter Sunday, with Volunteers being 'cheerfully unaware' of any countermanding mobilisation order.[49] For instance, Portlaoise-based Irish Volunteers felled telegraph poles and cut their wires along the Portlaoise–Waterford railway line on Sunday evening, disrupting communications and rail signals. They then removed 60 yards of track that included twelve 30-foot rails, 66 sleeper ties, and 208 bolts, and disposed them in the nearby Colt Wood, where they then sheltered from the rain. Two hours later, William Dalton, a railway porter at Maryborough (Portlaoise) station, began to inspect a reported block signal failure. He discovered the downed line but was driven from the scene by the Volunteers under 'the first shot fired in the Rising' before discovering the missing tracks. A dummy engine and brake carriage, carrying police and railwaymen, later derailed during a further investigation.[50]

Communication lines were cut, rails uprooted, bridges destroyed and barricades erected elsewhere throughout the week, including Kildare, Roscrea, Cavan, Longford, Enniscorthy and Galway City and its environs, demonstrating how the Volunteers' broad preparatory initiative focused on logistical disruption as well as establishing stiff defensive positions.[51] Despite these enterprises further afield, rebels failed to isolate the capital from material reserves, including troops from the Curragh military camp – the largest British military garrison in the country – and artillery from Athlone. From Monday afternoon, 'Military Specials' ferried soldiers between the Curragh and Kingsbridge, which bolstered Dublin's garrison of 400 soldiers to approximately 3,000 and delivered Major-General Lowe to the scene.[52] Widespread attempts to frustrate British communications and reinforcements at best delayed, but in most instances failed, to prevent Dublin's encirclement.

Trenching extended beyond industrial rail lines and commercial carriageways to pedestrian spaces, linking Dublin's urban war zone to the 'conflict now being waged on the Continent', one official reported to the *Central News*.[53] Seamus Kavanagh arrived at St Stephen's Green at around 1 p.m. on Easter Monday and proceeded to organise its defence.[54] He inspected the park's circumference and ordered trenches to be dug at the different gate entrances and barricades to be erected from commandeered bicycles, cars and cabs between St Stephen's Green and the nearby Hotel Russell.[55] James O'Shea and Jim Fox dug a trench facing down Dawson Street, 'putting some bushes around it as camouflage', as O'Shea recalled. Their post included a shelf for bombs and shotguns formed by 'cutting into the earth', extending the allegory of street barricades that appeared to rise out of the ground.[56] Wet weather complemented the Western Front simulation. Warming temperatures brought sporadic rain showers that reduced the trenches to slop and gave St Stephen's Green defenders 'a taste of Flanders trench life'.[57] Dublin experienced nearly twenty days of rain throughout April 1916; nearly two inches fell on 19 April, five days prior to the start of the Rising.[58] The rain let up to produce 'a beautiful night, gusty with wind, and packed with sailing clouds and stars' as rebels withdrew to the Royal College of Surgeons on Tuesday morning. They left St Stephen's Green 'an appalling picture of litter and earth and holes and damaged property'.[59]

A Carl von Clausewitz-inspired defence scheme sought to lure British reinforcements into fortified areas and inflict unacceptable casualty levels, resulting in a political settlement and recognition of the Irish Republic. But this strategy bore uneven results, proved difficult to coordinate and failed to neutralise British communications and reinforcements. Telegraph wires were downed or cut throughout the city and further afield, but key communication transfers remained intact. Developments were communicated to London via the Amiens Street Railway Telegraph Office, where British forces had established a command post.[60] Rebels failed to take Dublin Castle, a symbolically important and centrally strategic building representative of British intelligence and administration. Elsewhere, rebel success appeared accidental, or the result of British inflexibility. The Mount Street Bridge area was a particularly deadly nexus where rebels inflicted 'potentially catastrophic' casualties on the Sherwood Foresters, but ultimately failed to prevent the city's reinforcement from Kingstown harbour.[61] Other spaces reflected the Rising's class-based element and firmer ideological grounding. For instance, the occupation of Jacob's Biscuit Factory, the South Dublin Union and, particularly, William Martin Murphy's Metropole Hotel manifested James Connolly's attempts to link republicanism and labour, as some observers have noted.[62] Overall, preparing trenches, occupying buildings, cutting communication lines and erecting barricades primed Dublin for the type of confrontation Pearse, MacDonagh, Plunkett and Connolly had envisioned: one which might spare the city and its inhabitants from the British Army's destructive capacity and instead instigate a drawn-out street fight and guerrilla war throughout the country.[63] However, others anticipated that the rebellion would be suppressed with urgency and expediency, and the combined destructive impact of artillery, fire and looting would be devastating.

The Destruction of Dublin

The Easter Rising caused substantial urban destruction and produced scenes, sounds and smells foreign to nearly all its witnesses. The British Army's initial challenges to rebel positions, including unsuccessful cavalry and infantry assaults, misplaced impressions of rebel success. Reinforcements from Kingsbridge, the Curragh, Belfast, Templemore and Athlone quickly and decisively shifted favour to the British Army.[64] As the week progressed, artillery bombardment, steady machine-gun fire, ensuing fires, looting, the collapse of asbestos-lined tenements, human and animal casualties, and odours indicative of unattended death grounded the rebellion's ruinous scope.[65] Critically, artillery meant endgame. James Connolly's oft-cited prediction that capital would not destroy capital was offset by the concurrent realisation that 'if the British were ever compelled to use artillery in the "second city of the empire", they [the rebels] were doomed.'[66] In this sense, Fearghal McGarry has observed that the British Army's response was in many respects 'instinctual'. 'The rebels who went out to do battle on Easter Monday morning may have been marching towards the unknown, but they shared one expectation: that the British military response would be rapid and hard.'[67] In the absence of functioning civil authority (Lord Wimbourne was confined to Vice Regal Lodge, Under Secretary Matthew Nathan was isolated in Dublin Castle and Chief Secretary Augustine Birrell was in London), the military, under the command of Major-General Lowe, moved to subdue the insurrection quickly and definitively. General Sir John Maxwell brought equal determination to Dublin when he assumed command later in the week.

As the scope of insurrection came into focus, British commanders sent for reinforcements, secured strategic positions and fortified Dublin Castle, the administrative centre of colonial governance. Occupying the North Wall docklands and Amiens Street and Kingsbridge terminuses, for instance, prepared a peripheral operating ring around what were almost exclusively (and fatally) central rebel positions.[68] From College Green, Trinity College acted as 'a beacon to loose military units' and colonial soldiers on leave, who joined resident Officer Training Corps cadets and established a field battery behind its tall iron gates and proverbial ivory towers. Further south, soldiers entered the Shelbourne Hotel via its service entrance on Dawson Street, gaining the high ground as well as a commanding view of Citizen Army posts on St Stephen's Green and the College of Surgeons.

British High Command quickly pivoted from frontal attacks to sniping and siege manoeuvres.[69] Soldiers constructed their own barricades throughout the city, fortifying their positions while inflicting damage on private property and further congesting streets and lanes.[70] On Tuesday, snipers and machine gunners stationed around College Green, Parnell Square and Amiens Street peppered portions of Sackville Street; bullets shattered windows, hacked away at buildings' plaster and concrete facades, and shredded shop canopies.[71] Rebels took to burrowing between buildings to maintain communication lines and avoid drawing fire, often boring through thick brick and plaster to link entire building blocks. Arthur Agnew, Peadar Bracken and Joe Good withdrew from Kelly's 'Fort' at

O'Connell Bridge towards Middle Abbey Street in this way, emerging in Elverys several buildings away.[72]

Looting complicated the week's drama and spurred a wave of low-level destruction throughout Dublin's commercial districts. Opportunism converged on Sackville Street and its environs, where 'the 'underworld' of the city vandalised homes and sampled from various shops in what developed into a smash-and-grab orgy.[73] Ernie O'Malley later described Clery's department store as 'an ant heap' with 'men, women, and children swarming about'.[74] Deliberate and accidental crossfire,[75] and progressively unstable structures, failed to deter raiders whose safety, Desmond Fitzgerald noted, appeared to weigh 'against nothing in the scales against the opportunity [...] to go home with a sackful of boots'.[76] Excitement, curiosity and a collective sense of legal impunity encouraged the mob, some of whom quickly established a black market where lifted toys, boots and jewellery sold for cheap.[77] In one instance, young entrepreneurs on O'Connell Street charged 'a tuppence a look' for a view of the snipers in Trinity College through their magnifying prismatic glasses.[78] The absence of the Dublin Metropolitan Police (DMP), which had been withdrawn on Easter Monday after three of their number were killed, removed remaining civil bastions of consequence.[79] Looting insulated rebel headquarters and surrounding posts, and was concentrated within the Capel, Parnell and Marlborough Street perimeter bordered by the river, an area of roughly 120 acres. Several businesses seemed to receive special attention. Desmond Ryan was particularly blunt in his portrayal of the progressively invasive looting in the vicinity of Sackville Street:

> Looting begins. The plate-glass of Noblett's [confectioners] is shivered. The crowd breaks in. A gay shower of sweet-stuffs, chocolate boxes, huge slabs of toffee tosses over amongst the crazy mass. Tyler's [John Tyler and Sons Limited, boot manufacturers] suffers in its turn. The old women from the slums literally walk through the plate-glass panes. Heavy fragments of glass crash into their midst inflicting deep gashes and bloody hurts, but their greedy frenzy is unchecked.[80]

Claims later filed with the Property Losses (Ireland) Committee detailed the variety, quantity and value of items lifted, as well as the projected cost of repair.[81] Looters stuffed their cheeks and their pockets, raiding confectioners as well as jewellers. Others sought to outfit parlours with furniture and other goods. Fianna Phádraig messenger Seán O'Shea confronted several youths ferrying billiard cues, balls and other sports goods from Sackville Street towards Ringsend. He commandeered their loot and deposited it in the canal.[82] Tobacco was another popular item, and shops were raided for more than Woodbines or sweetened plugs. Purcell's, adjacent to the GPO at 68 Upper Sackville Street, was robbed of over £1,000 of tobacco stock in addition to its scales, shelves and display, which were not insured against 'hostilities, riots, civil commotion, or sack or pillage connected therewith'.[83]

Despite widespread civilian interaction, the insurrection failed to ignite (or unite) Ireland's working-class powder keg. Instead, as Bulmer Hobson recalled, the rebels' provoking spark fell 'into a puddle'.[84] Dublin's working class pillaged alongside its destitute, conduct believed to muddy the Rising's noble gesture in Pearse's eyes.[85] But rebel leadership had anticipated looting, and procedures had been issued to check it.[86] Volunteers doused raiders with water, threateningly levelled bayonets and dealt 'sturdy blows with rifle butts' and batons to disperse crowds.[87] Jeremiah O'Leary found the task difficult; around Earl

Street, Volunteers were swallowed by the 'dense, milling crowd' and became separated and powerless.[88] Civil efforts to disperse looters fared little better. Before his arrest and execution, writer, feminist and pacifist Francis Sheehy-Skeffington ascended a vacant tram near O'Connell Bridge to persuade crowds of people 'to be quiet and orderly, to go home quietly, to stay in their homes and to keep the peace'.[89] Nearby, Fathers O'Flanagan, Aloysius and Monahan exercised their religious authority to disperse crowds around the Pro-Cathedral and Marlborough Street, with greater success.[90]

Beyond the Rising's integrity, looters threatened to compromise rebel positions. Fires set at Lawrence's Photographic and Toy Emporium and Tyler's Boot Shop on Tuesday spread between the corners of Cathedral and Earl Street on which they stood.[91] Incendiarism had also ignited the Cable Shop Company and the True Form Shoe Shop, opposite the GPO, making several important rebel posts 'untenable'.[92] The Dublin Fire Brigade struggled to respond to the numerous calls they received, as rifle fire threatened their safety and thus hindered their work. As a result, fires grew and spread rapidly, aided by barricades that escorted flames across streets and loop-holed walls that connected buildings.[93] Artillery shelling ignited fires near the *Irish Times* Reserve Printing Office in Lower Abbey Street, which eventually claimed the entire block south to Eden Quay and compelled rebels to evacuate key positions in the area. The fires quickly spread north along Sackville Street. Oscar Traynor, who commanded Volunteer garrisons in the area, reported the following:

> I saw the barricade being hit; I saw the fire consuming it and I saw Keating's [bicycle shop] going up. Then Hoyt's [chemists] caught fire, and when Hoyt's caught fire the whole block up to Earl St. became involved. Hoyt's had a lot of turpentine and other inflammable stuff, and I saw the fire spread from there to Clery's [department store, whose] plate-glass windows [ran] molten into the channel from the terrific heat.[94]

The heat was so intense that fire-proof safes failed to prevent their contents from igniting, much to the lament of numerous solicitor firms.[95] Fire Captain Purcell also described the blaze, which appeared to pause momentarily within the extended height and thick walls of the Dublin Bread Company Restaurant at 6–7 Sackville Street: 'Little by little the smoke and flames gathered strength, and then burst through the ventilators and windows.'[96] On the scene, Seamus Daly simply recalled 'terrible dust and smoke and blaze' as the building collapsed on Thursday evening.[97]

Fire linked rebel experiences between central Dublin and outlying posts, which at times mimicked the chaos of Sackville Street. For instance, Clanwilliam House in Ballsbridge acted as a makeshift suburban headquarters for Irish Volunteers due to its strategic position in the Mount Street Bridge area overlooking Northumberland Road. Its integrity was short-lived. A 'shower of grenades' from the British Army ignited a fire that impelled evacuation and eventually burned the stately Victorian residence to its braces. This occurred despite guarantees given to the owner that his home would be evacuated unharmed.[98] For Joseph O'Connor and others at the scene, the burning of Clanwilliam House inaugurated 'a fearful nightmare of fires and explosions' that accelerated towards the week's end.[99] In some places, fire consumed more than timber and plaster, compounding its imprint and the magnitude of ecological pollution. Rebels intentionally burned the Linenhall barracks on Coleraine Street, north of the Four Courts, on Wednesday as it was deemed too large to occupy. 'Cans of oil and flammable paint [were] poured throughout the building' to act as chemical kindling. Fire engulfed stores of oil as it spread, which exploded and filled the air with thick smoke; Moore & Alexander's Chemists, adjacent to the barracks, was also consumed, resulting in a blaze that could be seen for miles. Seán Prendergast echoed O'Connor when he described this fire as a 'new and perhaps extremely frightful feature in the long series of thrills' during the week, something 'awesome, fearsome and amazing', 'a spectacle beyond description and comprehension':

> It resembled a huge burning furnace, a veritable inferno. The belching flames that shot skyward lit up a wide area and transformed an otherwise dark night into uncommonly lurid brightness, brighter even than daylight.

It is understandable that many were unable to grasp the Rising's destructive magnitude. Previous nineteenth-century rebellions had been exposed, prematurely executed, and contained with relative ease. In 1916, however, the Irish government responded with a force relative to the perceived threat.

Lord Wimbourne quickly announced martial law in an attempt to reassert control and end the rebellion. His declaration appeared in the *Irish Times* on Tuesday, 25 April, spurring further excitement and fresh rumours amongst Dubliners, whom James Stephens, an important contemporary witness to the week's events, observed to be 'animated and even gay [...] outside and around the areas of fire'.[100] British Army command committed to bombing principal rebel positions rather than risking excessive casualties in infantry assaults, a move the Cabinet deemed necessary for the quick suppression of the rebellion. General Maxwell was less diplomatic; he later described measures to suppress the rebellion to include the destruction of 'all buildings within any area occupied by rebels'.[101] Though articulated on Friday, this policy was put into effect the previous Wednesday. That morning, two artillery pieces (18-pound guns akin to those on the Western Front) were escorted from Trinity College and positioned on nearby Tara Street, facing Liberty Hall.[102] Additionally, two 12-pound guns mounted aboard the Royal Navy's 'armed yacht', *Helga*, arrived from Kingstown, fixed on Boland's Mill.[103] Artillery generated anxiety and shattered rebel positions. Vivacious street scenes gave way to 'the shouts of frenzied and excited people' as fragmentary and incendiary shells fell on the city, disfiguring the face of Dublin beyond the minor blemishes war preparations or opportunistic looting had produced.[104]

Direct and consequential damage eroded rebel positions, large and small. From Wednesday afternoon, Kelly's fishing tackle shop, which occupied a red brick building at the corner of Sackville Street and Bachelor's Walk, was 'pummelled' by machine-gun and artillery fire.[105] The obliteration of 'Kelly's Fort', a property the *Sinn Féin Rebellion Handbook* later identified as 'one of the most shot at and fully punctured premises in Dublin', was reduced to a shell shrouded 'in a cloud of red dust and smoke'.[106] James Stephens was on the scene to view its demise:

> From roof to the basement the building was bare as a dog kennel. There were no floors inside, there was nothing there but blank space; and on the ground within was the tumble and rubbish that had been roof and floors and furniture. Everything inside was smashed and pulverized into scrap and dust, and the only objects that had consistency and their ancient shape were the bricks that fell when the shells struck them.[107]

Liberty Hall was also shelled on Wednesday. A place of refuge during the 1913 Lockout and home to James Connolly's various newspapers, the building provided a space for both open and covert defiance prior to the rebellion; a banner that read 'We Serve Neither King nor Kaiser, But Ireland' adorned its cornice, while small scale munitions were produced inside. Combined fire from the *Helga* (based at Sir John Rogerson's Quay approximately 900 meters away) and Trinity College's field guns eventually reduced the building to a pockmarked facade.[108]

The GPO was discriminately targeted on Thursday, though not actually hit until around noon on Friday. Fires supplemented the British assault and worked to outflank rebel positions with uncanny sentience. 'The fire ate its way through several blocks,' reported a special correspondent, 'and although it was a costly method, it served to drive out the Sinn Féiners like so many rats out of an old mill.'[109] Adjacent flaming buildings on Henry Street ultimately ignited the GPO, accelerating the Rising's timetable as rebel headquarters threatened to collapse, or asphyxiate its defenders. Advancing fires also scorched remaining optimism within headquarters. Indeed, as the steel ring drew tighter, previously rationed food was distributed wholesale, Cumann na mBan women were ordered to evacuate and remaining ammunition was withdrawn.[110] On Saturday, April 29, Commander-in-Chief Patrick Pearse, accompanied by Elizabeth O'Farrell, surrendered to General Maxwell in an effort to prevent further civilian casualties, a capitulation that materialised throughout various commands over several days.

For the majority of Dubliners, the insurrection was an intimate and bewildering affair, one whose arch was observed in the reverberation of artillery, the crash of bricks and glass, and the infringement of smoke and fire. It was witnessed and processed through the intense sights, sounds and smells – exposures that grounded the scale and severity of destruction and helped to shape reaction, reflection and memory.

Sensing the Rising

Bombardment, fire and death produced sights, sounds and smells that triggered diverse emotional impressions. While ephemeral experiences, they nevertheless act as reconstructive gateways to memory and interpretation.[111] Aural experiences of the Easter Rising, for instance, allowed onlookers to align their immediate experiences with the visually iconic aftermath of destruction, personified in the Sackville Street fires.[112] In this regard, the rebellion created a unique sensory stamp, a 'sonic environment' that was relatively foreign to rebels and civilians alike, and recognisable to only a selection of British troops that had seen combat in Europe.[113] Space and class influenced this experience. Inner-city Dubliners, rebels and soldiers were exposed to deafening, repetitive noise, prolonged views of destruction and advancing decay, and concentrated ecological hazards – a distinct sensory experience from that of greater suburban Dublin. Nevertheless, those outside the immediate city centre also received the basic auditory indictors of conflict – explosions, artillery shelling, gunshots – that conveyed the Rising's progress and hinted at its potential outcome. For some, the mere sounds of war and the proximity of death transformed their views towards Irish nationalism and the Rising in general. Rebellion made a negligible impression on Ernie O'Malley at first; as he recalled, 'I had no feeling about it.' However, as 'the shelling and noise increased' – easily audible from his home in Glasnevin – it awoke a note of patriotism that overturned his previous indifference:

> In the evening I was in a whirl. I walked up and down the garden at the back of our house. Distant sounds of firing had new sounds that echoed in my head. They meant something personal; they made me angry. The men down there were right, that I felt sure of. [...] I was going to help them in some way.[114]

For O'Malley and many thousands of others, the noise of war was inescapable, even outside ground zero, which ultimately implicated all of Dublin as witness to rebellion. Rebels experienced and recalled the rebellion's sounds as indicators of its progression, often linking noise to the ebb, flow and overall pace of destruction. Individuals differentiated between the artillery that fell on and around Sackville Street, which reverberated throughout the city, and smaller rifle and machine-gun fire that chirped in short bursts day and night. Volunteer Seosamh de Brún explained the tide of military noise from his post at Jacob's Factory:

> Rifle and machine gun fire was continuous during the day only slackening towards nightfall when it became intermittent. The nights were sombre and awesome as we stood on guard we heard the noise of the improvised armour cars as they raced around the side streets reconnoitring our position. On Wednesday towards the middle of the week the firing increased in intensity, the crack of the artillery was heard above the rattle of machine gun fire and the loud bang of the Howth gun.[115]

Intermittent but persistent gunfire, the smashing of glass, construction of barricades, shouting and screaming, artillery, explosions and the roar of fire and, ultimately, firing squad volleys composed a unique orchestra that echoed throughout the city and its environs. Joseph O'Connor, in an appreciation that would have elated Marinetti's Futurists, confessed that he had 'enjoyed the artillery fire and took a pleasure in counting the interval between the flash and the noise of the explosion. [...] The bursting of grenades and the continuous machine-gun and rifle fire was quite another matter.'[116] These sounds guided many through the week's drama. Individuals were able to locate and gauge the conflict's intensity by these sounds of war, and to speculate from a distance the extent of damage. In the historically based fiction *The Wasted Island*, Eimar O'Duffy noted the swift abruptness of encroaching war, communicated through its sounds and concentration: 'To those who listened it seemed that the whole city must inevitably be destroyed, for what buildings could possibly survive the fearful tornado that smote upon their ears?'[117] In light of Ireland's tenuous relationship with the First World War, these 'sense' events did more than anything else to hammer home, to Dubliners at least, the situation on the continent. Both intimate observers and those removed from immediate danger became familiar with the noise of rebellion to the point that they were able to classify its sounds. James Stephens noted that by late Wednesday morning, 'the report of the various types of arms could be easily distinguished. There were rifles, machine guns, and very heavy cannon.'[118] Out-of-place volleys, misfires and explosions betrayed an eerily rhythmic soundscape, while rifle and ammunition patterns distinguished the rebel's assorted instruments from the near-uniform crack of British Army models.[119]

Evening stillness contrasted daytime commotion, but it was often deceptive and naturally varied by location. For instance, residents in Fitzwilliam Place, roughly a mile south of Sackville Street, remembered Wednesday night as mostly calm and beautiful – a 'dead silence' in which an insurrection was being fought: 'Hour after hour there was the buzzing and rattling and thudding of guns, and, but for the guns, silence.'[120] Elsewhere, there was 'stray shooting, then spells of silence'.[121] That same night, Ernest Jordison deposited his children in safety with family in Drogheda, Louth, before returning home to Clontarf – a two-to-three hour ride. Jordison, who managed the British Petroleum Company's Dublin operations, 'hardly met a soul the whole way home … everything was still and quiet.' Even from Santry, the Dublin guns were not enough to muffle the sound of corncrakes 'craking' in the fields along the road, or his bicycle upon the road, which 'made a clattering noise in the stillness of the night, all the way home'.[122] Space and proximity certainly lowered the Rising's destructive tones; from a distance, detonations and explosions produced but thuds and dull booms as opposed to crashes and explosions up close. However, the apocalyptic spectacle of Dublin's destruction was widely visible. Impressive flames, 'vivid over the city', beaconed Jordison's otherwise tranquil cycle home.[123] Like sound, the Rising's destructive impact was witnessed on various visual scales, from the dull glow of fire visible for miles to ruined building facades and rubble piled at the feet of more intimate observers. Such displays prompted comparison with the destruction of the Great War and iconised Dublin's ruin.

The sight of destruction grounded the rebellion's magnitude, foolhardiness and importance, evident in its immediate impressions carrying forward to later recollections. Witnesses commonly cited the intensity of fires, whose 'blaze' and 'glare' rose from Sackville Street to illuminate the night sky.[124] Fired chemical stores in the Linenhall barracks and an oil depot in Abbey Street contributed to the 'inferno', which melted plate glass and wreathed the city in smoke that was observable for miles.[125] Journalists struggled to convey the scale of ruin, or its parallel within recent history. One *Daily Chronicle* correspondent, confined to the North-Western Hotel on the North Wall, reported that he and others 'could see fires blazing furiously in the direction of Sackville Street':

> The whole sky was reddened by the glare of burning buildings, while dense masses of smoke were lit up by it. No such scene has been witnessed in the British Islands since the sack of Bristol in 1831. And the sack of Dublin in 1916 far outweighs that event in grim horror and fearful destruction of life and property.[126]

The following day, under a 'sky filled with black smoke', an *Illustrated Sunday Herald* reporter pronounced Dublin to be 'in a state of rebellion the like of which has never before been witnessed through all the sad history of Ireland, and which only has its parallel in some of the incidents in the great civil war of this country'.[127]

Conversely, the great 'pall of smoke' shrouding Dublin was glorified as it assisted in communicating the Rising's scale and importance.[128] From Jacob's Factory, John MacDonagh, brother of proclamation signatory Thomas MacDonagh, and his comrades felt 'heartened' by 'the glare in the sky from the fires which were raging'. '[I]t showed the magnitude of the rising,' he explained, 'which we knew would change the whole position of Ireland.'[129] Joseph V. Lawless also interpreted Dublin's destruction in triumphant tones.

His brief glance of Sackville Street, of 'the gaunt ruins of the GPO [...] outlined against the twilight sky, and still smoking heaps of masonry', revealed the force necessary to coerce a rebel surrender.[130] Beyond this core, the effects were often too much to bear. Members of the Boland's Mill garrison were 'unnerved' as they witnessed the terrible fires raging from the direction of Sackville Street.[131] Such expressive responses were indicative of the emotional investment many had made in the Rising, which fatigue and hunger had intensified. Ordinary Dubliners, to whom war had been 'brought home', exhibited diverse reactions throughout the week, which ranged from boredom to anxiety over when and where the next bombs would fall.[132] Their responses polarised as the extent of death and destruction came into focus.[133]

It may be said that Dublin's complete capitulation took several weeks, as various buildings smouldered, collapsed or were pulled down, and noxious smells continued to pollute the Capital. Several commercial photograph albums and commemorative handbooks memorialised the ruin as the rebellion's primary outcome.[134] In fact, some rebellion sites remained in ruin throughout the Irish Revolution, ghostly shells that venerated the Easter Rising. However, while Nora Connolly believed Dublin resembled 'photographs of bombed streets during the war', she experienced the scene more completely. It was, she said, the 'terrible smell of burning buildings and some rubber' that contributed to the Easter Rising's unique environmental experience.[135] These smells were easily distinguished against the city's typical discharge and helped to forge distinct impressions – impressions recalled in Bureau of Military History Witness Statements over 30 years later. For instance, Robert Brennan recalled that the 'smell of smoke from the charred ruins of the city' also produced a 'gloom' that seemed to hang over the capital.[136] Outside Dublin, 'fumes of charcoal, [and] the subtle smell of burning [...] wafted over on the soft summer breeze' to confirm news reports and gossip surrounding the week's events, in addition to the spring rain's inability to completely extinguish fires.[137]

An array of rebellion-related hosts delivered other distinct odours. Lifeless animals littered various locations; unable to be moved, interred or quarantined, their bodies stiffened and decayed as the week progressed. A horse killed near St Stephen's Green remained in place, 'stiff and lamentable', throughout the week.[138] A dead donkey blocked the road at Annesley Bridge near Fairview Park, 'swollen and decaying'.[139] Oscar Traynor and Fintan Murphy freed horses in the city centre when fire in the Metropole Hotel threatened their stables.[140] Sanitation officers later discovered the remains of 14 others, who had been trapped in their stalls in Henry Street and burned to death. '[I]nasmuch as they had lain in the place for several days,' the *Freeman's Journal* reported, 'the job of dealing with them was a particularly unpleasant one.'[141] Dogs and cats fell victim in large numbers as well. 'There is not a cat or a dog left alive in Camden Street,' witnessed one young girl. 'They are lying stiff out in the road and up on the roofs.'[142] In all senses, dead animals contributed to the Rising's 'odour of death', which American journalist Percival Phillips observed fell 'heavy on the morning air'.[143]

Death's omnipresence ensured that Dublin's 'nightmare' persisted.[144] Temporary graves dug in gardens and yards had concealed bodies during the rebellion, while burning buildings acted as makeshift crematoriums for their deceased occupants.[145] Moreover, exposed corpses, overcrowded hospitals and morgues, and cemeteries ill-prepared to process the dead produced a toxic atmosphere, raised concerns about public health and presented unique logistical and environmental problems, including exposure to infectious bodies. Several deceased civilians, casualties of a firefight between rebels and soldiers, littered the streets below Reginald Neville's hotel window. 'In the neighbourhood of the Custom House I saw at least eight women lying dead. Hundreds of others were wounded,' he wrote, 'but these were carried away for treatment in the City Hospitals.'[146] Indeed, the burden placed on hospitals was particularly acute as an unanticipated volume of patients, limited space (including beds and gurneys) and interruptions to gas, water and electricity pushed staff and facilities to their limits. This included treating the wounded and temporarily storing corpses until they were able to be removed for burial. The Richmond Hospital, positioned in a concentrated conflict zone behind the North Dublin Union on North Brunswick Street, operated at capacity to treat over 300 wounded.[147] Sixteen of these casualties 'were either brought in dead or died shortly after admission',[148] victims that transformed the buildings into overflowing 'deadhouses'. 'It was a gruesome sight,' an anonymous Cumann na mBan member recalled, 'to see the dead piled on top of each other in the morgues where there were not enough marble slabs on which to place the bodies.'[149] By 4 May, Dublin's city hospitals contained nearly 200 dead bodies.[150]

Other casualties simply remained where they fell, or were concealed in the rubble of collapsed structures, unaccounted for until clean-up efforts commenced. It was reported that 26 dead rebels were discovered in this way in the *Daily Express* offices opposite City Hall.[151] Other bodies were concealed as a precaution to protect the living and were perhaps not meant to be exhumed. In this sense, the *Strabane Chronicle* suggested that a true death toll from the Rising might never be known, 'as it is an open secret that scores of people were buried in backyards, patches of garden, and some out-of-the-way places' as a way for occupants or relatives to avoid being questioned by authorities.[152] Regardless of intent, death's distinctive odour betrayed many makeshift graves. For instance, on 10 May – over a week after the rebel surrender – young George Fitzgerald 'got a heavy smell' from the cellar of the pub on the corner of North King Street and Ann Street, where he had returned to his job as a porter. He traced the odour to the cellar, and there found blood and disturbed earth. Stacked in a shallow pit were the bodies of Patrick Bealen and James Healy, two of the fifteen victims discriminately killed when the military cleared the heavily fortified area.[153]

Further ad hoc burials were performed throughout the rebellion in an effort to remove the danger of decaying and potentially infectious bodies. British soldiers overtaking St Stephen's Green interred fallen rebels on the spot.[154] In the neighbouring Royal College of Surgeons, rebels converted the lecture theatre's sub-gallery into a makeshift morgue.[155] Several bodies were concealed in house gardens along Morehampton and Northumberland roads after rebels suffered casualties under heavy fire.[156] Francis Sheehy-Skeffington, Thomas Dickson and Patrick MacIntyre were buried in Portobello barracks after they were executed on 26 April. They, along with dead soldiers deposited throughout the week, were interred in sheets as coffins were difficult to obtain and generally unavailable (or inaccessible) as the rebellion progressed.[157] For example, the Dublin Castle Red Cross Hospital buried nearly 70 individuals in the Castle's rear garden, approximately 30 of whom were delivered from congested hospitals.[158] One member of the Castle's Voluntary Aid Detachment (VAD) described the logistical difficulty of processing the dead:

> Towards the end of the week the dead were so many they were brought in covered carts instead of ambulances. I saw a cart open once – about fifteen bodies, one on top of the other. It took time to carry them round to the mortuary, and sometimes as one passed two or three bodies would be lying near the side door, dressed in khaki, but so still, so stiff, the hands so blue, and the faces covered.[159]

As the anonymous witness intimated, burial was not always immediate or possible. Constable William Frith was killed by friendly fire inside Store Street Police Station on Thursday of Easter Week. A 'very heavy man', Frith was placed in the orderly room where he remained for four days before he was able to be coffined and transferred to Mt Jerome Cemetery.[160] Conversely, Paddy Whelan was shot and killed at his post in Boland's Mill the previous day and left under the third-storey window where he had fallen. Joseph O'Byrne explained that the delay in Whelan's interment was owed 'to lack of men and from the pressure of our more urgent duties, general fatigue and the necessity for keeping look-outs at several distant points of the building'. On Friday, O'Byrne, his brother Peter, and Willie Bruen fashioned a rough coffin and buried Whelan nearby, marking the makeshift grave with a wooden cross for later identification.[161] A coffin shortage and the danger of moving throughout the city prevented these and other bodies from being retrieved, or even temporarily interred. The Public Health Department viewed inadequate and temporary burials, with 'human remains lying in backyards',[162] 'lying on roofs or concealed in chimneys', as particularly hazardous, inciting fears of a potential health crisis.[163] On 2 May, Sanitary Inspectors began to comb the city, investigating rumours (and fears) of corpses concealed in roofs (which proved groundless), and notifying authorities as they discovered makeshift graves throughout the city.[164]

Like many others, Paddy Whelan was exhumed and reinterred in Glasnevin Cemetery in the days and weeks following the rebel surrender.[165] However, similar to its hospitals, Dublin's cemeteries were unprepared to receive the dead at the pace and, in many cases, the condition in which they arrived. Glasnevin's Superintendent, James Geary, applied 'powerful disinfectants' to safeguard against the scores of dead that arrived often 'uncoffined in lorries' and in 'distressing frequency'.[166] By 11 July, Glasnevin's gravediggers had interred approximately 250 bodies, many in plainclothes or wrapped in sheets and blankets. Many were later exhumed and reburied as caskets and plots became available.[167] Longstanding grievances over poor wages, long hours and generally unhealthy conditions that included 'hazard pay for exhuming corpses that have been buried for a long time'[168] led gravediggers to renew strikes at Dean's Grange and Glasnevin cemeteries,[169] which Dublin City Council attempted to mediate 'in the interests of Public Health'.[170] Discovery, unearthing and transportation of the dead, temporary burials, exhumation and final interment of rebellion victims continued throughout the summer and early autumn.

Beyond a politically transformative catalyst, the Easter Rising stimulated intense sensory experiences that heightened aspects of the conflict. Individuals experienced an unprecedented proximity to war, delivered via visual, aural and olfactory emissaries. Although we are unable to measure the rebellion's environmental impact against modern ecological scales, immediate impressions and recalled memory from witnesses suggest it was significant. Observers encountered this evidence in unique ways. Burnt, blackened walls, shattered glass and pockmarked facades erected intimate if temporary memorials to the week's devastation, while persistent, wandering smoke and scraps of 'charred and burnt paper' exhibited the Rising upon tangential neighbourhoods and beyond.[171] This is as true in contemporary accounts as it is in literary representations. For instance, contemplating the rebellion from his boyhood home in Glencoole, west of the city beyond Lucan, Eimar O'Duffy's fictional republican Stephen Ward locates the capital against the night, 'a dull red spot like a cooling cinder [...], and in the sky above it was a delicate glow.'[172] Although this description indicates the rebellion's embers to be dying, public opinion in Ireland and abroad soon came to interpret the Rising as the spark that ignited a popular nationalist revolution, which included additional episodes of concentrated urban destruction as well as the small-scale but widespread demolition of roads, railways, bridges and communications. As such, the unprecedented destructive experience of Easter 1916 presented inimitable bureaucratic challenges towards the assessment of damage, its cost and clean-up, and the complicated process of compensation.

The Cost of Rebellion

Images and descriptions of Dublin's devastation resonated in the Rising's aftermath. 'The havoc in Sackville Street is now complete,' wrote the *Belfast Newsletter*, 'that even those who are most familiar with the thoroughfare, recalling its old associations, can only form a vague mental picture of its now departed glories.'[173] Clearing and clean-up efforts contributed to post-rebellion noise and dust pollution as hundreds laboured amidst the curious, probing crowds. Workmen pulled down half-standing or damaged walls, sentinel chimneys and 'gaunt, towering sections of what had once been fashionable emporiums'. They were directed and aided by the Borough Surveyor's staff, the city engineer and Dublin Corporation's Paving Department (Dangerous Buildings staff), who played 'tug-of-war' to bring 'the tottering ruins to the ground with a crash that reverberated through the district and sent great columns of dust right across the wide street to rise in thick, grey clouds high above the masonry around'.[174] A 'Ratepayer of the City' was quick to praise such work, in particular that of the Dublin Fire Brigade, which cleared principal streets, contained and extinguished smouldering fires, 'pumped out flooded cellars' and removed previously inaccessible wounded civilians from homes.[175]

Municipally directed clearance occurred between 3 May and 9 June. The Women's National Health Association of Ireland and other groups coordinated an overlapping general clean-up week from 12–19 May.[176] Collective efforts attempted to conceal the 'disfiguring scars' of rebellion that shone across the face of Dublin. Homes and businesses in assorted neighbourhoods had been burned and looted, and barricades remained throughout the city (then attended by British soldiers); St Stephen's Green was sealed to all but the most daring souvenir seekers; and overturned vans, trams and carts presented obstacles, while blood stained the footpaths of more active conflict sites, such as at Mount Street Bridge and along Northumberland Road.[177] Sackville Street was prioritised for clean-up due to the extent of its damage, to end the moratorium on Dublin's commercial district, and to begin the process of compensation assessment. In July 1916, Dublin City Council recorded that, exclusive of the GPO, fire had destroyed approximately 240 properties during Easter Week, a significant increase from the 179 the press had previously identified in the immediate aftermath of the rebellion.[178] The most severe damage sites overlapped key rebel strongholds, looting sites and their adjacent surroundings. Select outliers, such as Arnotts department store, stood unscathed amidst otherwise wholesale destruction. Housing and small businesses accented larger instances of destruction: interconnected housing blocks and goods stores, such as Harbour Court, were entirely destroyed. Damage to Dublin's concentrated commercial sector was notable; over 150 premises were damaged or destroyed within the relatively small perimeter of Lower and Upper Sackville Street, Henry Street, Lower and Middle Abbey Street, Earl Street and Eden Quay.[179]

It is difficult to completely or accurately tally the true material and financial loss suffered as a result of the Easter Rising.[180] Looting, loss of trade, consequent damage to stock and expired stores extended the rebellion's total fiscal impact beyond what the government was willing to recognise and reimburse. London's ex gratia grant towards compensation had various limits and stipulations.[181] The complex process of collecting, assessing, categorising and indemnifying various claims occurred relatively quickly. Despite some complexities, approximate figures may be produced from the claims and assessments of the Dublin Fire and Property Losses Association, and the subsequent Goulding Commission.

In response to the significant material losses suffered during the rebellion, several leading businessmen formed the Dublin Fire and Property Losses Association in May 1916. Chaired by the heavily invested William Martin Murphy, the committee's deputation met with several influential government figures and lobbied for swift and fair compensation to their firms.[182] By late May 1916, the Association's membership had submitted 1,500 claims totalling £2.5 million,[183] while claims filed with Dublin Corporation under the Malicious Injuries Act equalled £4 million.[184] The following month, Sir Robert Chalmers, the newly appointed Under Secretary, selected a government committee, headed by Sir William Goulding, to investigate the nature and extent of property loss articulated by the Dublin Fire and Property Losses Association.[185] Dubbed the Property Losses (Ireland) Committee, they received over 7,000 claims amounting to £2.7 million; ineligible, withdrawn claims, those filed after the deadline, and claims submitted by individuals implicated in the Rising reduced the recommended compensation to £1.8 million. The Committee also withheld assessment of select government properties, such as the GPO and Linenhall barracks. Many other claims, however, illustrate the banal extent to which even minor property had been damaged or destroyed, and what Dublin traders believed to be fair compensation. Overall, the Goulding Committee attempted to navigate many of the 'thorny issues of the scale of compensation' that had arisen since the Rising's end.[186] It specifically challenged the government's adopted compensation scale, which was calibrated to reflect hypothetical rates of insurance coverage in the event of accidental fire.[187] James Healy, the Commission's secretary, presented the collected view that:

> To limit the loss admissible in insured cases to the amount of the insurance would not adequately meet the special circumstances. For nearly a week the buildings fired, or that caught fire, were allowed to burn themselves out, as the fire brigade could not venture on duty, the police had been withdrawn, and the owners were prevented from approaching their burning premises. As a result nothing could be done in most cases to check the fires, or to salve any of the property in the buildings affected.[188]

Other outstanding financial issues contributed to this complexity. City departments had bills to settle, which added to their overall operating cost and slowed post-Rising urban regeneration. For example, Dublin Corporation's Dangerous Buildings Branch encumbered an additional £306 in their post-Rising structural assessments and demolition, while the Paving Department was £1,617 over budget after repairing numerous damaged footpaths.[189] There was also unofficial pushback from the Irish Executive regarding issues surrounding liability and funding. Removing barricades in Herberton Lane, which had obstructed traffic since the rebellion's conclusion, would add 19 shillings to the rates, an expense Captain Slaugher at the Chief Secretary's Lodge believed should be met through civil funds.[190] Salaries were paid despite overextended budgets, and the city continued its clean-up and sanitation efforts; the Cleansing Committee approved full payment to its staff despite interruption to normal operating hours, while John Fennelly was paid double-time for his work in collecting unburied bodies throughout the city.[191] Comparing refuse removal statements in 1915 and 1916 shows a marked increase in the number of loads needed to dispose street refuse, dustbin refuse and miscellaneous garbage after the Easter Rising.[192] Against overdrawn operational funds, Dublin Corporation, which lost £16,000 in tax payments in 1916 owing to destroyed property, sought other solutions to offset the cost of rebuilding.[193]

Several individuals and organisations emerged to relieve the financial stress and begin to restore the city. The National Relief Fund provided £5,000 in emergency funds during the first two weeks of May to relieve unemployment for those affected by the Rising, while the Lord Mayor's Fund, or Mansion House Fund, financed works projects that progressed the waste removal and sanitation process.[194] In June, the Lord Mayor, James Gallagher, acknowledged the fund's diverse patrons, which included the Dublin Jewish Board of Guarding (£50), the Dublin Distiller's Company (£50), and Lieutenant Col. Hutchinson Poe (£10), who had previously officered the Irish National Volunteers and canvassed for enlistment in the British Army.[195] International relief was also generated, most notably in the United States. Irish-born tenor John McCormack organised a fundraising concert at New York City's Century Opera House that earned the Lord Mayor's fund £1,650.[196]

Conclusion

The 1916 Easter Rising transformed Ireland in unforeseen ways. To many, the destruction Dublin suffered was a testament to the ferocity with which Britain managed (and disciplined) its empire. Rebellion and its suppression moved many moderate political outlooks towards republicanism and mobilised thousands of previously unaffiliated men and women to the cause of Irish independence. Environmental damage oversaw this transformation and occurred in the background of additional efforts to eject British authority by force between 1919 and 1921. The skeletal buildings of Sackville Street silently attested to the influence of grand ideals, while 'little wooden kiosks', erected along the frontage of ruined commercial blocks, indicated that Dublin had survived and would recover.[197]

Dublin's destruction is irrevocably linked with the Irish Republic's foundation – a sacrifice attuned to salvation's contemporary interpretation. Many of the thousands of individuals who later joined the revolutionary movement looked to 1916 and its leaders for inspiration, and were converted to (or strengthened in) the belief that suffering must precede redemption. A vantage reading of such iconoclasm strips 1916 of its exclusivity, instead portraying it as the foundational episode of concentrated urban destruction and environmental contamination within the broader Irish revolutionary period.

NOTES

1. *Irish Independent*, 19 Mar. 1916; *The Sinn Féin Rebellion Handbook. Easter 1916* 5 (Compiled by the *Weekly Irish Times*, Dublin, 1917 edn); Paul Rouse, 'How Leix won the All-Ireland hurling championship of 1915', in *Century Ireland* (blog), http://www.rte.ie/centuryireland/index.php/articles/how-leix-won-the-all-ireland-hurling-championship-of-1915, accessed 8 October 2022.
2. Cumann na mBan member Aine Ryan, who was employed with Malachy Scally's drapery shop on William Street, remembered Tullamore as 'not very Nationalist' at the time, with 'ladies knitting socks for the soldiers at the front, organizing flag days'. She also recalled 'a large "separation" element' in the town comprised of women whose husbands, sons and brothers were serving in the British Army who 'created a disturbance' when receiving their separation allowance. Statement of Áine Ni Riain (Aine Ryan), Bureau of Military History [hereafter BMH], Witness Statement [hereafter WS] 887, p. 3.
3. See categorised enlistment returns, John Redmond papers, National Library of Ireland [hereafter NLI], Ms 15,259. For Irish enlistment motivations, see David Fitzpatrick, 'The logic of collective sacrifice: Ireland and the British army, 1914–1918', in *The Historical Journal*, 38:4 (1995), pp 1017–30; David Fitzpatrick, 'Home front and everyday life', in John Horne (ed.), *Our War: Ireland and the Great War* (Dublin: Royal Irish Academy, 2008), pp 131–42.
4. The *Fermanagh Herald* described the hall as being 'besieged by a hostile crowd'. *Fermanagh Herald*, 25 Mar. 1916; *Kerry Sentinel*, 25 Mar. 1916.
5. Statement of Peadar Bracken, BMH, WS 12, p. 1; joint statements of James Clarke, Frank J. Brennan and Henry McNally, BMH, WS 49, pp 1–2.
6. *Connaught Telegraph*, 25 Mar. 1916; *Kerry Weekly Reporter*, 25 Mar. 1916; *Donegal News*, 1 Apr. 1916; *Freeman's Journal*, 5 Apr. 1916.
7. Those arrested on 23 March 1916 were Edward Downes, Francis Brennan, John Martin, Thomas Hogan, Thomas Duggan, James Clarke, John Spain, John Delaney and Joseph Graham. Joint Statement of James Clarke, Frank J. Brennan and Henry McNally, BMH, WS 49.
8. Inspector General's monthly report for March 1916, 'Activities of Political and Secret Societies', Nevil Chamberlain to Under Secretary, 13 Apr. 1916, The National Archives, Kew [hereafter TNA] (CO 904/99).
9. Statement of Seamus Brennan, BMH, WS 48.
10. *Connaught Telegraph*, 25 Mar. 1916; *Belfast Newsletter*, 5 Apr. 1916; *Evening Herald*, 21 Mar. 1916; Statement of Peadar Bracken, BMH, WS 12.
11. *Irish Independent*, 23 Mar. 1916.
12. See, for instance, details of a Protestant-led attack on an Ancient Order of Hibernians hall in Breagh, Armagh, on 31 March 1916, during which 'a party of about two hundred men armed with rifles and shotguns and carrying picks and sledge hammers [...] completely demolished the walls of a new Hall [...] being built between an Orange Hall and a Masonic Hall in the centre of a Protestant locality.' Inspector General's monthly report for March 1916, TNA (CO 904/99).
13. Statements of Andrew McDonnell, BMH, WS 1768, pp 31–2; Patrick Caldwell, BMH, WS 638, pp 4–5; Francis Daly, BMH, WS 278, pp 1–5; and Ruaidhri Henderson, BMH, WS 1686, p. 1.
14. Statement of Seamus Reader, BMH, WS 627, p. 9.
15. Statement of Michael O'Flanagan, BMH, WS 800, pp 7–9.
16. Statement of Andrew McDonnell, BMH, WS 1768, p. 32.
17. Addendum to statement of Mrs Catherine Rooney (Byrne), BMH, WS 648, p. 1.
18. Diarmaid Ferriter, *The Transformation of Ireland 1900–2000* (London: Profile Books, 2005), pp 141–2. The Cluny bomb factory was aided by Sean Price, Vincent Gogan, Richard Gogan, S. P.

O'Reilly, Josie O'Rourke, W. P. Ryan and P. J. Corless. Statements of Francis Daly, BMH, WS 278, pp 1–5; and Seamus Daly, BMH, WS 360, p. 16. For acquisition of lead and its various stores in Dublin, see Francis Daly, BMH, WS 278, pp 1–5. Charles Townshend referred to the 'seizure of explosives' as indicating 'a new mode of combat'. Townshend, *The Republic: The Fight for Irish Independence* (London: Allen Lane, 2013), p. 79.

19. The Royal Commission of Inquiry on the Rising identified the theft of explosives between 1913 and 1915 as cases which were 'considered to indicate the intention to commit outrages on persons or buildings'. *Sinn Féin Rebellion Handbook: Easter, 1916; A Complete and Connected Narrative of the Rising, with Detailed Accounts of the Fighting at All Points* (Dublin: *Weekly Irish Times*, 1917), p. 152.

20. *Sunday Independent*, 6 Feb. 1916; see also, Inspector General's monthly report for January, Neville Chamberlain to Under Secretary, 14 Feb. 1916, TNA (CO 904/99).

21. McCabe was acquitted though no evidence was presented for the defence and the accused claimed the explosives were 'for fishing'. Samuel Chadwich, chief chemist at Knyoch's, determined the amount of explosives to be insufficient to do any serious structural damage and would, 'if exploded along the side of a river [...] kill the fish'. *The Liberator* (Tralee), 5 Feb. 1916, p. 3; *Irish Independent*, 5 Feb. 1916, p. 5; *Irish Examiner*, 5 Feb. 1916, p. 6. See also Inspector General's monthly report for January, Neville Chamberlain to Under Secretary, 14 Feb. 1916, TNA (CO 904/99).

22. 'Cotton and Explosives', *Anglo-Celt*, 12 Feb. 1916.

23. The War Office outlined several potential invasion scenarios. A hypothetical nationalist *levée en masse* also appeared doubtful, due in part to the significant divergence in outlook, membership and arms between the Irish Volunteers and the National Volunteers. On RIC home defence during the Great War, see Jérôme aan de Wiel, *The Irish Factor 1899–1919: Ireland's Strategic and Diplomatic Importance for Foreign Powers* (Dublin: Irish Academic Press, 2011), pp 158–209; and Justin Dolan Stover, 'Periphery of war or first line of defence? Ireland prepares for invasion (1900–1915)', in *Francia: Forschungen zur Westeuropäischen Geschichte* 40 (2013), pp 385–96.

24. Charles Townshend, *Easter 1916: The Irish Rebellion* (London: Penguin, 2006), pp 80–3.

25. Ibid., p. 84.

26. Inspector General's monthly reports for September; October; and November, Neville Chamberlain to Under Secretary, 13 Oct. 1915, 13 Nov. 1915, and 14 Dec. 1915, TNA (CO 904/98).

27. Inspector General's monthly report for February 1916, Neville Chamberlain to Under Secretary, 14 Mar. 1916, TNA (CO 904/99).

28. A pre-Rising report from Major General Ivor Price set Irish Volunteer membership and arms at 10,000 and 4,800, respectively. Townshend, *Easter 1916*, p. 143.

29. Townshend, *Easter 1916*, pp 143–5.

30. For an overview of the intrigue surrounding Eoin MacNeill's marginalisation from the Volunteer leadership, Bulmer Hobson's arrest and the cancellation of Sunday manoeuvres, see Townshend, *Easter 1916*, pp 135–8.

31. Statements of James Kavanagh, BMH, WS 889; Michael O'Reilly, BMH, WS 886; and Sean MacEntee, BMH, WS 1052, p. 42; *Kerry News*, 1 May 1916.

32. Statement of Oscar Traynor, BMH, WS 340, p.15; Derek Molyneux and Darren Kelly, *When the Clock Struck in 1916: Close-Quarter Combat in the Easter Rising* (Cork: The Collins Press, 2015), p. 228.

33. Townshend refers to it as 'not part of a long-prepared plan intended to launch the rebellion, but a last-minute improvisation'. *Easter 1916*, p. 155. Roy Foster, too, states 'The chaotic and last-minute nature of the leaders' deliberations was reflected in the way that the insurrection began.' R. F. Foster, *Vivid Faces: The Revolutionary Generation in Ireland 1890–1923* (New York: W. W. Norton & Company, Inc., 2015), p. 227; Ferriter, *Transformation of Ireland*, p. 147.

34. Molyneux & Kelly, *When the Clock Struck in 1916*, pp 9–22; Eamon Murphy, 'The raid on the magazine fort, Phoenix Park, Easter Monday 1916', in *The History of Na Fianna Éireann*, https://fiannaeireannhistory.wordpress.com, accessed 16 September 2016.

35. Fearghal McGarry, *The Rising: Ireland, Easter 1916* (New York: Oxford University Press, 2011), p. 138; Molyneux & Kelly, *When the Clock Struck in 1916*, p. 21. Soldiers and the fire brigade extinguished small fires in the fort by Tuesday. *Belfast Newsletter*, 4 May 1916; *Irish Examiner*, 3 May 1916.

36. Molyneux & Kelly, *When the Clock Struck in 1916*, p. 171.

37. *Leitrim Observer*, 13 May 1916. The same methods were applied in April 1922, when the republican IRA occupied the buildings. Ronan Keane, 'A mass of crumbling ruins: The destruction of the Four

Courts in June 1922', in Caroline Costello (ed.), *The Four Courts: 200 Years: Essays to Commemorate the Bicentenary of the Four Courts* (Dublin, 1996), p. 161.
38. Statement of Francis X. Coghlan, BMH, WS 1760, p. 2; Molyneux & Kelly, *When the Clock Struck in 1916*, pp 169–70.
39. Statement of Ignatius Callender, BMH, WS 923, p. 8.
40. Statement of Francis X. Coghlan, BMH, WS 1760, p. 4. For further details as to the variety and quantity of items used to stock barricades, see The Property Losses (Ireland) Committee, 1916 (PLIC) files at the National Archive of Ireland, http://centenaries.nationalarchives.ie/centenaries/plic/index.jsp.
41. *Irish Independent*, 13 May 1916.
42. *Kerry Weekly Reporter*, 6 May 1916.
43. Claim of Kathleen Gregg, National Archives of Ireland [hereafter NAI], Property Losses (Ireland) Commission [hereafter PLIC]/1/0798; D. Devine & Sons, PLIC/1/4763. Crown forces also utilised personal property as barriers throughout the city and occupied commercial and residential space. For example, Lieutenants Murphy and Kennedy instructed Inniskilling Fusiliers under their command to prepare a barricade in Lower Gardiner Street from goods raided from Redmond & Co. Pawnbroker & Jewellers, which included fifteen beds and three tables. Claim of Laurence Redmond, 96 Lower Gardiner Street, NAI, PLIC/1/1304. Rose Dunne also claimed damage for a feather bed she had pledged at Redmonds. She received £1.10. PLIC/1/5184.
44. Statement of Sean O'Keefe, BMH, WS 188, p. 6.
45. Statement of Joseph O'Connor, BMH, WS 157, p. 27.
46. Sean O'Keefe, BMH, WS 188, pp 7–8; Molyneux & Kelly, *When the Clock Struck in 1916*, p. 46.
47. For coverage of attacks on rail lines and bridges, see *The Liberator* (Tralee), 2 May 1916; *Sinn Féin Rebellion Handbook: Easter, 1916*, pp 31–2; Townshend, *Easter 1916*, pp 178, 216; Statements of Richard Hayes, BMH, WS 79, pp 3–4; and Francis Daly, BMH, WS 278, p. 10.
48. 'The railways during the Rising', in *Sinn Féin Rebellion Handbook: Easter, 1916*, p. 31.
49. McGarry, *The Rising*, pp 139–41.
50. Statement of Patrick J. Ramsbottom, BMH, WS 1046, pp 5–15. Volunteers involved included Laurence Brady, Thomas F. Brady, Patrick Muldowney, Colm Houlihan and Michael Sheridan; see also, *Nationalist and Leinster Times*, 28 Oct. 1918; *Leinster Express*, 29 Apr. 1916. At time of operations, RIC returns for Queen's Co. show 36 Irish National Volunteer branches with 3,159 members, and one Irish Volunteer branch with 30 members.
51. *Leinster Express*, 29 Apr. 1916; Inspector General's monthly report for April [1 April–31 May], Neville Chamberlain to Under Secretary, 15 June 1916, TNA (CO 904/99).
52. Unknown [General Manager's Office, Kingsbridge] to Unknown [Chief Secretary's Office], 5 May 1916 (Irish Railway Record Society, Sinn Féin Rebellion files); Townshend, *Easter 1916*, pp 183, 186; McGarry, *The Rising*, p. 181.
53. 'Munition factory official's graphic story', *Irish Examiner*, 4 May 1916, p. 5; *Kerry Advocate*, 6 May 1916.
54. Barricading streets and public spaces inspired select observations of continuity between the Irish rebellion and France's revolutionary past. Some took liberty with the analogy. The *Northhampton Chronicle* reported: 'The rebels barricaded St. Stephen's Green with motor-cars and tramcars, as in the French Revolution.' To this, the *Donegal News* mocked: 'The 1789 models of motor-cars and tramcars are of course out of date by now.' (*Donegal News*, 27 May 1916). *Le Figaro* presented the garrison as *un Fort Chabrol*, paralleling the park's fortification and defence with Jules Guérin's Parisian stronghold during the Dreyfus affair. '[T]hey are now desperate,' the paper concluded, and 'remain inaccessible to all means of conviction other than force.' *Le Figaro*, 30 Apr. 1916.
55. Statement of Seamus Kavanagh, BMH, WS 1670; 'Introduction and Afterword by John A. Murphy', in James Stephens, *The Insurrection in Dublin* (England: Colin Smythe Ltd, 1916; New York: Barnes & Noble Books, 1999), pp 16–18, 20.
56. Statement of James O'Shea, BMH, WS 733, pp 126–7.
57. McGarry, *The Rising*, p. 167.
58. British Meteorological and Magnetic Year Book, 1917 (–22), issued as a supplement to the weekly weather report (vol. xxxiv – new series), Meteorological Office, London, 14 June 1918.
59. Sandra Spillane, 'Weather Easter 1916, Sunday 23 to Saturday 29 April 1916,' in *Met Eireann Historical Note* 7 (12 April 2016), pp 15–29; Stephens, *The Insurrection in Dublin*, pp 31–4; *Kerry Weekly Reporter*, 6 May 1916.

60. Diarmaid Ferriter, *A Nation and Not a Rabble: The Irish Revolution 1913–1923* (London: Profile Books, 2015), p. 157.
61. Townshend, *Easter 1916*, pp 196–8.
62. Foster, *Vivid Faces*, p. 231; Ferriter, *Transformation*, p. 143; Lauren Arrington, 'Socialist republican discourse and the 1916 Easter Rising: The occupation of Jacob's Biscuit Factory and the South Dublin Union explained', in *Journal of British Studies* 53:4 (October 2014), pp 992–1010.
63. Townshend, *Easter 1916*, p. 198.
64. *The Sinn Féin Rebellion Handbook: Easter 1916*, pp 592–3.
65. On the other hand, Donal O'Hannigan recorded that Connolly believed, 'in the event of a rebellion and if the English used artillery against the rebels that it would be equivalent to recognition that they were fighting the armed forces of another country and that other nations would recognize us as such accordingly.' Statement of Donal O'Hannigan, BMH, WS 161, p. 8.
66. McGarry, *The Rising*, pp 191–2, citing Bob de Coeur, who heard it from Liam Ó Briain; Townshend, *Easter 1916*, p. 209.
67. McGarry, *The Rising*, pp 181–2.
68. For observations criticising rebel strategy, see McGarry, *The Rising*, pp 184–5, and Ferriter, *A Nation and Not a Rabble*, pp 155–6.
69. Molyneux and Kelly, *When the Clock Struck in 1916*, p. 228.
70. See various claims from Property Losses (Ireland) Committee, especially PLIC/1/6425; PLIC/1/4123; and PLIC/1/1998.
71. Molyneux and Kelly, *When the Clock Struck in 1916*, p. 232.
72. Statement of Arthur P. Agnew, BMH, WS 152, p. 4; *The Sinn Féin Rebellion Handbook*, p. 12. Kevin McCabe recalled how 'Some of these walls at Clery's were three feet thick.' Statement of Kevin McCabe, BMH, WS 926, p. 8.
73. *The Sinn Féin Rebellion Handbook*, p. 9; Townshend, *Easter 1916*, pp 264–5.
74. Ernie O'Malley, *Army Without Banners: The Adventures of an Irish Volunteer* (Cambridge, Massachusetts: The Riverside Press, 1937), p. 28.
75. Men such as Arthur Agnew were under orders that 'looters were to be stopped and made drop their loot on the street. If they failed to do this they were to be shot.' Statement of Arthur Agnew, BMH, WS 152, pp 4–5; statement of Seán O'Shea, BMH, WS 129, np, labelled under 'Q'.
76. Desmond Fitzgerald, *Desmond's Rising: Memoirs 1913 to Easter 1916* (Dublin: Liberties Press, 1968; 2006), p. 139; McGarry, *Easter 1916*, p. 148.
77. Gustave le Bon, *The Crowd: A Study of the Popular Mind* (London: T. Fisher Unwin, 1896), pp 12–20. More recently, Charles Tilly described looting as 'Opportunism' occurring 'as a consequence of shielding from routine surveillance and repression, individuals or clusters of individuals use immediately damaging means to pursue ends that would be unavailable or forbidden to them under other circumstances.' The withdrawal of the DMP on Monday of Easter Week certainly freed many looters from normal social restraints. Charles Tilly, *The Politics of Collective Violence* (New York: Cambridge University Press, 2003), p. 131.
78. O Malley, *Army Without Banners*, p. 31.
79. McGarry, *Easter 1916*, p. 187.
80. Statements of Desmond Ryan, BMH, WS 724, p. 10; and Right Rev. Monsignor Curran, BMH, WS 687, p. 44.
81. 'Compensating for the Rising: The papers of the Property Losses (Ireland) Committee, 1916', in *History Ireland* 21, http://www.historyireland.com/20th-century-contemporary-history/compensating-for-the-rising-the-papers-of-the-property-losses-ireland-committee-1916/, accessed 8 October 2022.
82. Statement of Sean O'Shea, BMH, WS 129, np, labelled under 'Q'. [from page 35, question 'Q-Looting' from BMH 'Questionnaire on The Rising of Easter Week 1916 and Associated Events'].
83. PLIC/1/0495.
84. Statement of Bulmer Hobson, BMH, WS 81, pp 6–7.
85. 'P. H. Pearse, on behalf of the Provisional Government, to the Citizens of Dublin', in *The Sinn Féin Rebellion Handbook*, p. 4a.
86. McGarry, *The Rising*, pp 144–5; statement of William O'Brien, BMH, WS 1766, p. 2.
87. Statements of Desmond Ryan, BMH, WS 724, p. 10; and Arthur Agnew, BMH, WS 152, pp 4–5.
88. Statements of Jeremiah Joseph O'Leary, BMH, WS 1108, p. 17; and Mrs Geraldine Dillon, Sister of Joseph Mary Plunkett, BMH, WS 358, p. 18.

89. Statement of Eileen Costello (née Drury), BMH, WS 1184.
90. Statements of Michael Staines, BMH, WS 284, p. 14; and Father Augustine, BMH, WS 920, p. 15.
91. Statements of William O'Brien, BMH WS 1766, p. 3; Ruaidhri Henderson (son of Frank Henderson), BMH, WS 1686, p. 8; and Brenda Malone, BMH, WS 926, p. 9; *Irish Examiner*, 21 Mar. 2016; *The Sinn Féin Rebellion Handbook*, pp 9–10.
92. Statement of Ruaidhri Henderson (son of Frank Henderson), BMH, WS 1686, p. 8; the *Annual Report for the Year 1916*, submitted by Thomas Purcell, Chief Officer of the Dublin Fire Brigade; Donal O'Fallon, 'The denizens of the slums' and 'Looting during the Easter Rising', *Come here to me!*, 4 Oct. 2015.
93. *The Sinn Féin Rebellion Handbook*, p. 34.
94. Statement of Oscar Traynor, BMH, WS 340, pp 16–17.
95. 'Loss of title deeds', in *The Sinn Féin Rebellion Handbook*, p. 245; see also, 'Final report of Goulding Commission', http://centenaries.nationalarchives.ie/centenaries/plic/Final%20Report%20of%20the%20PLIC.pdf.
96. *The Sinn Féin Rebellion Handbook*, pp 34–5.
97. Statement of Seamus Daly, BMH, WS 360, pp 39–40.
98. McGarry, *The Rising*, p. 198; statement of Joseph O'Connor, BMH, WS 157, p. 33.
99. Statement of Joseph O'Connor, BMH, WS 157, p. 35.
100. James Stephens, *The Insurrection in Dublin*, p. 39.
101. 'Sir John Maxwell adopts rigorous measures', in *The Sinn Féin Rebellion Handbook*, p. 41; Townshend, *Easter 1916*, p. 208.
102. Molyneux and Kelly, *When the Clock Struck in 1916*, p. 233; McGarry, *Easter 1916*, p. 191.
103. British forces were ultimately able to establish and reinforce field artillery batteries in the north Dublin neighbourhood of Phibsborough and at Trinity College, in the heart of the city.
104. 'The Dublin trouble', by Albert George Fletcher-Desborough [BA, Lewis Gun instructor], BMH, WS 1604, appendix 2, as replicated from *The Stage*, 25 May 1916.
105. Property Losses (Ireland) Commission, NAI, PLIC/1/0495. Statement of Eamonn Bulfin, BMH, WS 497, pp 8–9.
106. 'The capture of "Kelly's Fort"', in *The Sinn Féin Rebellion Handbook*, p. 287; Townshend, *Easter 1916*, pp 209–10.
107. Stephens, *The Insurrection in Dublin*, pp 43–4, 46; Molyneux and Kelly, *When the Clock Struck in 1916*, p. 228; Townshend, *Easter 1916*, p. 210.
108. McGarry, *The Rising*, p. 191.
109. *Kilkenny People*, 6 May 1916.
110. Townshend, *Easter 1916*, pp 210–11; *Kilkenny People*, 6 May 1916.
111. Jonathan Reinarz, *Past Scents: Historical Perspectives on Smell* (Urbana, Chicago, and Springfield: University of Illinois Press, 2014), pp 3–5.
112. Leslie Morris, 'The sound of memory', in *The German Quarterly* 74:4 (Autumn 2001), p. 368.
113. Carolyn Birdsall, *Nazi Soundscapes: Sound, Technology and Urban Space in Germany, 1933–1945* (Amsterdam: Amsterdam University Press, 2012), p. 12.
114. O'Malley, *Army Without Banners*, p. 33.
115. Statements of Seosamh de Brún, BMH, WS 312, p. 11; and Seamus Robinson, BMH, WS 156, p. 17: 'My first recollection of Wednesday was hearing the sound of artillery fire and with the aid of a home-made periscope we saw a boat in the river just beyond the railway bridge shelling Liberty Hall.'
116. Statement of Joseph O'Connor, BMH, WS 157, p. 35; see also, Garret Keizer, *The Unwanted Sound of Everything We Want: A Book About Noise* (New York: PublicAffairs, 2010), p. 118.
117. Eimar O'Duffy, *The Wasted Island* (Miami: Hardpress Publishing, 2013; reprinted from Dublin, Martin Lester, Limited, 1919), p. 467.
118. Stephens, *The Insurrection in Dublin*, pp 41, 51–2.
119. O'Malley, *Army Without Banners*, p. 35.
120. Stephens, *The Insurrection in Dublin*, pp 54–5.
121. O'Malley, *Army Without Banners*, p. 29.
122. Statement of Ernest Jordison, BMH, WS 1691, p. 8.
123. Ibid.
124. Statements of Min Ryan (Mrs Richard Mulcahy), BMH, WS 399, p. 20; and Seosamh de Brún, BMH, WS 312, p. 11; Stephens, *The Insurrection in Dublin*, pp 60–2.

125. Foster, *Vivid Faces*, pp 242–3.
126. (From the 'Daily Chronicle') Special Correspondent-Copyright, *Irish Examiner*, 3 May 1916.
127. *Kerryman*, 6 May 1916.
128. *Kilkenny People*, 6 May 1916; statement of Gerald Doyle, BMH, WS 1511, p. 14; Foster, *Vivid Faces*, p. 243.
129. Statement of John McDonagh, BMH, WS, 532, p. 13; McGarry, *The Rising*, p. 202; *Nationalist and Leinster Times*, 6 May 1916.
130. Statement of Joseph V. Lawless, BMH, WS 1043, p. 144.
131. Townshend, *Easter 1916*, p. 201, cited from Donnelly, 'Thou shall not pass – Ireland's challenge to the British Forces at Mount Street Bridge, Easter 1916' (Irish Military Archives, CD 62/3/7); *Kerry News*, 3 May 1916.
132. *Belfast Newsletter*, 4 May 1916; McGarry, *The Rising*, pp 196–7. McGarry also notes how others simply continued with their work and employment (p. 199), and that civilians within the military cordon could 'feel the silence' between bombs (p. 200). *Western People*, 13 May 1916.
133. Ferriter, *A Nation and Not a Rabble*, pp 162–3.
134. Ibid., pp 167–8; see also, *The Record of the Irish Rebellion* (Irish Life), *Dublin and the Sinn Féin Rising* (Wilson, Hartness and Co.), *Sinn Féin Revolt Illustrated* (Hely's Ltd), *Dublin After Six Days' Insurrection* (Mecredy, Percy & Co., Ltd).
135. Statement of Nora O'Brien, née Connolly, BMH, WS 286, p. 47.
136. Statement of Robert Brennan, BMH, WS 779, pp 130–1.
137. *Cork Examiner*, 3 May 1916. As the *Anglo-Celt* recorded, 'Despite the continuous rainfall for three days in Dublin some of the fires in the wrecked premises were burning on Monday.' *Anglo-Celt*, 13 May 1916.
138. Stephens, *The Insurrection in Dublin*, p. 38. McGarry, *The Rising*, p. 184.
139. Statement of Ernest R. Jordison, BMH, WS 1691, pp 7, 9.
140. Statements of Oscar Traynor, BMH, WS 340, pp 17–18; and Fintan Murphy, BMH, WS 370, p. 6.
141. *Freeman's Journal*, 10 May 1916.
142. Stephens, *The Insurrection in Dublin*, p. 61.
143. *Leitrim Observer*, 13 May 1916.
144. *Evening Herald*, 4 May 1916.
145. McGarry, *The Rising*, p. 197.
146. *Ulster Herald*, 6 May 1916; *Donegal News*, 6 May 1916; *Anglo-Celt*, 6 May 1916.
147. Pádraig Yeates, *A City in Turmoil: Dublin 1919–1921* (London: Gill & MacMillan, Ltd, 2012).
148. *Irish Independent*, 11 May 1916; *Irish Examiner*, 3 May 1916.
149. 'A member of Cumann na mBan', *Gaelic American*, 18 Nov. 1916, in Ruth Taillon, *When History Was Made: The Women of 1916* (Belfast, 1999), p. 88; McGarry, *The Rising*, p. 198.
150. *Belfast Newsletter*, 4 May 1916; see also, *Ulster Herald*, 6 May 1916.
151. *Belfast Newsletter*, 4 May 1916; *Irish Examiner*, 13 May 1916
152. *Strabane Chronicle*, 13 May 1916.
153. *The Sinn Féin Rebellion Handbook*, p. 28; *Kerry Sentinel*, 17 May 1916; 'The North King Street massacre, Dublin 1916', http://www.theirishstory.com/2012/04/13/the-north-king-street-massacre-dublin-1916/#.WNQ-Z461t4k, accessed 8 October 2022.
154. *Irish Examiner*, 4 May 1916; *Irish Independent*, 26 Oct. 1916; 'On Saturday 8 bodies were disinterred at Dublin Castle and one at Trinity College. Of these 3 are believed to be men named Keogh, Byrne, Geoghegan, and Byrne. The remainder have not been identified', *Irish Independent*, 24 May 1916.
155. *The Sinn Féin Rebellion Handbook*, p. 19.
156. *Anglo-Celt*, 13 May 1916; Ferriter, *A Nation and Not a Rabble*, p. 155; *Irish Independent*, 20 May 1916.
157. *The Sinn Féin Rebellion Handbook*, pp 102–8, 211, 224.
158. Ibid., p. 236.
159. Ibid., p. 17; 'An anonymous VAD', *Blackwood's Magazine*, Dec. 1916, in Angela Bourke, Siobhán Kilfeather, Maria Luddy, Margaret Mac Curtain, Geradine Meaney, Máirín Ni Dhonnchadha, Mary O'Dowd and Clair Wills (eds), *The Field Day Anthology of Irish Writing* V, Irish Women's Writing and Traditions (New York: New York University Press, 2002), pp 108–10.

160. *Kerryman*, 26 Aug. 1916; http://irish-police.com/easter-rising-1916/, accessed 8 October 2022; *Evening Herald*, 31 July 1916.
161. Statement of Joseph M. O'Byrne, BMH, WS 160, p. 8; Molyneux and Kelly, *When the Clock Struck in 1916*, pp 66, 85, 87.
162. *Irish Independent*, 8 May 1916.
163. *Limerick Leader*, 8 May 1916.
164. *Sunday Independent*, 7 May 1916.
165. *The Sinn Féin Rebellion Handbook*, pp 59–60.
166. *Evening Herald*, 6 May 1916.
167. *The Sinn Féin Rebellion Handbook*, pp 59–61; *Sunday Independent*, 7 May 1916.
168. 'Gravediggers on strike at Glasnevin', *Century Ireland*, http://www.rte.ie/centuryireland/index.php/articles/gravediggers-on-strike-at-glasnevin, accessed 8 October 2022.
169. *Freeman's Journal*, 13 Oct. 1916; *Evening Herald*, 14 Aug. 1916; *Anglo-Celt*, 26 Aug. 1916; Donal O'Fallon, 'The striking gravediggers', *Come Here to Me!*, 25 Apr. 2016, https://comeheretome.com/2016/04/25/the-striking-gravediggers/, accessed 8 October 2022.
170. Dublin City Archives, Dublin City Council Minutes, 'Glasnevin cemetery – strike of gravediggers', 1916, 764a, p. 832.
171. Stephens, *The Insurrection in Dublin*, p. 60.
172. O'Duffy, *The Wasted Island*, p. 483; see also, Frances Flanagan 'Against insurrection: Eimar O'Duffy and the memory of the 1916 Rising', in *Irish Studies in Britain* (Newcastle upon Tyne: Cambridge Scholars Publishing, 2010), p. 109; Jonathan Bolton, *Blighted Beginnings* (Lewisburg: Bucknell University Press, 2010), p. 31.
173. *Belfast Newsletter*, 4 May, 28 June 1916.
174. *Irish Independent*, 8 May 1916; *Belfast Newsletter*, 4 May 1916; Dublin City Archives, Dublin City Council Minutes, 'Payment to employees engaged in demolition of destroyed property', II, 1916, p. 711; see also, 'Collapse of a public-house: The scene of recent fighting: Report of the paving committee', 31 July 1916; *Belfast Newsletter*, 1 June 1916.
175. 'A ratepayer of the city to the editor', *Freemans Journal*, 8 June 1916.
176. Dublin City Archives, Dublin City Council Minutes, 'Report of the cleansing committee, no. 208: Breviate for three months, ending 30th June', III, 1916, p. 287; 'Payment to employees engaged in demolition of destroyed property', II, 1916, p. 477.
177. *Belfast Newsletter*, 4 May 1916.
178. Dublin City Archives, Dublin City Council Minutes, 'Report of the paving committee RE: Demolition of buildings in devastated area, and payments to employees for overtime in connection with the work', 31 July 1916; *Belfast Newsletter*, 4 May 1916; Daithí Ó Corráin, '"They blew up the best portion of our city and ... it is their duty to replace it": Compensation and reconstruction in the aftermath of the 1916 Rising', in *Irish Historical Studies* XXXIX:154 (November 2014), p. 275, fn 18 citing Tom Geraghty and Trevor Whitehead, *the Dublin Fire Brigade: A History of the Brigade and the Emergencies* (Dublin, 2004), p. 148.
179. Ibid.
180. Early estimates varied. For instance, by 4 May the *Evening Herald* set the value of buildings destroyed on the west side of O'Connell Street at £1.1 million (*Evening Herald*, 4 May 1916). On 6 May, the *Kerry Advocate* cited £1 million in damage to both east and west sides of O'Connell Street, with loss of stock £3/4 million. For same story, see also *Kerry Press*, 4 May 1916.
181. *Limerick Leader*, 17 May 1916.
182. 'Compensation to property owners (Dublin),' House of Commons Debate 82, 10 May 1916, pp 629–30; *Belfast Newsletter*, 9 May 1916; *Freeman's Journal*, 13 May 1916; *The Sinn Féin Rebellion Handbook*, pp 249–50; Ó Corráin, '"They blew up the best portion of our city and ... it is their duty to replace it"', pp 277–9.
183. Ó Corráin, '"They blew up the best portion of our city and ... it is their duty to replace it"', p. 278; *Irish Times*, 20 May 1916. £2.5 million remains a fairly accepted figure amongst historians. See Ferriter, *A Nation and Not a Rabble*, p. 158.
184. *Belfast Newsletter*, 18 May 1916.
185. Goulding was joined by Mr William E. Osborn, of Messrs Selfe and Co., London, and Mr Samuel J. Pipkin, General Manager of the Atlas Assurance Co., Ltd.

186. Ó Corráin, "'They blew up the best portion of our city and … it is their duty to replace it'" p. 274; Property Losses (Ireland) Committee: Report of Committee, 7 Apr. 1917, NAI; *Irish Examiner*, 15 May 1916; *Belfast Newsletter*, 18 May 1916.

187. 'Compensation to Property Owners (Dublin)', House of Commons Debate, 10 May 1916, 82 cc 2692–3.

It was reported on 17 May, five days after the last executions in Kilmainham Gaol, that 'the State will assume liability to the amount of the insurance for the destruction of buildings and their contents in Dublin during the recent outbreak. This liability covers looting.' Donal O'Fallon, 'The "denizens of the slums" and looting during the Easter Rising', *Come here to me!*, 4 Oct. 2015, https://comeheretome.com/2015/10/04/the-denizens-of-the-slums-and-looting-during-the-easter-rising/, accessed 8 October 2022.

188. James Healy (Secretary) to Lord Wimbourne, Property Losses (Ireland) Committee, 1916, Report of Committee, 7 Apr. 1917 (NAI, PLIC), pp 4–5.

189. Dublin City Archives, Dublin City Council Minutes, 'Report of the paving committee: Breviate for the quarter ended 30th June 1916', 1916.

190. Dublin Corporation Council Minutes, 1916, p. 87.

191. Dublin City Archives, Dublin City Council Minutes, 'Report of the paving committee: Breviate for the quarter ended 30th June 1916', 1916.

192. Dublin City Archives, 'Report from Francis Purcell, Captain, Dublin Fire Brigade, 26 July 1916'.

193. Ó Corráin, "'They blew up the best portion of our city and … it is their duty to replace it'", p. 288; *Irish Independent*, 20 May 1916; *The Sinn Féin Rebellion Handbook*, p. 246.

194. Joseph V. O'Brien, *Dear, Dirty Dublin: A City in Distress, 1899–1916* (California: University of California Press, 1982), p. 264; *The Sinn Féin Rebellion Handbook*, p. 244.

195. *Southern Star*, 22 Aug. 1914.

196. *Freeman's Journal*, 7 June 1916; *New York Times*, 7 May 1916; see also, 'Brandon Tynan's entertainment at the Criterion nets $2,000', *New York Times*, 20 May 1916.

197. *Belfast Newsletter*, 28 June 1916.

Chapter Two

Contested Spaces & Militarised Landscapes

Introduction

Dublin trains struggled to deliver racegoers to Punchestown in April 1917. Although attendance for the annual horse festival was recorded as moderate, 'almost as nothing' compared to pre-war years, many still flocked to the races.[1] Hotels were booked with visitors anxious to enjoy the sporting holiday, and guests unable to travel by motor or rail hired hackney carriages for transport to Kildare.[2] Racegoers also took time to play tourist at the capital's preserved rebellion sites.[3] Site-seers paraded in the shadow of ruins, viewing the 'stark devastation'. Extensive clean-up efforts, the restoration of utilities and the erection of temporary shopfronts returned functionality to Dublin's commercial district. Nevertheless, the city remained scarred, a graphic complement to the ideological divergence the Easter Rising exposed in Irish nationalist politics the previous year. 'Nobody can glance at O'Connell Street and say the city has had a recuperative year,' the *Sunday Independent* observed. 'Rain and plasterers have done much to obliterate bullet marks and shell rents. But nothing has risen from the ashes.'[4] This narrative kept to the paper's critical view of the rebellion and its leaders but was not entirely accurate. Indeed, select sites such as the GPO and Liberty Hall had yet to be completely cleared or restored, but they nevertheless served an important function. They operated as venerated monuments, mobilised for the Irish nationalist cause in the belief that sacrifice precipitated salvation. In another sense, they maintained a sense of war's destructive capacity and its impact on civilian lives.

Unionists, nationalists and embryonic republicans had each distorted civic space prior to 1916. Military geographies were in fact everywhere, and behaviours of resistance were many.[5] Leisure yachts had carried rifles to the ports of Larne and Howth in 1914, newsagents and tobacco shops sold 'seditious' literature, and public halls and fields were enlisted for paramilitary drills and shooting exercises. Similar transformations continued in the post-Rising years. Republicans, as well as constitutional nationalists and unionists, each appropriated public and commercial spaces for political rallies. Geographies of republican resistance, specifically, challenged existing power dynamics on various scales, in ephemeral and more permanent instalments, and were often carried out in plain sight 'under the noses of the oppressor'.[6] Throughout the country, politicised vandalism, organised protest and memorial events publicised this changing nationalist attitude. Each instance worked to challenge or alter existing social and political boundaries, and at times redefined spatial identities.

Demonstrations & Public Space

In December 1916, the British Government released the remaining rebellion detainees from Frongoch internment camp in Wales, and hundreds of men returned to Ireland.

Amnesty not only reflected a shift in the government's approach to the 'Irish question', but it also presented the Irish Parliamentary Party (IPP), members of which had lobbied for rebels' release, the opportunity to shore up nationalist support in the face of rising republican populism.[7] Internment had provoked an ideological awakening in internees, their families, and in nationalism generally. Mass incarceration had lumped together approximately 2,000 rebels, sympathisers and suspects, many of whom became radicalised in the company of veteran separatists.[8] For many, Britain's response to the Easter Rising validated the Fenian physical force philosophy and the union of violence and politics in public life.[9] Amnesty and release failed to reconcile nationalist political outlooks to the IPP or make palpable the notion of conscription, as was evident towards the Easter Rising's first anniversary.[10] Released men revamped Sinn Féin and the Irish Volunteers. 'The last is gone back again to old Ireland,' went a contemporary Frongoch tune, 'to prepare once again for a fight to the death.'[11]

Dublin Castle recognised this threat and the Irish penchant for nationalist commemoration and demonstration. As Easter 1917 approached, the Chief Secretary, Henry Duke, monitored political developments and warned the War Cabinet of potential trouble.[12] Officials followed Count George Noble Plunkett's candidacy for the North Roscommon vacancy, documenting Sinn Féin convert Laurence Ginnell's flamboyant canvassing on his behalf.[13] Plunkett's comfortable win in February set a foundation for Sinn Féin's parliamentary abstention policy and platform for complete independence, which subsequent by-elections developed.[14] Irish Volunteer membership, arms and activity were also watched and recorded (when possible), with monthly returns forwarded to the Under Secretary, William Byrne. St Patrick's Day parades demonstrated that the organisation was alive and well, although the number of spectators in several locations exceeded marching Volunteers.[15] Nevertheless, both Church and State quickly moved to reclaim public and pious atmospheres. Anticipating 'collision' between soldiers and the Irish Volunteers, Lt Gen. Sir Bryan Mahon proclaimed public meetings and processions in Dublin from 22 April to 13 May.[16] Senior religious figures exercised their authority to counter Sinn Féin's influence on young priests.[17] In Cork, Bishop Cohalan filtered instructions through his clergy to refuse memorial Masses for those who died as a result of rebellion, 'as they would only lead to conflict and disorder'.[18] As such, restricting public gatherings and the laity's desire to venerate the Rising's dead extended the role of civic, public and religious spaces as sites of protest.

By April 1917, such dictates appeared purely reactionary. Attempts to check republicans' appropriation of public space, ceremony and political methods failed to deter their appeal and broadly reinforced accusations of a British police state.[19] Timothy McMahon explained how Gaelic League's occupation of public space for *feiseanna* and cultural processions worked to 'reconfigure images of the existing social order', assimilating witnesses and elevating the League's mission in the process.[20] The same might be observed of popular republicanism after 1916. Although the Rising's anniversary passed 'without any serious disturbance', the Inspector General noted that it was evident 1916's Easter embers had not passed to ash.[21] Memorial cards featuring the executed proclamation signatories were widely sold, while black silk armbands and republican tri-colour badges publicly exhibited sympathy to their cause.[22] Churches throughout Ireland, spanning Belfast, Cork, Dungannon, Drogheda, Limerick and elsewhere, held Mass 'for the repose of the souls of the Insurgents', in direct defiance of the Catholic hierarchy.[23] In Dublin, roughly 100 Cumann na mBan women laid tri-colour-trimmed wreaths over select graves at Glasnevin Cemetery and offered prayers in Irish, which doubled as an act of cultural defiance.[24] The tri-colour was a subtle yet versatile tool of insubordination that frustrated authorities. Flags were erected 'on the roofs of buildings, on old ruins, and on telegraph poles and high trees', taunting irritated police who were unable to procure ladders or haul them down. Crowds cheered 'rebel rags' fixed to the GPO and run up Nelson's Pillar during Easter Week commemorations. Staying true to the rebellion, the rowdy crowd recreated scenes of damage to commercial property. On Tuesday, vandals broke shop windows on Sackville Street and tore placards from tramcars. The city again provided fodder for its own turmoil. '[Y]oung men wearing rebel colours' weaponised debris from buildings damaged the previous year, hurling bricks and other material at unarmed soldiers at Eden Quay. Police baton charges and bitterly cold weather eventually subdued the commotion.[25] In Cork, Jerome Buckley, Con O'Regan and their Volunteer comrades affixed tri-colours to the highest points in the district, Mourneabbey Castle and a tall tree in Analeentha, to commemorate the rebellion. Unable to reach the flag, constables felled the tree. Police in County Tyrone followed suit and downed a large tree they were unwilling (or unable) to scale.[26] Limerick Volunteers honoured Con Colbert by raising flags atop the trees leading into Athea village, where the executed rebel leader had spent his youth. They sawed the top branches on their descent and hid all ladders in the vicinity to prevent removal.[27] Overall, it was reported that over 250 republican flags were displayed at 165 separate locations in April 1917, a subtle yet widespread defiance that renegotiated and politicised public space throughout Ireland.[28]

Vandalism and public demonstrations reinforced popular disaffection and nurtured the republican movement. They also brought pressure to bear on the British Government on issues ranging from the treatment of Irish political prisoners to conscription, which at times led to violence and the destruction of property.[29] For example, in June 1917, Colonial Secretary and Conservative Party leader Andrew Bonar Law announced that Lewes prison would release 29 Irish prisoners, whose status as political offenders had been recognised. Nationalists celebrated in various ways. Those in Strabane and Waterford ignited tar barrels and lit bonfires as a show of solidarity with the prisoners and their cause.[30] Cohesion was also apparent in Dublin, where thousands of prisoners' families and friends 'mobilised' to welcome their arrival. Áine Ceannt spent the night at the North Wall docks before crossing to Westland Row (Pearse) Station, where 117 combined prisoners arrived the next morning.[31] The liberated were led on a 'triumphal procession' to O'Mahoney's hotel, passing the GPO; 'a different scene to [...] being smuggled out of Ireland in the dead of night, and sent on cattle boats to England', Ceannt recalled.[32] In addition to a changing political climate, Ceannt's experience illustrates a confrontation with convention and power in other ways. First, as it contested women's domestic reserve within nationalist Ireland's traditionally 'masculine political landscape', and second, as it radically feminised Irish public spaces, such as docklands, streets and train stations.[33]

Dublin was but one of the centres of festivity where, William Murphy observes, 'flag-waving, war-piping, torchlight-bearing and, occasionally, stone-throwing crowds demonstrated the capacity of prisoners to bring people onto the streets.'[34] Nowhere was this more evident than in Cork, where Sinn Féin supporters, numbering 4,000–5,000, converged on the Great Southern and Western Railway terminus, 'of which they took complete possession', to receive J. J. Walsh, Diarmuid Lynch, David Kent, Maurice Brennan, Fergus O'Connor, William Tobin, Con Donovan and Thomas Hunter.[35] Walsh's memoir, *Recollections of a Rebel*, detailed the mood:

> Thousands of hurlers and footballers, all in uniform and the former carrying hurleys; handballers, boxers, youth organisations, volunteers, and about a dozen bands, stretched mile after mile along the Glanmire Road. Without doubt, it was one of the greatest parades ever seen in the City by the Lee. [...] No man, friend or foe, who saw that amazing demonstration could have had any doubts in his mind but that Rebellion had triumphed, that defiance of alien government had won the day.[36]

Shortly after departing the train platform, the crowd attacked Cork City Gaol and smashed its windows to contact Defence of the Realm Act (DORA) prisoners serving sentences inside.[37] It then moved into town, wrecking the local British Army recruiting office and disabling the courthouse's fire ladder (after using it to establish republican colours atop the building). A stand-off between republicans and soldiers' families preceded clashes with police that left one man, Abraham Allen, dead from a bayonet wound. Thirty others were admitted to hospital.[38] Rioting in Patrick Street later that evening damaged storefront windows and prompted looting before heavy rain and military relief quieted the city.[39]

Commemorative demonstrations and impulsive receptions fed nationalist enthusiasm and augmented a growing popular front. Prevailing excitement fed republican political rallies in 1917 and 1918 as well, where violence and the destruction of property often manifested as aversions to British rule.[40] Éamon de Valera's election to parliament for East Clare, for example, animated a politically charged crowd that proceeded to stone Ballybunion RIC barracks in Kerry on 11 July 1917, breaking several windows.[41] The following January, Loughrea Quarter Sessions awarded John Darcy £7 compensation for his horse, which had been deshod, shaved, painted green, and had 'Up De Valera!' written across its side.[42] Just as occupying and controlling public space exhibited republican agency, withdrawal from conventional political arenas and arguments shaped an alternative platform. For instance, Sinn Féin's absence from the Irish Convention, where conventional political interests – including constitutional nationalists as well as unionists – met over nine months between July 1917 and March 1918 to discuss the future of Irish self-government under the Home Rule model, presented an alternative solution to the 'Irish question'. Its own all-Ireland convention in October 1917 underscored this exclusivity.[43] The reorganisation of the Irish Volunteers mirrored this political development but was not necessarily its exact reflection. Similar to Gaelic League branches, Gaelic renaissance literary groups and Gaelic Athletic Association (GAA) clubs in previous decades, Sinn Féin, Cumann na mBan and the Irish Volunteers claimed distinction despite overlapping membership, personified most clearly in de Valera's election to president of both Sinn Féin and the Irish Volunteers in October 1917.[44] The continued threat of conscription in Ireland further aligned politics and militancy, 'dovetailing', in the words of IRA Chief-of-Staff Richard Mulcahy, 'Government-Army relations' in Dublin.[45] The overlap held electioneering value. Sinn Féin imported hundreds of Irish Volunteers for the South Armagh election, who arrived in Newry in military uniform carrying hurleys and bearing what the *Freeman's Journal* described as 'a distinct rural appearance'.[46] Others descended on the Waterford City elections in March 1918, which prompted further questions as to how the 'party machine' was transporting, housing and maintaining its mobile political army.[47] 'Demonstration politics' expanded both Sinn Féin membership and Volunteer rolls throughout the 1917–18 period[48]; growth, Fr Eugene Nevin explained, that showed separatist Ireland had not had all its eggs in the political basket.[49]

The government reassigned key roles in the Irish Executive in an effort to appease nationalist fervour and prevent another rebellion, at least for the remainder of the war. Lord Wimbourne retained the Lieutenancy while H. E. Duke, 'a political lightweight', was selected as Chief Secretary. Three Irishmen headed the top security and legal positions: Sirs Joseph Byrne, Bryan Mahon and James O'Connor filled the roles of RIC Inspector General, Commander-in-Chief of Irish forces and Attorney General, respectively.[50] However, in February 1918, Duke communicated that Sinn Féin was making his administration impossible. Arrests for offenses under DORA often made a spectacle of the legal process and failed to produce conviction. Defendants rejected the Crown's authority in Ireland, a performance that played well for the movement. Inspector General Byrne summarised the growing pattern of dissent that had spread from the streets to the courtroom:

> The Republican and mischievous doctrine publicly preached by Sinn Féin leaders, and disseminated by their journals, has given rise to widespread disloyalty and defiance of authority among the rising generation. Mere boys now commonly defy the Police, and when charged in Court declare themselves citizens of the Irish Republic, or soldiers of the Irish Republican Army, and refuse to acknowledge the jurisdiction of the Magistrates.[51]

Prosecutors were not deterred, and they proceeded under pretext to curtail the republican movement. From 1918, special inquisitorial procedure areas, special juries, martial law and evolved manifestations of the Defence of the Realm Act – notably Defence of the Realm Regulations (DRR) and the Restoration of Order in Ireland Regulations (ROIR) – were applied with protracted scope.[52] More direct precautionary measures went into effect. In May 1918, 51 members of the Sinn Féin and Irish Volunteer leadership were removed from public life, arrested and interned under the pretext of a 'German Plot'.[53] Furthermore, in July, the Criminal Law and Procedure (Ireland) Act 1887 was expanded. The Irish Volunteers, Sinn Féin and the Gaelic League were proclaimed illegal and their public meetings and general visibility were suppressed, while the country remained in a state of 'acute political unrest'.[54]

Though it varied by location, government suppression, mounting fear of conscription, and the coupling of Home Rule with conscription in Ireland further stirred Irish *résistance en masse*, which manifested from many quarters, in many forms and on various scales.[55] The Irish Labour Party directed a 'down tools' protest prior to Easter 1918 that spanned from Derry to Cork, while Dublin Trade Unionists' anti-conscription pledge received over 100,000 signatures – approximately the number of available, non-essential, military-aged Irishmen that the Irish Office in London had identified in early 1916.[56] This is somewhat misleading. A parliamentary report in November 1916 stated that '40% of those who had not yet enlisted were unfit.'[57] Unlike military service, there was no physical examination that barred a signature on an anti-conscription pledge. Women protested conscription in Ireland by threatening to withhold labour. More specifically, 40,000 Irishwomen pledged to refuse to fill the positions of men dismissed from their work for resisting conscription, and Cumann na mBan established a 'Green Cross' corps in anticipation of violence that an enforced draft would initiate.[58] Irish bishops validated the Irish Anti-Conscription Committee's protests through their added support.[59] Other anti-conscription demonstrations sought to not only resist Ireland's contribution to the current war effort, but to efface installations that honoured past wars, colonial figures and marks of ascendancy. Nationalists assaulted monuments commemorating British wars and religious markers during the period, sometimes repeatedly. In mid-April 1918, four allegedly drunk Irish Volunteers destroyed 23 Church of Ireland tombstones at Ballinatone, Wicklow – sacrilege erroneously linked to German influence that, Judge Ralph Brereton Barry noted, 'a few years ago [...] would have been impossible in Ireland'.[60] In December, explosives damaged a large commemorative Celtic cross dedicated to the Boer War in Cork; it was again assaulted in November 1919, and a larger portion of its base blown away.[61] Nuala Johnson explains public monuments as guiding a particular civic education, through which they espouse a particular political and cultural meaning.[62] As Yvonne Whelan succinctly wrote: 'Public monuments are not merely ornamental features of the urban landscape but rather highly symbolic signifiers that confer meaning on a city and transform neutral places into ideologically charged sites.'[63] Hence, nationalist attacks on the statues of individuals and monuments believed to represent Ireland's dispossession and coercion suggest a layered cultural protest. As such, long-standing discontent was often exorcised in a burst of destructive activity. One of the most layered examples of destruction occurred in Galway City prior to the civil war. In May 1922, labour advocates led demonstrators to Eyre Square, where they removed a bronze statue of Lord Dunkellin, paraded it to Nimmo's Pier and then deposited it in Galway Bay. On the surface, Dunkellin was an obvious target as he embodied many characteristics nationalists had come to despise: he was a British Army veteran who fought in the Crimean War and later served the colonial executive in India. However, the Dunkellin statue may have acted as a surrogate mark. Protest against Galway's slums, landlordism and unemployment had activated the mob, and Dunkellin's brother, Hubert de Burgh-Canning (Marquis of Clanricarde), was remembered as one of the worst landlords in Ireland.[64] 'Let it go boys,' Jim Larkin remarked, 'and may the devil and all rotten landlordism go with it.'[65] To ensure its permanent banishment from public space, Galway's poor and working class recovered the statue from the bay, sawed its arms and legs off, and sunk it again.[66] In the least, this event highlights a reactionary protest. However, like the statue and the life it represented, its destruction contested the emblems of power and memory it embodied.[67]

Republicans defaced statues, plaques and monuments as a challenge to the British State and in an effort to revise its colonial narrative. These actions went both ways as effigies commemorating nationalist milestones fell at the hands of military and police. In October 1920, a monument to Bartholomew Teeling, who was hanged for his role in the 1798 rebellion, was badly damaged outside Collooney, Sligo. Erected for the 1898 centenary, the statue portrayed Teeling with his right arm extended skyward, into which someone placed a Sinn Féin flag. Unable to remove the flag, military and police Auxiliaries opened fire on the statue and blew off Teeling's upstretched arm. In Youghal, a marble statue of Father Peter O'Neill was wrenched from its perch in Green Park and toppled. O'Neill, who was flogged and hanged by British soldiers in 1798, suffered a second, metaphorical death when the statue was decapitated upon its collapse.[68] Bombs dislocated the Croppy Boy pikeman from atop the 1798 monument in Tralee in April 1921, and caused serious damage to surrounding homes and businesses. Further dismemberment saw its pike, head, arms and legs smashed and stolen away.[69] Bandon's Maid of Erin was defaced with paint on the Manchester Martyrs anniversary in November 1920, and was split in two the following spring, its granite column smashed.[70] The military's escalated response characterised an important dynamic of the period. While republican flags or public rallies altered a space's physical integrity or political meaning, Crown forces often destroyed the space or its objects in an attempt to maintain their previous meaning. Dublin in ruins had remained a city of the Empire; the stump of a tree upon which republican colours had flown remained rooted in a United Kingdom; and Teeling's mangled statue would remain only as it recalled the failure of 1798, rather than the promise of 1916. As David Fitzpatrick noted, after 1916, the political status quo animated a reactionary political 'mood'. Tri-colour flag planting (and removal) was one outlet that showed how spaces were politicised and controlled.[71]

Crown forces also countered attempts to craft the narrative of more recent events. In Miltown Malbay, Clare, police and military confronted demonstrators that gathered to celebrate hunger strikers' release from Mountjoy Prison in April 1920.[72] Three men, Patrick Hennessy, John O'Loughlin and Thomas O'Leary, were shot and killed in the process. Crosses were erected to mark the spot on which they died, a place called Canada Cross, and each identified the men as having done so 'in the cause of Ireland'.[73] For four consecutive weeks, locals converged on Canada Cross following Sunday Mass to recite the rosary, consecrating the otherwise pedestrian intersection as nationalist holy ground.[74] Authorities removed the crosses in August, in what the *Cork Examiner* labelled a 'wanton act of desecration' that intensified civilian hostility in a region where locals were already refusing to sell food and fuel to police.[75] Similarly, mourning cards listing the murders of George Clancy, the Mayor of Limerick, and Michael O'Callaghan, the former mayor, who were shot in their homes in early May 1921, were removed from Limerick City Hall during curfew hours.[76]

It is perhaps too complex a reading to suggest that vandalism acted as a vehicle for cultural recovery, or a reiteration of state authority. Sites of memory certainly projected a subjective social and political value system – an imposed moral landscape – but their targeting was as much guided by location and convenience as by popular memory. It is also difficult to frame the battle for public space as binary. Ireland's geography of remembrance was diverse, often divisive, and further complicated by the memory of the Great War and nationalist and republican counter-narratives that had emerged to challenge it.[77] In this sense, public space served as a platform for compliance and dissent as well as indifference. Defacing or destroying statuary or icons exhibited attempts to reclaim or control historical narrative, a practice that continued in the decades following independence. In addition to public space, private, corporate and industrial spaces served to rearm and supply the republican movement.

A Conspicuous Cache: Building an Arsenal

Few instances of destruction occurred throughout 1918 that would resemble the types or scale of environmental damage inflicted during the War of Independence.[78] Cattle driving and maiming and agrarian-directed arson were far more prevalent, particularly in Connacht, as anti-grazier sentiment resurfaced.[79] The republican arsenal was similarly unbalanced. Weapons, whether in the hands of civilians, stored in safe houses or in IRA dumps, or in production in private homes, called further attention to revolutionary Ireland as an increasingly militarised place. The number of arms in the country after the Easter Rising is difficult to pin, but a tally compiled by police in February 1917 provides a starting point.[80] Though at most an estimate, it reported that the majority of arms were in Ulster (1,003), specifically in County Tyrone (595) and the cities of Belfast (217) and Londonderry (102). Munster totalled 827 rifles, with Cork's East Riding district claiming the majority (304).[81] To expand these resources, Volunteers raided police patrols, barracks and quarries for arms and explosives, and soldiers were occasionally persuaded to sell or surrender their weapons.[82] Volunteers favoured soft targets as evidenced by the overwhelmingly lopsided raids on civilian targets (434) as opposed to police (16) and military (25) over a 16-month period from January 1919 to April 1920.[83] People often willingly passed shotguns, sporting rifles and ammunition to local Volunteer companies, and lingering members of John Redmond's Irish National Volunteers continued to defect (with their rifles) to the 'rump' Volunteer faction, as they had done since 1915.[84]

Volunteers were not always able to successfully negotiate a peaceful transfer of arms. In February 1919, for example, three masked men raided the home of John Drislane, a Cork farmer, and demanded his gun. Drislane explained that it was hidden outside and motioned the men to the door. He then locked them out, retrieved his gun from inside the house and opened fire on the invaders, driving them away.[85] The West Limerick Brigade also appropriated guns from local farmers, but avoided a potential Drislane episode by pillaging houses on Sundays while residents were away at Mass.[86] Animals were often unwitting accomplices. The Kilbeacanty Company delayed their raid on the home of Thomas Burke, a local pro-British Galway farmer, until he had gone fowling. Nearby, the gamekeeper for Lord Gough's neighbouring estate at Lough Cutra, 'a tough, strong and exceedingly active Scotsman', fortified the residence against raids. The company lured him away, Thomas Keely recalled, by asking him to call on a sick horse.[87] More prosperous raids for arms, such as the Collinstown Aerodrome caper in March 1919, were rare,[88] and the 'mere trickle' of arms procured by 'devious methods' were unable to sate Volunteers' demands on a national scale.[89] Rifles were essential to ambushes and raids, but explosives were far more versatile. As such, companies pivoted towards obtaining explosive material and manufacturing their own bombs and grenades. The need to mine roads, breach perimeter walls and open fortified buildings prior to an engagement, or in aid of it, made them an indispensable accompaniment. Their acquisition very much depended on local knowledge of stores and deposits, such as quarries, engineer stores and transport sheds, as well as arranging a means to transport and conceal them. Volunteers enlisted the expertise of surveyors, engineers and miners, while university students studying for chemistry and engineering degrees proved invaluable in their knowledge of, and access to, laboratory chemicals.[90]

From 1918, IRA engineers directed the demolition of transportation routes, bridges and buildings for the construction of field defences, make-shift bridges and trenches; for identifying and collecting mineral and chemical supplies to be used in explosives; and for acquiring basic training in mechanical and electrical engineering.[91] Similar to the build-up of explosives and their manufacture prior to Easter 1916, explosive material – mainly gelignite, guncotton, blasting caps and fuses – were lifted from local sources, refined in private homes and commercial shops, and distributed or hidden for later use. Several heists throughout 1918 show the extent to which Volunteers were able to locate and acquire large quantities of materials. For instance, armed men robbed DeSelby Quarries in April 1918, making off with gelignite, blasting powder and fuses.[92] The same week, Volunteers forced open the magazine at a barytes mine near Bantry, Cork, and made away with 150 lbs of gelignite and 200 lbs of additional explosive materials.[93] Train stations and public carriages provided for smuggling and exchange. Jerry Golden met Seamus Robinson at Amiens St Station (Connolly Station) in June 1918, where he received three suitcases brought from Belfast. Golden took the cases to his home on the nearby Botanic Avenue, where he found that his comrades had already laid out nearly 100 empty biscuit tins to act as explosives casing, each waiting to receive a ration of the gelignite hidden in the suitcases.[94]

Concealing war material within ordinary objects further militarised banal spaces and routine experiences, but the method was not infallible. Long before travellers were asked if they had packed their own bags and knew their contents, Aliens Officers and Customs Officials inspected luggage cases and questioned their escorts; 35 lbs of gelignite, 15 lbs pounds of monarkite explosives, detonators, ammunition and revolvers were discovered in Michael Callaghan's suitcases in Scotland en route to Belfast in July 1918. Ironically, instruction letters also found on his person advised that 'parcels [of explosives] should be taken as ordinary luggage – that was the only way there was.'[95]

Raids on materials in transit or in storage dispersed legal implications beyond an individual courier. Amiens St Station was also the site of a large IRA raid in September 1918, where explosive materials again arrived from Belfast, spending the night in a goods shed under the guard of a single unarmed Dublin Metropolitan Police constable.[96] Dublin Brigade's E Company were instructed to remove the explosives to the adjacent Oriel Street. 'The number of boxes was so great,' Frank Henderson recalled, 'that a large number had to be mobilized.'[97] *An t-Óglach* afterwards boasted that 1,000 lbs of gelignite had been captured in the raid. The heist certainly made an impression in government circles. As the German war effort collapsed in November, the Chief Secretary for Ireland, Edward Shortt, reminded the House of Commons that danger still loomed in the form of the IRA:

> There is the question, again, of the Irish Volunteers, who are dominated to-day by the Irish Republican Brotherhood, and the question of their activities has once more arisen. When I tell the House that they had made preparations for fresh acts of violence, violence of the most serious description, and that only last week at one of their headquarters there was seized sufficient of [sic] high explosives, with fuses all prepared—and the experts are examining to see where they were prepared—sufficient to have blown up the whole of Belfast and Dublin. That element is still there.[98]

John Dillon, leader of the IPP after the death of John Redmond, criticised the Chief Secretary's assessment as a 'grotesque exaggeration' and asked why the government hadn't moved against the assailants whom 'everyone in Dublin' knew had explosives stashed in Rutland Square (Parnell Square).[99] The IPP leader's question appears contradictory given that, a month prior to the Amiens St Station raid, Dillon criticised the military for repossessing and rationing explosives for road works. As Shortt explained at that time, it was a necessary precaution given the existing national circumstances.[100]

These circumstances coalesced at Soloheadbeg, Tipperary, in January 1919. It is uncertain whether the South Tipperary Volunteers that crouched along Cranitch's field on the by-road to Soloheadbeg quarry intended to take the lives of two policemen in addition to the 160 lbs consignment of gelignite they escorted. However, the result nonetheless suggests the ambush was something more than an 'accidental start' to the revolution, as Seamus Robinson later labelled it.[101] Instead, it indicated the IRA's initiative and autonomy, a conscious assertion of force to differentiate itself from Dáil Éireann, which convened the same day.[102] 'A Tipperary Volunteer' reconciled each viewpoint in a letter reprinted in *An t-Óglach*, where he placed the killing of constables McDonnell and O'Connell as an act of self-defence: 'The men who seized the explosives at Soloheadbeg risked their lives for Ireland in order to get war material to assist and defend Ireland's freedom.'[103] Such 'assistance' had preceded the Soloheadbeg ambush, generally viewed as the start of military hostilities against British forces in Ireland, by nearly a year. In this context, preparative actions such as raids for arms and explosives, and the militarisation of public and private space, suggests we consider an earlier designator as well as a revision of the nature and definition of what was contemporarily viewed as 'active service'. On the other hand, the killing of constables McDonnell and O'Connell elicited shock that previous public protests or raids for arms failed to register.[104] The British Government's reaction was similarly distinct: south Tipperary was declared a special military area, martial law was applied, and permits for the use of explosives for quarrying were severely restricted.[105] In Dublin, police offered anywhere from £1 to £50 for information leading to the recovery of stolen explosives.[106] After Soloheadbeg, officials reclassified otherwise industrious mining instruments as tools of war. Explosives continued to hold value throughout the revolutionary period, and the unique circumstances of their theft, transport and refinement expanded the militarised landscape.

Unlike Soloheadbeg, encounters were mostly non-violent; some were especially courteous. For example, in April 1918, Volunteers intercepted two surveyors transporting 250 lbs of gelignite in Wexford, held them in a nearby wood as the explosives were driven away and unloaded, returned their car, released them and departed.[107] Intelligence work secured further material from unconventional places. Volunteers seized half a ton of gelignite from a steam drifter anchored at Arklow, Wicklow, in February 1920. Kynoch's factory had liquidated its overhead after ceasing production following the Great War and was preparing to ship the material to England.[108] Other coastal targets included Mizen Head lighthouse in Cork, and Hook lighthouse in Wexford, where Thomas Howlett recalled that the newfound resources animated the local company, making it feel as if it were 'on a war footing'.[109]

The Lord Lieutenant, Sir John French, acknowledged that by April 1920 the IRA possessed a significant amount of explosive material. However, its application was, he told a *Chicago Tribune* reporter in London, limited to 'rough bombs of the jampot type', that is, 'non-metropolitan' fragmentation grenades made from tin cans stuffed with nails.[110] While patronising, the Viceroy was correct. Like the bombs they produced, Volunteers' grasp of chemical engineering was either effectual or benign. Several university students and professionals within the IRA worked to close this gap. At University College Dublin, postgraduate chemistry student James O'Donovan and his professor secretly produced mercury fulminate, a primary explosive sensitive to heat and friction.[111] In Cork, Ray Kennedy, MSc, a chemistry demonstrator at University College Cork (UCC), distributed sulphuric acid and ammonium chlorate to small canister bombs to equip local companies.[112] Another UCC student, Michael V. O'Donoghue, regularly lectured Volunteers on engineering demolition at the Maylor St Club (which doubled as an IRA bomb factory) and the Thomas Ashe Hall. Both operated behind a Gaelic League facade.[113] From mid-1918, IRA General Headquarters (GHQ) pressed for simple, inexpensive bombs able to be produced by unskilled hands in great quantity.[114] *An t-Óglach* featured instructions for effective use of explosives, the nature, care and potential of gelignite, and methods on the use of chemical gas.[115] Rory O'Connor, Director of Engineering on the Volunteer General Staff, inspected potential production sites; by 1921, GHQ prioritised explosives training, circulating handbooks and pamphlets and organising training retreats.[116] Throughout November 1921, Lord Massey's home, Grantstown Hall, hosted a particularly intensive training course for all company engineers within the Third Tipperary Brigade. Instruction in engine repair, mechanical work, electricity, mines and explosives generated an atmosphere reminiscent of a marriage between Ford Motor Company and the Electricity Supply Board, Seamus Babington later recalled.[117]

Small-scale, amateur bomb factories superimposed explosives production onto homes, businesses and, consequently, unsuspecting neighbourhoods. Dave Higgins's home in Ballylegane, Waterford, was selected as a bomb factory as it was the only house in the parish never raided by British forces.[118] Similarly, Second Cork Brigade Engineer Daniel Daly used his home in Glanmore for making bombs – 'these were made with ordinary tin canisters, some cement, pieces of old metal from old pots, etc., and a half stick of gelignite to which a piece of fuse was affixed.' Daly's was selected as it was in a quiet part of the country.[119] Operations in Blackrock were removed to Glencullen House, an abandoned manor in the Dublin hills, where Andrew McDonnell and members of the Second Dublin Brigade resumed work in May 1921.[120]

Many unsuspecting people were exposed to the danger of police raids or accidental explosions, as manufacture proceeded near or in homes and businesses and adjacent to foot paths. Police evacuated the homes around Messrs Heron & Lawless at 198 Parnell Street, Dublin, in December 1920, after it was discovered that the cycle shop fronted an IRA bomb factory. It is unknown whether John Dillon, who had previously identified the area as a well-known bomb-making site, offered comment. However, a Dublin Castle report described the bomb factory and its manufacturing process:

> The loading was done in an extremely dangerous and haphazard manner. Boxes of detonators were lying all over the place, whilst loose powder was scattered on the table and mixed up will all kinds of cartridges. [...] Sacks full of gelignite, annonite, and other explosives were lying about the workshop. [...] It is remarkable that no accident has occurred during the filling process and the manufacture of detonation units. Had such an explosion taken place it would undoubtedly have involved the whole block of buildings, and the loss of life would have been very heavy.[121]

Joseph Lawless was in Collinstown Interment Camp when he learned of the factory's discovery. While he conceded its output to be 'the crudest form of a bomb and little removed from the cocoa tins we had used in 1916', an Intelligence Officer at the camp enthusiastically praised 'the skill and ingenuity he had seen displayed in the production of these bombs, and the bombs themselves were, he said, most excellent productions'.[122] The

Irish Independent conceded as much in its coverage of an explosion in Cork the previous year at which 'no little ingenuity and skill' was displayed.[123] 'The Cork Explosion' received continuous coverage throughout May 1919, due in no small part to it having occurred in the ground-level kitchen of a three-storey tenement house on a prominent city street. The blast injured several people in the building and on the street, including Volunteers Dick Murphy, Seán O'Connell and Michael Tobin, and their associates Mrs McMahon, Jeremiah Downey, Timothy Hegarty and Cissie Moore. Twenty-nine-year-old Tobin later died in hospital from shock and excessive burns. An upstairs lodger, Mrs Buckley, was not home at the time of the detonation; her children were but escaped unharmed.[124] Like weapons dumps or arms concealed on one's person, bomb making militarised public and private space and endangered civilians, including women and children. While guns responded to even the most untrained shooter, bomb building, no matter how rudimentary, required a degree of knowledge and skill.

As the Cork explosion demonstrated, the IRA comprised many inexperienced engineers who often operated beyond their knowledge or training. Some were quite aware of their shortcomings. Michael Ryan reflected on his appointment as East Waterford Brigade Engineer Officer in early 1921 as 'the worst possible choice':

> I was not yet 18 years of age, and I had little or no knowledge of explosives and certainly no leadership. It may have been that because of my employment with Messrs. John Hearne & Son, Builders, I was presumed to know a little about Building and Civil Engineering. [...] It will be appreciated that, as these were the days before broadcasting and the advent of a radio set in every home, [...] electricity was one of the mysteries of life.[125]

In May 1921, Ryan was tasked to destroy a bridge on the main road between Waterford and Dungarvan; 'an unholy mess was made of the job', and the bridge suffered only minor damage. The mishap proved fortuitous, however, as a pipeline that carried water from the nearby Knockaderry reservoir was laid along the bridge. Destroying it would have interrupted local water distribution, 'and the consequences would not have been pleasant'.[126] Bernard Kilbride, an Assistant Surveyor for Longford County Council, observed that when materials failed to detonate or acted in unanticipated ways, the fault was almost always due to a lack of technical knowledge on the part of the engineer.[127] In many instances, the IRA's general lack of experience or technical knowledge in explosives may have saved many innocent lives.

Building the Volunteer arsenal altered established associative dynamics. An idle shotgun revised the importance of a rustic country home; explosives legitimised mining stores, surveyors and their guard as military targets; and acculturated spaces, such as university laboratories, bicycle shops and kitchens, were reimagined as bomb factories. In their reimaged nature, these objects and spaces became platforms for revolutionary activity.[128] The concept also applied to state officials and Crown forces. Sinn Féin's new political dictate reordered social behaviour, displacing those it deemed hostile to republican separatism. Local excommunication took many forms, including social boycott, a denial of services and the destruction of homes and property. These substitute targets aligned to the IRA's ordnance and dictation of public order, but their ruin was nevertheless felt on personal and social levels as well.

Social Environments

Drilling, preparing natural landscapes for ambush, transporting arms and explosives from dumps to assault sites, raiding, cutting communication wires and burning enemy structures greatly expanded Ireland's militarised geography. In turn, these acts displaced familiar spatial and temporal boundaries amongst both civilians and combatants.[129] Chris Pearson explained that combatants and non-combatants co-exist (often unwillingly) within militarised landscapes, which produce 'contact zones' where military activity invades private spheres: 'For militarized landscapes are places of contact, tension and negotiation between civilians and the military, soldiers and the environment, and between humans and non-humans.'[130] In addition to its impact on rural and urban landscapes, the intimate, liminal and incessantly destructive nature of guerrilla warfare in Ireland also altered existing social environments, deconstructing the relationships and identities they hosted.[131] This was particularly true of individuals and groups whose political and religious convictions provoked the republican program, for whom the dual experience of physical and social displacement coalesced. Many were marginalised against the growing popularity of Sinn Féin and the arbitration for political space in post-Rising Ireland. Nevertheless, the contact zones that emerged during of the War of Independence hosted more violent, intimate negotiations.

The IRA intimidated and punished those who violated republican public social etiquette, which essentially comprised housing, serving or extending graces to policemen and those labelled political and religious dissidents. Eroding the social foundations of these groups significantly altered communal dynamics. Specifically, it weakened police authority and public resistance to republicanism. Pressure came to bear on constables to leave the force, and on their families to persuade the same. *An t-Óglach* encouraged local initiative towards this end, which Dáil Éireann sanctioned as national policy. Proclamations distributed throughout County Clare in September 1919 listed various offences treasonous to the Irish Republic, which included 'having intercourse with the Police or Military, supplying them with goods or transport, assisting them in their investigations' – conditions echoed in numerous notices posted near barracks throughout the month.[132] Lodging constables was also forbidden and carried a penalty of destruction of the boarding house.[133] Sometimes orders were communicated directly. Landlords in the small Clare village of Corofin refused to let vacant houses to police and their families after they received threatening letters. In Youghal, Cork, the IRA hand-delivered instructions to landlords that delineated which loyalties were to be observed. They read:

> Fellow Irishman, You are unfortunate to have taken up the attitude you have. Why harbour police, soldiers, and coastguards[?]. It is regretted you associate with the enemies of our country. You are hereby warned to cease communication with those class of people, otherwise you must be dealt with as an enemy of Ireland. If you value your life get rid of them from your house, and obey the laws of your country. [signed] Intelligence Branch, I.R.A.[134]

The program had a powerful effect, as one policeman's letter to the *Constabulary Gazette* had already established:

> Dear Editor, I do not know that you are aware that there never was a time in the history of

the Force that there was less respect for the Irish policeman than there is at present. Nobody respects them, and nobody fears them, and they are not wanted in any society. [...] He [a constable] is not welcome in the locality he was reared in – his actions have been well circulated there. [...] He is met by ingratitude on one side, on the other by contempt.[135]

The local church also failed to provide sanctuary for policemen and their families. For instance, republicans removed the dedicated police pew at Monroe Chapel, a Roman Catholic church in Tipperary, in April 1920, forcing humiliated constables and their families to kneel on the bare floor amidst parishioners' muffled laughter. The same occurred at Kilcommon Catholic Church in Newport, 20 miles south. In an attempt to mediate, the parish priest suggested constables should perhaps 'refrain from attending Divine Service for some time'.[136] Graffiti and social animus politicised the churchyard and often shamed the bereaved. Mrs Wallace was publicly mocked as she made her way to Mass shortly after the death of her husband, an RIC sergeant shot and killed aboard a Cork-bound train in May 1919.[137] Subtle changes made to familiar landscapes were both intimidating and ominous. The following year, for example, 'Kilmovee R.I.C. – R.I.P.' and the drawing of a coffin and revolver hanging on the church gate greeted the faithful as they arrived at Sunday Mass.[138] Equally suggestive, the IRA prepared grave plots on the property of landlords and graziers, which threatened the ultimate penalty. Though it largely featured within agrarian conflicts, the practice was extended to the homes of non-compliant civilians and state officials.[139] In essence, threatening letters and public warnings eroded the familiar sanctuary of select private and public spaces. For constables' wives and children, social excommunication could be a very traumatic experience.

Resident families presented unique difficulties when IRA men assaulted the barracks they called home. Attacking barracks meant home invasion and a reimagining of domestic spaces as military targets. A policeman's family not only complicated a building's destruction but also the moral dimensions of the republican program, though they rarely delayed operations or deterred evictors. Attitudes varied from company to company, but in the majority of interactions, Volunteers simply ejected tenants and burned the building. This most often occurred in the midnight hours when terrified women and children were banished to the night's frigid embrace, which hostile neighbours' equally cold response often intensified. Mrs Reddy and her child were ordered out of a Monaghan barracks at gunpoint at 3 a.m. on 26 April 1920, before their bedding, clothing and furniture were soaked with petrol and ignited. No fewer than 17 families experienced a similar ordeal over the course of a week in May 1920, as part of more coordinated movements against vacated barracks where policemen's families remained. Some endured not only the trauma of violent eviction but also the slow destruction of their property. Mrs Mullally attempted to depart from the burning police hut in which she resided at Lissycasey, Clare, but was detained by Volunteers who made her spend the night in a warehouse adjacent to the smouldering ruins of her former home.[140] Elsewhere, Mrs Collins and her eight children willingly returned to what remained of the basement of her destroyed barrack home, so that the children 'might not be completely deprived of a night's sleep'.[141]

Despite apparent indifference, republicans often observed a degree of courtesy towards inhabitants who had made the barracks their home.[142] For instance, raiders removed the sergeant's wife, as well as her furniture and valuables, to a safe location before destroying

Ballyfarnon barracks in County Roscommon.[143] The same occurred in Farnaght, Leitrim, where Mrs Gilroy, her eight children, and their belongings were withdrawn and accommodated in an adjacent house before the barracks was burned. It was the second effort to destroy the building; a 'tender-hearted' commandant had overturned the assault ('failed to carry out his orders') three weeks prior.[144] These actions exhibit how the symbolic and pragmatic destruction of state property was habitually prioritised over harming its inhabitants – part of an observable live-and-let-live policy extended to those who co-operated with the IRA.[145] Elsewhere, communities rallied to support the IRA's victims. As in republican areas, politics, religion and the possibility of retaliation informed local responses. For example, hundreds offered support to the displaced victims of an IRA attack on the barracks in Cullybackey, Antrim, a predominantly Protestant, unionist 'loyal neighbourhood'.[146] Civility had its limits, however, particularly from those who feared reprisal. Neighbours denied shelter to a sergeant's wife and children after they were evicted from a County Clare police station shortly after Christmas in 1919. The family wandered the cold countryside until they found shelter in Ennis, 12 miles away, the following afternoon.[147] Elsewhere, Sergeant Terence McDermott's wife and three children remained in Ballivor barracks in County Meath after police were withdrawn in October 1919. Insulated within a row of houses at the centre of the village, the family had furnished five rooms during their fifteen-year residence.[148] Only the piano and bookcase were removed before the building was burned, and Mrs McDermott was publicly ridiculed during her compensation hearing after she told the court of the sentimental loss of her possessions, which included religious magazines and her son's football medals.[149] Overall, effacing barracks aimed to eliminate state security structures and to manufacture psychological distress in the locality, compounding, as Inspector General William Byrne ironically remarked, Ireland's 'highly inflammable condition'. A 'Sergeant's Wife' spoke even more plainly to the *Irish Independent* about the enduring hardship of policemen and their families: 'Big pay is no good if your life is a hell upon earth.'[150]

Beyond policemen and their families, the individuals and businesses that supplied them (willingly or unwillingly) became targets by association, their commerce boycotted.[151] Again, public notices and private letters warned against being 'on friendly terms with the police'.[152] Offenders were punished through their property and livelihoods, which a reduced police presence allowed with impunity in more remote, rural areas.[153] Publicans in Kerry and Limerick reported extensive damage to their premises in June 1920, which resulted from their continued association with constables; Miss Redmond's public house in Wicklow was rechristened an 'R.I.C. Bar' on similar grounds.[154] In some places, previous agrarian activism guided destructive processes and intimidation. 'Old methods were simply applied to a new cause', Brian Hughes observed, with restrictions on food, fuel and transport exacerbating police distress and discomfort.[155] Turf was a particularly versatile victim of the police boycott. Local supplies were burned, buried or broken up to prevent them heating barracks.[156] Vehicles and animals that conveyed turf and other goods were also immobilised. In Donegal, farmer Neil Harkin's cart was dismantled and its wheel thrown into a lake to prevent him supplying any more turf to police.[157] Bernard McGinley and members of the IRA's Creeslough Company disabled another cart by sawing its axel shaft, and later burned a lorry used to deliver goods and mail to the RIC.[158] Autopsies conducted on two horses in Downpatrick revealed arsenic in their intestinal tracts; their owner, P. J. Kelly, frequently lodged police in his hotel. James Doyle's horse bled to death after suffering a malicious cut on its leg in retaliation for moving a constable's furniture.[159] Serving dead policemen was also disciplined. Michael McCarthy's hearse was burned after he delivered Constable Patrick Carey, who was killed in an ambush near Tuam, to his family plot in Skibbereen in July 1920.[160]

The IRA worked to ensure that damaged and destroyed landscapes remained in the public eye. Tradesmen were regularly cautioned against repairing damaged barracks, renovating apartments or outfitting cottages meant for police occupation. Louis Hodkinson was contracted to paint a District Inspector's apartments in Bruff, Limerick, but was warned that doing so would bring 'great risk to yourself and your employees'. The home of a Waterford carpenter named Kelly was raided shortly after he had made repairs to the local RIC barracks, which made him 'unpopular' in the locality.[161] Such acts worked to deny space and alter and enforce social relationships within a locality; the process looked backwards as well as forwards. In Cashel, Tipperary, Charles Clarke was threatened for seeking repair to Holycross barracks, which he owned, and for entertaining the division and allotment of his farmland for ex-soldiers.[162] Intimidating landlords and suppliers and denying their means to conduct business, the IRA purged the Irish constabulary from necessary quarters and essential services. This accounted for nearly 500 reported instances of police–supplier intimidation between March 1920 and July 1921, encounters that altered countless local partnerships and very often left small, though personally impactful, trails of destruction.[163] The social isolation it enforced was arguably more divisive, particularly when we consider the degree to which Irish police had been integrated into local communities since the early twentieth century.[164]

Conclusion

Republicans continued to use Ireland's civic spaces as platforms for dissent in the immediate post-Rising years. While these transformations were often subtle or temporary, they nevertheless demonstrated continued opposition to British rule. Public defiance manifested in various ways, from flying republican tri-colours to resisting conscription and ostracising police, which resulted in both temporary and permanent damages to Irish landscapes. Additional challenges targeted Britain's colonial legacy, which the damage to numerous statues and memorials to landlords, improvers and politicians throughout Ireland reinforced. Their defacing revised what many nationalists believed to be a sanitised narrative that underwrote centuries-long political and cultural suppression. Such sentiments manifested in covert activities to stock and outfit the IRA private homes and farms; known arsenals were relieved of loose firearms, while quarries, chemists and motor garages were raided for explosives and chemicals for bomb making. The process militarised these spaces and implicated surrounding areas where weapons were stored or refined, an overlap that ultimately dissolved previously understood spatial boundaries. As the next chapter shows, the fluid nature of guerrilla warfare further eroded civilian–military distinctions, while at the same time compounding the Irish revolution's environmental impacts.

NOTES

1. *Nationalist and Leinster Times*, 28 Apr. 1917; *Irish Independent*, 25 Apr. 1917.
2. *Evening Herald*, 24 Apr. 1917.
3. Ibid., 28 Apr. 1917.
4. *Sunday Independent*, 22 Apr. 1917.
5. Chris Pearson, 'Researching militarized landscapes: A literature review on war and the militarization of the environment', in *Landscape Research* 37:1 (February 2012), pp 115–33. Pearson defines militarised landscapes as 'sites that are partially or fully mobilized to achieve military aims'. My use here is less contained and far more fluid; quoting Rachel Woodward, 'military geographies are everywhere', Pearson, p. 116.
6. Steve Pile, 'Introduction: Opposition, political identities, and spaces of resistance', in *Geographies of Resistance* (New York: Routledge, 1997), p. 1.
7. Diarmaid Ferriter, 'The 1916 prisoners released on Christmas Eve', *Irish Times*, 24 Dec. 2016, https://www.irishtimes.com/opinion/diarmaid-ferriter-the-1916-prisoners-released-on-christmas-eve-1.2915580, accessed 8 October 2022; Ronan McGreevy, 'Home for Christmas – An Irishman's diary on the release of republican prisoners from Frongoch in 1916', *Irish Times*, 19 Dec. 2016, https://www.irishtimes.com/opinion/home-for-christmas-an-irishman-s-diary-on-the-release-of-republican-prisoners-from-frongoch-in-1916-1.2910274, accessed 8 October 2022; see also, Eunan O'Halpin, 'Historical revision XX: H. E. Duke and the Irish Administration, 1916–18', in *Irish Historical Studies* 22:88 (September 1981), p. 364.
8. J. J. Lee, *Ireland, 1912–1985: Politics and Society* (Cambridge: Cambridge University Press, 1989), p. 37.
9. Charles Townshend, *Political Violence in Ireland Since 1848* (New York: Oxford University Press, 1984), p. 312; David Fitzpatrick, *Politics and Irish Life 1913–1921: Provincial Experience of War and Revolution* (Cork: Cork University Press, 1998 edition), p. 109. Mark Duncan, 'Between armed rebellion and democratic revolution: The Irish Question in 1917', in *Century Ireland*, https://www.rte.ie/centuryireland/, s.d., accessed 8 October 2022.
10. Amongst the War Cabinet's views towards releasing interned prisoners were that there was more danger, in a political sense, in keeping them interned, and that release would help in the application of compulsory service being extended to Ireland. Also, amnesty was viewed as a necessary predicate to any workable implementation of the Home Rule Bill and the Irish Convention. War Cabinet minutes, 21 Dec. 1916, TNA (CAB 23/1/14); H. E. Duke, 21 Dec. 1916, ibid/appendix; ibid., 22 May 1917, CAB 23/2/143(72); ibid., 24 May 1917, CAB 23/2/145(11); ibid., CAB 23/3/163(19); *Irish Independent*, 11 June 1917.
11. Inspector General's report for February 1917, Joseph Byrne to Under Secretary (William Byrne), TNA (CO 904/102).
12. Chief Secretary's report to War Cabinet, 15 Mar. 1917, TNA (CAB 23/2/97(22)).
13. 'Sinn Féin meetings 1917, 'The Sinn Féin Movement', speeches from Strokestown (19 January), Boyle (20 January), Arigna (23 January), Tarmonbarry (25 January) and Elphin (28 January), TNA (CO 904/23/3). See also, 'War Cabinet minutes', 19 Feb. 1917, TNA (CAB 23/1/73 (12)). Ginnell was later prosecuted for inflammatory speech in May 1919. Inspector General's report for May 1919, Assistant Inspector General to Under Secretary, TNA (CO 904/109).
14. *Kerry News*, 23 Apr. 1917; Inspector General's report, Byrne to US, 15 Mar. 1918, TNA (CO 904/105).
15. 'Sinn Féin Volunteer Parades, St Patrick's Day, 1917', TNA (CO 904/23/3).
16. *Irish Independent*, 23 Apr. 1917; *Southern Star*, 28 Apr. 1917; Inspector General's report for January 1917, Joseph Byrne to William Byrne, TNA (CO 904/102).
17. Fitzpatrick, *Politics and Irish Life*, p. 118.
18. Ibid.
19. Ibid., p. 107.
20. Timothy G. McMahon, *Grand Opportunity: The Gaelic Revival and Irish Society, 1893–1910* (Syracuse: Syracuse University Press, 2008), pp 155–6.
21. Inspector General's report for April 1917, TNA (CO 904/102).
22. *Belfast Newsletter*, 25 Apr. 1917.

23. *Drogheda Independent*, 14 Apr. 1917; *Belfast Newsletter*, 24 Apr. 1916; see also, statements of M. J. Curran, BMH, WS 687, pp 195–6; and Madge Daly, BMH, WS 855, p. 5; 'Lively scenes in Cork', *Belfast Newsletter*, 10 Apr. 1917; *Derry Journal*, 18 Apr. 1917.
24. *Freeman's Journal*, 9 Apr. 1917. Bystander victims were also commemorated, though often privately and with a view towards repose rather than political antagonism: 'In sad and loving memory of John Byrne [...] who died [...] from gunshot wounds accidentally received in Rebellion riots. Sweet Jesus have mercy on his soul. [...] Inserted by his loving wife and children', *Evening Herald*, 26 Apr. 1917.
25. *Belfast Newsletter*, 10 Apr. 1917.
26. The flag on Mourneabbey Castle remained in place until it was destroyed by the elements. Statements of Jerome Buckley, BMH, WS 1063, pp 4–5; Cornelius O'Regan, BMH, WS 1200, p. 4; Edward Dolan, BMH, WS 1078, p. 3; and Henry O'Keeffe, BMH, WS 1315, p. 1; *Belfast Newsletter*, 27 Apr. 1917.
27. Mossie Harnett (ed. James H. Joy), *Victory and Woe: The West Limerick Brigade in the War of Independence* (Dublin: University College Dublin Press, 2002), pp 19–20. Around the same time, authorities removed another rebel flag from the municipal buildings of Sligo's county seat. Imitating a practice they had struggled to counter, police affixed a Union Jack high on the building's tower. *Evening Herald*, 30 Oct. 1920. A similar incident occurred in Tipperary Town in 1919. See Nuala Johnson, *Geography of Remembrance*, pp 69–70.
28. Inspector General's report for April 1917, TNA (CO 904/102).
29. William Murphy, *Political Imprisonment and the Irish, 1912 –1921* (Oxford: Oxford University Press, 2014), pp 70–6.
30. *Cork Examiner*, 18 June 1917; *Irish Independent*, 18 June 1917; Diarmaid Ferriter, *A Nation and Not a Rabble: The Irish Revolution 1913–1923* (London: Profile Books, 2015), p. 170. *Belfast Newsletter* cited only 20 released from Lewes Gaol. *Belfast Newsletter*, 18 June 1917.
31. *Ulster Herald*, 23 June 1917.
32. Statement of Áine Ceannt, BMH, WS 264, pp 50–1; Murphy, *Political Imprisonment and the Irish*, p. 57.
33. Lorraine Dowler, 'Amazonian landscapes: Gender, war, and historical repetition', in Colin Flint (ed.), *The Geography of War and Peace: From Death Camps to Diplomats* (Oxford: Oxford University Press, 2005), pp 136–8.
34. Murphy, *Political Imprisonment*, p. 77.
35. Inspector General's report for June 1917, Joseph Byrne to William Byrne, 9 July 1917, TNA (CO 904/103). Source matched against J. J. Walsh's recollection of events, which places the release in August 1917.
36. J. J. Walsh, *Recollections of a Rebel* (Tralee: The Kerryman Ltd, 1944), pp 44–6; see also, *Cork Examiner*, 25 June 1917. Walsh's contemporaries corrected several of his statements, mainly inaccurate dates and details, while also expanding on the destructive by-product of this enthusiastic reception. Statement of Ralph P. Keyes, BMH, WS 128, pp 1–2; statement of John Joseph Scollan, BMH, WS 341, pp 1–2.
37. *Belfast Newsletter*, 25 June 1917.
38. *Limerick Leader*, 27 June 1917; statement of Jerome Coughlan, BMH, WS 1568, p. 2; *Derry Journal*, 27 June 1917.
39. *Evening Herald*, 25 June 1917. Shops included Messers P. D. Buckley, tobacconist; Jas. Hayes, provision merchant; Teape, jeweler; Cotter, outfitter; Haynes, fishing and tackle; Grant and Co., drapers; Harringtons, chemist; Thompsons, confectioners; Lipton's, general provisions; Alcock's, grocers; and Elverys, outfitters.
40. J. J. Lee, *Ireland*, p. 38.
41. One young man, Daniel Scanlon, was killed in confrontation with police; but this episode, like the assault on Cork Gaol earlier that year, was consequential to the collective mood rather than indicative of coordinated rebellion. Inspector General's report for July 1917, Joseph Byrne to William Byrne, 14 Aug. 1917, TNA (CO 904/103); *The Liberator* (Tralee), 10 July 1917; *Kerry Evening Post*, 14 July 1917.
42. *Kerry People*, 12 Jan. 1918. The press noted: 'The affair was said to have its origin in local displeasure with the C.D.B. in whose service Darcy was.'

43. Arthur Griffith on 'British Parliament renounced by Sinn Féin', Report of the Proceedings of the Sinn Féin Convention, 25–26 October, 1917, TNA (CO 904/23/5), pp 6–10; Townshend, *Political Violence in Ireland*, p. 319. Political rallies continued throughout 1918, particularly following the arrest of Sinn Féin leaders under the guise of the 'German Plot', by-elections and the general election. Ferriter, *A Nation and Not a Rabble*, p. 177.
44. Statement of Patrick O'Brien, BMH, WS 812, pp 1–2; Tim McMahon, *Grand Opportunity: The Gaelic Revival and Irish Society, 1893–1910* (New York: Syracuse University Press, 2008), pp 85–126; Harnett, *Victory and Woe*, p. 20; Justin Dolan Stover, 'Modern Celtic nationalism in the period of the Great War: Establishing transnational connections', in Deborah Furchtgott, Georgia Henley and Matthew Holmberg (eds), *Proceedings of the Harvard Celtic Colloquium* XXXII (2012), pp 286–301.
45. Richard Mulcahy, 'Conscription and the General Headquarters' staff', in *Capuchin Annual* (1968), p. 395; Townshend, *Political Violence in Ireland*, p. 317; *Freeman's Journal*, 1 Feb. 1918.
46. *Freeman's Journal*, 1 Feb. 1918.
47. Reprinted from the *Dundalk Democrat*: 'What has Sinn Féin spent on South Armagh? Probably not less than £10,000. To bring that army of 1,000 "Volunteers" from Clare, Kerry, and Limerick and keep them in Dundalk and Newry must have cost some thousands.' *Freeman's Journal*, 4 Feb. 1918; *Freeman's Journal*, 21 Mar. 1918.
48. Ferriter states: 'The Representation of the People Act had expanded the electorate from 700,000 to 1.93 million, with women over the age of thirty with the requisite property qualifications allowed to vote for the first time.' Ferriter, *A Nation and Not a Rabble*, pp 179–80; Townshend, *Political Violence in Ireland*, p. 312; see also, Richard Mulcahy, 'Conscription and the General Headquarters' staff', in *Capuchin Annual* (1968), p. 384; Florence O'Donoghue, 'Volunteer "Actions" in 1918', in *Capuchin Annual* (1968), pp 340–4; and Townshend, *Political Violence in Ireland*, pp 320–1.
49. Specifically, 'We have not all our eggs in the one basket; we have our own selves; we have Sinn Féin. No country ever regained its lost independence that had not men ready to dare and die for it.' *Derry Journal*, 4 Mar. 1918; *Irish Independent*, 2 Mar. 1918; see also, statement of Fr Eugene Nevin, CP, BMH, WS 1605, p. 20–2.
50. O'Halpin, 'H. E. Duke and the Irish administration', pp 362–3; Townshend, *Political Violence in Ireland*, citing Memo by Chief Secretary, 19 Feb. 1918 (note 3), pp 324–5.
51. Inspector General's report for March 1918, J. Byrne to Under Secretary, 13 Apr. 1918, TNA (CO 904/105).
52. Colm Campbell, *Emergency Law in Ireland, 1918–1925* (New York: Oxford University Press, 1994), pp 13–24, particularly, p. 15 on DORA, sections 9AA and 29B.
53. Inspector General's report for May 1918, J. Byrne to Under Secretary, 11 June 1918, TNA (CO 904/106). For specific files on Dowling and the 'German Plot', see 'Case of Dowling (prisoner) July 1918, notes from court martial', Irish Military Archives (George Gavan Duffy collection, CD 45/15/2); Michael McKeogh, 'Casement, Germany and the World War', in *Catholic Bulletin* xviii (October 1928), pp 1043–4.
54. Inspector General's report for July 1918, Byrne to Under Secretary, 9 Aug. 1918, TNA (904/106); *Donegal News*, 6 July 1918.
55. Pádraig Yeates writes 'Prevailing anti-conscription sentiment aligned public opinion, including that of Unionists, and underscored the geneses of various protests, raids, and military demonstrations throughout 1918.' Pádraig Yeates, *A City in Wartime – Dublin 1914–1918: The Easter Rising 1916* (eBook edition).
56. *Irish Independent*, 24 Apr. 1918; see also, Inspector General's report June 1918, TNA (CO 904/106).
57. Patrick Callan, 'Recruiting for the British Army in Ireland during the First World War', in *Irish Sword* 17 (Summer 1987), p. 56.
58. *Donegal News*, 15 June 1918.
59. 'All Nationalists combine for defence', *Strabane Chronicle*, 27 Apr. 1918.
60. *Skibbereen Eagle*, 22 June 1918. For reports of similar damage, see *Strabane Chronicle*, 4 May 1918, and *Donegal News*, 4 May 1918.
61. *Cork Examiner*, 30 Dec. 1918; *Kerryman*, 4 Jan. 1919; Inspector General's report for November 1919, J. Byrne to Under Secretary (James Macmahon), TNA (CO 904/110).
62. Nuala C. Johnson, 'Mapping monuments: The shaping of public space and cultural identities', in *Visual Communication* 1:3 (2002), p. 293, citing N. C. Johnson, 'Sculpting heroic histories: Celebrating

the centenary of the 1798 rebellion in Ireland', in *Transactions of the Institute of British Geographers* 19 (1994), pp 78–93, and N. C. Johnson, 'Cast in stone: Monuments, geography and nationalism', in *Environment and Planning D: Society and Space* 13 (1995), pp 51–65.
63. Yvonne Whelan, 'The construction and destruction of a colonial landscape: Monuments to British monarchs in Dublin before and after independence', in *Journal of Historical Geography* 28:4 (2002), p. 508.
64. Ronnie O'Gorman, 'Woodford stood up to the power of Lord Clanricarde', *Galway Advertiser*, 6 May 2010. Alternatively, a statue of Fr Patrick Costello, a Woodford Parish Priest who helped maintain the people during evictions, was honoured with a marble alter erected in St Michael's Church, Ballinasloe, his former assignment. Statement of Lawrence Flynn, BMH, WS 1061, p. 1; Maud Gonne publicly projected these images into Parnell Square in 1897 to protest Queen Victoria's Diamond Jubilee, extending their public exposure. Fintan Cullen, 'Marketing national sentiment: Lantern slides of evictions in late nineteenth-century Ireland', in *History Workshop Journal* 54 (Autumn 2002) pp 162–79 (material from pp 163–4). See also, statements of Laurence Flynn, BMH, WS 1061; and Lawrence Garvey, BMH, WS 1062. Police had used battering rams to evict tenants on his Woodford estate during the late nineteenth-century Land War, which circulated throughout Ireland as part of *Ireland in the Magic Lantern*, a collection of sixty images documenting tenant evictions.
65. Kernan Andrews, 'The Galway MP who got thrown in the river', *Advertiser*, 5 Sept. 2017, https://www.advertiser.ie/galway/article/94889/the-galway-mp-who-got-thrown-in-the-river, accessed 8 October 2022.
66. *Irish Independent*, 27 May 1922.
67. Nuala Johnson, 'Mapping monuments: The shaping of public space and cultural identities', in *Visual Communication* 1:293 (2002), p. 293.
68. *Irish Independent*, 17 May 1920. In Bantry the previous night, 'the dwelling house and public house and carpenter's shop occupied by Mr. Michael O'Donovan, a strong adherent of Sinn Féin, were smashed on Friday night.' The O'Neill statue had been a point of controversy for soldiers visiting Youghal on holidays after the war.
69. *Freeman's Journal*, 21 Apr. 1921
70. *Belfast Newsletter*, 16 Apr. 1921; *Skibbereen Eagle*, 16 Apr. 1921.
71. Fitzpatrick, *Politics and Irish Life*, pp 111, 119.
72. *Irish Independent*, 16 Apr. 1920; *Skibbereen Eagle*, 17 Apr. 1920.
73. They were buried in Killatrain, Ballard. *Irish Independent*, 19 Apr. 1920.
74. Statements of Anthony Malone, BMH, WS 1076, p. 7; and Edward Lynch, BMH, WS 1333, pp 4–5.
75. *Cork Examiner*, 10 Aug. 1920; statement of Anthony Malone, BMH, WS 1076, p. 7.
76. *Evening Herald*, 9 Mar. 1921; *Meath Chronicle*, 12 Mar. 1921.
77. Nuala Johnson, *Ireland, the Great War and the Geography of Remembrance* (Cambridge: Cambridge University Press, 2003), pp 11–14.
78. C. J. C. Street writes: 'In the first nine months of 1918 there were 112 outrages, of which 59 were attributable, in the opinion of the police, to Sinn Féin. In the last three months of 1918 only 21 outrages were committed, and only two of these were due to Sinn Féin.' Street, *Administration of Ireland*, pp 52–3.
79. See 'Criminal Injuries Ireland Act and Local Government (Ireland) Act, 1898', proceedings; Inspector General's reports throughout 1918, especially for May 1918, TNA (CO 904/106–7).
80. J. Byrne to Under Secretary, TNA (CO 904/29/2).
81. Irish Volunteers: Return of Arms to 28 February 1917, TNA (CO 904/29/2).
82. Florence O'Donoghue, 'Volunteer "actions" in 1918', *Capuchin Annual*, 1968, p. 343; statements of Gerald Byrne, BMH, WS 668, p. 5; William McNamara, BMH, WS 1135, p. 14; Michael Healy, BMH, WS 1064, p. 8; Richard Walsh, BMH, WS 400, p. 141; and Garry Holohan, BMH, WS 328, p. 23.
83. 'Return showing by periods the outrages attributed to the Sinn Féin movement from 1st January, 1919, to 30th April, 1920.' Chief Secretary's Office, Dublin Castle, 15 May 1920, HMSO, 1920 [Cmd 709].
84. Townshend, *The Republic*, p. 104; Transfer of rifles from the National to the Irish Volunteers, various dates c. 1915, TNA (CO 904/29); statements of Dan Corkery, BMH, WS 93; and D. O'Sullivan, 6 Nov. 1915, National Library of Ireland (Maurice Moore papers, s10548/5); *Freeman's Journal*, 16

Aug. 1915; *Irish Times*, 16 Aug. 1915; Byrne to Duke, 3 Aug. 1917; *Irish Daily Independent*, 17 Aug. 1917; Ben Novick, 'The arming of Ireland: Gun-running and the Great War, 1915–16', in Adrian Gregory and Senia Paseta (eds), *Ireland and the Great War: 'A War to Unite Us All'?* (Manchester: Manchester University Press, 2002), pp 103–4.
85. Inspector General's report for February 1919, J. Byrne to James Macmahon, TNA (CO 904/108).
86. Harnett, *Victory and Woe*, pp 31–2. For raiding during Divine Service, see TNA (CO 904/108), raiding of Mrs Roberts, Ballincollig, Cork, ER, on 23 February; raid on police barrack at Araglen, Fermoy, Cork, on 20 April.
87. Statement of Thomas Keely, BMH, WS 1491.
88. Inspector General's report for March 1919, Byrne to US, 15 Apr. 1919, TNA (CO 904/108). Other raids were not as successful, and some outright failures. See Charles Hanon, PhD UCD 1989, 'The Irish Volunteers and the concepts of military service and defence 1913–1924', pp 193–4.
89. Statement of Joseph V. Lawless, BMH, WS 1043, p. 242.
90. See statements of Michael V. O'Donoghue, BMH, WS 1741; Bernard J. Kilbride, BMH, WS 1165; Seamus Babington (referencing Hodnett), BMH, WS 1595; and Michael Ryan, BMH, WS 1709.
91. Townshend, *The Republic*, p. 77; *An t-Óglach*, 15 Aug. 1918.
92. *Belfast Newsletter*, 23 Apr. 1918. Located outside Dublin, the site had been raided two years prior in preparation for the 1916 Easter Rising.
93. *Cork Examiner*, 26 Apr. 1918; *Skibbereen Eagle*, 27 Apr. 1918.
94. Statement of Jerry Golden, BMH, WS 522, p. 8.
95. *Irish Independent*, 11 Sept. 1918.
96. *An t-Óglach*, 30 Sept. 1918.
97. Statement of Frank Henderson, BMH, WS 821, pp 47–9. See also, statement of Vincent Byrne, BMH, WS 423.
98. H. C. Deb. (5 Nov. 1918), vol. 110, col. 1984.
99. *Cork Examiner*, 14 Nov. 1918.
100. H. C. Deb. (8 Aug. 1918), vol. 109, col. 1521.
101. Statement of Seumas Robinson, BMH, WS 1721, p. 23.
102. Charles Townshend, *The British Campaign in Ireland 1919–1921: The Development of Political and Military Policies* (Oxford: Oxford University Press, 1975), p. 16, citing Dan Breen, *My Fight for Irish Freedom*, pp 32–3.
103. *An t-Óglach*, Feb. 1919.
104. Similar to crosses erected and brought down at Miltown Malbay, Clare, following the killing of three nationalists, two crosses marking the place where Constables McDonnell and O'Connell were killed were thereafter removed by unknown parties. *Kerryman*, 10 May 1919.
105. *Cork Examiner*, 22 Jan. 1919; E. A. Hackett, Co. Surveyor for South Tipperary. Soloheadbeg raid secured 160 lbs of gelignite. 'As a result of this lamentable outrage,' says Mr Hackett, 'nearly all my preparations for the repair of the roads west of Tipperary which were urgently needed and on the point of bearing good fruit, will be nullified.' *Irish Independent*, 12 Feb. 1919.
106. *The Liberator* (Tralee), 19 Apr. 1919.
107. *Belfast Newsletter*, 20 Apr. 1918.
108. *Belfast Newsletter*, 9 Feb. 1920; *Evening Herald*, 7 Feb. 1920.
109. *Belfast Newsletter*, 19 May 1920; activities intensified after the raid, he explained, which included road trenching, tree felling and cutting telephone wires. Statement of Thomas Howlett, BMH, WS 1429, p. 3.
110. The *Daily News* publishes the following account of an interview with Mr. John S. Steele, the London correspondent of the *Chicago Tribune*. *Irish Independent*, 10 Apr. 1920. See also, Phillip Stigger, '1668: Numerous matters relating to grenades', in *Journal of the Society for Army Historical Research* 81:326 (Summer 2003), pp 168–77 (especially p. 172).
111. Kautt, *Ambushes*, p. 162.
112. Statement of Michael V. O'Donoghue, BMH, WS 1741, p. 50.
113. Ibid., p. 70.
114. Statement of Joseph V. Lawless, BMH, WS 1043, p. 243.
115. See *An t-Óglach*, 1 Mar. 1920 (2:6); 15 March 1920 (2:7); 1 June 1920 (2:12); and 3 June 1922 (4:2).

116. Statement of Michael Ryan, BMH, WS 170, p. 29.
117. Statements of Seamus Babington, BMH, WS 1595, p. 153; and James (Seumas) Hickey, BMH, WS 1218, p. 15.
118. Statement of John Joseph Hogan, BMH, WS 1030, p. 4.
119. Statement of Daniel Daly, BMH, WS, 743, p. 3.
120. Statement of Andrew McDonnell, BMH., WS 1768, pp 64–7.
121. *Freeman's Journal*, 13 Dec. 1920; statement of John Plunkett, BMH, WS 865, p. 22.
122. Statement of Joseph Lawless, BMH, WS 1043, p. 357. The Dublin Castle report claims experts were unsure of a new bomb that utilised 'a glass vessel or capsule', while Lawless recorded 'To avoid corrosion of the detonator by the nitro-glycerine of the gelignite, a piece of glass tubing was set in the middle of the explosive charge to keep the copper case of the detonator out of contact with it, the top of the explosive outside the ends of the glass tube being sealed with wax.' He also stated that Parnell Street factory did not load the explosives on site, only constructed the casing, pp 243–8.
123. *Irish Independent*, 30 May 1919.
124. *Irish Independent*, 30 Apr. 1919; *Cork Examiner*, 22 May 1919; statement of Sean O'Connell, BMH, WS 1706, pp 3–4. See also, 'Bomb factory discovered after Cork house explosion', *Century Ireland* (https://www.rte.ie/centuryireland/index.php/articles/bomb-factory-discovered-after-cork-house-explosion).
125. Statement of Michael Ryan, BMH, WS 1709, pp 22–3.
126. Ibid., p. 28.
127. Bernard J. Kilbride, BMH, WS 1165, p. 5.
128. Ethel Crowley, *Land Matters: Power Struggles in Rural Ireland* (Dublin: The Lilliput Press, 2006), p. 131.
129. Pearson, 'Researching militarized landscapes', citing Woodward (2004), p. 3 and Westing (1980), p. 191; Brian Graham, 'The imagining of place: Representation and identity in contemporary Ireland', in Graham, *In Search of Ireland*, p. 193.
130. Pearson, 'Researching militarized landscapes' p. 126.
131. Ibid., p. 116, citing J. Schofield, *Combat Archaeology: Material Culture and Modern Conflict* (London, 2005), p. 44.
132. Inspector General's report for September 1919, J. Byrne to Macmahon, 15 Oct. 1919, TNA (CO 904/110). A notice was found posted near Rearcross barracks that persons associating with police would forfeit their lives and that animals and vehicles placed at their disposal would be destroyed. 7 Sept. 1919, TNA (CO 904/110).
133. August 1919, Clare. On 11 August, Michael Casey, draper, received a letter threatening that his house at Miltown Malbay would be burned unless he evicted one of his tenants, a local Constable. Inspector General's Monthly Report for Aug. 1919, Byrne, 15 Sept. 1919 NAI (CO 904/109).
134. Outrage reports for week ending 29 August 1920, County Cork, TNA (CO 904/149).
135. *Constabulary Gazette*, 25 Jan. 1919.
136. Outrage reports, County Tipperary, TNA (CO 904/148).
137. Inspector General's monthly report for May 1919, n.d., TNA (CO 904/109).
138. 16 May 1920, Kilmovee, Mayo, TNA (CO 906/19). Hughes notes the tradition of the threatening letter, citing W. J. Lowe, 'The war Against the R.I.C., 1919–21', in Éire-Ireland, 37:3/4 (Fall/Winter 2002), pp 99, 102; Vaughan, *Landlords and Tenants*, pp 150–6, quoted in Hughes, *Defying the IRA?*, pp 26–7.
139. 'Gates were removed, graves dug, and headstones erected on a grazing farm in Sligo.' *Anglo-Celt*, 3 Feb. 1917; 'Land war spreading. Clare involved. "Arbitration" by Sinn Féin Courts.' *The Times*, 3 May 1920, p. 15.
140. Dublin Castle outrage reports, TNA (CO 904/148); *Cork Examiner*, 31 Dec. 1919.
141. *Cork Examiner*, 14 May 1920.
142. 'Munster and Leinster: Raiders show courtesy', *Irish Independent*, 6 Apr. 1920.
143. Statement of Thomas Lavin, BMH, WS 1001, p. 4; *Drogheda Independent*, 10 Apr. 1920; *Connacht Tribune*, 16 July 1921.
144. Outrage reports, TNA (CO 904/148); *Leitrim Observer*, 10 Apr. 1920; statement of Patrick Doherty, BMH, WS 1195, p. 7. Apparently not all of the Gilroy's furniture was spared. Sergeant Gilroy was compensated £275 for furniture burned at Leitrim barracks at the Carrick-on-Shannon quarter sessions. *Fermanagh Herald*, 9 Oct. 1920. 'When those engaged in the burning called at Rantogue

they intimated their business to the wife of the sergeant, who occupied the barrack, and gave her 15 minutes to clear out. After providing accommodation for her and removing all her furniture and effects they set the building on fire.' *Leitrim Observer*, 10 Apr. 1920. 'Married police in several cases were served with notices to leave their houses.' Kerry, CO 904/112 for June 1920. 'Mrs. Churchill, a police sergeant's wife, resided in Graenagh Barracks, and the armed masked raiders gave her a brief period to take away her belongings. She took refuge in a neighbouring house.' *Irish Independent*, 6 Apr. 1920; see also, statement of Thomas Lavin, BMH WS 1001, p. 4; see also, 'Maynooth barracks burned', *Drogheda Independent*, 3 Apr. 1920; 'Big barrack raid', *Drogheda Independent*, 10 Apr. 1920; 'Co. Wexford burnings', *Cork Examiner*, 14 May 1920.

145. This extended to Civic Guard as well. When the IRA burned Rathowen barracks in Westmeath on 11 March 1923, it allowed Guards to collect belongings and evacuate. *Belfast Newsletter*, 13 Mar. 1923.

146. *Belfast Newsletter*, 31 May 1920.

147. Inspector General's report for December 1919, 13 Jan. 1920, TNA (CO 904/110).

148. Statement of Seamus Finn, BMH, WS 901, pp 10–11.

149. *Anglo-Celt*, 8 Nov. 1919; *Meath Chronicle*, 22 May 1920.

150. 'Dilemma of sergeants' wives', A. G. to the editor, *Irish Independent*, 27 Nov. 1919.

151. Tipperary, NR: 'Threatening and boycotting notices were prevalent and in several districts the police were obliged to commandeer food.' July 1920; Roscommon: 'Five vacated police barracks were burned ... [Police] were largely boycotted in Boyle, Ballaghadereen, Strokestown and to a less extent Roscommon. Food supplies were refused and had to be commandeered.' Inspector General's monthly report for July 1920, TNA (CO 904/112).

152. Dublin Castle outrage reports, TNA (CO 904/150). See especially, 25 Mar. 1921: 'Garage and motor car property of Miss Polly Hamilton, were destroyed by fire. Owner is on friendly terms with the police, and drove them in the car.'

153. Republican police and courts slowly assumed legal duties in certain evacuated areas and patrolled agrarian crime. Inspector General's report for June 1920, TNA (CO 904/112).

154. Dublin Castle outrage reports, TNA (CO 904/148).

155. Hughes, *Defying the IRA?*, p. 23. Notes the program to withhold goods observable as early as 1918, which accelerated in all forms by 1920. See also, R. F. Foster, *Modern Ireland 1600–1972* (London: Allen Lane (Penguin Press), 1988), pp 499–500.

156. Various incidents include Galway, ER, Portumna. 2 Apr. 1920, TNA (CO 904/148); Roscommon, 3 June 1920, TNA (CO 904/148); County Galway, 1 June 1920, TNA (CO 904/148); and Fermanagh, 30 June 1920, TNA (CO 904/148); statement of Daniel O'Sullivan, BMH, WS 1191, p. 4.

157. Dublin Castle outrage reports, Donegal, 17/18 June 1920, TNA (CO 904/148).

158. Statement of Bernard McGinley, BMH, WS 1482, p. 6; Dublin Castle outrage reports, Kildare, 17 May 1920, TNA (CO 904/148).

159. Dublin Castle outrage reports, June 1920, TNA (CO 904/148); ibid., TNA (CO 904/149); Kautt, *Ambushes*, p. 78.

160. *Cork Examiner*, 26 July 1920; Dublin Castle outrage reports, 23 July 1920, TNA (CO 904/149); *Tralee Liberator*, 24 July 1920.

161. Dublin Castle outrage reports, Waterford: at 9:30 p.m. on 13 Nov. 1920, the house of M. Kelly. See also, Wicklow, TNA (CO 904/150); Limerick City: at 10:15 p.m. on 28 Nov. 1920, Louis Hodkinson, TNA (CO 904/149).

162. Dublin Castle outrage reports, Tipperary, 26 July 1920, TNA (CO 904/149).

163. Reported outrages compiled from Dublin Castle outrage reports, TNA (CO 904/148–150). Nearly 70 per cent of reported intimidation incidents (345/497) occurred between April and August 1920; see also, Hughes, *Defying the IRA?*, p. 26. In regards to defying the IRA, Tom Barry said of loyalists: 'Active hostility to the IRA and active support of the British Forces were now not only dangerous games but also very expensive ones.' Tom Barry, *Guerrilla Days in Ireland* (Dublin: Anvil Books, 1995 edition), p. 118.

164. Elizabeth Malcom calculated 588 constables died as a result of revolutionary violence between 1919 and 1922, with upwards of 700 having been wounded. While only 17 of these deaths occurred in 1919, by that summer, Kent Fedorowich highlights, 'the IRA was formulating and initiating a systematic terrorist campaign.' British authority initially responded by evacuating police from remote

rural police stations to concentrate them in larger town centres. In response, the IRA directed attacks against vacated barracks on an unprecedented scale that resulted in their widespread destruction. Elizabeth Malcolm, *The Irish Policeman, 1822–1922: A Life* (Dublin: Four Courts Press, 2006), p. 199; Kent Fedorowich, 'The problems of disbandment: The Royal Irish Constabulary and imperial migration, 1919– 29', in *Irish Historical Studies*, xxx:117 (May 1996), p. 90; Street, *Administration in Ireland*, pp 27–8; Richard Abbott, *Police Casualties in Ireland* (Cork: Mercier Press, 2000), p. 55; statement of James Reilly, BMH, WS 1593, p. 6.

CHAPTER THREE

IRELAND'S FIFTH COLUMN: ENVIRONMENT & LANDSCAPE IN THE WAR OF INDEPENDENCE

INTRODUCTION

The 1916 Easter Rising inaugurated a distinct turn in the suppression of Irish insurrections. Notwithstanding the failure of an anticipated nationwide insurgency, rebels had prepared Dublin's urban landscape for an intimate and local conflict but were met with a disproportionately industrial response. Incendiary artillery shells and machine guns reduced large portions of the Irish capital city to smoking rubble, which many witnesses likened to contemporary scenes from war-torn Belgium and France. While Easter Week symbolically extended the Western Front to Sackville Street, the war ended without another comparable experience. Yet various Irish towns experienced similarly disproportionate replies throughout the Anglo-Irish War, or War of Independence, between 1919 and 1921; reprisals for the murder of Crown forces, ambushes, and attacks on state authority. Many occurred in response to the IRA's loosely coordinated war strategy: to disrupt and alter Ireland's urban and rural landscapes in order to stage ambushes, raid for arms and generally frustrate British forces. Examining the environmental framework of this strategy highlights how the IRA perceived landscapes and climate as tools for waging war. Integrating environmental considerations builds upon the foundational work that established the geography, patterns and pace of revolutionary violence in Ireland at local, county and national levels during the period. It attempts, in its own way, to examine revolutionary violence differently by emphasising the nature, extent and severity of damage done to natural and built environments by the IRA. As such, efforts are made here to highlight evidence hidden in plain sight – to compile and animate Irish landscapes as features that contributed to, and experienced, revolutionary violence.

There is no lack of evidence in this regard. The difficulty remains in divining a comprehensive environmental experience from IRA operations that manipulated, damaged or despoiled built and natural features. Irish geographies and the infrastructure that connected them suffered low-level injuries at a near-daily pace throughout the War of Independence period. Bridges were sabotaged to disrupt traffic and prevent pursuit by Crown forces, consequently affecting underlying waterways and adding stress to adjacent routes. Roads were effectively trenched, mined or flooded to reduce mobility, and Crown forces often pressed local populations to repair them. To the same end, boundary markers, such as fences and stonewalls, were overthrown and scattered upon roads. Trees and hedges were comprehensively exploited as obstacles in rural ambushes and as complements to attacks on police barracks. They were felled to herd enemy convoys into ambush zones or to prevent their retreat or reinforcement. The number of trees felled in the service of the Irish Republic is hard to determine, and the ecological impact remains elusive. Volunteer companies often cited road-blocking operations as continuous, or too numerous to tally. These acts reframed these spaces as war zones, as the previous chapter introduced. Like public and private spaces repurposed or commandeered for political rallies or munitions work, manipulated landscapes were enlisted and transfigured towards revolutionary political purposes.

Towards 'Active Service'

Not everyone could be a gunman. Scarcity of arms and ammunition made it impossible, and only a select few within the typical IRA demographic pursued the opportunity.[1] Many who remained in the movement found it difficult to transition from the protesting, parading and soft defiance of the 1917–18 period to active service between 1919 and 1921. Moral attitudes towards killing, the fear of imprisonment, death or losing one's job or business, and potential reprisals against families and communities influenced participation and compliance and caused even devout republicans to withdraw.[2] Others perceived the receding conscription crisis and subsequent Armistice to have ended their tour of duty, and Volunteer officers noted a general thinning of ranks throughout autumn 1918. Farm work and family life competed for time and energy. As David Fitzpatrick summarised: 'As long as there were cows to milk, hay to save, and women to order about, the vast majority of Volunteers would have to remain part-timers, on the plains.'[3]

The quartermaster's ability to arm and outfit a Volunteer company certainly influenced retention,[4] but militant republicanism also required ancillary actors. Various Brigade Activity Reports (BAR) detail support roles in acquiring tools, weapons and chemicals, retrieving and transporting arms, mines and petrol from dumps, and scouting, running interference and communicating intelligence. Overlooking these efforts when examining the finer dynamics of interpersonal violence may be permissible, but the observation that there was 'not much these men could do for the organization, since there were virtually no arms to fight with', distorts the reality of guerrilla warfare at this time.[5] These were, Seán O'Faoláin recalled, 'undemanding if essential jobs', and the majority of Volunteers remained in support roles even after autumn 1920, when the IRA strategy pivoted towards direct engagement with British forces.[6] As the BAR detail, the number of trenching and barricading parties who worked to alter natural landscapes was significantly larger than active service gunmen, sometimes several times over depending on an operation's sophistication and foresight. Localities that carried out revolutionary violence remained consistent with those that had demonstrated acts of non-violent public defiance in 1917 to 1918. In both cases, Peter Hart argued: 'Local initiative and organization were the deciding factors, not guns'[7]; to paraphrase Fitzpatrick, to participate in the independence movement involved risk calculated at the personal, collective and financial levels, regardless of activity.[8]

Since January 1918, *An t-Óglach*, the journal of the Irish Volunteers that carried both propaganda and training instructions, had emphasised the importance of preparation and adaptability. 'An army must develop its resources, tabulate its collected information, and always be, as far as possible, in a state of preparedness. A military organization comprises many and various departments and activities.'[9] This process included developing broader landscape awareness as well as attaining the tools and skills to transform roads, railways and entire towns into war environments. For instance, the West Limerick Brigade held a mock assault on an isolated, yet still inhabited, police barracks.[10] A contemporary GHQ pamphlet directed those in rural areas to employ 'tactical measures' towards resistance.[11] Barricades and sabotage were to render roads and railways useless; boulders, trees and flooding would block tunnels and bridges; telegraph lines and signal boxes were to be cut and wrecked; and cars would be immobilised and petrol stores drained. Each altered the landscape in physically minor, though strategically significant, ways. As Crown forces travelled in bicycle patrols, motor transport and troop trains, widespread landscape preparation sought to frustrate enemy mobility, communication and supply lines. As police noted, 'murder and sporadic raids on barracks' were 'more compatible' with rebels' military equipment.[12] Rebel resistance embraced a mantra of utility, tapping into Volunteers' practicality: 'no weapon should be despised; [...] a hay fork is quite as good as a rifle and bayonet [and] a scythe-blade securely lashed with wire to a pole is equal to a hay fork.'[13]

More violent acts intersected a rising public temperament. Talk of 'shooting policemen, attacking their barracks, blowing up bridges and other acts of sabotage' circulated at public meetings throughout the summer of 1918.[14] These were neither idle threats nor speculative paranoia.[15] In December, Charles Hurley was court martialled for possessing ammunition and 'a manuscript plan of attack on the police barrack' in Castletownbere, Cork, where, the prosecution attested, Hurley planned to cut communication wires, blow up nearby railway lines and bridges and destroy 'every building there'.[16] Sporadic acts of landscape sabotage throughout 1918 complemented raids for weapons and explosives, all of which occurred in the background of Sinn Féin's political advancement. This 'new mode of combat' reinforced violence within the emerging nationalist political program, and the Irish Executive took note.[17] RIC Inspector General Byrne anticipated expanded destructive activity following Sinn Féin's monumental victory in the 1918 general election, in which Sinn Féin unseated the IPP to capture the majority of Irish seats in the House of Commons. Though 'not sufficiently equipped to take the field against troops', Byrne believed the Irish Volunteers to possess the ability to do 'a vast amount of damage'.[18] 'In each locality where arrests had been made,' he continued, 'particulars had been found of bridges to be cut down and of careful military plans.'[19] An ominous indication of the nature of guerrilla warfare in Ireland can be seen in these captured documents and early activity.

Prior to assaults, from autumn 1919 Volunteer companies manipulated landscapes surrounding police barracks, tax record offices and other centres of state authority. Most occurred without sanction from GHQ in Dublin, whose control of local brigades and battalions was tenuous.[20] As such, scattered activity and attacks against property initiated a war scenario earlier than some historians have acknowledged, generally recognised to have commenced in early 1920.[21] A House of Commons report attributed over 100 instances of arson and malicious injury to property to 'Sinn Féin outrages' for 1919. Statistical returns for non-agrarian criminal offences identified 671 injuries to property cases, which had risen significantly from previous years.[22] 1920 and 1921 represent the revolution's deadliest and most destructive years prior to the civil war. They also helped construct historical memory of flying columns, ambushes and men 'on the run' from unfettered British militarism. Such writing identified guerrilla warfare as enforcing a moral geography that permitted republican Ireland to level the playing field against a numerically and materially superior opponent. For example, W. A. Ballinger's *Rebellion* places Professor Martin and would-be revolutionary Terence McKeon in conversation prior to the Easter Rising, where Martin saw the rebellion as 'lost before it's begun'. However, he prophesised eventual victory in its aftermath: 'Then will be the time for a proper war, for a war waged throughout the country and not in a single city, a war with no mercy, of shots in the back and bombs by night.'[23] A passing scene in this lesser-known semi-centennial fiction, Martin's 'proper war' was decentralised, fought in darkness and as incessant in its execution as it was crude in its methods. Many contemporary experiences obviously informed Ballinger's narrative and can be seen in recollections from British forces as well. In his memoir *Kwab-O-Kayal*, Major General L. A. Hawes, Staff Captain for the Sixth Division in Cork, recalled the general attitude toward IRA ambushes: 'The soldiers despised the Sinn Féiners. They never came into the open. All the shooting was in the back from behind walls.'[24] With exceptions, this very much reflected the IRA's ideal approach to warfare: selective and prepared engagements in which the technical and numerical superiority of British forces were offset. The Irish landscape enabled this type of war.

LAY OF THE LAND

Irish landscapes have historically served as obstacles to conquest and platforms for resistance. Bogs and forests acted as natural buffers against outside influence, and colonial officials equated a landscape's inaccessibility with sedition and crime.[25] English legislation identified the need for clearance and improvement in Ireland from as early as the thirteenth century, as Irish woods, bog lands and mountains presented 'vicious spaces at the margins of civility'.[26] Tudor conquest undertook timber clearing, road development and bridge building to aid the Plantation and improvement in various forms.[27] Efforts in Ireland emulated earlier clearance and enclosure strategies in Scotland, with infrastructure transporting Anglo-Dublin's political and cultural influence beyond the Pale. However, progress and influence were uneven. Noted eighteenth-century English agriculturalist and travel writer Arthur Young praised the Irish road network as having developed despite the country's otherwise embryonic state.[28] Victorian railway expansion supplemented links between major cities, while Carlo 'Charles' Bianconi's 'bian' routes filled gaps in more remote locations.

Despite an overall improvement in roads and railways throughout the nineteenth century, many western localities remained 'poorly served'.[29] The extension of 'administrative geographies' helped to align isolated communities into a broader colonial standard. Standardised property valuation, census taking, public works mapping and post office networks extended state bureaucracy and surveillance in this regard, while a dedicated Irish constabulary burrowed itself into nearly every aspect of Irish life.[30] Transportation and communication continued to expand. By 1922, motor registration and petrol duties maintained 60,000 miles of Irish roads.[31] Over 3,000 miles of rail lines extended from Dublin out to provincial bases at Belfast, Galway and Cork. Roughly 2,500 rail bridges spanned various points along Ireland's 1,500 miles of navigable waterways, which carried traffic to and from principal ports at Arklow, Belfast, Cork, Drogheda, Dublin, Foynes, Limerick, New Ross and Waterford.[32] Wireless transmission stations and meteorological observation points at Malin Head, Crookhaven, Valentia, Seaview, Larne, Carnsore Point, Ballybunion and Clifden complemented this arterial network.[33]

Irish infrastructure continued to serve colonial oversight throughout the revolutionary period, but often failed to meet essential deployment, supply and mobility standards in the face of inadequate transport and greatly deteriorated roads. George Fletcher's 1922 survey of Connacht confirmed as much: 'The roads, being repaired with limestone (the only available rock) are generally bad – dusty in summer, sticky in winter, and rutty all the time.'[34] The War Office identified military transport as inadequate well into 1920.[35] General Sir Nevil Macready, Commanding Forces in Ireland, pressed the British Cabinet for additional lorries, vans, armoured cars and motorcycles that would, he believed, reduce logistical gaps and increase local capabilities throughout Ireland.[36] Macready's petition overlapped a general munitions strike that operated between May and December 1920, during which dock and railway workers refused to transport British troops and military equipment. The strike froze distribution of vital equipment and personnel and influenced the military's reliance on motor vehicles that operated independent of striking conductors and labourers.[37] Autonomous mobility solutions contributed to an increasingly militarised landscape. The RIC Depot in Dublin was reconfigured and expanded to store additional clothing and equipment, and garages were constructed to shelter and service motor vehicles. In September 1920, the Irish Executive assumed control of the Centre for Motor Transport in the Phoenix Park. The Department of Public Works oversaw this and other construction. It built additional garages at military centres and police barracks throughout the country, and converted a wartime aerodrome at Gormanston and camps at Newtownards into supplementary constabulary depots. These renovations were not cheap. The buildings required significant improvements that included extended dormitories and kitchen facilities, water supply and lighting, and other amendments estimated to cost over £50,000.[38] The arrival of lorries, cars, vans, ambulances and motorcycles throughout 1920 filled these garages and other stations. A total of 2,240 mobile vehicles were in use by the end of the year, more than doubling those in service in May.[39] In essence, the British military installed and equipped its own transportation and supply terminals, immune to Irish labour disputes or republican sentiment, set to operate primarily upon roads.

However, Ireland's roads, 'still primitive by the time of the conflict', could not sustain heavy military traffic and quickly deteriorated from excessive use.[40] Moreover, their integrity outside Dublin and Belfast – the only locations at the time that were asphalted, paved or maintained to the necessary standard – varied considerably, particularly in wet weather. While nearly 5,000 miles of compacted, bituminous-bound roads stretched across England, Wales and Scotland, Ireland remained 'in the depths of the backwoods regarding the road question'.[41] Muddy or 'boggy' sections of roads that lacked proper drainage, macadam or supplementary limestone frequently ensnared heavy lorries. Conversely, compacted or potholed roads often broke weak or overburdened axels, a hazard that affected transport ranging from bicycles to Ford touring cars to armoured cars and lorries.[42] In some areas, poor road conditions negated the advantages of British motor transport altogether. Officers of the 5th Divisional area identified only two functioning main roads within their command: Maryborough (Portlaoise) to Dublin and Athlone to Dublin. The remainder of the area was 'covered by a haphazard network of narrow second and third-class roads', which officers recognised as favouring guerrilla activity:

> This narrowness of the roads, and the many patches of bogland over which they cross, have

> assisted Sinn Féin greatly, since Christmas, 1920, to interrupt our road communications by blowing up bridges, cutting trenches and trees, and also to select suitable places for ambush on lorries and convoys.[43]

Excessive motor traffic and poor weather compounded road damage to the degree that even animals struggled to maintain footing.[44] Sligo Corporation recorded that military lorries had cut up a local road so deeply that 'you could bury a horse in some of the ruts.'[45] On the whole, Irish roads were not necessarily overburdened by the volume of military traffic, which hardly neared the 'heavy' category established by civil engineers at the time, but deteriorated as a result of a sizable increase in the frequency of traffic and increased rebel trenching, which neutralised the benefits of compacted sediment even after being refilled. The situation worsened to such a degree that, as William Kautt observed, by May 1921 'it was easier [for British forces] to travel around the island by sea' than to attempt to navigate over land.[46] The Irish landscape disadvantaged mechanised patrols in other ways: their engines grumbled throughout an otherwise industrially mute countryside[47], they kicked up dust that betrayed position, and narrow, winding roads and single carriage bridges slowed pace and limited forward sightlines.[48] Modern warfare's more recent innovations contributed little to the situation.[49] Tanks lumbered through urban centres to showcase British military might and the ability to ram doors, but were of little use beyond public spectacle. Armoured cars were too few and too heavy to be effective on Irish roads. Both had been 'developed to meet a conventional threat in a conventional war'.[50] Conspicuous overkill was lost on Ireland, where combatants, fronts and objectives ignored convention.

Aeroplanes were mobilised in response to extensive road trenching and railway sabotage,[51] but they were only marginally effective and never contributed to counter-insurgency strategy in the ways successive commanders envisioned.[52] Lord French imagined intimidating war birds nested in each Irish province, strafing guerrillas whose play at war would erode in the face of real combat. General Macready saw precise air support unbound from recent wartime limitations in France, able to fly freely at low altitudes to identify and engage rebels. Certain realities grounded these ambitions. Mainly, it was argued that pilots could not be responsible for filtering (loyal) civilians from combatants, and that the potential public backlash for wrongful deaths would be politically harmful.[53]

Bird and beast offered simpler solutions. In January 1920, Irish command requested homing pigeons and mobile courier stations to circumvent intelligence leaks and dead communication lines throughout Ireland. By August, eight horse-drawn pigeon lofts had been distributed to commands at Killarney, Galway, Killybegs (Donegal) and Waterford.[54] Horses were mobilised to overcome poor road conditions and extend Crown forces beyond conventional routes, but even this proved difficult in certain areas.[55] Cavalry operated along open fields, bogs and hedges to beat out concealed republicans, while soldiers occupied nearby villages and blocked roads to prevent their flight.[56] Toward July 1921, horse-led round-ups combed previously inaccessible landscapes, notably mountainous regions and county borderlands.[57] Coordinated operations conducted 'on a war-like scale' brought in hundreds and at times thousands of suspects.[58] The IRA responded to the use of pigeons and horses by destroying their lofts, stables and food supplies.[59] It attacked a government remount farm outside Dublin in December 1920, setting fire to stabling and hay sheds that resulted in approximately £20,000 worth of damage. Volunteers returned the following spring to complete the job, destroying a railway supply wagon and two tons of oats.[60]

Ireland's dated and ill-maintained road system curtailed mobility in various ways and frustrated Britain's inherent logistical superiority.[61] Manipulating and destroying built and natural features, such as trees, bridges and roads, compounded this frustration. These activities certainly occupied what David Fitzpatrick saw as Irish nationalism's 'rural preoccupation', but their impact extended beyond the immediate damage site and often brought retributive punishment.[62]

IRELAND'S FIFTH COLUMN

Ireland's diverse natural features dictated the geography of revolutionary violence. Woods, mountains and rivers, elevation and curves in the road, and proximity to urban centres influenced the scope and pace of obstruction, offered routes for evasion, and formed a nexus at which environmental damage and interpersonal violence intersected.[63] The widespread and diverse damage to Irish landscapes shows that environmental engineering was indispensable to republican militancy and revised the scope of active service for women as well as men. For Crown forces, road obstructions distinguished the Irish landscape as a tool of war and further eroded the boundary between Irish civilians and rebels.

Barricading occurred almost continuously throughout the Irish War of Independence. *An t-Óglach* observed the need for general obstruction, but as Crown forces pivoted from passive defence to more active patrol, the journal identified specific factors that would determine a barricade's site, size and material:

> If by blocking the roads we can destroy the columns mobility we place the enemy again where he started and render him immobile. But blocking a road is not as simple as it looks; there are many points to be studied in order to block it in the most effective manner – for that alone is any good. First of all we must consider the nature of the column to be stopped – for the barricade will depend on this. The column may consist of infantry in lorries, of cyclists, of cavalry, of armoured cars, of tanks, or of combinations of these arms. What will stop one of these will not stop all, and what would be needed to stop the most formidable would be a waste of time against the others. Similarly we must consider the best place for the barricade, and this will depend on many things – where materials are available, where the road is suitable, how far out it is necessary to stop the column. Only when these factors are taken into account can we be certain of stopping any column in time.[64]

As such, obstructions were not equally distributed, and their type varied as regarded the road being blocked and enemy mobility and concentration. Geographically, barricades overlapped the geographies of violence examined by David Fitzpatrick, Peter Hart and Joost Augusteijn.[65] Memoirs, newspaper reports and compensation files locate concentrations of activity in relation to ambushes, often with rationale behind felling trees or digging trenches at specific points. Destruction was most often an act unto itself. Records illustrate that IRA companies perpetually and repeatedly altered their surroundings. Narrative evidence from the Bureau of Military History Witness Statements and the BAR show that for the majority of IRA and Cumann na mBan members, the better part of their service was spent in preparing attacks rather than in executing them, extensive work that often overlooked details beyond an operation's location and participants. In this sense, Volunteers described their work in indefinite terms and on floating timelines. For instance, those in Pallasgreen, Limerick, reported blocking roads and cutting communication wires once a week throughout the entire War of Independence period.[66] Road trenching and tree felling went hand-in-hand toward this end, but knocking and scattering stone walls, roadside gates, farm machinery and carts, and demolishing bridges (often without the assistance of explosives) also impeded mobility, dictated control and demonstrated a locality's contribution to the movement.[67] This was no small task: coordinated acts often required widespread logistical organisation and muscle as they could extend for miles beyond an ambush point.[68] The resulting scale of disruptive, destructive activity quickly outpaced the government's ability (or necessity) to report it in detail.[69] Volunteer statements were equally vague. David Hall and the Meath IRA destroyed 'about twenty bridges in the area' by the time of the Truce, 'all on the main arteries used by the enemy'.[70] In Carlow, John McGill and his comrades 'knocked' bridges and felled one or two trees each week from autumn 1920. 'When we got information that the military lorries used other roads, we blocked them immediately,' he recalled, concluding, 'I don't think there is any need to go into details of these operations, as every one of them had the same preparation, the same labour and watchfulness.'[71]

By 1921, various companies reported that 'extensive' road blocking occurred 'constantly' throughout their battalions.[72] Transport was completely paralysed in more active areas, such as in Bandon, Cork, and Trim, Meath, as the IRA prevented movement *in toto* by demolishing or barricading all available routes.[73] Police in Killaloe, Clare, were resigned to bicycles as motor transport was deemed 'useless' due to blocking; the *Freeman's Journal* praised donkeys as the sole method for navigating trenches and felled trees.[74] IRA companies employed road obstruction as a form of resistance, a 'safe and popular amusement for the IRA',[75] but it was also a political statement. Open trenches and felled trees exhibited republican control of a region, or at the very least its continued presence. Bodyke in East Clare was deemed an IRA safe haven as all routes entering the village were blocked,[76] and impassable roads throughout Tipperary permitted IRA meetings to be held with regularity.[77]

Not all landscapes or features were complicit. In the case of roads, compaction and drainage – how difficult it was to dig – influenced trench location, size and the labour required. Most times, labourers outnumbered the succeeding gunmen. For example, sixty men from two companies were required to move 1,200 cubic feet of earth to open a large trench at Boherash Cross between Mallow and Buttevant, Cork, in March 1921.[78] Smaller pits, artificial fencing, large stones and short ridges in the road required fewer hands to destroy and were effective in diverting lorries towards larger traps. Other methods were more deceptive. Simon Donnelly concealed trenches with small brush and dirt to give an impression of safe passage.[79] Engineering schemata captured during the civil war show how road traps had evolved since 1919.[80] One featured a trap-door mechanism where a wooden plank was balanced on a central beam over a six-foot wide trench, camouflaged with mud or road dust, and would collapse when triggered.[81] British forces came to recognise widespread and innovative obstruction as a significant military achievement. More so, given the degree of local government compliance (genuine or coerced) that refused to vote funds towards road repairs.[82] After the establishment of the Irish Free State, local government looked to the British Treasury to compensate roads and bridges damaged from frequent and heavy military traffic, including hauling timber for military purposes, and trenching. Collectively, over 90 claims were filed that totalled nearly £600,000. Clare County Council, for instance, claimed nearly £120,000 on behalf of nine rural districts for damage to 103 bridges, 5 culverts, 90 gullets (by-roads) and 3 walls, and for the repair of 160 trenches.[83] The War Office denied liability, and Treasury officials summarised a Damage to Property (Compensation) Act 1923 clause that precluded payments to county or local government authorities.[84]

Like road trenching, tree felling was practised throughout the revolutionary period and was widespread. Ireland's forests suffered insignificant injury compared to the vast woodlands processed to serve industrialised armies and annihilated by their artillery in the First World War. However, like much of the damage during the Irish Revolution, the destruction of trees should be considered relative to the small-scale, non-industrial and predominantly rural conflict. In this sense, the volume of mature trees felled by the IRA was widespread and constant. Axes and saws were more readily available than rifles, which permitted opportunities to contribute to the cause without the moral burden of killing. Moreover, a volunteer army that sawed trees by hand under the cover of darkness to block country roads permitted a sense of romanticism to prevail in Ireland against the disillusionment of the mechanised evisceration of nature experienced along the Western Front.[85]

Though Ireland was denuded to a considerable extent by the early twentieth century, trees remained roadside features, alongside other territorial markers that included hedges, berm edges, ditches and loose stone walls. Unlike trenches, which were regularly dug, filled and reopened in the same locations, trees were single-use obstacles. Their removal permanently altered the landscape within a generation as saplings rooted in their place, or as part of larger afforestation programs in the 1920s, required decades to mature. Native and imported species cut included alder, ash, aspen, birch, oak, elm and willow, which varied by location. Volunteers considered several factors when selecting trees to fell, including trunk diameter and density and the labour needed to construct an effective barricade. Smaller calliper (younger) trees were more easily cut but could also be cleared with similar ease; older growth trees were more effectual barriers but took longer to fell due to their size and potential for irregular growths and knots. Ornamental and commercially grown trees were also cut, most often extracted as tribute for political offenses. In one instance, John Begley refused to donate towards the construction of a Sinn Féin hall near his home in Glashakeenleen, Cork, in December 1919. In reply, several young larch trees within his plantation were cut (and his dog shot). Arboreal tribute continued to be extracted from estates and plantations through the civil war and was widespread in Munster and Connacht.[86]

The ability to fell trees quickly and efficiently varied considerably between companies where distinctions in talent were recognised. Officers ordered 'experts' for a barricading job in Cork in December 1920, where six roads that converged on Kilbrittain needed to be blocked prior to an assault on the barracks: 'On that dark night experience was necessary to get some of the heavy trees down quickly in the required positions.'[87] A rural or urban background often influenced a Volunteer's aptitude towards soldering. In preparing for an attack on the RIC barracks at Clerihan, Tipperary, men from rural companies led cutting parties and supervised their urban comrades. 'Townsmen would not have the same knowledge of, or skill in, the cutting and felling of trees as their country brethren,' Timothy

Tierney explained.[88] Other service highlighted the rural–urban distinction. A Free State intelligence report filed during the civil war, for instance, judged Dublin-based republicans unit assigned to Tipperary to be 'unskilled to the work. The majority of this unit are small weak lads who cannot stand the continuous marching.'[89] Like road trenching, techniques for felling and staging trees evolved throughout the period. Their use in deception was particularly valuable. Following an assault, Volunteers used trees to obstruct one route in hopes that it would attract police or military investigation and pursuit, while they withdrew down another.[90] Even outwardly, clear routes were potentially dangerous. Volunteers use heavy gauge wire to link partially cut trees on either side of a road where unsuspecting vehicles triggered their collapse.[91] Such methods were far from failproof. Crown forces ignored (or failed to discover) bait trees along false retreat routes, and at times the IRA accidentally triggered its own traps.[92] Regardless, whether orchestrated towards a raid for arms, to allow for withdrawal, or to host an ambush, trenching, tree felling and other road obstacles required skill, extensive preparation and widespread participation. Two examples on either end of the War of Independence period demonstrate this process in greater detail.

The Cork IRA attacked the King's Shropshire Light Infantry outside the Wesleyan Church in Fermoy in September 1919, 'one of the first, if not the first, major activity of the IRA', Joseph Morgan claimed.[93] Nearly 70 Volunteers participated.[94] Some monitored soldiers' movements in the months preceding the event, noting routines and habits: Annie Barrett, a supervising telephonist at Mallow Post Office, passed intelligence to local IRA officers; Leo Callaghan hired a grey Buick touring car.[95] On the morning of 7 September, Liam Lynch sounded a whistle, the soldiers were relieved of their rifles (15 in total), one soldier was killed in the process, and the Volunteers withdrew east toward Waterford. 'Pursuit rendered difficult', the *Skibbereen Eagle* reported after a pursuit party encountered trees scattered on the Fermoy–Tallow road.[96] However, the report withheld vital nuance, which John Fanning and Leo Callaghan inserted decades after the event. Rather than being dropped immediately, the trees felled to prevent pursuit had been sawn earlier that morning and suspended upright. When the Volunteers passed through Carrigabrick village, they were released onto the road.[97]

In the years that followed, Crown forces came to lament the Irish environment. Excessive foliage and overgrowth frustrated troops attempting to locate and detain rebels during a March 1921 round-up operation in County Roscommon. Captain Roger Grenville Peek was said to have promised to 'return and burn every bit of brush and cover on the mountain side'.[98] He was not afforded the opportunity. Shortly after the round-up, he, Lieutenant John Harold Tennant and several others on patrol were killed in an ambush at Scramogue, outside Strokestown.[99] In this instance, the Roscommon brigade exploited the area's natural surroundings and topography to dictate the engagement. Again, a habitual travel routine was observed, trees prevented retreat or reinforcement, and a sharp bend on the Strokestown–Longford road provided a point of attack insulated by stonewalls, houses and a small wood at the base of Slieve Bawn.[100]

Like many other similar engagements, Fermoy and Scramogue reshaped Irish environments beyond fallen trees and disturbed earth. Compounded environmental damage and contamination, coupled with the inestimable personal grief and communal distress of those directly affected, defy the tidy column heads used to categorise interpersonal violence within the record. The 'Wesleyan raid' at Fermoy instigated unofficial reprisals in

Ireland.[101] Reprisals, examined in greater detail in the next chapter, multiplied the scope of destruction and increased civilian suffering and loss. The killing of Private William Jones in Fermoy elicited an attack on the town; 'not unnatural,' *The London Times* contextualised, 'though there can be no excuse for it.'[102] Nevertheless, the soldiers that carried out the 'Methodical Wrecking' felt they had an excuse. They 'tried to get a bit of their own back for their comrade', Colonel Dobbs explained.[103] Jones, a young soldier set to be wed after his approaching discharge, was shot by a 'gang of locals, sitting lounging around – in ambush',[104] 'a damned dirty trick', General Peter Strickland conceded.[105] He died in the home of Mrs Foster, the minister's wife, in a town that boasted a distinct British military tradition.[106] A pound of flesh was claimed in turn, taken in the form of looting and broken glass. Some of the buildings sacked belonged to jurors that had failed to produce a satisfactory verdict: murder.[107] The 'avenging tour' claimed an estimated £2,000 in broken plate glass, with the loss of property projected at £3,000. Messrs Tyler was looted of 2,000 pairs of boots.[108] The Shropshire regiment had received notoriety for its service in the Great War; ironically, its revenge on Fermoy transformed the town into 'one of the battered towns common the Western Front during the progress of the war. [...] the scene is one of general desolation.'[109]

Derivative destruction also followed the Scramogue ambush. After the assault, Volunteers doused the soldiers' lorry with petrol and ignited it, burning away its rubber tyres, lubricants and remaining fuel, and left it on the road.[110] In retaliation, Crown forces destroyed a house that had served as a sniping post, destruction that contributed to County Roscommon's running total of £284,317 in claims for malicious damage to property.[111] Fermoy and Scramogue could be exchanged for a number of ambushes and retaliations that escalated a 'tit-for-tat cycle of violence' during the period.[112] Ireland's built environment suffered under this distinct archetype. Destruction was often retributory, commonly committed with anonymity and focused on vulnerable targets.

Reclaiming the Built Environment

Ireland's natural landscapes offered platforms and materials to carry out attacks and ambushes, but Crown forces adapted. Police patrols began to carry saws and hatchets to clear downed trees, with dynamite in reserve for larger barriers.[113] Bicycle patrols manoeuvred between obstacles, and lorries travelled in groups of two or three, equidistant between wide gaps to avoid bottlenecking at an obstacle.[114] Adaptation also followed the IRA's transition from collecting war material to direct attacks on individuals and buildings, which accelerated towards the end of 1919.[115] Steel shutters, sandbags and barbed wire reinforced vulnerable police barracks and courthouses, which were commonly set within rowed housing or sat alone as detached, often remote buildings. While destruction perpetuated ongoing low-volume damage to the natural environment, the IRA's targets – RIC barracks, rural police huts and urban stations, income tax and rates offices, courthouses, and the homes, businesses and property of those deemed political and class enemies – exemplified Britain's colonial presence in one form or another. Police registered as an omnipresent threat to the republican movement due to their widespread presence and intelligence network. These factors prioritised their marginalisation and destruction. As Diarmaid Ferriter noted, policemen's intimacy with the local community, vital for peacekeeping, ultimately staged their decline.[116] A coeval precis justified hostility towards

Irish police in these terms, as 'the force was the backbone of the British Government in Ireland.' Addressing Dáil Éireann in April 1919, Eoin MacNeill labelled the RIC 'a force of spies ... a force of traitors ... a force of perjurers':

> I say these things, not that your feelings might be roused, but to convince you of the necessity that exists why you should take such measures as will make police government in this country by the enemy impossible.

Éamon de Valera branded policemen 'England's janissaries' – a standing army loyal to the Crown. 'They are the eyes and ears of the enemy.'[117] As such, the social marginalisation of police and the destruction of their barracks was as much a political protest as it was practical military exercise. Even unsuccessful attacks, where the IRA retired without raiding or destroying a building, nonetheless discouraged authority, bolstered republican morale and provided exercise for future attempts.[118] Towards this, Derek Gladwin reinforced the fact that wartime obstacles include both human and non-human elements, an 'interlinking networks of the social and environmental'.[119] As such, the IRA's destruction of the built environment altered landscapes and ecologies while at the same time disrupting various social environments.

While attacks on police barracks occurred as early as April 1918, coordinated assaults against RIC barracks first occurred in Munster, where 17 buildings were attacked between January and August 1919. Activity extended to counties Armagh, Down, Derry and Monaghan, which experienced attacks during the same period.[120] Filtered through contemporary language, rebel 'outrage' described a wide range of destructive and violent activity, including firing at and into barracks, raids for arms, and the complete destruction of buildings, typically through arson or explosives. In response, Dublin Castle withdrew constables from smaller posts and consolidated larger towns.[121]

Approximately 75 police stations and huts closed between August and December 1919.[122] Some had been raided and remained vulnerable, while others were too small or insignificant to defend. The Inspector General categorised areas in Sligo in these terms, where stations 'were too few and the force too small to cope with the state of affairs prevailing'.[123] Four closed in August at Clogher, Keash, Ross and Templehouse.[124] Limerick stations at Herbertstown, Elton and Knocklong also closed the same month. Each had maintained but a few constables, four on average, and were within six miles of the District HQ at Bruff.[125] Difficult topography and isolation also prompted closures. The Dingle peninsula was nearly devoid of police presence: 'Its geographical position and the limited number of roads made it very difficult to police'.[126] West Galway also featured 'wide areas [...] without police and under the control of Sinn Féin.'[127] Notes from a raid on a two-man station at Maam in Connemara detailed how the barracks' exposed position, 'situated in an isolated lake and mountain district, with a wood at the back', favoured attackers.[128] In spite of their actual utility, withdrawing police from barracks and huts altered the perception of security in an area.

Multiple barrack closures in counties Antrim (6), Kilkenny (11), Sligo (4), Tyrone (7) and Wexford (9) throughout November 1919 further reduced police presence, intimated republican control and altered the local security dynamic. By summer 1920, nearly a third of RIC barracks had been evacuated from areas authorities deemed 'too hot to hold'.[129]

Approximately 700 barracks were closed through January 1921, representing over 50 per cent of those in operation just two years before.[130] Police withdrawal was seen as an 'unfortunate [...] course', one that, authorities conceded, 'caused apprehension among law abiding citizens in the localities affected who feel that they are left without adequate protection'.[131] The *Irish Independent* interpreted abdication in more explicit terms: as an act that abandoned civilians 'to the *de facto* supremacy of revolution'.[132] 'Every deserted barrack or hut,' the *Irish Times* added, 'is an advertisement for the physical triumph of sedition.'[133] Contemporary fiction *Tales of the RIC* explained the retreat as a 'game of seesaw':

> The movements of the flying columns of the IRA [...] have always corresponded accurately to the amount of police and military pressure brought to bear on them, which pressure has continually fluctuated in agreement to the whims and brain-waves of the politicians in power. [...] [Conversely,] Extra pressure, more rigid enforcement of existing restrictions on movement, and increased military activity have always resulted in a general stampede of flying columns to the mountains of the west, where the gunman could rest in comparative safety, and swagger about among the simple and ignorant mountain-folk to their hearts' content.[134]

A response to the republican show-of-force and shifting government policy, abandoned barracks also presented training opportunities for aspirant soldiers whose 'amateur enthusiasm' could operate 'in a climate of relative innocence'.[135] Of the 38 barracks closed in November 1919, the IRA destroyed at least 24 the following spring.[136] Attacking the built environment guided more significant outcomes: it was a social exercise, validating and often personally transformative. In Limerick, for instance, Mossie Harnett and his comrades organised a *céilí* – 'a night of frolic and fun' – to mark the burning of an abandoned barrack at Tounafulla.[137] Innocence faded as Volunteers flirted with local women and handled petrol for the first time.

Petrol and liquid paraffin were principal catalysts throughout the Irish Revolution, aiding the ignition and spread of destructive fires and compounding ecological contamination in several forms. Environmental historians of war have categorised fire as a tool of pre-industrial conflict; a destructive weapon that also benefitted agriculture through clearance and soil enrichment.[138] Coupled with chemical accelerants, however, fire is reassigned to modern industrial conflicts. For the IRA, petrol was versatile and fuelled assaults on police barracks in various ways. It filled canisters and bottles that were lit and thrown into buildings, it was pumped through holes bored in walls and roofs, or it was sprinkled throughout a building and ignited. Straw, cotton and flax tow were saturated in petrol to offset potentially damp conditions, while dry thatch and timber construction offered ready tinder.[139] Like rifles and explosives, the IRA acquired petrol from various sources; large quantities came from Anglo-American Oil Company depots throughout Ireland.[140] While it was a valued commodity, larger stores were also neutralised to prevent their use by Crown forces, as general acts of sabotage, or in protest over motor permits and petrol tax – acts that resulted in concentrated ground pollution. Over 400 gallons of petrol were emptied onto the ground in Sligo in March 1920.[141] The following June, the IRA intentionally spilled 4,000 gallons of petrol that were bound for the Royal Air Force at Oranmore.[142]

Petrol was an efficient stimulus, but Volunteers noted its inferiority to paraffin and the two were often used in combination. 'There were so many barracks burned that our boys were quite efficient at the job,' Sean Farrelly recalled:

It was found that petrol by itself was no use. It would just go off in a flame without lighting the material. Paraffin was the stuff to get them going. It was just dabbed on the floors, then sprinkled with a little petrol and very soon after being ignited we were assured of a complete job.[143]

Petrol and paraffin supplemented existing caches of gelignite, nitrates and other explosive chemicals to diversify the republican arsenal. As a countermeasure, the Home Office attempted to dam the flow of explosive chemicals to Ireland under the Firearms Act 1920. The Chief Inspector of Explosives, A. Cooper-Key, wrote to over 80 chemical salt manufacturers throughout Britain explaining that circumstances in Ireland were such that substantial orders from Ireland should be treated as suspect, that 'there is very good reason to believe that these orders form part of an organized attempt to obtain munitions of all kinds.'[144]

Empty barracks and access to incendiary chemicals prompted an extensive arson campaign that reconfigured the colonial landscape. Contemporary reports attempted to accurately assess the number and severity of burnings, but figures were often given as approximates, particularly during periods of frequent and intense destruction.[145] Government outrage reports indicate that nearly 300 barracks, courthouses and tax offices were raided or burned over a two-week period that bordered the Easter Rising's fourth anniversary, 29 March–11 April, 1920.[146] A more focused evaluation might centre on the Easter holiday alone, when seemingly coordinated destruction unfolded on a national level. On 3–4 April, 1920, upwards of 200 police barracks, 'one hated symbol of English rule', were converted to 'tombstones of British prestige in Ireland'.[147] Various extensions of state bureaucracy and security were likewise targeted, including courthouses, tax offices and coast guard stations. When buildings could not be burned, their contents were stolen or destroyed. Volunteers routinely burned property, tax and excise records in order to disrupt assessment, collection, record-keeping, and local government in general. The act performed as revolutionary metaphor in some ways: an Irish *Grande Peur,* widespread and fervent, marked a more violent turn against the State. Fiscal records and rate books from 18 Irish counties were stolen, ripped up or burned on the spot over Easter 1920, *'render*ing to cinders the things that are Caesar's', the *Freeman's Journal* reported.[148] Pensions and Inland Revenue offices from Belfast to Cork were destroyed along with their financial files, while revenue, customs and excise, and pensions officials in Cork City claimed over £114,000 in destroyed property, ruined record books and lost supplies following the Easter assault.[149] Elsewhere, rate collections were projected to be 'paralysed for months to come' after raids and arson, and government officials in Galway assessed the cost of repairing buildings damaged from forced entry and the manhours required to restore financial records at £300,000.[150] Records were often destroyed in a performative manner that complemented a wider drama. In Oldcastle, Meath, a cortege escorted records to the local cemetery where they were ceremoniously 'cremated'.[151] Volunteers tied a local tax collector named Patton to a tree outside his office in Ballyshannon, Donegal, to witness his tax accounts drowned in the River Erne.[152] Some officials attended to their duties in spite of intimidation and destruction, though often under military protection. A Resident Magistrate and Clerk in Cloyne, Cork, conducted quarter sessions hearings 'under the canopy of Heaven' after the courthouse was partially destroyed by fire.[153]

A second destructive surge began on 12 May 1920, which claimed a further 88 barracks and 34 tax offices. 'The work left uncompleted at Easter was finished,' the *Westmeath Independent* observed, at times in 'a leisurely but thoroughly efficient manner'.[154] Inclusive, this brief period accounted for approximately 350 destroyed barracks and nearly 100 tax office raids.[155] Notably inactive areas, such as in Mayo, east Galway and south Roscommon, registered few destroyed barracks but were nevertheless disturbed. Agrarian violence preoccupied many young men and women in the region, who drove cattle off large estates and downed field walls and fences, demarcating possession.[156] Further destructive periods occurred between June and August 1920, and April and May 1921, when the IRA assaulted homes and businesses, infrastructure, and commercial and agricultural goods with greater frequency.[157] Dublin Castle statistics recorded 540 barracks destroyed and 268 damaged through 23 April 1921.[158] Outwardly, apolitical installations were not spared. Of the 151 coast guard stations in Ireland, 83 had been destroyed by 1922.[159]

Incendiarism aided IRA operations and maintained the general disruption of British rule. This included pre-emptive and preventative arson in Ireland and abroad. Besides structures framing state authority or security, Volunteers pre-emptively burned private homes and estates, empty buildings, hotels, castles and workhouses to prevent their occupation by police or soldiers.[160] These acts also served as diversions for other assaults and as bait for police or soldiers to investigate.[161] For example, the Third Tipperary Brigade burned a Cashel courthouse in May 1920 under the pretence that it was to be occupied by the military, then awaited investigation from the local police whom they had hoped to lure away from their stronghold.[162] However, police came to recognise the ruse. In Galway, Portumna constables ignored a fire that claimed 10 tons of hay, a horse and 25 feet of a shed adjacent to their barracks. The building belonged to a man named Reilly who, with the help of some locals, worked to extinguish the flamed and salvage his property. 'As there is no animus against Reilly,' a District Inspector reported, 'the only motive that can be assigned to the crime is that the fire was caused to induce the police to leave the Barracks to quench the flames.'[163]

Significant ruin occurred outside Ireland as well. The IRA in Britain initiated a 'counter destruction' campaign to offset Crown reprisals against Irish homes and property, to bring light to the situation in Ireland, and to reciprocate arson's psychological effects on English cities.[164] 'The ordinary English people couldn't have cared less about what was happening in Ireland,' John Pinkman explained, 'being unconcerned about the reports of murder and destruction there.'[165] In late November 1920, the Liverpool IRA set fire to stores near Gladstone Dock.[166] Its initial plan was to burn thousands of barrels of resin, but revised targets were equally flammable. Massive stores of oak, mahogany, poplar, sugar and cotton steered fire along a nearly nine-mile strip of the Liverpool warehouse district. Approximately fourteen warehouses and four timber yards were destroyed, and there was over £400,000 of damage.[167] The IRA continued to operate in the region, where it destroyed numerous farm buildings, material stores and telegraph wires outside Liverpool and Manchester the following year. '[S]everal gangs of incendiaries' incinerated agricultural stock that ranged in form and scale from a single hay rick to '200 tons of straw, wheat, peas, and beans'.[168] Police assigned guilt to the Irish republican movement even when perpetrators could not be identified or apprehended. Concurrent instances of arson, abandoned bottles that smelled of paraffin and petrol, and targets located within cycling distance to known Irish communities and seasonal Irish labour populations evidenced guilt, though these methods were not entirely accurate.[169] Nevertheless, the destruction of agricultural stock, buildings and implements accounted for nearly half of the IRA's 239 operations in Britain, which occurred between late November 1920 and 11 July 1921 and primarily affected the midlands and northern England. Gerard Noonan's extensive analysis concluded that 'parts of Britain saw more I.R.A. operations than some areas of Ireland.'[170] This is true in a certain sense, though it may discount the diversity, consistency and saturation of landscape manipulation and environmental damage in Ireland. Despite notable spikes in IRA assaults on the built environment, an overall negative trend can be observed beginning the summer of 1920. This was due to the fact that many strategic and high-priority targets had already been destroyed; as the Inspector General observed for June 1920, 'Sinn Féin has practically completed its campaign of burning police barracks and destroying Government property.'[171]

While IRA methods produced physical ruin, they also shaped more intimate damage. Destruction battered the human senses and assaults elicited distress and panic in civilians. However, for Crown forces and State officials, silence could be an unsettling sensation. Dead telecommunication lines or transmission difficulties often foreshadowed an attack, but the exact targets or timeframes remained unclear. On one occasion, downed communication lines disconnected Tralee from north Kerry in March 1920. Anxiety and rumour prompted an investigation of the region that located trenches, stone barricades, a broken bridge and felled trees in several villages leading north toward Listowel, the work of approximately 200 men from local companies.[172] What the *Belfast Newsletter* later labelled 'The Cutting Epidemic' had its genesis during the 1918 Conscription Crisis and continued throughout the revolution, altering the aural environment as an indispensable tool of the republican guerrilla war.[173] Silencing techniques remained fairly constant throughout the period.[174] Volunteers destroyed communication instruments on the spot, snipped telegraph and telephone wires and cut support poles, often in remote or otherwise unnavigable sections of line where detection and repair were difficult. When hand tools failed (thick wire snapped John McCormack's hedge cutters 'at the rivet'),[175] or risk prevented cutting (Edward Fullerton, Hughie Carrol and Dan O'Hare clung to a telegraph pole after a Newry district train swept away their ladder),[176] weighted ropes hauled wires to the ground.[177] At times, however, more extreme measures were required that betrayed attempts at stealth. As an example, Donegal telegraph poles were 'blown out of the ground' in April 1920 as part of the widespread assault over Easter.[178] Outrage reports reveal that nearly 1,200 post office telegraphs were damaged or destroyed between June 1920 and July 1921.[179] The British military only established a wireless communication network in late 1921, months after the declaration of truce.[180] Destruction, intelligence leaks and the volume of communications, which pigeon couriers failed to service, had illustrated the need for this transition. In County Cork alone the Postmaster General reported 356 instances of damage to, or destruction of, communication wires, infrastructure and operating tools between the autumn of 1919 and 11 July 1921. Activity was so widespread and constant that entries only occasionally recorded a definitive number of wires and instruments destroyed. And while compensation for damage to communication equipment accounted for only 2.7 per cent of claims (£15,958), it contributed nearly 50 per cent to the total reported instances of damage to Crown property during this period.[181]

Guerrilla action could also produce deafening sounds. Despite the desire to maintain quiet and preserve an element of surprise (Volunteers closing on their target often removed their shoes to ensure silence),[182] assaults on barracks often proceeded as blunt confrontations between cut stone walls, reinforced windows and amateur explosives. The ordnance that destroyed the barracks in the small village of Ballytrain, Monaghan, for instance, exploded with memorable force. One witness, Sergeant Lawton, told the *Freeman's Journal* he had recently observed 200 lbs of gelignite detonated at a local quarry, 'but that was nothing to the explosion when the barracks was blown up.'[183] Likewise, a mine placed outside an Armagh station in late April 1920 detonated with a force that did more damage to surrounding houses than the intended target. Another in Tipperary, at Holycross, was audible in Thurles over four miles away.[184] Defending constables were 'rocked and reeled as if there was an earthquake', but the exterior gable wall was only slightly damaged, and the raid was eventually abandoned.[185]

Civilians sensed war differently; violent noise underscored events they were often hostage to observe. This was the experience of the Beasley family when the Cork IRA billeted in their home outside Bandon before an ambush. In March 1921, the family hosted 'a fine, jolly lot of fellows [who] made themselves quite at home. They cooked some meals, and then they played cards, and some went into the front room, played the piano and sang.' Miss Beasley spent the subsequent ambush face down in a backroom, processing the assault through the din it produced: the ascending, rhymical popping of military lorry engines, dirt and stone crunching under tyres that navigated a turn in the road, and gunfire that exploded from various points on her farm. 'There were several loud explosions like bombs, and one bigger than the others shook the house. It was terrifying. After about 15 minutes there was a lull, and it began again and lasted about 20 minutes.' The experience lingered for hours as the lorries burned on the roadside. In her work on Holocaust memory, Leslie Morris probed 'the echo of the sound of memory' and asked whether we can examine formative sounds of an era or experience, or 'speak of a site of memory as a sound of memory'.[186] The Irish Revolution was certainly remembered in this way, with the War of Independence period performing a broad spectrum of scales, timbres and tempos.[187]

Environment, Climate & Conflict

Irish environments experienced continuous manipulation and destruction throughout the Irish Revolution. This chapter has surveyed some of the IRA's work during the War of Independence, which included the basic tenants of landscape preparation, obstruction and incendiarism against select natural and urban environments. Numerous episodes fall outside this dedicated view, including counter-revolutionary, punitive damage and social disruption committed by Crown forces, and low-level agrarian unrest and civil-war violence that often occurred in the fog of war and political transition. These are the subjects of subsequent chapters. The underlying observation here is that republican forces enlisted Ireland's landscapes towards obstructing and combating the British State and in doing so inflicted an unprecedented degree of environmental damage.

It is not enough to simply observe that the IRA's campaign yielded damage to Ireland's natural and built-up landscapes. It should instead be recognised that felling trees to block roads or burning barracks or tax offices essentially renegotiated Ireland's territoriality; that is, environmental damage, however small or static, was an act of resistance that challenged political power and control as well as Ireland's colonial legacy.[188] Aspects of military control, such as the occupation of space, were similarly challenged. Low-level, consistent destruction and the occasional ambush or assassination reaffirmed the republic on levels both physical and metaphysical. Trenched roads, silent communication lines and the charred barrack foundations sustained a 'banal terrorism' that indicated to civilians and Crown forces that the republic was living, its army active.[189] In this respect, unremarkable day-to-day environmental destruction underpinned the revolution's more celebrated violent exploits. Each created co-operative zones of violence, or a 'system of shared presence', that conveyed the impression that Crown forces controlled little more than the ground on which they stood.[190]

The frequency, geography and saturation of destructive activity supports this argument, but a comprehensive analysis or representation is both conceptually problematic and difficult to present.[191] David Fitzpatrick and Peter Hart identified several obstacles to navigating the geography of Irish nationalism and revolutionary violence.[192] Steve Pile warned that even observed and recorded expressions of resistance, such as vandalism, protest and military-style engagement, produce only crudely suggestive geographies of resistance.[193] An environmental analysis faces similar difficulties. The amount of evidence for environmental damage is overwhelming yet inexact, particularly as we consider that multiple incidents of varying scale occurred throughout Ireland on the same day, often in the same locale. It is also scattered and imprecise. Much like the countless un- and under-reported raids, robberies, assaults and acts of vandalism that occurred throughout the period, environmental collateral was often ignored or generalised as a preface to interpersonal violence. The Bureau of Military History Witness Statements – closed to Fitzpatrick, available in hardcopy to Hart, and fully digitised for myself – reflect these shortcomings. Corroborating these narratives with other available source material presents a deeper impression of IRA landscape manipulation during the War of Independence with which we may observe the types and patterns of damage and test its distribution and intensity against established patterns of revolutionary violence.

Local and regional influences, such as an area's previous alignment to nationalist organisations or ties to the British economy or relevant urbanisation, have helped to explain manifestations of republican violence during the War of Independence. Erhard Rumpf (1977), David Fitzpatrick (1978), Charles Townshend (1979) and Tom Garvin (1983) produced durable studies from which later scholars, notably Peter Hart (1997), Joost Augusteijn (2007) and Marie Coleman (2013), qualified their own explanations for revolutionary behaviour.[194] Consensus suggests that raids, engagements, killings and broadly inclusive 'outrages' were most present in the province of Munster, least in Ulster.[195] Garvin contended that the most active regions ran through a swath of the 'middle west', which spanned from Fermanagh to Cork and included smaller 'theatres' of war around a Cavan–Sligo interchange. Incorporating the civil war period, Hart broadened this scope to include Roscommon, Longford and Westmeath.[196] Though it applies many of the same sources that informed preceding studies, the impressive spatial representations within the *Atlas of the Irish Revolution* help us to further understand the complex 'process by which individuals, through interaction with their environment, became revolutionaries'.[197] Observing these influences in the literal sense pivots from Augusteijn's implied social contexts to emphasise how many men and women interpreted 'helping the cause of national emancipation' to mean cutting wires, sawing trees and digging trenches.[198]

My research sampled 2,183 instances of landscape manipulation and ensuing damage to the built and natural environment on a daily basis from 1 January 1919 to 11 July 1921. Destruction of the built environment (1,120 occurrences) stands out amongst other categories due to its publicisation and long financial paper trail, but its prominence amongst all types of damage is somewhat artificial. As Hart explained of a 'bullets and bombs' methodology, if an incident was significant then it was reported. As such, injuries, deaths and significant physical destruction are much easier to verify. Conversely, the widespread preparations that preceded both aborted and executed ambushes were often too numerous to record, 'mundane' details incompatible with the 'thrilling exploits' that followed.[199] Like death and destruction, damage to the natural environment through tree felling (93 instances), to communication infrastructure (401), to roads and railways (85), to mobility in the form of destroyed cars and lorries (107), and to personal property in general (384) is only accountable when it was reported. Those included in this sample were often reported at the individual level or, in the case of trees and trenches, represent numerous individual points of damage as a single instance of damage. Extensive files produced through various reparations for malicious injury grants and indemnity acts permit a more focused view, but a true representation remains an estimate at best.

Rate of Damage to the Built Environment per 10,000 people				
County	**Rate**	**County**	**Rate**
Cork	7.8	Wexford	2.63
Meath	5.53	Galway	2.3
Westmeath	5.16	Fermanagh	2.26
Clare	4.79	Mayo	2.23
Tipperary	4.72	Monaghan	1.95
King's (Offaly)	4.39	Carlow	1.93
Queen's (Laois)	4.39	Wicklow	1.81
Limerick	4.33	Louth	1.72
Roscommon	4.15	Donegal	1.48
Sligo	4.04	Cavan	1.2
Waterford	3.57	Down	1.17
Kilkenny	3.33	Tyrone	0.98
Longford	3.19	Londonderry	0.64
Kerry	2.88	Dublin	0.5
Kildare	2.85	Armagh	0.49
Leitrim	2.67		

Nevertheless, what is available suggests that environmental damage was significantly aligned to the established geography of revolution. Again, Munster was by far the most active province in regards to landscape damage or destruction during the period (1,414 instances), followed by Leinster (423), Connacht (210) and Ulster (136). County Cork registered higher instances of damage (1,063) than Leinster, Connacht and Ulster combined (769), and five of the ten most damaged counties were in Munster. Geographically, Garvin's 'middle west' region should be adjusted south and west to begin at Sligo–Roscommon–Longford, as Fermanagh, Cavan and Leitrim registered relatively lower damage totals. Accounting for population, the rate of damage to the built environment per 10,000 inhabitants is tabled above.

Finally, what can be said about the relationship between environmental manipulation and interpersonal violence? Was environmental damage a predictable precursor or outcome of IRA violence, or merely the product of a standing order to disrupt British rule? Landscapes were often primed for ambushes that never occurred; while evidencing activity in an area, it did not evidence violence. However, correlating Peter Hart's data for the rate of IRA violence by county per 10,000 inhabitants with the rate of total damage for each province in overlapping periods reveals strong positive correlation (Leinster: .678; Ulster: .678; Munster: .794; Connacht: .821). In short, the geography and concentration of conflict differed due to an area's ability to host that violence. This validates Michael Brennan's complaint of soldiering 'in level country' where there was little cover to aid operations, but it confronts other views that terrain may have been a local inhibitor of IRA activity but failed to project a nationwide model.[200]

Examining Irish climate data and short-term weather patterns pushes this analysis further.[201] Irish weather was impartial to the conflict and compounded the adversity of difficult terrains for all combatants.[202] Long-term precipitation records show the War of Independence period to have experienced extreme weather fluctuation. Autumn 1919 was documented as the fourth driest on record between the years 1850 and 1922.[203] This was reversed in 1920 as wet, cold weather persisted throughout the year. One Belfast weather observer categorised the entire month of January as 'one of heavy rain and storm'; similar reports came from the opposite end of the country in Cork.[204] Adverse conditions continued into the spring and summer of 1920, saturating Ireland's already poor roads and threatening the harvest. Tipperary received rain nearly every day between April and May – weather 'more like January than the first day of summer' that transformed the whole of Ireland into a 'regular swamp'.[205] In late May, Athlone received 1.5 inches of rain in an hour.[206] July featured 'rain, rain, rain, with such results as inevitably follow upon a cold, wet and unseasonable, mid-summer month'; the *Drogheda Independent* judged August to be the 'worst on record'.[207] This continued into autumn. 6.5 inches of rain fell throughout October 1920, exceeding the documented monthly average over the previous 45 years.[208] Overall, 1920 was unseasonably wet and cold, and weather remained 'wild, wet and stormy' into early 1921.[209]

While it was not uncommon for rainfall to exceed historic averages throughout the 1919–1922 period, data suggests that extreme weather did not stymy guerrilla activity. In fact, some of the conflict's most materially destructive months were also its most wet and mild. Detrimental to conventional warfare and modern industrialised conflicts, overcast skies, poor visibility and generally lousy conditions facilitated guerrilla activity. For example, the most destructive month in the sample, April 1920 ('cloudy, cold and cheerless'), hosted 22 days of rainfall that produced 3.54 inches of water, slightly above average for the period but 146% of the 35-year average.[210] In fact, April initiated a destructive period that produced 952 instances of damage through August 1920, a 5-month span that received 20 days of rain and just over 3 inches of rainfall per month on average, whose typical daily temperature averaged 53°F (11°C). Conversely, a second surge between March and July 1921 occurred in ideal conditions. The IRA committed 776 instances of damage over a period that experienced an average of just over 2 inches of rain over 13 days. June 1921 stands as an outlier in this illustration. The month registered 253 instances of damage that came off in brilliant Irish weather: less than an inch of rain over 6.5 days, just 24 per cent of the long-term average. The table below accounts these figures.[211]

Combined Meteorological Rainfall Values Averaged from North & South District Station Returns January 1920–July 1921			
Month	Total Instances of Damage	Rainfall (inches)	Days of Rain
January 1920	36	5.435	26.5
February 1920	45	2.675	20
March 1920	36	3.815	22
April 1920	344	3.54	22
May 1920	163	3.51	22.5
June 1920	198	2.11	14.5
July 1920	122	4.135	25.5
August 1920	125	2.39	15.5
September 1920	59	2.89	20.5
October 1920	27	5.14	16
November 1920	36	3.815	21
December 1920	54	8.87	19
January 1921	50	4.175	27
February 1921	77	1.57	10.5
March 1921	110	3.645	26
April 1921	80	1.005	11.5
May 1921	137	2.165	9
June 1921	253	0.375	6.5
July 1921	196	3.68	15.5

As one of several potentially detrimental environmental variables, abnormally poor weather did not deter guerrilla activity. However, an adverse climate did complicate duties and extract casualties. For the Volunteer organisers traversing the country, rain-soaked, muddy backroads often proved as challenging as the companies they attempted to discipline. Ernie O'Malley was frequently caught out in the rain, in the dark, and consequently disoriented. O'Malley's weary body paid 'the penance of a bicycle' to organise inactive areas nestled within 'the rugged wild nature of the land'.[212] Brighid O'Mullane was a cycle courier for the IRA and organised Cumann na mBan branches between April 1920 and March 1921, cycling up to 40 miles a day in some instances and in all types of weather.[213]

Weather was impartial to rank, assignment, age and sex. Many caught out in the rain often suffered a 'severe wetting' and became susceptible to respiratory infection, which typically manifested as pulmonary tuberculosis or bronchial pneumonia. Illness could claim life quickly or prevent recovery long after one's service concluded. Anastasia Nevin was in 'excellent health' prior to her service, which required 'long journeys in rain and cold and long periods of strain on despatch and observation work', from which she developed bronchial asthma.[214] Nora Wallace was another such case. She contracted tuberculosis as a result of her service to the Cork IRA in 1921, and she endured comparable 'strain, hardship and exposure' in aid to the republican cause during the civil war. Her condition persisted, and in 1934 doctors found scar tissue on her lung casing that indicated pleural thickening, collapsed lobes and partial diaphragm paralysis.[215] Similarly, in early February 1921, Joseph Collins posted all-night sentry duty in 'exceptionally bad' weather. Corroborative evidence from multiple sources recalled the particular night as 'one of the worst in memory, wet and cold'; 'so bad that the rain came through the thatched roofs'. Collins was consequently 'drenched, and with water running out of his boots'.[216] He contracted pneumonia, registered a high fever and died within a week. His parents filed his pension application posthumously, in which it is noted how his father had struggled to maintain the family farm following the death of his eldest son, and how Joseph's premature death 'had such an effect on his mother that she got a nervous attack and broke down in health from which she has never recovered'.[217]

While not its detriment, poor weather complicated guerrilla activity. Rain-soaked IRA scouts and couriers fell ill from exposure, and some died as a result. The War of Independence caused significant damage to the built and natural environment, which began to heal after building debris was cleared, trenches filled and fires extinguished. However, many of the environment's human victims endured irreversible loss, injury or compromised health for many years after the war's conclusion.

Conclusion

This chapter has presented three broad concepts towards an environmental understanding of the War of Independence. First, it argued that the term 'active service' requires revision. Traditionally equated with IRA 'flying columns', the designation overlooks essential labour, scouting and logistics contributions. Though military pensions were awarded for this work, its incorporation into the revolutionary narrative allows new voices to emerge and new insights to be gained. Second, that IRA guerrilla activity produced widespread, perpetual instances of landscape damage, contamination and destruction. Its patterns, pace and concertation greatly overlap those of interpersonal violence during the period, suggesting that environmental manipulation was a likely precursor to revolutionary violence. Finally, the Irish climate was shown to have experienced unusually wet weather during the revolution's most active months. This is a particularly interesting point as poor weather is typically a battle retardant, at least in conflicts of the period. Heavy rain failed to neutralise the guerrilla war in Ireland, although it did attend disease and impairment in Irishmen and women that lasted well beyond the conflict.

The Easter Rising inaugurated large, coordinated landscape manipulation and resulted in widespread urban destruction. During the War of Independence, the IRA concentrated on destroying select individual buildings and stores, aided by a steady campaign of obstruction and disruption. This, too, was met with retaliation. From 1919, the British Army, RIC and its Auxiliary forces targeted a variety of private and commercial spaces in their pursuit and harassment of rebels. These included private homes, meeting halls, farms, markets and co-operative dairy creameries – civilian property that amplified the conflict's moral tone and environmental impact.

NOTES

1. Augusteijn outlined the typical Volunteer: young, Catholic, working or middle-class. Officers tended to be older than the rank-and-file, from urban areas and better educated. Joost Augusteijn, *From Public Defiance to Guerilla Warfare: The Experience of Ordinary Volunteers in the Irish War of Independence, 1916–1921* (Kildare: Irish Academic Press, 1996), p. 75; Foster remarked, 'IRA activists came from the youth of the small towns, and the rural lower middle classes; unlike the Volunteer movement at large, the eldest sons or local notables from the strong-farming and shopkeeping classes were not prominent, whereas the unattached, younger "men of no property" were.' R. F. Foster, *Modern Ireland 1600–1972* (London: Penguin Press, 1988), p. 500.
2. Augusteijn, *From Public Defiance to Guerrilla Warfare*, pp 69–72; further, David Fitzpatrick identified participation in the revolution (in various forms) to involve risk calculated at the personal, collective and financial levels. David Fitzpatrick, 'The geography of Irish nationalism 1910–1921', in *Past & Present* 78 (February 1978), pp 114–15.
3. David Fitzpatrick, *Politics and Irish Life 1913–1921: Provincial Experiences of War and Revolution* (Cork: Cork University Press, 1977; 1998), p. 180.
4. Peter Hart, 'The geography of revolution in Ireland 1917–1923', in *Past & Present* 155:1 (May 1997), p. 156.
5. Augusteijn, *From Public Defiance to Guerrilla Warfare*, p. 69.
6. Seán O'Faoláin, *Vive Moi* (Boston, Toronto: Little, Brown and Company, 1963), p. 175.
7. Peter Hart, *The I.R.A. at War 1916–1923* (Oxford University Press, 2003; 2005), p. 44.
8. Fitzpatrick, 'The geography of Irish nationalism', p. 115.
9. 'Notes on training', *An t-Óglach*, 15 Aug. 1918, p. 2.
10. Mossie Harnett (ed. James H. Joy), *Victory and Woe: The West Limerick Brigade in the War of Independence* (Dublin: University College Dublin Press, 2002), p. 29.
11. C. J. C. Street, 'Measures for combating conscription', in *The Administration of Ireland, 1920* (London: Philip Allan & Col, 1921), pp 58–61.
12. Inspector General's report for January 1920, Smith to Under Secretary, 14 Feb. 1920, TNA (CO 904/111).
13. C. J. C. Street, 'Measures for combating conscription', pp 58–61.
14. Inspector General's report for April 1918, J. Byrne to W. Byrne, 11 May 1918, TNA (CO 904/105).
15. Statement of Denis O'Brien, BMH, WS 1306, p. 2.
16. *Killarney Echo and South Kerry Chronicle*, 21 Dec. 1918; *Irish Examiner*, 9 Jan. 1919; 'Cork's War of Independence Fatality Register' entry for Charlie Hurley, http://theirishrevolution.ie, accessed 8 October 2022; Inspector General's report for December 1918, J. Byrne to Under Secretary, 11 Jan. 1919, TNA (CO 904/107).
17. Charles Townshend, *The Republic: The Fight for Irish Independence, 1918–1923* (London: Penguin Books, 2013), pp 76–81; on the changing mode of combat, see ibid., p. 79.
18. Inspector General's report for December 1918, Byrne to US, 11 Jan. 1919, TNA (CO 904/107).
19. The danger of armed rebellion still persisted. In May 1919, Dublin Castle reported to the War Cabinet in London that there were '4,000 armed Volunteers in Dublin district alone'. Draft minutes of a meeting of the War Cabinet held at 10 Downing Street, 14 May 1919, TNA (CAB23/15).
20. Dorothy Macardle, *The Republic*, pp 291, 307, 353.
21. Joost Augusteijn, 'Military conflict in the War of Independence', in John Crowley, Donal Ó Drisceoil, Mike Murphy and John Borgonovo (eds), *Atlas of the Irish Revolution* (Cork: Cork University Press, 2017), p. 351; Michael Hopkinson, *The Irish War of Independence* (Dublin: Gill & Macmillan, 2004) p. 25; Hughes, *Defying the IRA?*, p. 13; Augusteijn, *From Public Defiance to Guerrilla Warfare*, p. 69. Though Britain was reluctant to classify its counter-insurgency as a war, the American Commission on Conditions in Ireland, citing the 1907 Hague Convention, identified destroyed property as a significant qualifier for such status. Albert Coyle (transcriber and annotator), *Evidence on Conditions in Ireland Comprising the Complete Testimony, Affidavits and Exhibits Presented Before the American Commission on Conditions in Ireland* (Washington, DC, 1921), pp 46–7.
22. Previous year returns were for 1917: 215; and for 1918: 285. Street, *The Administration of Ireland*, p. 62.
23. W. A. Ballinger, *Rebellion*, pp 169–70.

24. *Kwab-O-Kayal (The Memoirs and Dreams of an Ordinary Soldier)*, Major General L. A. Hawes, Staff Captain, Cork District, 1919, IWM (87/41/1), p. 69. Hawes denounced the morality of republican ambush and included criticism from the Catholic Church: 'Some even ventured to attack the whole conduct of the Irish Republican Army, condemning murders, kidnapping and arson, and denouncing ambushes as cowardly and criminal.', p. 177; Dr. Cohalan said in his Pastoral that 'ambushers take very little risk to themselves', and the Archbishop of Tuam denounced ambushers as 'criminal'. *Western News*, 5 Mar. 1921.
25. Nigel Everett, *The Woods of Ireland* (Dublin: Four Courts Press, 2015 paperback edn), pp 5, 53.
26. Everett, *Woods*, pp 19, 52.
27. Frank Mitchell and Michael Ryan, *Reading the Irish Landscape* (Dublin: Town House and Country House, 1997 edn), p. 317; Everett, *The Woods of Ireland*, pp 18, 46–8; William J. Smyth, 'A plurality of Irelands: Regions, societies, and mentalities', in Brian Graham (ed.), *In Search of Ireland: A Cultural Geography* (New York: Routledge, 1998 edn), pp 31–6; Patrick J. Duffy, *Exploring the History and Heritage of Irish Landscapes* (Dublin: Four Courts Press, 2007), p. 37.
28. T. W. Freeman, *Ireland: Its Physical, Historical, Social and Economic Geography* (New York: E. P. Dutton & Co. Inc., 1942), p. 238.
29. Duffy, *Irish Landscapes*, p. 141.
30. Duffy, *Irish Landscapes*, p. 96. The Irish constabulary, honoured with the prefix 'Royal' following its suppression of the 1867 rebellion. Police records gradually bureaucratised an inventory of Irish customs and temperament. Revolutionary France provided context for contemporary critics who interpreted professional police in Ireland as government spies and conceivable agents of repression. Elizabeth Malcolm, *The Irish Policeman 1822–1922: A Life* (Dublin: Four Courts Press, 2006), p. 42.
31. Horace Piggott and Robert J. Finch, *Dent's Historical and Economic Geographies: Great Britain and Ireland* (London: J. M. Dent & Sons Ltd, 1922), pp 112–13.
32. W. H. Kautt, *Ambushes and Armour*, p. 53.
33. Piggott and Finch, *Dent's Historical and Economic Geographies*, pp 168–9.
34. George Fletcher, *Connaught* (Cambridge: Cambridge University Press, 1922), p. 9.
35. Charles Townshend, *The British Campaign in Ireland 1919–1921: The Development of Political and Military Policies* (Oxford: Oxford University Press, 1975), pp 55–8. See also, Sheehan, *Hearts & Mines*, pp 24–7, 84–5.
36. Cabinet conclusions, 19 May 1920, TNA (CAB 23/21(12)), Appendix II; Keith Jeffrey underscored the vitality of such logistical capacity. Keith Jeffery, 'Forward', in W. H. Kautt, *Ambushes and Armour: The Irish Rebellion, 1919–1921* (Dublin: Irish Academic Press, 2010), p. xv; see also, Townshend, *The British Campaign in Ireland*, pp 83–4.
37. Kautt's overview is unparalleled in this regard. Kautt, *Ambushes and Armour*, pp 53–5, 60; Townshend, *The British Campaign in Ireland*, pp 176–7.
38. 'Appendix A: Details of voted and special services (Naval, Military and Police Buildings)', in *Public Works, Ireland: Eighty-Ninth Annual Report of the Commissioners of Public Works in Ireland: With Appendices for the Year Ending 31 March 1921* (Dublin: His Majesty's Stationary Office, 1921), p. 10.
39. Kautt, *Ambushes and Armour*, pp 62–5.
40. W. H. Kautt deduced a 7.5-ton maximum limit operating on maintained roads that included the vehicle and its cargo. *Ambushes and Armour*, pp 55, 63. By definition of the Committee of British Engineers reporting to the Third Road Congress, 'Heavy Traffic' was defined as 250–600 vehicles per day. Ireland perhaps experienced 'Light Traffic' – 70 vehicles a day – though this is also doubtful. Heavy as comparable to road materials, conditions and typical use. Sellars, 'The tarring of roads', p. 53.
41. J. F. Delany, 'The tarring of roads', in *Transactions of the Institution of Civil Engineers of Ireland* 41–2 (1915–16) (3 January 1916), pp 41–2, 44, 48.
42. Townshend, *The British Campaign in Ireland*, pp 176–7. Rolls Royce was the only car unable to be heard from a distance. Kautt, *Ambushes and Armour*, p. 98.
43. William Sheehan, *Hearts & Mines*, pp 10–12.
44. Kautt, *Ambushes and Armour*, p. 160.
45. Alderman John Jinks, 'Sligo corporation', *Sligo Champion*, 21 Feb. 1920.
46. Kautt *Ambushes and Armour*, p. 130.
47. Statement of Brighid O'Mullane, BMH, WS 450, p. 26.

48. Kautt, *Ambushes and Armour*, pp 53–5; Pattison, 'The British Army's effectiveness in the Irish campaign 1919–1921', p. 95.
49. Charles Townshend, *The Republic*, p. 153.
50. Kautt, *Ambushes and Armour*, p. 42.
51. Report: Air reconnaissance carried out on 29 June 1922, TNA (WO 35/92).
52. Pattison, 'The British Army's effectiveness in the Irish campaign 1919–1921', pp 95, 97, citing Townshend, *The British Campaign in Ireland*, p. 171. See also, Sheehan, *Hearts & Mines*, pp 85–6, 89.
53. Charles Townshend, *The Republic*, pp 11, 143, 152–4. Sheehan, *A Hard Local War*, pp 140–4. Aeroplanes continued to inform military strategy in Ireland even after the Anglo-Irish Treaty had been signed. For example, Dublin Command planned a half-hour aerial bombardment on the Four Courts in late June 1922, to be followed by artillery and tank assaults. 'Proposed plan for attack on the Four Courts', G. F. Boyd to HQ Dublin District, Parkgate, TNA (WO 35/92). Hopkinson, *Green Against Green*, pp 115–20.
54. Lofts redistributed: Killybegs to Londonderry (26 Oct. 1920); Renmore Barracks, Galway, to Boyle (1 Oct. 1920). Wagon units featured two loftmen, a small table and chairs, pigeon lofts and corn feed. TNA (WO 35/180A); *Freeman's Journal*, 6 Aug. 1920. For an overview of Britain's mobilisation of pigeons during the First World War, see Jilly Cooper, *Animals in War* (London: William Heinemann Let, 1983), pp 72–7.
55. Kautt, *Ambushes and Armour*, p. 160.
56. Sheehan, *Hearts & Mines*, pp 24–5, 89–93; *Leinster Leader*, 2 Apr. 1921; 'Report on Operations 16/17th February, 1921', A. C. Halahan, Essex Reg., 18 Feb. 1921, TNA (WO 35/88B, Part II: Conflicts 1920 Nov. 6 – 1921 Aug. 26).
57. Soldiers commandeered horses to conduct 'round up' searches for wanted men. This was particularly the case in Tralee, Co. Kerry, in February 1921. *Irish Examiner*, 11 Feb. 1921; *Belfast Newsletter* 11 Feb. 1921; *Evening Herald*, 15 Feb. 1921.
58. *Freeman's Journal*, 7 June 1921, *Connaught Telegraph*, 11 June 1921; *Irish Independent*, 11 June 1921; *Irish Independent*, 17 June 1921; *Drogheda Independent*, 25 June 1921.
59. *Evening Herald*, 29 Dec. 1920; ibid., 6 Nov. 1920; 'Homing pigeons taken', *Irish Independent*, 30 Apr. 1921; *Ulster Herald*, 20 Nov. 1920. Intercepted documents outlined the IRA's intention to shoot army horses and mules, eliminating mobility and conveyance. Authorities would offset the potential losses by seizing animals from local Sinn Féin sympathisers. Sheehan, *Hearts & Mines*, p. 72.
60. Statements of Walter Brown, BMH, WS 1436, pp 11–12; and Seamus Finn, BMH, WS 1060, p.
50. See also, *Belfast Newsletter*, 10 Dec. 1920; *Irish Independent*, 28 Apr. 1921.
61. Ireland's own natural and built landscapes worked against certain numerical and military advantages in many ways. The IRA's counter-mobility campaign developed opposite Britain's material build-up and revised counter-insurgency policy. See Kautt, *Ambushes and Armour*, pp 18, 95, 157.
62. David Fitzpatrick, 'The geography of Irish nationalism 1910–1921', in *Past & Present* 78 (February 1978), pp 130–1.
63. Hart, 'Geography', pp 146, 158–9; Michael Hopkinson, *The Irish War of Independence*, p. 200.
64. 'Flying columns', *An t-Óglach*, 1 June 1920.
65. Returns to the fundamental question of motivation and participation. John Shouldice explained: 'Volunteers who did not have weapons (due to supply available) or who could not use weapons well were tasked with trenching roads, felling trees, blowing up bridges, acting as scouts or carried dispatches.' Statement of John F. Shouldice, BMH, WS 679, p. 24; The bridge on the main Athlone-Ballinasloe Road at Summerhill was demolished using crowbars and pickaxes. Statement of Patrick Lennon, BMH, WS 1336, p. 7.
66. Irish Military Archives, Military Service Pension Collection (MA/MSPC/A/11).
67. Statements of William Walsh, BMH, WS 974, p. 2; and Cornelius Kelleher, BMH, WS 1654, p. 6.
68. Abbott, *Police Casualties*, p. 55; Inspector General's report for January 1920, TNA (CO 904/111); Dublin Castle outrage reports (throughout), TNA (CO 904/148).
69. See destructive activity in Donegal and Mayo for July 1920 as being a 'daily occurrence' in Inspector General's monthly report for July 1920, TNA (CO 904/112).
70. Statements of David Hall, BMH, WS 1539, p. 17; and Michael O'Donnell, BMH, WS 1145, p. 8.
71. Statements of John McGill, BMH, WS 1616, p. 5; and Bartholomew Flynn, BMH, WS 1552, p.
11. Officers later informed the Military Pensions Board that it would be 'impossible' to produce a

2. Mounted photograph, possibly taken from Henry Street, of the rear of the GPO showing extensive structural damage; many of the buildings on Moore Street and Henry Street have been totally demolished. Nelson's Pillar is silhouetted against the skyline. Reproduced by kind permission of UCD Archives, Desmond FitzGerald Photographs P80/PH/1.

3. Mounted photograph of a soldier on duty outside a ruined building, possibly near the Munster and Leinster Bank on Sackville Street; the gables of other badly damaged buildings are visible in the background. Reproduced by kind permission of UCD Archives, Desmond FitzGerald Photographs P80/PH/3.

4. Two mounted photographs (with some differences of detail) of very badly damaged buildings, possibly on Sackville Street; the foreground contains twisted metal including the remains of a tram and a sign advertising Nestle's. Reproduced by kind permission of UCD Archives, Desmond FitzGerald Photographs P80/PH/10.

5. Photograph of a burned-out building, possibly the creamery in Ballymacelligott, County Kerry; the roof has collapsed at one end and the interior has been gutted; a water tank is lying on the grass outside; a sign on the side of the building which is partially fire-damaged reads, 'The Ballymacelligott Cooperative Agricultural...'. Reproduced by kind permission of UCD Archives, Desmond FitzGerald Photographs P80/PH/15.

6. Destruction in Cork after the official reprisal of the city. Reproduced by kind permission of the Imperial War Museum, Major General Peter Strickland Collection, Q107757.

7. Photograph of a group of men viewing the gutted interior of an imposing entrance hall surrounded by debris. The caption reads: 'Labour Commission and Cork LCC, Town Hall, Cork.' Reproduced by kind permission of UCD Archives, Desmond FitzGerald Photographs P80/PH/18.

8. British Army road cleaning operations. Reproduced by kind permission of the Imperial War Museum, Major General Peter Strickland Collection, Q107765.

9. British Army road cleaning operations. Reproduced by kind permission of the Imperial War Museum, Major General Peter Strickland Collection, Q107766.

10. British Army road cleaning operations at Carrignovac, 10 June 1921. Reproduced by kind permission of the Imperial War Museum, Major General Peter Strickland Collection, Q107762.

11. British Army troops at the bridge near Kinsale blown up by the IRA. Reproduced by kind permission of the Imperial War Museum, Major General Peter Strickland Collection, Q071704.

12. British troops standing on the remains of a bridge in Clydagh Valley, Reproduced by kind permission of the Imperial War Museum, Major General Peter Strickland Collection, Q107769.

13. Remains of Dripsey Bridge, County Cork after IRA action, showing an Intelligence car, Reproduced by kind permission of the Imperial War Museum, Major General Peter Strickland Collection, Q10760.

14. British Army officers inspecting damage to a bridge on the Ballinspittle road (inflicted by the IRA), whilst local labourers are employed in repairs. Reproduced by kind permission of the Imperial War Museum, Major General Peter Strickland Collection, Q071706.

15. Photograph by W. D. Hogan of the ruined interior of the Four Courts. Debris and broken pillars lie around. The imposing statue of a judge has been badly damaged. Reproduced by kind permission of UCD Archives, Desmond FitzGerald Photographs P80/PH/32.

16. Photograph by W. D. Hogan of a gentleman standing in the ruins of part of the Four Courts surrounded by debris and broken pillars. He is holding what is possibly the remnant of a document from the explosion in the treasury of the PRO. Reproduced by kind permission of UCD Archives, Desmond FitzGerald Photographs P80/PH/33.

17. Photograph by W. D. Hogan of the gutted interior of a building; the interior consists of a mass of twisted metal; through the breached walls a more imposing building, also damaged, is visible [possibly the mezzanine storage treasury of the Public Record Office although the window apertures are church-like]. Reproduced by kind permission of UCD Archives, Desmond FitzGerald Photographs P80/PH/97.

list of members taking part in active destruction in Tipperary due to their extensive activities. Con Spain could not recall anything important: 'Apart from the cutting of roads and the felling of trees as barricades, I cannot recall anything of any importance having occurred in April 1921.' Statement of Con Spain, BMH, WS 1464, p. 12.

72. These activities generated annoyance as well as genuine impediment. British Army officers of the 5th Division described obstructions in the midlands as more of an annoyance than a threat, a 'safe and popular amusement for the IRA'. William Sheehan, *Hearts & Mines*, pp 74–5.

73. The entire Kilpatrick Company undertook this work each night and some days throughout early 1921. See statements of Michael Riordan, BMH, WS 1638. p. 21; David Hall, BMH, WS 1539, p. 7; and Con Kelleher, BMH, WS 1654, pp 9–11.

74. General Cork to Irish Command, Parkgate, 21 Mar. 1921, TNA (WO 35/88B); *Freeman's Journal*, 7 June 1921.

75. Sheehan, *Hearts & Mines*, pp 74–5.

76. Statement of Michael Gleeson, BMH, WS 1288, p. 10.

77. Irish Military Archive, Military Service Pensions Collection (MSPC/A/19).

78. Statement of Leo Callaghan, BMH, WS 978, p. 20.

79. Statement of Simon Donnelly, BMH, WS 481, p. 26; see also, 'Donegal roads damaged. Trenches dug to entrap military', *Belfast Newsletter*, 29 Nov. 1920.

80. IRA, GHQ Documents D/Engineering. No indication in records as to place or date of capture, various dates, July 1922 onward, Irish Military Archives (Captured Documents, Lot No. 229).

81. However, sophisticated design often required time and material. Amidst the republican IRA's withdrawal west, Rory O'Connor instructed battalions to revisit methods 'on the old basis, i.e., as existed during the War with Britain'. Director/Engineering to Battalion Commandant, 5 Nov. 1922 (MA, Captured Documents, Lot No. 229). See also, Seán O'Faoláin, *Vive Moi*, p. 195.

82. Kautt, *Ambushes and Armour*, p. 130; see also, TNA (PRO 141/93).

83. 'County Surveyor's estimate for war loss – Clare County Council' 27, 31 Mar. 1922, TNA (FIN/1/1661).

84. Unknown to McElligot, Dept. of Finance, 15 Aug. 1924, TNA (FIN/1/1661).

85. Michael Hopkinson, *War of Independence*, conclusion.

86. RIC Inspector General's report for December 1919, to Under Secretary, 13 Jan. 1920, TNA (CO 904/110).

87. Joint statement of James O'Mahony, Denis Crowley and John Fitzgerald, BMH, WS 560, p. 15.

88. Statement of Timothy Tierney, BMH, WS 1227, p. 5.

89. Oglaigh na h-Eireann, 'Weekly intelligence report: Irregular forces', Irish Military Archives (CW-OPS-10-05).

90. Statements of Seán Moylan, BMH, WS 838, p. 169; and Thomas Barry, BMH, WS 430, p. 12.

91. Statements of John O'Riordan, BMH, WS 1117, p. 3; Seán E. Walshe, BMH, WS 1363, p. 5–6; and James McKeon, BMH, WS 436, pp 17–18.

92. Statements of Seán E. Walshe, BMH, WS 1363, p. 5–6; James McKeon, BMH, WS 436, p. 17–18; Edmond Power, BMH, WS 1130, p. 12; John Walsh, BMH, WS 966, p. 22; and David Hall, BMH, WS 1539, p. 17.

93. Statement of Joseph P. Morgan, BMH, WS 1097, p. 4.

94. George Power to Pensions Board, 15 July 1935, Irish Military Archives, Military Service Pensions Collection (MA/MSPC/A/2(1)).

95. Statements of Patrick Ahern, BMH, WS 1003; Annie Barrett, BMH, WS 1133; and Leo Callaghan, BMH, WS 978.

96. *Skibbereen Eagle*, 13 Sept. 1919.

97. Statements of John Fanning, BMH, WS 990, p. 10; and Leo Callaghan, BMH, WS 978, p. 4.

98. Statement of Frank Simons, BMH, WS 770, pp 22–5.

99. *Belfast Newsletter*, 24 Mar. 1921; *Evening Herald*, 24 Mar. 1921; *Irish Examiner*, 24 Mar. 1921; *Connaught Telegraph*, 26 Mar. 1921. See also, Brigade Activity Reports, North Roscommon Brigade (MA/MSPC/A/31(1)). In his reflective history of the period, the Earl of Midleton, uncle to the slain Captain Peek, summarised the situation in 1921: 'The British Government, who had won the war on the Continent, were being outwitted at every turn in Ireland. Not a single raid by the organized troops had been successful for many months; the number of rebels captured *flagrante delicto* was negligible; scores of British officers had been sacrificed.' William St John Fremantle Brodrick

Midleton, *Ireland: Dupe or Heroine* (London: William Heinemann, 1932), p. 155. See also, statement of Patrick Mullooly, BMH, WS 1086, p. 39.
100. Statement of Martin Fallon, BMH, WS 1121, pp 12–15.
101. William Sheehan, *A Hard Local War: The British Army and the Guerrilla War in Cork 1919–1921* (Dublin: The History Press Ireland, 2011; 2017), pp 24–8. Refers to his section on the subject as 'The Origin of Reprisals'.
102. *The Times* (London), 10 Sept. 1919. Peter Hart assessed: 'Soldiers' frustrations with this situation could not be contained indefinitely.' Hart, *The IRA and its enemies*, p. 63.
103. *Irish Independent* 10 Sept. 1919.
104. Sheehan, *A Hard Local War*, pp 24–5.
105. Ibid., p. 40.
106. *The Times* (London), 9 Sept. 1919.
107. Ibid., 10 Sept. 1919; *Kerry Weekly Reporter*, 13 Sept. 1919.
108. *Kerry Weekly Reporter*, 13 Sept. 1919.
109. Ibid.; *Donegal News*, 13 Sept. 1919.
110. Seán Leavy, BMH, WS 954.
111. Statement of Martin Fallow, BMH, WS 1121, p. 14; *Sunday Independent*, 27 Mar. 1921; *Irish Independent*, 4 Apr. 1921.
112. Peter Hart, *IRA and Its Enemies*, pp 79, 100–1.
113. *Irish Examiner*, 20 Jan. 1920.
114. Sheehan, *Hearts & Mines*, p. 63. See also, statement of Frank Simmons, BMH, WS 770, p. 23.
115. For explanation of 'people's war' framework, see Kautt, *Ambushes and Armour*, p. 12.
116. Ferriter, *A Nation and Not a Rabble: The Irish Revolution 1913–1923* (London, 2015), pp 190–1.
117. Royal Irish Constabulary: RIC Boycott, 1919, Irish Military Archives (A/0385); Dáil Éireann debate F:6, 1st Dáil, 10 Apr. 1919; notes from a 2 September 1917 speech by Éamon de Valera. Inspector General's report for September 1917, 12 Oct. 1917, TNA (CO 904/104). For observations of outrages and 'Sinn Féin conspiracy to render government impossible by terrorizing the Police', see Inspector General's report for July 1919, TNA (CO 904/109).
118. Oppenheimer, *The Urban Guerrilla*, pp 74–5.
119. Derek Gladwin, 'Topobiographical inquiry: Lived spaces, place-based experiences, and ecologies', in Justin Dolan Stover and Kelly Sullivan (eds), *Éire-Ireland: An Interdisciplinary Journal of Irish Studies*, Special Issue: Ireland and the Environment 55:3–4 (Fall/Winter 2020), pp 129–49.
120. House of Commons Debate 119, 14 Aug. 1919, cc 1663-6W. Barracks' location, inhabitants and potential for reinforcement dictated the pace, ferocity and geographic intensity of their destruction. Attacks waned in light of more aggressive resistance, reinforcement and adaptation throughout later 1920 and, as Joost Augusteijn has noted, in predominantly loyalist neighbourhoods. Augusteijn, 'Military conflict in the War of Independence', p. 352. See also, statement of Seán McConville, BMH, WS 495, pp 6–8; Joseph McKenna, *Guerrilla Warfare*, p. 131.
121. The Inspector General stated: 'Many of the more isolated police barracks have had to be closed in order to augment the force in the remainder for defensive purposes, and to enable patrols to be strengthened.' RIC Inspector General's report for November 1919, TNA (CO 904/110).
122. Evidence taken from daily newspapers, RIC Inspector General's monthly reports to Dublin Castle. Two posts were opened during the period in Tynagh, Galway, and Annacarthy, Tipperary.
123. For instance, the Inspector General reported: 'The police [in Sligo] [...] have almost ceased to exist, and could do little more than hold their barracks.' Inspector General's report for August 1920, TNA (CO 904/112).
124. *Kilkenny People*, 29 Nov. 1919
125. *The Nationalist* (Tipperary), 23 Aug. 1919; *Freeman's Journal*, 19 Aug. 1919; *Irish Examiner*, 16 Aug. 1919.
126. Inspector General's report for July 1920, TNA (CO 904/112).
127. District Inspector claimed that 'stations reduced from 60 to 20 by August.' Inspector General's report for August 1920, TNA (CO 904/112).
128. Ibid.; *Freeman's Journal*, 13 Nov. 1919.
129. Kautt, *Ambushes and Armour*, p. 79.
130. Augusteijn, 'Military conflict in the War of Independence', p. 351; David M. Leeson, 'The Royal Irish Constabulary, Black and Tans and Auxiliaries', in *Atlas of the Irish Revolution*, pp 373, 377.

131. RIC Inspector General's report for November 1919, TNA (CO 904/110). By December 1919, 'the police [were] largely dependent on military aid in the performance of duties.' RIC Inspector General's report for December 1919, TNA (CO 904/110); *Leitrim Observer*, 10 Apr. 1920; *Sligo Champion*, 10 Apr. 1920. See also, Dominic Price, *The Flame and the Candle*, p .69.
132. *Irish Independent*, 6 Apr. 1920.
133. Ibid.; *Leitrim Observer*, 10 Apr. 1920.
134. *Tales of the RIC*, p. 262–3.
135. Conor McNamara, *War and Revolution in the West of Ireland*, p 122.
136. Almost every location had boarded around four men with the exceptions of Garrylawn and Mooncoin, Kilkenny, which had five, and Dervock, Antrim, where census returns showed four women to reside. PRONI/FIN/18/1/85; *Ulster Herald*, 5 June 1920; *Belfast Newsletter*, 14 May 1920; *Strabane Chronicle*, 15 May 1920; *Leitrim Observer*, 10 Apr. 1920; *Irish Examiner*, 14 May 1920; *Freeman's Journal*, 22 May 1920; Inspector General's monthly report for June 1920, TNA (CO 904/112); statement of Thomas Treacy, BMH, WS 590, p. 58. Ambiguity around Sligo: reports show Ross Hut closed in 1919 but no record of it being burned, while Rosses Point shows no record of closure but does have record of being burned. *Leitrim Observer*, 10 Apr. 1920; *Sligo Champion*, 10 Apr. 1920.
137. Harnett, *Victory and Woe*, p. 34; *Kerry Weekly Reporter*, 3 Apr. 1920; *The Liberator* (Tralee), 30 Mar. 1920.
138. Richard P. Tucker, 'The impact of warfare on the natural world: A historical survey', in Tucker and Russell (eds), *Natural Enemy, Natural Ally*, p. 17; Judith A Bennett, 'Pests and disease in the pacific war: Crossing the line', in ibid., p. 217.
139. Dublin Castle outrage reports, TNA (CO 904/148).
140. Donnelly, 'Big House burnings', p. 169. See also, 'Raid on American oil company's store', statement of Michael Murphy, BMH, WS 1547, p. 27.
141. *Sligo Champion*, 6 Mar. 1920; *Irish Independent*, 11 Mar. 1920.
142. Inspector General's monthly report for June 1920, TNA (CO 904/112).
143. Statement of Seán Farrelly, BMH, WS 1734, p. 9.
144. 'Prohibition of importation of certain chemicals into Ireland', A. Cooper-Key, Major, HM Chief Inspector of Explosives to the heads of various explosives firms, 24 Nov. 1921, TNA (HO 351/75).
145. The *Drogheda Independent* reported 218 barracks attacked, 'the great majority being wholly destroyed either by fire or explosives'. *The Leitrim Observer* reported 153 barracks destroyed. Both published 10 Apr. 1920; *Kerry People* and other papers echoed this.
146. *Freeman's Journal*, 5 Apr. 1920; *Drogheda Independent*, 10 Apr. 1920. Dublin Castle outrage reports, TNA (CO 904/148). See also, 'Crime in Ireland', H. C. Deb. (26 Apr. 1920), vol 128, cc 957–95.
147. Harnett, *Victory and Woe*, p. 34. Irish Bishops most certainly disapproved of both activities. Rev. Dr Browne, 'preaching at Macroom, referred to the widespread destruction of barracks and of property general in Ireland, saying he did not see how this would bring them any nearer emancipation.' *Irish Independent*, 10 June 1920. The Bishop of Ross, Rev. Dr Kelly, also condemned 'a number of young hotheads who want war'. *Nenagh News*, 31 July 1920; 'What the "Irish Times" says on the matter', *Leitrim Observer*, 10 Apr. 1920. Newspaper reports remarked on the coordination of burnings, but detailed nationwide coordination appears unlikely. Some Volunteer units only discovered the extent of the Easter arson campaign through the press. See also, statement of Martin Fallon, BMH, WS 1121, p. 4.
148. This far exceeds other accounts of the period. As Abbott writes: 'In March and April, the attacks on RIC barracks increased dramatically, with approximately 150 being burned on the night of 5/6 April 1920 alone. The campaign accelerated, with official figures recording that between 1 January 1919 and 30 June 1920 the number of barracks attacked was as follows: Vacated Barracks – destroyed: 351. damaged: 105. Occupied Barracks – destroyed: 15. damaged: 25.' Abbott, *Police Casualties in Ireland*, pp 55–6, citing Street, *Administration in Ireland*. See also, *Freeman's Journal*, 5 Apr. 1920; *Drogheda Independent*, 10 Apr. 1920; Dublin Castle outrage reports, TNA (CO 904/148).
149. 'Crown property, or the property of Crown employees', Entries for Boro' of Cork, 3 Apr. 1920, TNA (CO 905/14).
150. 'Official records destroyed in fifty offices', *Drogheda Independent*, 10 Apr. 1920. 'In the House of Commons, Mr Henry, answering Col. Ashley, said that three buildings in Ireland, occupied wholly or part for the purpose of income tax administration, have been destroyed. Of these, two, valued

provisionally at £25,000, were Government buildings, and one, valued provisionally at £4,000, was privately owned.' *The Liberator* (Tralee), 15 May 1920.

151. *Meath Chronicle*, 22 May 1920.

152. *Irish Examiner*, 7 Apr. 1920; *Sligo Champion*, 10 Apr. 1920; *Ulster Herald*, 15 May 1920.

153. *Kerry Weekly Reporter*, 29 May 1920.

154. *Westmeath Independent*, 15 May 1920.

155. These are the numbers Col O'Callaghan Westropp, JP, presented to the Clare Farmers Association in mid-May, and very nearly match my own research (329 total barrack burnings and Income Tax Office raids), *Ulster Herald*, 22 May 1920; *Irish Independent*, 15 May 1920; 'Nearly 400 barracks burned. Reported yesterday: 6; Total: 393', *Irish Independent*, 28 May 1920. The *Irish Independent* reported that over 400 barracks were destroyed between Easter and mid-June 1920. *Irish Independent*, 15 June 1920.

156. Dominic Price, *The Flame and the Candle*, pp 69–71.

157. *Belfast Newsletter*, 16 Apr. 1921. Later, Free State and anti-treaty republican forces occupied remaining barracks evacuated following the RIC's disbandment – an improvised changing of the guard as representative of local initiative as it was of political division. For change of barracks in County Clare, see *Irish Examiner*, 11 Apr. 1922. Further, see Irish Military Archives (CW/OPS/01/01/28).

158. *Freeman's Journal*, 30 Apr. 1921.

159. Property transferred from the British to the Free State Government, n.d., NAI (OPW/1/18/2/7). See also, *Connacht Tribute*, 11 Dec. 1920.

160. Military service pensions collection, Irish Military Archives (MA/MSPC/A/11; MSPC/A/14); statement of John O'Driscoll, BMH, WS 1250, p. 8.

161. Statement of Denis Prendiville, BMH, WS 1106, p. 9.

162. Operations carried out by members of 1st Btn, 3rd Tipp Brigade: Burning of courthouse, Cashel in May 1920, Irish Military Archives (MSPC/A/11; MSPC/A/14).

163. 'Malicious burning of hay – Woodford', J. Wheally to Inspector General Royal Irish Constabulary, 30 Oct. 1920, TNA (WO/35/88B).

164. O'Malley, *On Another Man's Wound*, p. 241. Gerald Noonan, *The IRA in Britain, 1919–1923: 'In the Heart of Enemy Lines'* (Liverpool: Liverpool University Press, 2014), pp 138–40.

165. Statement of Bernard Meehan, BMH, WS 1513, pp 5–6.

166. John A. Pinkman, (ed. Francis E. Maguire), *In the Legion of the Vanguard* (Dublin: Mercier Press, 1998), p. 35.

167. Pinkman, *Legion*, pp 37–8; Noonan, *The IRA in Britain*, p. 142; statement of Bernard Meehan, BMH, WS 1513, p. 6; Bootle County Borough, return showing loss or damage occasioned during the period 1 Jan. 1919–14 Jan. 1922 and attributable to persons actuated by Irish political motives, TNA (FIN/1/1589).

168. Noonan, *The IRA in Britain* p. 136; statement of Bernard Meehan, BMH, WS 1513, pp 6–12; excerpts from *Evening Express* (Liverpool), 10 Mar. 1921; TNA (FIN/1/1589).

169. Extracts from an 'Agreement between the British Government and the Irish Free State Government' in 1925 fixed indemnity at £1,000,000. Free State Minister for Defence, Richard Mulcahy, identified which operations the IRA were responsible for, reducing claims by half. See TNA (FIN/1/1589).

170. Noonan, *The IRA in Britain*, pp 166–68.

171. Inspector General's report for June 1920, TNA (CO 904/112). By June, Volunteers had destroyed 366 barracks and damaged an additional 130. Abbott, *Police Casualties*, pp 55–8.

172. *The Liberator* (Tralee), 13 Mar. 1920; statements of Timothy Houlihan, BMH, WS 969, p. 3; William McCabe, BMH, WS 1212, p. 5; Patrick Joseph McElligott, BMH, WS 1013, p. 6. The attack was directed at Ballybunion RIC barracks but failed and was abandoned after two hours.

173. *Belfast Newsletter*, 9 Feb. 1921.

174. Statement of Thomas Brennan, BMH, WS 1104, p. 18.

175. Statement of John McCormack, BMH, WS 1371, p. 3.

176. Statement of Edward Fullerton, BMH, WS 890, p. 5.

177. Excerpt comes from 'Tactical measures' section on how to resist conscription but applies thereafter. Street, *Administration of Ireland*, p. 60.

178. *Ulster Herald*, 10 Apr. 1920; *Leitrim Observer*, 10 Apr. 1920.

179. See various outrage reports, particularly County Kilkenny, 30/31 May 1920; King's County (Offaly), 2 June 1920; County Down, 2 June 1920, Dublin Castle outrage reports, TNA (CO 904/148); statement of Laurence Redmond, BMH, WS 1010, p. 5. For record of this practice during the Easter Rising see Street, *Administration in Ireland*, pp 28–32, passim.
180. Gordon Pattison, 'The British Army's effectiveness in the Irish campaign 1919–1921 and the lessons for modern counterinsurgency operations, with special reference to C31 aspects', in *Cornwallis XIV: Analysis of Societal Conflict and Counter-Insurgency Workshop* (Vienna, 2009), p. 99.
181. Crown property, or the property of Crown employees, TNA (CO 905/14).
182. Seán Ó Faoláin, *Vive Moi*, p. 199; Soldiers patrolling the Kilbrittain district surprised an IRA scouting party by wrapping their boots in sandbags to muffle their approach. Report on operations 16/17 February 1921, A. C. Halahan, Essex Reg., 18 Feb. 1921, TNA (WO 35/88B).
183. *Freeman's Journal*, 16 Feb. 1920.
184. Statement of Frank Donnelly, BMH, WS 941, p. 5; *Freeman's Journal*, 26 Apr. 1920; *Irish Examiner*, 26 May 1920.
185. *Nenagh Guardian*, 24 Jan. 1920; statements of James Leahy, BMH, WS 1454, p. 23; and Jerry Ryan, BMH, WS 1487, pp 6–8. Constables later returned the deafening courtesy by concealing explosives in the barrack prior to its evacuation that ignited when Volunteers burned it in late June 1921. *Irish Examiner*, 28 June 1921; statement of Thomas F. Meagher, BMH, WS 1541, p. 8.
186. Leslie Morris, 'The sound of memory', in *The German Quarterly* 74:4 (Fall 2001), p. 368.
187. *Nenagh Guardian*, 26 Mar. 1921.
188. 'Territoriality' refers to the 'social construction of spaces by political processes that act as platforms for the expression of power'. Colin Flint, 'Introduction', in Colin Flint (ed.), *The Geography of War and Peace: From Death Camps to Diplomats* (New York: Oxford University Press, 2005), pp 5–6.
189. Colin Flint, *The Geography of War and Peace*, p. 6; see also, Katz, 'Banal terrorism: Spatial fetishism and everyday insecurity', in Derek Gregory and Allan Pred (eds), *Violent Geographies: Fear, Terror, and Political Violence* (New York: Routledge, 2007), p. 350.
190. Jeremy Black, 'Geographies of war: The recent historical background', in Colin Flint (ed.), *The Geography of War and Peace: From Death Camps to Diplomats* (New York: Oxford University Press, 2005, p. 24.
191. Ibid., p. 24.
192. David Fitzpatrick, 'The geography of Irish nationalism 1910–1921', in *Past & Present* 78 (February 1978), pp 114–16; Peter Hart, 'The geography of revolution in Ireland 1917–1923', p. 143–5.
193. Steve Pile, 'Introduction: Opposition, political identities, and spaces of resistance', in *Geographies of Resistance* (New York: Routledge, 1997), p. 2.
194. Other notable observations from these studies identify preceding disturbance or land hunger in areas that later exhibited revolutionary violence (Fitzpatrick, 'The geography of Irish nationalism 1910–1921', pp 118–19; Townshend, 'The Irish Republican Army and the development of guerrilla warfare, 1916–1921', in *The English Historical Review* 94:371 (1979), pp 332–3); that passive resistance (belonging to nationalist organisations and voting patterns) overlapped the active revolution (violence) (Fitzpatrick, 'The geography of Irish nationalism', p. 122), the distinct rurality of activity (ibid., p. 130), later balanced by Hart and Coleman's noting of correlative urban activity (Hart, *The IRA at War*, pp 114–16; Marie Coleman, *The Irish Revolution, 1916–1923*, pp 149–51) and the deterrence in concentration of Protestant or loyal populations (Garvin, *The Evolution of Irish Nationalist Politics*, pp 122–23); and the availability of arms as deterring activity (Hart, 'The geography of revolution in Ireland 1917–1923', pp 154–7).
195. Fitzpatrick, 'The geography of Irish nationalism 1910–1921', p. 116.
196. Hart, 'The geography of revolution in Ireland 1917–1923', p. 154.
197. Joost Augusteijn, 'Accounting for the emergence of violent activism among Irish revolutionaries, 1919–21', in *Irish Historical Studies* 35:139 (May 2007), p. 333.
198. Fitzpatrick, 'The geography of Irish nationalism 1910–1921', p. 114; Hart: 'The geography of revolution in Ireland 1917–1923', p. 144.
199. Hart, *The IRA and its Enemies*, pp 321–2.
200. Garvin, *The Evolution of Irish Nationalist Politics*, p. 125. As Hart concluded, 'terrain may well have made a difference in some areas under specific local circumstances, but it was not an important factor nation-wide.' Hart, 'The geography of revolution in Ireland 1917–1923', p. 159.

201. Harold Winters, Gerald G. Galloway, Jr, William Reynolds and David W. Rhyne, *Battling the Elements: Weather and Terrain in the Conduct of War* (Baltimore: The Johns Hopkins University Press, 1998), p. 75.

202. The *Green Howards' Gazette*, a regimental publication, published one soldiers view: 'everything in Ireland is sad looking, the weather remains truly Irish and there is always a look of depression on the face of an Irishman.' *Green Howards' Gazette*, Nov. 1920, p. 142; Benjamin Laurence Butler, 'The British Army in Ireland 1916–1921: A social and cultural history', Doctoral thesis, University of Hull (February 2007), p. 41.

203. Simon Noone, Conor Murphy, John Coll, Tom Matthews, Donal Mullan, Robert Wilby and Seamus Walsh, 'Homogenization and analysis of an expanded long-term monthly rainfall network for the Island of Ireland (1850–2010)', in *International Journal of Climatology* 36:8 (2015), pp 2837, 2851.

204. 'Rainfall for January, 1920', C. Firth, Cavehill Road, Belfast-Observer, *Belfast Newsletter*, 3 Feb. 1920; 'Weather in Cork,' *Irish Examiner*, 3 Jan. 1920.

205. 'Bad Weather and Tillage Outlook,' *Irish Examiner*, 8 May 1920.

206. *Meteorological Magazine* 55:653 (June 1920), p. 83.

207. *Drogheda Independent*, 14 Aug. 1920.

208. 'Rainfall for October, 1920', C. Firth, Cavehill Road, Belfast-Observer, *Belfast Newsletter*, 4 Nov. 1920.

209. Volunteers recalled a bitterly cold and wet winter in 1920/21. Statements of James Duggan, BMH, WS 875, p. 2; Patrick O'Reilly, BMH, WS 1650, p. 21; and Peadar de Barra, BMH, WS 853, p. 14.

210. *Meteorological Magazine* 55:652 (May 1920), p. 59.

211. *British Meteorological and Magnetic Year Book*, 1917 (–22), issued as a supplement to the weekly weather report (vol. xxxiv – new series) (Meteorological Office: London, 14 June 1918).

212. O'Malley, *On Another Man's Wound*, pp 104, 109.

213. Sworn statement made before the Advisory Committee, by Bridgit O'Mullane, 30 June 1937, Irish Military Archives, Military Service Pensions Collection (MSP34REF1178, SPC, File 1178, p. 2); Statement of Brighid O'Mullane, BMH, WS 450, p. 26. Furthermore, Seán Moylan engaged 'long distance cycling on bad roads in all weathers'. Statement of Seán Moylan, BMH, WS 838, p. 18.

214. Statement of Anastasia Nevin, 31 Nov. 1941, Irish Military Archives, Military Service Pensions Collection (DP11207), p. 17.

215. Pension of Gratuity, Miss Nora Wallace, signed by T. J. Crowley, 15 May 1934, Irish Military Archives, Military Service Pensions Collection (34D2124).

216. Patrick Collins to Minister for Defence, 31 May 1939; Francis O'Keeffe to unknown, 25 May 1939; statement of Thomas J. Kennelly. 6 Mar. 1942, Irish Military Archives, Military Service Pensions Collection (DP10122). David Joseph Conroy also fell ill from exposure. In his witness statement to the BMH in 1953 he, too, recalled being out in Clare on 'that very stormy night', after which his health was 'indifferent for some months'. Statement of David Joseph Conroy, BMH, WS 809, p. 9.

217. Edmond Stack to unknown, 22 Apr. 1939, Irish Military Archives, Military Service Pensions Collection (DP10122).

CHAPTER FOUR

'THE CURSE OF ANANIAS GREENWOOD': CROWN FORCE REPRISALS & DISPLACEMENT[1]

INTRODUCTION

In May 1920, one month after his appointment as Chief Secretary for Ireland, Sir Hamar Greenwood hosted a deputation from the Association of Municipal Authorities in Ireland at the Viceregal Lodge in the Phoenix Park, Dublin. They sat to discuss the Irish housing question; specifically, how the lack of money, labour and materials made it difficult to meet housing demands throughout the country. The Chief Secretary agreed that new house construction was a necessity, and promised to speak to the Chancellor of the Exchequer, Austen Chamberlain, to secure 'further assistance as would give a spurt to the building throughout the entire country'.[2] Proposals continued throughout the summer in the form of government-backed loans and locally directed surveying and construction.[3] The need for new housing development and planning reform in Ireland, particularly in rural areas and within cities' clustered tenement blocks, was not a new or novel concern. It had featured prominently in public discourse and parliamentary debate since the Famine; at times, dilapidated urban dwellings were framed as a catalyst to lawlessness and rebellion.[4] Proposals for post-war reconstruction also prioritised housing as a means to honour the service of Irish Great War veterans, alleviate widespread unemployment and assuage labour activism to which, by 1920, a steady stream of demobilised men had contributed.[5] Ironically, the founding of Ireland's revolutionary parliament, Dáil Éireann, and Sinn Féin's growing influence over local government prevented the Housing (Ireland) Act 1919 – a mechanism designed to address social housing concerns and by extension curb political extremism – from functioning.[6] But the Association's appeal to the Chief Secretary to tackle Irish housing was satirical in its own right. By May 1920, newspapers and relief agencies reported that Crown forces had damaged approximately 90 Irish towns in acts of retaliatory justice, as reprisals for IRA outrages. Just as Home Rule literature politicised inadequate housing prior to the Irish Revolution, the destruction of homes and businesses became politicised and propagandised during that conflict. Though separated by time and circumstances, both Home Rulers and Irish republicans yearned for the economic production and social stability self-government would presumably stimulate. During the War of Independence, however, reprisals on homes and businesses of Irish people destroyed existing infrastructure and demonstrated the British Government's apathy towards the actions of the Crown forces in the face of IRA terror.

From 1919, the British Army and the RIC and its Auxiliary supplement targeted a variety of private and commercial spaces in their pursuit and harassment of Irish republicans. Violence against Crown forces intensified throughout 1920 in the form of ambushes and assassinations. These forces countered with indiscriminate and arbitrary retaliation against the civilian population and their property in an effort to erode republican support within affected communities. These highly destructive and disruptive acts internationalised Ireland's independence movement in unprecedented ways by calling into question Lloyd George's Irish policy and generating criticism of Britain's moral position in the post-war world. But these experiences of violence resonated in more impactful ways across Ireland, experiences that the eventual cessation of hostilities in July 1921 failed to quell. In addition to extensive property loss, reprisals claimed 'uncounted victims': individuals and families who lost their livelihoods, prospects and security with the destruction of their homes and businesses.[7] Countless others suffered from anxiety and traumatic stress as a result of frequent raids and the violation of private space. The fact that encounters went beyond the considerations of post-revolution compensation tribunals only exacerbated those effects.

This chapter considers the impact of Crown force reprisals in several ways. In a broad sense, it focuses on the physical destruction of landscapes as both spontaneous retributive acts and as premeditated instruments of British policy in Ireland. In a more focused turn, it frames reprisals as processes of physical and emotional displacement aligned to a policy of environmental terror. These incidents had both immediate and enduring economic consequences, as illustrated by a survey of damage to commercial districts and home-run shops, and attacks on Ireland's budding co-operative creameries.

'COORDINATED DESTRUCTION'

Throughout 1919 and the first half of 1920, the British Cabinet viewed IRA raids, ambushes and assassinations as criminal outrages rather than acts of war, and pursued justice against what it perceived to be a small but dedicated 'murder gang' within the civilian legal framework.[8] Though popularly applied to any punitive attack on civic or personal property, the term 'reprisal' evolved throughout Sir Hamar Greenwood's tenure as Chief Secretary. Episodes of impassioned Crown force retaliation against civilians, which occurred as early as September 1919, were 'unofficial', occurring independently at the local level rather than as part of a governing police policy. RIC Inspector General Joseph Byrne voiced his concern about effective command structure and discipline at this time, noting that it would be difficult for police officers to regulate the ex-soldiers being recruited to bolster their ranks. Byrne's fears proved to be well founded, as an ineffectual and unenforceable discipline structure often failed to de-escalate or redirect impulses for rogue justice throughout 1920.[9]

While unofficial reprisals drew criticism from certain government circles, they were tolerated on the grounds of policemen's situational stress, and even encouraged as the only means through which the IRA could be defeated.[10] The term 'unofficial' also conveyed a sense of deferred rightfulness.[11] This was demonstrated in how men were psychologically affected by war conditions in Ireland, and how the British Government saw reprisals as a likely outcome in those conditions. A deep sense of fear lurked behind vicious bravado; 'the men [troops and police] were in a savage condition of nervousness,' Dorothy Macardle explained, 'expecting an ambush at every corner.'[12] F. S. L. Lyons and others, notably Richard Bennett, also observed that combat conditions in Ireland were wholly unique from veterans' experiences of the Great War, and affected 'a greater strain than service in France'.[13] Likewise, Diarmaid Ferriter suggests that 'the IRA's ability to choose and vary ambush sites left them [Irish police] physically and psychologically vulnerable.'[14] Irregular warfare in unfamiliar territory elevated already heightened tensions as Crown forces attempted to uncover and suppress revolutionary activity. Lieutenant-General Hugh Jeudwine, Commander of the Fifth Division in Ireland, understood the pathology of revenge amongst men 'driven half mad by seeing their comrades shot down in cold blood'.[15] Similarly, Winston Churchill, Secretary of State for War, could not find blame in the actions of men who had been 'goaded' into retaliation.[16] General Macready, who disapproved of reprisals as unfavourable substitutes for martial law, acknowledged the desire to avenge the death of a comrade as being 'in the proper nature of things'. He also recognised that reprisals functioned as a means of avoiding even greater indiscipline in the ranks: 'If we punish the men for revenging the murder of their officers we shall have mutiny,' he informed Sir Henry Wilson in September 1920, 'and quite right too.'[17] The policemen's newspaper, *The Weekly Summary*, carried the view that while reprisals were 'wrong' and bad for morale and discipline, they were 'the result of the brutal, cowardly murder of police officers by assassins, who take shelter behind the screen of terrorism and intimidation which they have created'.[18] Acts of reprisal were frequently contextualised and excused on these grounds.

Impulses toward reprisals were born out of frustration in pursuing and prosecuting rebels, and in response to the IRA's escalation of revolutionary violence throughout 1920. As Crown courts failed to function, police were withdrawn from isolated areas and attacks on RIC barracks continued apace throughout the first half of 1920; the Coalition Government resurrected Gladstonian precedent of political conciliation and coercion to navigate the Irish situation.[19] However, the release of hunger strikers from Dublin's Mountjoy Prison in April and the Government of Ireland Act 1920 (to establish separate Home Rule parliaments) were ultimately ineffective gestures. Along harder lines, Greenwood introduced the Restoration of Order in Ireland Act 1920 (ROIA) in early August. The Act effectively extended the Defence of the Realm Act's wartime provisions, authorised internment and empowered courts-martial trials in active republican areas.[20] It also provided for military courts of inquiry to replace coroner's inquests into IRA killings. This was because the government believed the moderate rulings by coroner's inquests on capital offenses often reflected sympathy with the republican movement or intimidation by it. According to Charles Townshend and Peter Hart, the ROIA marked Greenwood's 'loss of patience with conciliation' and the birth of a 'consistent counter-insurgency regime', respectively.[21]

The ROIA was initially effective against the IRA, whose sabotage and assassination campaign had gained momentum throughout the summer of 1920. The War Office produced search reports that detailed the date, place and objectives of raids, and any instances of damage to private property, which occupants were required to corroborate. Conversely, republican publicity produced weekly counts of 'raids', 'sabotage' and 'militarism' that recounted violations of personal space, destruction of property and general aggression towards the Irish people, respectively.

It is difficult to produce an accurate tally of unofficial reprisals. Crown force destruction of property materialised in many forms, including buildings being 'shot up', arson, looting and the ruin of agricultural stock. A town being 'sacked' or 'partially' sacked referred to 'generalised attacks [...] and implied a measure of looting'.[22] Inaccuracies and omissions, as well as exaggerations and misreporting, complicate accurate calculations. What is obtainable, however, is a view towards steadily expanding reprisal activity, which accelerated after July 1920. Contemporary sources nevertheless attempted to present the number of reprisals and their locations. For instance, the *Irish Bulletin*, an echo chamber for republican propaganda, listed 'Ninety Irish towns ravaged in twelve months'.[23] The following year, the American Commission on Conditions in Ireland published its findings in which it cited 133 towns and villages burned, sacked or 'shot-up' over five months, May–October 1920. In 1921, the Dáil Éireann Publicity Department produced a list of reprisals that included 346 incidents between September 1919 and February 1921, which included 79 'official reprisals' that occurred in counties under martial law during the first two months of 1921.[24]

David Leeson has analysed reprisals within the Register of Crime for the province of Connacht, which detailed crime against persons and property in the counties of Galway, Leitrim, Mayo, Roscommon and Sligo between July and December 1920. While his findings for Connacht confirm an overall escalation in the destruction of property over these six months, counties measuring the greatest destruction (Sligo, Galway (West Riding) and Roscommon) registered fewer instances of attacks on property in December than in preceding months. Destruction in Mayo and Galway (East Riding) – which registered the fewest attacks on property overall – also declined after October.[25] By Leeson's own admission, 'the Register of Crime is neither complete nor completely candid.'[26] What the Register makes clear, however, is that attacks on property overshadowed attacks on persons, 190 accounts to 36, illustrating a tendency towards attacks on the built environment over interpersonal violence.

The back-and-forth or reciprocal dynamics of collective violence help to frame a theoretical understanding for reprisals.[27] Charles Tilly identified several factors that contribute to 'coordinated destruction', under which reprisals may be classified. These include a failed political consensus, a concentration of violent actors in a given area, and prevailing 'conspiratorial terror' – clandestine violence against persons, objects and sites of state control.[28] Acts of large-scale destructive retribution shaped the political landscape as well. Their immediate political impact highlighted 'the vulnerability of apparently insuperable powers', reactionary destruction of a frustrated body of men. Reprisals, and both the immediate and compound damage they produced, sought to restore parity between Crown forces and the IRA, or more accurately, the Irish people. In another sense, reprisals resulted from the government's inability to suppress Sinn Féin and the IRA as well as maintain the governing and policing functions they had assumed throughout 1920. Although overlap existed between the threat of IRA 'conspiratorial terror' and 'government-backed terror', asymmetry between personnel and destructive capacity permitted Crown forces more opportunities for meaningful destruction.[29]

Several factors contributed to the pace and geography of Crown force reprisals, which included increased IRA activity in certain localities and its shift towards mobile fighting units, or 'flying columns'.[30] Reprisals that occurred prior to the ROIR were fewer than those executed after July 1920; 'official' reprisals marked out homes and businesses for destruction after martial law came into effect in December 1920 and was extended in January 1921. This trend suggests, in essence, that legal pretext suspended certain practical barriers to both reactionary retribution and premeditated anarchy, but nevertheless failed to satisfy sanguine desires for revenge. An exhaustive tally of property destroyed by Crown forces under the auspices of restoring government, suppressing political terror and deterring republican activity is beyond the scope of this chapter. The variety of, motivations for, and resulting suffering from reprisals does not require an inventory in order to understand their impact, however. While the details of certain previously neglected environmental inquiries (such as the destruction's strain on sanitation and building professions, or the acquisition or repurposing and transportation of construction material) may be factually interesting, such a detailed survey busies an already complex topic. Instead, frequency, scale and narratives of destruction better represent the experience of reprisals because they illustrate the saturation of revolutionary activity and its impacts in a given region. Republican ambushes and assassinations 'aroused passions', triggered 'anger' and provoked a sense and feeling of entitlement to revenge amongst Crown forces, which included Irish police (old RIC), the Auxiliary Division RIC (from August 1920), soldiers and the notorious Black and Tans.[31]

Observers labelled the Black and Tans – men that augmented the RIC from March 1920 – as low-life drunkards whose violent excesses personified the Great War's brutalising effects. Where dramatist Shaw Desmond described Irish constables as merely 'Ireland's black janizaries', Black and Tans were 'Gentlemen of Fortune [and] exceedingly brave and reckless fighting material [...] with a contempt for human life, their own as well as others [...].' They were an 'Irish bogeyman for many generations of Irish children'.[32] However, David Leeson advances that the inability to trace the service records of these men, or to examine their lives prior to the First World War, complicates our ability to attribute their conduct in Ireland to wartime trauma and post-traumatic stress.[33] Witness statements, propaganda and media that reported their behaviour nonetheless crafted and reinforced the perception that their ungovernable behaviour resulted from 'shell shock'. Contemporary Britain was broadly aware of this behaviour after September 1920, as relief society and inquiry tours published their reports in the English press. The *Manchester Guardian News Bulletin* produced the following report in early September:

> There is one aspect of Irish crime [...] that is not fully realised in this country because it is utterly alien to our ordinary conception of law and government, that is the systematic destruction committed by the soldiers and constabulary. Every allowance may well be made for the provocation received. [...] Yet day after day this goes on in Ireland. Town after town is 'shot up', shops are looted, liquor stores are rifled, houses burnt, the inhabitants of the whole town or village driven by indiscriminate fusillade into the cellars for safety.[34]

Shocking headlines and graphic depictions of death and destruction failed to gain widespread traction in Britain. The journalist Philip Gibbs attributed this apathy to war-weariness on the part of the British public, whereas Susan Kingsley Kent saw news of reprisals as reigniting national trauma surrounding the Amritsar massacre in India, which the general public sought to avoid.[35]

But large-scale destruction eventually roused anti-reprisal sentiment, if only to argue for the maintenance of Britain moral standing in the post-war world. News of reprisals began to generate protest in political and literary circles. The Anti-Reprisals Association, for instance, was formed in November 1920 as a group averse to 'frightfulness as policy'. It condemned 'acts of barbarism' and sought to preserve Britain's honour amongst its allies in the post-war world.[36] Similar sentiments emerged in the international community as 'ungentlemanly behaviour over a few short months' on the part of Crown forces quickly created a powerful lore in its own right.[37]

How did Crown force reprisals impact Irish environments and disrupt commercial life? How did their processes dislocate individuals from a sense of place and security within their own homes and communities? These questions push an analysis of reprisals beyond their immediate political narrative to consider their varied immediate and compounded consequences.[38]

'Unofficial', 'haphazard' reprisals proceeded from September 1919; the Shropshire Regiment's assault on Fermoy, Cork, where 'indiscriminate wreckage' claimed 'more than fifty shop fronts' at an estimated cost of nearly £6,500, marked their inauguration.[39] Two additional incidents occurred in Cork in 1919. Members of the Essex Regiment 'partially sacked' Kinsale on 22 October, while the Shropshire regiment, which had been relocated from Fermoy, rioted in King Street and St Luke's district in Cork City on 10 November, breaking doors and plate-glass shop windows.[40] The military were confined to barracks for Armistice Day and later transferred to the Curragh.

Irish citizens were intimately affected by reprisals throughout 1920. For instance, on the evening of 20 January, the Urban District Council Chairman, Denis Morgan, sheltered alongside his pregnant wife and their son in their home in Thurles, Tipperary, which was 'shot up' (to use a typical, contemporary description) after the murder of Constable Luke Finnegan. Morgan recounted the evening's horrors to the American Commission on Conditions in Ireland.

> I placed my wife and the little boy flat on the floor. [...] My wife, in her condition, being within two weeks of her confinement, was in a terror-stricken state. [...] We could not stir from the position we were in because we did not know at what moment it would break out again. So that we had to lie on the stone floor all night.[41]

The next day, Morgan surveyed the damage to his home. 'Inside the rooms the ceilings were all torn and the woodwork was all shattered. There was debris lying on the floor and all around.'[42] Members of the English Labour Commission encountered scenes of destruction, 'worse than Flanders', when they visited Thurles as part of their tour of Ireland to ascertain the nature and severity of British military suppression.[43] Reprisal also affected businesses in the predominantly agricultural town of Thurles. Plate-glass and smaller windows in Friar Street were smashed and 'most of the houses in Main Street were wrecked'; this included a hardware shop, drapery house, hotel, public house and the offices of the *Star* newspaper, contributing to an estimated £3,000 in damage.[44]

General environmental damaged increased throughout the spring of 1920 as the frequency of reprisals gained momentum opposite the IRA arson campaign. Reprisal clusters were also present. Violence revisited Thurles on two separate occasions in March, and the house of Ellen McCarthy, whose son Michael was a member of the local Urban Council, Sinn Féin and the Irish Volunteers, was bombed and burned in May.[45] Home wrecking and violence occurred at nearby Bouladuff twice between March and April, while Kilcommon and Reiska, also outside Thurles, were similarly terrorised.[46] Limerick experienced significant commercial damage in late May that included widespread glass-breaking and the destruction of M'Birney & Co. drapers and John Daly's bakery.[47]

The scale of destruction increased throughout the summer of 1920. Soldiers attacked Fermoy once more in late June, operating from Kilworth camp nearby. Coordinated destruction transformed the town into one that witnesses said resembled 'some place on the Western Front in the last war after a period of bombardment', retaliation for the IRA's kidnapping of General Lucas.[48] Soldiers smashed dozens of plate-glass windows and looted and tossed goods into the road. Compensation claims from the incident totalled £20,000, but the reprisal had much more damning effects.[49] Many of the premises wrecked on this occasion had also suffered losses during the previous year's reprisals and had yet to receive compensation, the *Cork Examiner* reported.[50] Furthermore, homes in Artillery Quay and Patrick Street were destroyed, displacing men, women and children who had no connection to the soldiers' motivation, during the kidnapping of General Cuthbert Lucas by the IRA on 26 June 1920.[51] The Bishop of Cloyne, Cork native Dr Robert Browne, visited Fermoy in the aftermath to give comfort and sympathy to residents who had lost their homes and property.[52]

Reprisal on Tuam, Galway, 'got out of hand' in July following the murder of Constables Burke and Carey. An estimated £100,000 in damage occurred in which the town hall and several businesses were burned.[53] Crown forces ignited the Canney Brothers Drapery with the family inside, while 'practically all business premises in Shop Street' suffered some form of damage. Touring the town the following day, Constable John Joseph Caddan, a 19-year-old recruit from Limerick, observed three large buildings burned to their foundation walls.[54] Indeed, the reprisal carried out on Tuam drew harsher criticism than the ambush at nearby Gallagh that had prompted it.[55] Reflecting on the cycles of violence gripping Ireland, the Archbishop of Tuam, Dr Thomas Gilmartin, wrote of Ireland as 'the theatre of misgovernment, injustice, violence, and terrorism, one wrong leading to another, and all making up a lurid chapter of crime, counter-crime, and retaliation.'[56]

This cycle of violence and destruction continued throughout August 1920 as soldiers descended on Doon in east Limerick after an IRA ambush near the border at Cashel. A half-dozen homes were damaged and several shops were raided.[57] Attacks on police prompted further arson and sabotage in Limerick City, the village of Hospital, Limerick, and Tralee, Kerry.[58] The mayor of Limerick, Michael O'Callaghan, wrote to General Macready 'with the cries of women and children whose houses have been wrecked, ringing in my ears, with the smouldering ruins of once prosperous business houses before my eyes' to convey that one could not 'plead ignorance' as to what was taking place under his supreme command.[59] In a more cynical tone, the chairman of Oranmore Urban Council questioned the purpose of condemning the damage wrought on his town on 21 August. Dr Walsh 'did not see any use in it. That was what they used to do long ago, and this was a useless resolution.'[60] The nature of damage in Oranmore was particularly petty. Mrs Keane lost approximately £5,000 worth of property, which included several hens 'whose necks had been wrung off' and strewn about her back garden. Arson, looting and shooting into residences, so typical of reprisals at this time, compelled residents to flee to the mountains and surrounding fields.[61] In late August, an IRA attack on the Cameron Highlanders at Cobh prompted glass-breaking and looting in Queenstown that claimed about £10,000 in property damage, including up to 100 plate-glass windows.[62]

Unofficial reprisals throughout the summer of 1920 created political frustration on all levels of government. It became increasingly clear that the administration and security of Ireland was in a state of overall chaos.[63] John Borgonovo and Gabriel Doherty point to a letter from Brigadier-General Cyril Prescott-Decie, divisional police commissioner for north Munster, to John Taylor, assistant Under Secretary in Dublin Castle, dated 1 June 1920, as encouraging unauthorised reprisals and assassination of republican leaders at this time.[64] In a similar vein, a 'pep-talk' from Lieutenant-Colonel Gerald Smyth to constables at Listowel, Kerry, apparently encouraged murder with impunity. The fallout from these statements included public criticism and police resignations, and ultimately motivated IRA members to murder Smyth the following month.[65] David Fitzpatrick contextualised Decie's letter, noting that it did not advocate any *new* policy of assassination by Crown forces. He also pointed out that Smyth's address emphasised the fact that constables could in fact pre-empt an ambush by shooting first.[66]

Crown force destruction increased after August 1920 once the Restoration of Order in Ireland Act went into effect. The first phase of this acceleration occurred between September and October. Reprisals had become so common by this time that news or rumour of IRA activity in a locality was enough to spark fear of a potential reprisal.[67] In Roscommon, for instance, one resident envisioned an 'orgy of bomb, bullet, and petrol' after the IRA shot dead one constable and wounded another near Frenchpark. Shortly after this ambush, uniformed men began to amass and hoard petrol reserves in nearby Ballaghaderreen, which they later used for widespread arson. Heavy rainfall helped locals beat back flames that affected nearly every business in the town, but not before causing over £100,000 in damage.[68]

Spikes in destructive Crown force activity continued from late September through to the end of 1920, and represented some of the worst examples of damage to the built environment of the period. Alongside reprisals, Britain's attempts to restore order involved a war on Irish homes, women and children.[69]

War on the Home

Destructive acts, ranging from sabotage to vandalism to wholesale ruin, established property damage as a typical feature of Irish life throughout the 18 months that preceded the Truce of July 1921. This destruction had a profound impact on how contemporaries and survivors constructed the memory of the conflict, and how traumatic experiences further shaped nationalist politics at the time. But what made the experience of reprisals traumatic on a national scale? How did they engender fear in those who never actually experienced them? Reprisals 'abruptly dislodged' the 'patterned meanings' of individuals, families, groups and communities through psychological, physical and environmental violence.[70] In other words, this form of violence eroded the comforts and security of private space, where known individuals visited and resided. A sense of anxiety emerged in their place whereby Irish citizens anticipated home raids and searches by Crown forces, as well as the potential expulsion from and arson of their homes or other property. By creating this type of blanket fear and anxiety, reprisals generated more 'insecurity, fear, and general distrust' than actual material damage.[71] Irish men, women and children who endured broken glass, home invasions and burned town centres each contributed to a collective sense of national trauma. Environmental destruction shaped this trauma to such a degree that the stories of raids and reprisal produced a 'sense of shock and fear' on a par with the actual event.[72]

Christina Horan claimed she was 11 years old when she developed partial paralysis of her left hand and foot. Her family lived on French Quay in Cork, where their home hosted 'continuous raids' between 1919 and 1921. She explained the connection in her application to the Army Pensions Board: 'I was very nervous as a result of this continual raiding. [...] Everything in the house was smashed. My nerves are bad since.' In 1938, Drs Thomas Crofts and George Hegarty confirmed for the board that Horan 'was in perfect health up to 1920 when, following on shock and fright which she got from constant raids by 'Black and Tans' [...], she developed partial paralysis.'[73] Dr T. Donovan added that Horan suffered epileptic fits after 'the terrifying raids'. 'She will never be fit to work. Her disability is due to terror caused by raids.'[74] Maighread Bean Uí Luasa (Margaret Lucey) wrote to underscore the family's nationalist credentials in hopes of influencing a favourable decision. She wrote of Christina's mother, Agnes, and her active role in Cumann na mBan; and of her father, who was caretaker of the Thomas Ashe Sinn Féin Club hall before his death in 1918.[75]

It would not be difficult to view Horan's condition as genuine on its own. Evidence from the period shows how prevailing conditions influenced a general social nervousness.[76] But the Board was not satisfied that Christina's condition was the result of shock due to Crown force raids. And they were correct. Further medical analysis in 1954 revealed that Horan had, in fact, 'been totally incapacitated since the age of 6 years'. Despite being rejected by the Army Pensions Board, Christina Horan's application is nevertheless valuable in other respects. Whether the Horans truly believed Christina's condition developed from raids, or they were using her condition to secure a pension, the family was clearly attuned to prevailing post-independence sentiment regarding raids and reprisals and understood how to appeal to emotion. The sheer number of raids throughout the period minted the experience of home invasion and terror as cultural currency, one used to garner sympathy or, perhaps, influence the outcome of a pension application.[77]

Linda Connolly has shown that Irish society's willingness to remember shapes the collective memory of the revolutionary period. The subject of sexual violence against women during the Irish Revolution, for instance, has experienced a selective amnesia.[78] Intuition, however, connected the invasion or destruction of Irish homes with the plight of women and children.[79] In August 1920, Annot Erskine Robinson and Ellen Wilkinson led a body of Women's International League members to investigate atrocities in Ireland and, as Robinson testified, the alleged 'suffering of the women and children'. When the acting chairman of the American Commission on Conditions in Ireland asked how she had come to hear of such suffering, she replied:

> Well, of course, it is perfectly obvious, is it not, that when it is reported in the newspapers that homes were being destroyed, that women and children are going to suffer? I do not know that there was any particular statement of that suffering in the newspapers, but perhaps it was but our own imaginations that led us to know that what was happening there would cause suffering among the women and children. We knew that reprisals had occurred, and that they would fall hardest upon the women and children.[80]

Other dynamics of violence, including raids and reprisals, restrictions on public space and curfews, reinforced narratives of victimhood that, for many, evidenced the conflict's one-sided moral dimensions.[81] This was overwhelmingly true in the case of raids and reprisals, whose narratives established and reinforced experiences of violation, terror and destruction distinct from IRA assaults on barracks, courthouses or lighthouses. IRA violence against these structures could induce terror – particularly if the sergeant's family remained in residence after policemen had vacated, as the previous chapters have shown – but the cost to the State was comparatively negligible. A home, on the other hand, was more than a physical space. It could symbolise something more: safety, repose, an escape from the outside world. Raids gradually shifted sites of violence towards the civilian home.[82]

Raids on Irish homes contribute to a broader transnational experience that views conflict-driven evictions, communal displacement and the wilful destruction of homes as acts of 'domicide'.[83] In this sense, Christopher Harker distinguished the destruction of a house from that of a home, where violence permeates 'the extensive economic, political, cultural and social geographies (and temporalities)'.[84] Katherine Brickell further theorised the home as a physical place that both separates and shelters one from public life, but which simultaneously embodies inhabitants' politics, culture and customs.[85] Sociological perspective argues that structures function beyond their intended use in this way. Like natural landscapes, private dwellings, public buildings and communal spaces constitute environments from which individuals develop and claim identity and personal attachment.[86] Homes, for instance, were places where personal touches in furniture, photographs and mementos, as well as their arrangement and display, encased an intimate portrait of the individual or family, politics and leisure.[87] Further, individual rooms compartmentalised function and communicated certain boundaries. Those designated and outfitted for confidential, affectionate or vulnerable acts, such as bedrooms, might feature any combination of elements meant to comfort, conceal or protect its occupants and the private acts of sex, birth and motherhood that occurred therein.

Raids operated within the spectrum of environmental terror: physically invasive and often destructive assaults on private spaces and the sentimental and functional objects within.[88] Their regularity throughout the period, reconstructed from *Irish Bulletin* weekly reports, illustrates the scale of this terror. From available data it may be shown that an average of approximately 155 raids occurred daily in Ireland throughout 1920, with significant spikes appearing in the summer and towards December. This does not account for the number of homes raided, however, as individual residences were raided multiple times throughout the period.[89]

Cáit O'Callaghan's witness statement to the Bureau of Military History reconstructed her experience of raids and the emotionally charged atmosphere they created. Police targeted her husband, Michael O'Callaghan, then Mayor of Limerick, for search and interrogation several times between late August 1920 and March 1921 due to his republican politics and public presence. Cáit described searches of Irish homes as 'commonplace' but no less painful experiences, and detailed their invasive and destructive nature:

> A search means carpets pulled up, presses, wardrobes, cupboards and beds pulled out and ransacked, writing desks rifled, private letters read aloud and commented on, jeering questions put to an unarmed man, the humiliation of the women of the house standing for hours in their night clothes and hastily-donned dressing gowns.[90]

O'Callaghan's memory of the second raid of her home on 8 February 1921 was harder to recall, 'for it was like a nightmare.' Police 'rushed about, shouting and pulling things out, overturning vases, jeering at the long agony of Terence McSwiney [sic, who perished in Brixton prison the previous November after 74 days on hunger strike], threatening to put a speedy end to my husband's propaganda, yelling that there was no God, God was dead, asking me how I would like my house to "go up" [in flames]'.[91] A third raid occurred two weeks later when female searchers segregated Cáit and the maid from Michael, who was interrogated in the dining room. 'The women searched the wardrobes, linen press, cupboards, drawers, beds, etc., etc., very carefully. Even the heels of my boots and the shoes and hems of my gowns were examined.' The circumstances of this particular raid – the second in a fortnight, conducted late at night and intentionally disruptive – caused her 'great humiliation'.[92] 'It may be true [...] that some wars have ennobling effects even upon the conqueror;' Erskine Childers wrote in *The Daily News* in March 1921 that 'this kind of war has none.' A fourth raid the following month resulted in Michael O'Callaghan's murder.[93] The O'Callaghan's experience was precisely the type that engendered broad fear and anxiety – multiple raids on the family home, the demeaning of objects, sentiments and beliefs they held dear, and finally murder.

Many men were 'on the run' to avoid a similar fate. Going 'on the run' was certainly necessary as police increased their presence and pressure in Irish communities. Life on the lam also brought with it a degree of separation anxiety.[94] It is important to understand women's association with the home in this regard. Irish family roles were in many ways tethered to a sense of 'collective compliance' to ensure economic and social prosperity. While not definitively gendered, men and women played different roles as 'providers and nurturers', respectively, which corresponded to prevailing outlooks on the public and private spheres.[95] The option to absent oneself from the home, however, highlights further gender disparity between Irishmen's and women's war experiences. Men's withdrawal left women, children and elderly family members to confront police and military personnel. Galway IRA member Michael Hayes characterised women's service in these circumstances: 'I would say that their most difficult assignment was to have to remain in their own homes and there, along with their parents, meet the masked raiders who came to threaten and bully and burn out their homes.'[96] As Margaret Ward maintained, being 'on the run' was also the ultimate fate of women and children burned out of their homes or driven away during reprisals. Undeniably, 'those who suffered the worst were those who remained at home.'[97]

Mary Clancy, a founding member of Cumann na mBan, endured several raids on her home over the course of two years. Two of these occurred in the absence of her husband, George, the Mayor of Limerick. In one instance, soldiers raided her home at 3 a.m. on a cold night in November 1919. The violation entailed the military officer searching every inch of the house and back garden, 'even the hen run'.[98] Clancy traded the experience's initial trauma for a sense of perpetual anxiety and fear when the officer informed her that he would come again. 'Nightly expecting another raid my husband [then on the run] and myself had not very much rest for the next few months.'[99] The next visit eventually occurred in early December 1920, during which police again 'spread throughout the house, even invading the privacy of the room in which my mother and father were in bed.' A police cadet sat on a table, 'dangling his legs', while he leisurely hurled abuse at Clancy, accusing the family of aiding murder and threatening to 'blow the place to pieces'. The police then ordered Clancy and the maid to walk on a photograph of the local Irish Volunteer company. When both women refused, the presiding RIC sergeant stomped on the photo himself, removed it from its broken frame and burned it.[100] Female searchers then arrived and subjected Clancy, her 70-year-old mother and the young maid to 'the humiliation of being searched while the men went through the house and ransacked every corner of it'.[101]

Raids and reprisals violated intimate spaces, such as bedrooms and their contents, and places of comfort and respite, such as sitting rooms. As a result, they displaced a sense of emotional security that induced shock and trauma. Robert Brennan was hiding in a neighbour's house in 1920 when a raid occurred on his own home two doors away. 'I thought of Una and our three little girls,' he recalled, 'and bitterly realised I could do nothing for them.' The next morning Brennan found his wife standing at a window, 'pale and silent':

> I had never seen her so near a break. She had been crying. They had kept her downstairs all night away from the children and they had grilled her and our eldest child, Emer, aged nine, for hours, on my activities and whereabouts [...]. The two younger children, Maeve [...] and Deirdre [...], were hysterical, which was not to be wondered at.[102]

The homes, businesses and civic buildings and spaces that comprise a town also constitute a cultural landscape. The lived experiences within these spaces shape associative narratives of place. Patrick Duffy highlights the concept of a 'vernacular landscape' where the physical landscape and local community both inherit and produce cultural memory.[103] In this context, raids dislocated people from their previously lived experiences of home. The experiences of a raid created a sense of emotional captivity within one's own home and community, where the rumble of a lorry, a 'thunder of knocks', a pronounced English accent spouting 'a demand in vile language', or news of an IRA ambush triggered rumour and fear of imagined consequences.[104]

The hostile sounds of raids and reprisals sustained a distinct sonic landscape that further eroded a sense of security in the home and invoked a common emotional experience.[105] Newspapers, pamphlets and transcripts from aid societies and political inquiries highlighted this militarised soundscape. To Erskine Childers, Dáil Éireann's Minister of Propaganda, 'a typical night in Dublin' included 'weird cavalcades' of lorries, tanks, and armoured cars, that 'muster in fleets' after curfew to conduct raids on the homes of 'women and terrified children'.[106] In September 1920, Mallow was 'awakened by the arrival [...] of three motor lorries whose occupants cheered as they entered the town'.[107] Robert Lynd, literary editor of the *London Daily News*, identified the noise of military vehicles as complementing the war cries of their passengers. In October 1920, he published a pamphlet that stressed the intimidating tone and language of the Black and Tans: 'Descending on a village in the midnight hours, they announce their presence by fiendish yells. [...] to the accompaniment of savage yells [they] set to work.'[108] The *Irish Independent* reported:

> Several of the men [who attacked Lahinch] had pronounced English accents, plainly audible in the shouting. Inhabitants were terror-stricken, and fled in dozens to the sandhills to the north of the town with their little ones and household goods. The miserable night was spent in the moonlight.[109]

Republican playwright Seán O'Casey later differentiated between shouting and violent action in *Plough and the Stars*. 'Tans, thought Sean, for the Tommies would not shout so soullessly, nor smash the glass panels so suddenly.'[110] After touring Ireland, the British Labour Commission to Ireland concluded, 'months of oppression, coercion, and physical violence cannot but have far-reaching effects upon the people who suffer under them.'

> It is clear that the terrorism which prevails has had serious effects upon the health of the people. We may leave out of account the obvious consequences likely to follow to the members of a household who have been the horrified witnesses of bloodshed and violence in their own homes, and consider the effects of the terror upon those who have never experienced such an ordeal. There is medical testimony to show that the fear inspired by 'Black and Tans' and Auxiliary Police has had the most adverse effects upon pregnant women. Children naturally suffer from the effects of terror-laden atmosphere, and we are informed that the number of cases of such diseases as St. Vitus' dance has considerably increased. A large section of the population is 'all nerves'.[111]

'St Vitus' dance' was a colloquial term for Sydenham's chorea, an autoimmune disorder that caused the body to spasm and jerk rapidly. Its perceived connection to frayed nerves shows that in the public mind, raids severely impacted both mind and body.[112]

The violation and destruction of Irish homes established a shared emotional experience amongst victims.[113] In broad terms, raids and reprisals can be seen as acts of environmental manipulation that exhibit the forced transfer of spatial control and meaning. In this context, it is not unreasonable to view their invasive and destructive nature in the same light, though on different spatial scales. The physical damage caused by raids and reprisals is difficult to segregate from their economic and psychological impacts. Many of the reprisals conducted through to the Truce of July 1921 were of a scale, ferocity and destructive nature that left lasting emotional and economic effects. The day-to-day raids and militarism accompanying these reprisals reinforced and exacerbated an already tense atmosphere.

Economic Damage

Crown force raids and reprisals targeted shops, businesses and co-operative societies in order to disrupt the local economy and intimidate Irishmen and women against supporting republicanism. The business community feared reprisals for several reasons. First, reprisals threatened their physical premises and stock. Economic targets were highly visible, often centrally located, and subject to additional scrutiny if the owners were known republican sympathisers, though this was not always the case. Second, destruction of property meant loss of trade. Shopkeepers' ability to reopen their businesses after an attack depended on compensation from official channels to pay for reconstruction, which was often either delayed or, if paid at all, reduced from initial estimates. The time it took to rebuild or reopen also delayed shopkeepers' potential profits. Third, the implementation of martial law in some areas contributed to further loss of trade, as restrictions were placed on fairs, markets and operating hours. While violence against individuals often shapes our perception of conflict, it is also important to recognise how material loss, economic interference and restrictions on communal space attacked both the economic and political community.[114]

The destruction of property and public constraints stemming from martial law were of ongoing concern to Ireland's business communities. Diarmaid Ferriter pointed to the *Freeman's Journal* of January 1919, immediately following the Soloheadbeg ambush, which stated that local businesses were worried about 'military law in the area, as it is feared it is to lead to dislocation of their business.'[115] The Department of Agriculture and Technical Instruction (DATI) had the same reaction later that year when martial law threatened to restrict fairs and markets. The DATI told the Chief Secretary, Ian MacPherson, that those 'hit hardest' would be 'the decent, industrious section of the people' and would have knock-on effects on the propertied and 'respectable farming class'.[116] Martial law constraints began to take a toll in Tipperary by November 1919. Restrictions on the bi-monthly Fethard pig market, for instance, reported a 'big loss' to the town.[117] James Dwyer, Chairman of the Roscrea Rural District Council, spelled out the importance of the Roscrea weekly market for the Under Secretary. He noted that the market offered a wide variety of farm produce and was an important source for procuring fuel for the home. Many poor people used turf and timber rather than coal, he explained, which they were typically able to purchase at the market. The Roscrea market also hosted farmers from adjacent counties, broadening its economic footprint.[118] Restrictions also affected communities in County Clare. Mr G. de L. Willis pointed out that limits on fairs inflicted 'most serious loss on entirely innocent people'. While the government hoped these restrictions would deter crime, Willis noted that the opposite was more likely true: that constraints on public markets irritated the general population to the point that it 'tends to increase the risk of crime and outrages by the discontented or criminal'.[119] Inasmuch as martial law aimed to limit interaction and communal space, it also punished elements of the political community perceived to support and conceal the republican movement.

Restrictions on trading spaces and punitive reprisals coalesced in attacks on the co-operative rural industry, which occurred in the 'systematised' destruction of creameries.[120] The co-operative dairy movement had been founded in the 1880s under the direction of Sir Horace Plunkett, who aimed to cultivate Irish 'national character' via socio-economic reform and technical education.[121] Co-operative creameries were a feature of the Irish rural economy, particularly throughout Munster's 'Golden Vale' and in the northern dairying region that stretched from Sligo to Antrim. The movement boasted over 1,000 agricultural societies by 1920, with 316 co-operative creameries registered with the Irish Agricultural Organisation Society (IAOS) by spring 1921.[122] Their destruction politicised an ostensibly non-political agricultural entity.[123] The American Commission on Relief in Ireland registered creameries amongst the most important categories of destroyed property because they served a vital role in local rural economies.[124] George Russell (Æ), who lent his literary talents to editing two IAOS journals (the *Irish Homestead* and the *Irish Statesman*), argued along similar lines. In 'A Plea for Justice', he identified how Crown forces targeted creameries with the intent of hurting the community at large[125]:

> Why have these economic organisations been specially attacked? Because they have hundreds of members, and if barracks have been burned or police have been killed or wounded in the lamentable strife now being waged in Ireland, and if the armed forces of the Crown cannot capture those actually guilty of the offences, the policy of reprisals, condoned by the spokesmen of the Government, has led to the wrecking of any enterprise in the neighbourhood

the destruction of which would inflict widespread injury and hurt the interests of the greatest number of people.[126]

Sperling's Journal, a non-political English business publication, echoed Russell, explaining that the 'the most effective means of punishing everyone in that district is to destroy the creamery which furnishes them with a market for their milk.'[127] The *Irish Homestead* recognised the symbiotic economic connection and further explained that Irish traders and wholesalers were unwilling to stock goods for fear they would be destroyed in reprisals, a policy by which 'the Government are strangling trade both in Great Britain and Ireland.'[128]

Crown forces viewed co-operative dairying as a convenient cover for IRA activity, and creameries themselves as nodes for the exchange of guns and intelligence.[129] The American Commission's inspection tour between February and March 1921 identified that Crown forces destroyed or irreparably damaged approximately 55 creameries.[130] The significance of these losses has been debated. Proinnsias Breathnach argues that when set against the over 700 creameries (co-operative and private) in operation in Ireland in 1920, those destroyed appear negligible. Cyril Ehrlich also maintains that creameries did not contribute to the overall Irish economy in significant ways.[131] This analysis fails to consider the local impacts caused by their destruction, or the displacement experienced by the co-operative movement. The destruction of creameries sustained a war on the Irish people and the rural economy that was deeply felt within Ireland's dairy industry. Approximately 15,000 dairy farmers were affected by the destruction of roughly £250,000 worth of property. In his president's address to the IAOS in March 1921, Sir Horace Plunkett cited damage to creameries to have jeopardised roughly £1,000,000 in revenue.[132] The Annual Report for the year ending 31 March 1922 provided a clearer view of the impact of reprisals on Irish creameries: 'The losses our societies sustained were serious,' IAOS Vice President Rev. T. A. Finlay reported, 'too serious to be spoken of lightly.' An overall 27 per cent loss in trade from 1920 to 1921 was due, in part, to monetary inflation and a decline in prices (10 per cent loss), while a 17 per cent decrease in the volume of goods bought or sold by co-operative societies reflected 'the extent to which the operations of the societies were affected by the troubles through which the country was passing.'[133] Reprisals on Ireland's co-operative creameries affected farmers' ability to process milk, ultimately disrupting the rural economy.

Reprisals continued apace throughout September 1920. Revisited attacks occurred in Tuam and Galway City, where 'nightly terror by the imported police' prevailed, and where houses and establishments, such as the printing presses and machines of the *Galway Express*, were 'reduced to a state of wreckage'.[134] At the same time, Tullow, Carlow, endured what *The Belfast Newsletter* described as 'one of those appalling orgies of terrorism and destruction by uniformed men which have become of almost daily occurrence in Ireland', with damage estimated at £30,000.[135] Daily returns for 'sabotage' from the *Irish Bulletin* for August and September 1920 illustrate not only the frequency of Crown force damage, but also its saturation.

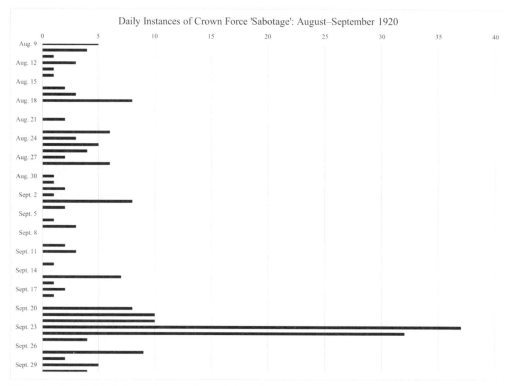

Daily Instances of Crown Force 'Sabotage': August–September 1920

The 'sack of Balbriggan', on the night of 20–21 September, was the crescendo of destruction in a month that experienced approximately 155 acts of Crown force sabotage. Ross O'Mahony and David Fitzpatrick untangled the complex dynamics of murder, reprisal and destruction in Balbriggan, which began after IRA members Michael Rock and William Corcoran murdered Head Constable Peter Burke and wounded his brother, Sergeant William Patrick Burke.[136] In response, Black and Tans and other policemen from the nearby Gormanstown training camp destroyed houses and businesses up and down Clonard Street, known as 'Sinn Féin row'.[137]

Of the 50 Balbriggan properties destroyed, just over half were private homes; shops, small businesses and pubs constituted the rest.[138] Beyond physical damage to the built environment, therefore, the reprisal created refugees and widespread unemployment. The *Belfast Newsletter* noted 'Pitiful scenes' of men, women and children 'on the roads leading from the town [...] fleeing to the country for refuge.'[139] The press reported a 'Nightly Exodus' of homeless men, women and children from Balbriggan, who took shelter 'under hedgerows, beside hay stacks and in old barns'.[140] The Balbriggan Relief Committee outfitted Walshe's flour mill as a temporary hostel to receive the destitute, but it was unable to fully address the need.[141] Refugees arrived in nearby Drogheda, with charity donations flowing into the city in the days that followed.[142] Others fled to Dublin, barefoot, 'scantily clad', carrying what possessions they could escape with and in many cases with nothing but the clothes on their backs.[143] A notorious folk ballad gave an impression of the reprisal's truly penetrating effects:

> The town of Balbriggan they burnt to the ground
> While the bullets like hailstones were whizzing around.[144]
> And women left homeless by this evil clan.
> They've waged war on children, the Bould Black an' Tan.[145]

A clearer picture of communal and economic displacement emerged in the aftermath of reprisal on Balbriggan. The deliberate destruction of Deede's, Templar & Co. hosiers meant unemployment for its 120 workers and nearly 300 others engaged in outwork. The Wood-Renton Commission later processed £83,727 in claims for the town, over half of which compensated Deede's. However, employees did not receive compensation for lost wages, though some found work with Smyth & Co., Balbriggan's other hosiery manufacturer. As the American Commission on Conditions in Ireland concluded, 'destruction of a factory brings destitution.'[146] Deede's was never able to recover and dissolved its Balbriggan operation in 1922.[147] The 'sack of Balbriggan' inaugurated a new phase in 'the Reign of Terror' that affixed reprisals in 'nationalist folklore' and brought the Anglo-Irish conflict more prominently into the British press.[148]

Balbriggan was the first of several devastating reprisals that took place throughout the autumn of 1920.[149] In County Clare, Crown forces attacked the towns of Miltown Malbay, Lahinch and Ennistymon in response to an ambush at Rineen, contributing to a broader 'season of terror'.[150] Mallow suffered in kind, with citizens fleeing in an exodus likened to scenes at Balbriggan.[151] The assault on Mallow in late September 1920 destroyed the historic town hall (which later received £12,186 under the Criminal and Malicious Injuries (Ireland) Act),[152] as well as up to 18 homes, the majority of which also served as businesses.[153] In fact, Crown forces deliberately sabotaged Mallow's economic engines. The burning of Cleeve's Factory added the milk condenser to a growing list of destruction that affected the local, regional and international economies.[154] This included Cleeve's other creamery at Knocklong, Limerick, which employed 50 men.[155] Cleeve's Mallow operation employed anywhere between 150 to 300 individuals, depending on the season, and distributed up to £600 a week in wages in the autumn.[156] Its destruction also tore at the town's social fabric and economic symbiosis. 'The men who worked there were heads of families, and all the wages from that factory were spent in that town. And so it was a great loss to the town,' recalled Frank Dempsey, Chairman of Mallow Urban Council.[157] In addition to the buildings, the attacks ruined Cleeve's valuable machinery, which a manager claimed would take up to ten years to replace.[158] Witnesses described the carnage, drawing comparisons to warzone scenes elsewhere.[159] '[W]hen one turned to the twisted, mangled, torn, distorted relics of what was but a few days ago one of the best equipped factories of its kind in Ireland,' the *Irish Independent* reported, '[...] some idea of the appalling destruction forced itself on the mind.'[160] Like many reprisal sites, direct witnesses and relief committees recorded their impressions. An Australian clergyman, Rev. M. D. Forrest, visited Mallow on 20 October to interview eyewitnesses and to take in the nature and extent of Mallow's 'criminal devastation'. He observed burned-out sections of the town where 'looting was carried on without the slightest restraint, and the military were indulging in the vilest language.'[161] Miss Ellen C. Wilkinson elaborated on the broader impact of Cleeve's creamery in Mallow, which was burned in October 1920: 'That was a pretty bad burning from the humane point of view,' she said, 'because people in Europe are dying for want of milk.'[162]

Police riots were mainly predicated on IRA outrages, which remained steady between October and December 1920, with significant spikes occurring throughout November.[163]

Week ending	Policemen Killed	Policemen Wounded	Policemen Threatened	Policemen Attacked but not Injured	TOTAL
26 Sept. 1920	10	4	3	6	23
3 Oct. 1920	7	6	1	8	22
10 Oct. 1920	2	5	3	8	18
17 Oct. 1920	5	5	4	3	17
24 Oct. 1920	3	5	3	3	14
31 Oct. 1920	5	5	7	1	18
7 Nov. 1920	12	26	1	7	46
14 Nov. 1920	5	8	0	8	21
21 Nov. 1920	3	1	0	2	6
28 Nov. 1920	2	7	4	7	20
5 Dec. 1920	19	5	0	5	29
12 Dec. 1920	0	13	0	4	17
19 Dec. 1920	7	7	0	5	19
26 Dec. 1920	1	3	1	3	8
2 Jan. 1921	5	9	2	5	21

These figures support what David Leeson and others have shown: that outrages triggered punitive responses that perpetuated a cycle of violence throughout the autumn of 1920.[164] The hallmarks of previous reprisals materialised in places such as Tubbercurry, Sligo, after an IRA attack on police killed District Inspector Brady and wounded another member of the force. These reprisals included destroyed homes ('There is scarcely a house that does not bear some evidence of attack.'), wrecked shops and creameries ('At one spot the debris [from the creamery] was a floating mass of liquid, presumably all that remained of the store of sugar.'), fear and exodus ('towards dusk people could be seen betaking themselves to the country and crowds of refugees were seeking the shelter of the convent.').[165] A similar report emerged from Kerry the following month after policemen were shot in Tralee, Killorglin, Causeway, Dingle, Abbeydorney and Ballyduff, and others were kidnapped at Tralee. A Special Commissioner to the *Irish Independent* estimated Kerry to be the most devastated county in Ireland at the time, which he evidenced by the tens of thousands of pounds in damage that had occurred and the generally nervous state of those he encountered on his tour.[166] Crown forces victimised various cities throughout County Cork in November and early December, yet Cork City was a particular hotbed of incendiarism, raids and arrests.[167] Martial law, which went into effect in Cork, Kerry, Limerick and Tipperary on 10 December, formally acknowledged that 'a state of armed insurrection exists' and considered those engaged in it as conducting war against the Crown.[168] Martial law meant censorship, curfew and restrictions on public space, conditions in place when an IRA ambush at Dillon's Cross, a neighbourhood in Cork City's north end, on 10 December prompted the largest and most destructive reprisal of the period.

'The burning of Cork' by RIC Auxiliaries caused an estimated £2 million in damage, including the destruction of Cork City Hall and the Carnegie Library. Corkonians felt the impact of reprisal more intimately in the destruction of homes, shops and businesses, and in the spectacle this destruction produced. Over 60 shops were looted and burned and an additional 20 were badly damaged.[169] Witnesses to the destruction compared the burning of Cork with the destruction of Dublin in 1916; Grant's in Cork revived the destruction of Clery's during Easter Week.[170] Britain's *Daily Chronicle's* presented an 'English pressman's views': 'I saw Dublin immediately after the rebellion, but, great though the damage was there [...], the picture presented now in this city's principal thoroughfare is more appalling.'[171] The *Freeman's Journal* also carried the comparison, which was appropriate in the fact that smouldering fires and smoke continued to fills the skies for days afterwards.[172] 'Jacques', reporting for the *Irish Independent*, struggled to navigate the city in the absence of familiar landmarks; the well-known shops of his childhood were 'nothing now but gaping voids and hissing steam. [...] Forrest's for furs. Forrest's for gloves! It looks like the battered outpost of a shell shattered area.'[173] For 'Jacques' and many others, the burning of Cork ruined more than commercial buildings and homes; it dislocated people from their city and the memories and lives that had been built there.

The destruction of Cork threw upwards of 2,000 people out of work and ushered in 'a new poor' from previously self-supporting classes that quickly outstripped local charity support and public appeal.[174] Cork Corporation agreed to form an unemployment committee to address the issue,[175] while the *Daily Chronicle* believed that money 'cannot cover the damage done or repair the loss, which will endure for many a day'.[176] The *Cork Examiner* was also unable to estimate a timeframe for recovery:

> It is much easier to destroy an industry than to build one up, and though that may sound like a platitude, its absolute truth has forcibly been brought home to many households in this city. The disaster that has befallen Cork, and the unemployment resulting from it, have set back the hands of the clock of local progress very considerably, and when the community will recover from the shock, the waste and the ruin is too speculative a question to be answered on the data available.[177]

Widespread distress continued into 1921. The Cork Distress Relief Committee received donations throughout the spring. In April, the Council of the Cork Incorporated Chamber of Commerce and Shipping called for funding for relief works and reconstruction projects to repair the city and relieve unemployment.[178] Reconstruction followed thanks to financial guarantees from the Irish Provisional Government in 1922; St Patrick's Street was restored by 1926, a new Cork Public Library appeared in 1930, and City Hall reopened in 1936.[179]

By 1921, the nature and scope of reprisals had changed. Martial law was extended to all of Munster in early January, after which environmental destruction and human displacement were formalised in the advent of 'official' reprisals, which marked out homes and businesses for demolition following IRA provocations. Michael Hopkinson considered the destruction of 191 houses as official reprisals through May 1921 a conservative figure.[180] Accompanying decrees required private homes, hotels and boarding houses to post occupancy lists, which prohibited loitering and restricted telegraphed and wireless communication. The keeping of a pigeon was allowed by permit. Major-General Strickland communicated that those who damaged government property or failed to prevent its damage would have their own property confiscated or destroyed. 'All persons,' he concluded, 'are therefore exhorted in their own interests to prevent such wanton damage.'[181] Major-General Sir F. Maurice, on the other hand, admonished the advent of official reprisals as 'a public admission that a policy of unofficial reprisals has failed and is in effect a condemnation of the whole system of placing the task of restoring order in the hands of irregular semi-military policy.'[182] English clergy demonised reprisals as 'only inflaming the wound',[183] while Mr R. E. Longfield of Mallow, 'an old Unionist', explained reprisals as merely swelling the 'Tide of Destruction.' 'Serious harm has been done,' he wrote to *The Spectator*, 'moral, material, and lasting. The mendacious historian of the future will, no doubt, class our excellent Tommies and splendid R.I.C. and the burning of 1921 with the Yeomanry and pitch caps of 1798.'[184] As the next chapter explores, reprisals framed political discourse at home and abroad, shaped popular memory of the period, and provided evidence of Irish nationalism's continued violent suppression.

Conclusion

Reprisals emerged as counter-insurgency methods in the face of IRA attacks on Crown forces, ultimately resulting in the destruction of Irish towns and broad terrorisation. Their motivation materialised from the stressful nature of guerrilla warfare, indiscipline and a faulted command structure, as well as a desire to avenge fallen comrades and to take revenge on Irish communities that supported the republican movement. This cycle of violence accelerated throughout the autumn of 1920, after the Restoration of Order in Ireland Act authorised more personally invasive and communally disruptive modes of policing. Destruction occurred on various scales, from window-breaking to wholesale arson. In between, police raids on Irish homes displaced individuals and families from familiar and intimate spaces, exacerbating a prevailing terror that often persisted in the absence of men who were 'on the run'. Commercial communities were dislocated in an economic sense as reprisals on creameries denied dairy farmers an outlet for their milk supply. As co-operative dairying sought to reform Irish rural character, attacks on creameries constituted a further attack on the Irish people. The same may be said of large-scale reprisals, such as those experienced in Balbriggan and Mallow, which not only destroyed commercial property but also threw many out of work.

NOTES

1. 'The curse of Ananias Greenwood: Over three thousand ruined buildings', in *The Irish Exile* 1:5 (July 1921), p. 5.
2. 'The Irish housing question', *The Irish Builder and Engineer*, 22 May 1920, p. 361.
3. 'Cabinet plan for faster housing', *The Irish Builder and Engineer*, 17 July 1920, p. 477.
4. See Ruth McManus, 'Taking the urban housing problem in the Irish Free State, 1922–1940', in *Urban History* 46:1 (2019), p. 62; F. H. A. Aalen, 'Public housing in Ireland, 1800–1921', in *Planning Perspectives* 2 (1987), pp 175–93.
5. Gordon Pattison, 'The British Army's effectiveness in the Irish campaign 1919–1921 and the lessons for modern counter-insurgency operations, with special reference to C31 aspects', in *Cornwallis XIV: Analysis of Societal Conflict and Counter-Insurgency Workshop* (Vienna, 2009), quoting Keith Jeffery, 'The British Army and internal security 1919–1939', in *The Historical Journal* 24:2 (1981), pp 377–97.
6. Ruth McManus, 'Taking the urban housing problem in the Irish Free State, 1922–1940', p. 35; F. S. L. Lyons, *Ireland Since the Famine* (London, 1985 edn), p. 407.
7. David Fitzpatrick, 'The price of Balbriggan', in David Fitzpatrick (ed.), *Terror in Ireland* (Dublin, 2012), p. 75.
8. John Ainsworth, 'British security policy in Ireland, 1920–1921', in *The Australian Journal of Irish Studies* (2001), p. 178.
9. David Leeson, *The Black and Tans: British Police and Auxiliaries in the Irish War of Independence, 1920–1921* (New York, 2011), p.24; Michael Hopkinson, *The Irish War of Independence* (Dublin, 2004 edn), p. 49; David Fitzpatrick, *The Two Irelands, 1912–1939* (Oxford, 1998), p. 90. For additional insight regarding discipline within Black and Tan and Auxiliary ranks, see 'Reprisals by troops in Ireland and effects on discipline', TNA (WO 32/9537).
10. Susan Kingsley Kent, *Aftershocks: Politics and Trauma in Britain, 1918–1931* (New York, 2009), p. 103; see also, Charles Townshend, *Political Violence in Ireland: Government and Resistance Since 1848* (New York, 1984 edn), p. 351.
11. Charles Tilly, *The Politics of Collective Violence* (New York, 2006 edn), p. 104.
12. Dorothy Macardle, *The Irish Republic* (Dublin, 1965 edn), p. 347.
13. Lyons, *Ireland Since the Famine*, pp 415–16; Richard Bennett, *The Black and Tans* (New York, 1959; 1995 edn), p. 68. Indeed, it is documented that many members of Crown forces developed acute psychological stress as a result of their service in Ireland. *Irish Independent*, 18 Oct. 1920.
14. Diarmaid Ferriter, *A Nation and Not a Rabble: The Irish Revolution 1913–1923* (London, 2015), p. 197.
15. Kent, *Aftershocks*, p. 104.
16. Ibid.
17. Ibid., pp 105–6.
18. 'What causes reprisals?', *The Weekly Summary* 9, 8 Oct. 1920, p. 1, cited from Ainsworth, 'British security policy in Ireland, 1920–1921', p. 179; see also, David Leeson, *The Black and Tans*, p. 214.
19. Lyons, *Ireland Since the Famine*, p. 413; Leeson, *The Black and Tans*, pp 8–9; Bennett, *The Black and Tans*, p. 82.
20. William Sheehan, *A Hard Local War: The British Army and the Guerrilla War in Cork 1919–1921* (Dublin, 2017 edn), p. 96.
21. Townshend, *Political Violence in Ireland*, p. 350; Peter Hart, *The IRA at War 1916–1923* (New York, 2005 edn), p. 84.
22. Joost Augusteijn, 'Military conflict in the War of Independence', in John Crowley, Donal Ó Drisceoil, Mike Murphy (eds) and John Borgonovo (associate ed.), *Atlas of the Irish Revolution* (Cork, 2017), footnote for figure 5b, p 354.
23. Macardle, *Irish Republic*, p. 353; *Irish Bulletin* 3:2, 28 Sept. 1920 is the most often cited source, which shows damage to 90 Irish towns over a 12-month period commencing September 1919. Others include *The Struggle of the Irish People: Address to the Congress of the United States, Adopted at the January Session of Dáil Éireann, 1921* (Government Printing Office, Washington, 1921), pp 14–20; Dáil Éireann publicity department, 'Map showing Irish towns and villages wholly or partly wrecked by English Forces from September 9th, 1919 to March 1st, 1921', UCD Archives, pp 0150–1336; see

also, Joost Augusteijn, 'Military conflict in the War of Independence', in *Atlas of the Irish Revolution*, pp 351–5.

24. *The Irish Exile*, citing *Irish Bulletin* of 6 June 1921: 'In the period January 1st 1921 to May 28th 1921, the cases of premises and property destroyed or damaged unofficially number 354 as against 162 official acts. By 1921, counties Cork, Kerry, Limerick, Tipperary, Clare, Kilkenny, Waterford, and Wexford were subject to martial law.'

25. Leeson, *The Black and Tans*, pp 158–66.

26. Ibid., p. 159.

27. Hart, *The IRA at War*, pp 75–6.

28. Tilly, *Politics of Collective Violence*, pp 102–4.

29. Ibid., p. 105.

30. Augusteijn, 'Military conflict in the War of Independence', p. 354; David Fitzpatrick, 'The geography of Irish nationalism 1910–1921', in *Past & Present* 78 (February 1978), p. 121.

31. Leeson, *Black and Tans*, pp 195–7.

32. Shaw Desmond, *The Drama of Sinn Féin* (New York, 1923), pp 232, 282.

33. Leeson, *The Black and Tans*, pp 88–9; David Leeson, 'The "scum of London's underworld"? British recruits for the Royal Irish Constabulary, 1920–21', in *Contemporary British History* 17:1 (2003), pp 1–38; Ferriter, *A Nation and Not a Rabble*, p. 197.

34. *Manchester Guardian News Bulletin*, 6 Sept. 1920, reproduced in *The Liberal Magazine*, 28 Oct. 1920, p. 518; see also, Ferriter, *A Nation and Not a Rabble*, pp 201–5.

35. Kent, *Aftershocks*, pp 117–18.

36. 'An anti-reprisals agitation', *Irish Independent*, 13 Nov. 1920; 'Anti-reprisals crusade', *Freeman's Journal*, 16 Nov. 1920.

37. Bennett, *The Black and Tans*, p. 38.

38. For instance, William Sheehan explained clashes between soldiers and civilians in Cork and 'unofficial' reprisals as comprising 'an unofficial war … an almost primitive struggle for the possession of public space, and on occasion for the control of local women'. Sheehan, *A Hard Local War*, p. 24.

39. Macardle, *The Irish Republic*, p. 377.

40. *Cork Examiner*, 5 Nov. 1919; *Evening Herald*, 11 Nov. 1919; *Irish Independent*, 13 Nov. 1919; *Irish Bulletin*, 14 Nov. 1919.

41. Albert Coyle (Official Reporter to the Commission), *Evidence on Conditions in Ireland: Comprising Testimony, Affidavits and Exhibits Presented before The American Commission on Conditions in Ireland* (Washington, DC, 1921), p. 15.

42. Ibid.

43. *Evening Herald*, 21 Jan. 1920; Coyle, *Evidence on Conditions in Ireland*, p. 18.

44. *Evening Herald*, 21 Jan. 1920.

45. *Irish Independent*, 14 May 1920; *Freeman's Journal*, 15 May 1920.

46. *Fermanagh Herald*, 3 Apr. 1920; *Evening Echo*, 30 Mar. 1920; *The Liberator* (Tralee), 17 Apr. 1920; *Evening Herald*, 28 Apr. 1920.

47. *Kerry Weekly Reporter*, 29 May 1920.

48. James S. Donnelly, Jr, '"Unofficial" British reprisals and IRA provocations, 1919–20: The cases of three Cork towns', in *Éire-Ireland*, 45:1 (2010), p. 170, quoting *Cork Examiner*, 29 June 1920.

49. Ibid., p. 158, 170–1, 174, quoting *Irish Independent*, 16 Sept. 1919, and *Cork Examiner*, 29 June 1920.

50. *Cork Examiner*, 29 June 1920.

51. Pauline Murphy, 'The amazing story of General Lucas and his kidnapping by the IRA in Cork', *Irish Independent*, 27 June 2020.

52. *Cork Examiner*, 13 July 1920.

53. *Kerryman*, 24 July 1920. Tuam Rural District Council adjusted its claim and requested £71,951 from Dublin Castle to address the damage. *Irish Independent*, 18 Oct. 1920.

54. Coyle, *Evidence on Conditions in Ireland*, p. 408.

55. William Henry, *Blood for Blood: The Black and Tan War in Galway* (Cork, 2012), pp 67–8, 70.

56. 'Moral guidance for Rebels', *Belfast Newsletter*, 18 Sept. 1920.

57. *Cork Examiner*, 10 Aug. 1920; *Kerry Weekly Reporter*, 14 Aug. 1920. The *Offaly Independent* reported 200 soldiers were involved in the raid. *Offaly Independent*, 14 Aug. 1920.

58. *The Wicklow News-Letter and Arklow Reporter*, 21 Aug. 1920.

59. *Cork Examiner*, 23 Aug. 1920.
60. *Connacht Tribune*, 28 Aug. 1920.
61. *Skibbereen Eagle*, 28 Aug. 1920.
62. *Belfast Newsletter*, 30 Aug. 1920.
63. Hopkinson, *Irish War of Independence*, pp 59–61.
64. John Borgonovo and Gabriel Doherty, 'Smoking gun? British government policy and RIC reprisals, summer 1920', in *History Ireland*, 17:2 (March/April 2009).
65. Ibid.
66. 'RIC reprisals, summer 1920', David Fitzpatrick to Editors, *History Ireland* 17:3 (May/June 2009).
67. Report of The Labour Commission to Ireland (London, 1921), p. 33; see also, *Freemans Journal*, 25 June 1921.
68. *Westmeath Independent*, 11 Sept. 1920; *Irish Independent*, 18 Oct. 1920; *Anglo-Celt*, 25 Sept. 1920.
69. Macardle, *The Irish Republic*, p. 354.
70. Siniša Malešević, *The Sociology of War and Violence* (Cambridge, 2010), p. 66.
71. Carl Schmitt (trans. C. J. Miller), *Theory of the Partisan* (1962; 2021 edn), p. 60. Schmitt discusses the impacts of terror and counter-terror on social structures. While speaking the impacts of terrorism on greater fears, the example may be applied towards public outlook towards reprisals.
72. Malešević, *The Sociology of War and Violence*, pp 66–7.
73. Memo, George F. Hegarty, 25 Mar. 1938; Thomas Crofts to Frank Aiken, 11 Feb. 1938, Irish Military Archives, Military Service Pension Collection (Sp. G14).
74. Memo, Dr T. Donovan, 24 Mar. 1938, Irish Military Archives, Military Service Pension Collection (Sp. G14).
75. Maighread Bean Uí Luasa to Dept. of Defense, 6 Nov. 1940, Irish Military Archives, Military Service Pension Collection (Sp. G14).
76. In December 1920, Senator Norris interrogated John Charles Clarke on the effects of raids. See Coyle, 'Continuous terrorism causes nervous breakdowns', in *Evidence on Conditions in Ireland*, p. 710; see also, 'Worse than air raids', *Irish Independent*, 12 Nov. 1920.
77. *The Irish Bulletin* reported that 11 raids on Irish homes occurred in 1917, 260 in 1918, 13,782 in 1919, and as of March 1920, 1,239 raids had taken place. 'Sixty-five thousand raids for 1920?' *Irish Bulletin* 1, 16 Mar. 1920, p. 359. American Commission on Conditions in Ireland published: 'Summary of British atrocities' with 'Raids on private houses: 11 in 1917; 260 in 1918; 13,782 in 1919; 24,171 in 1920'. Coyle, *Evidence on Conditions in Ireland*, p. 1060.
78. Linda Connolly, 'Towards a further understanding of the sexual and gender-based violence women experienced in the Irish Revolution', in *Women and the Irish Revolution: Feminism, Activism, Violence* (Kildare, 2020), p. 103.
79. Various sources point to Crown force raids and interrogation tactics as a 'war on women and children'. Coyle, *Evidence on Conditions in Ireland*, pp 124, 1041.
80. Ibid., p. 531.
81. Malešević adds insight from A. D. Smith that societies at war 'require coherent and believable narratives' that easily distinguish between 'rational and irrational' forms of violence. Malešević, *The Sociology of War and Violence*. p. 67.
82. Cecilia M. Bailliet's article examining US forces in Iraq and the use of house raids as a counter-insurgency tactic speaks to parallels with raids during the Irish Revolution. Mainly, that 'the intrusion into private homes and the disruption of family life during house raids raises many concerns, as "war amongst the people" becomes even more intimately "war in the home".' Cecilia M. Bailliet, '"War in the home": An exposition of protection issues pertaining to the use of house raids in counterinsurgency operations', in *Journal of Military Ethics* 6:3 (2007), p. 174.
83. J. D. Porteous and S. Smith, *Domicide: The Global Destruction of Home* (Montreal, 2001), p. 12.
84. Christopher Harker, *Transactions of the Institute of British Geographers* 34:3 (July 2009), p. 324.
85. Katherine Brickell, 'Geopolitics of home', in *Geography Compass* 6:10 (2012), p. 575.
86. Alexander B. Murphy and Douglas L. Johnson, 'Introduction: Encounters with environment and place', in Murphy and Johnson (eds), *Cultural Encounters with the Environment: Enduring and Evolving Geographic Themes* (Lanham, 2000), pp 10–12.
87. Caitriona Clear, 'Chapter nine: Houses, food, clothes', in *Social Change and Everyday Life in Ireland, 1850–1922*, pp 142–58.

88. David Fitzpatrick, 'The price of Balbriggan', pp 75–101. For an exploration of meaning attached to physical spaces and objects, see Phillip L. Wagner and Marvin Mikesell, 'Cultural encounters with the environment', in Phillip L. Wagner and Marvin Mikesell (eds), *Readings in Cultural Geography* (Chicago, 1962) pp 3–4, 9–10.
89. Statistics compiled from reprinted editions of the *Irish Bulletin* volume 1, 12 July 1919–1 May 1920 (Cork, 2012); volume 2, 3 May 1920–31 Aug.1920 (Belfast, 2014); and volume 3, 1 Sept. 1920–1 Jan. 1921 (Belfast, 2015).
90. Statement of Cait O'Callaghan, BMH, WS 688, p. 9.
91. Statement of Cait O'Callaghan, BMH, WS 688, p. 16.
92. Ibid. pp 17–18.
93. 'The Limerick military inquiry', *Irish Independent*, 15 Mar. 1921.
94. Justin Dolan Stover, 'Families, vulnerability and sexual violence during the Irish Revolution', in Jennifer Evans and Ciara Meehan (eds), *Perceptions of Pregnancy from the Seventeenth to the Twentieth Century* (Switzerland, 2017), pp 57–75; statement of Joseph Lawless, BMH, WS 1043, p. 157.
95. Lindsey Earner-Byrne and Diane Urquhart, 'Gender roles in Ireland since 1740', in Eugenio F. Biagini and Mary E. Daly (eds), *The Cambridge Social History of Modern Ireland* (Cambridge, 2017) pp 312–14.
96. Statement of Michael Hayes, BMH, WS 1173, p. 14.
97. Margaret Ward, *Unmanageable Revolutionaries: Women and Irish Nationalism* (London, 1989; 1995 edn), p. 143.
98. On significance of the hen run comment: 'Built environments also deal with settings greater than the level of scale of buildings. Spaces immediately adjacent to buildings can facilitate or hinder a great number of human activities, some desired (e.g., social interaction, children's play, car parking, gardening) and others mostly to be avoided (e.g., crime, noise, disorder, pollution). As with other settings, the design, control and distribution of such spaces is part of a social process (Gehl, 1987). Furthermore, spaces external to buildings but relevant to them extend outwards – sometimes quite far. The pattern of usage of the block (or other defined space on which a building is located) is typically the next greater scale of human relevance, but neighborhoods and communities are vital referents as well.' Riley E. Dunlap and William Michelson (eds), *Handbook of Environmental Sociology* (Westport, Connecticut: Greenwood Press, 2002), p. 4.
99. Statement of Mary Clancy, BMH, WS 806, pp 9–11.
100. The 'demoralising effects of coercion, repression, and reprisals' in Tralee later that autumn, where residents were subjected to 'petty tyranny', made to 'denounce the Pope, to spit on photographs of Mr. de Valera'. Report of The Labour Commission to Ireland, pp 31, 33.
101. Statement of Mary Clancy, BMH, WS 806, p. 11.
102. Stover, 'Families, vulnerability and sexual violence during the Irish Revolution', pp 66–7; statement of Robert Brennan, BMH, WS 779 (section 3), p. 593; '"Where is he?" Residence of Mr. R. Brennan raided – Also Dr. Kathleen Lynn's', *Sunday Independent*, 29 Feb. 1920.
103. Patrick J. Duffy, *Exploring the History and Heritage of Irish Landscapes* (Dublin, 2007), pp 210–11.
104. Erskine Childers, 'What it means to women', in *Military Rule in Ireland: A Series of Eight Articles Contributed to The Daily News March–May 1920* (Dublin, 1920), p. 9; see also, 'A night of terror', *Offaly Independent*, 24 Jan. 1920; 'Lorries disturb the silence of the night in Dublin and the South', *Freeman's Journal*, 2 Feb. 1920; 'Galway residents' alarming experience', *Freeman's Journal*, 28 Oct. 1920; 'Reprisals and promise of more', *Irish Independent*, 5 Nov. 1920.
105. Jan Plamper, *The History of Emotions: An Introduction* (Oxford University Press, 2015), p. 35.
106. Childers, *Military Rule in Ireland*, p. 6.
107. *Irish Independent*, 30 Sept. 1920
108. Robert Lynd, '"Hellish reprisals" in Ireland' (London: Liberal Publication Department; Roberts and Leete, Ltd, October 1920), n.p.; see also, 'Wake up, American editors!', in *News Letter of the Friends of Irish Freedom National Bureau of Information* 2:17 (October 1920), p. 3.
109. *Irish Independent*, 24 Sept. 1920.
110. Ferriter, *A Nation and Not a Rabble*, p. 196–7, citing Sean O'Casey, *Autobiographies: Volume 2* (London, 1980), pp 40–1.
111. 'The results of the Government's policy (1): The health of the people', Report of the Labour Commission to Ireland, p.54.

112. Contemporary references to St Vitus' dance appear in the press, principally in medical advertisements for rheumatism relief and nerve pain. There is a reference in the BMH witness statements to men on the run contracting scabies and 'scratching themselves as if they had St. Vitus dance'. Statement of Patrick J. Casey, BMH, WS 1148, p. 15(b).
113. William Michelson and Willem van Vliet, 'Theory and the sociological study of the built environment', in Riley E. Dunlap and William Michelson (eds), *Handbook of Environmental Sociology* (Westport, Connecticut, 2002), p. 83; see also, Sherry Ahrentzen, 'Socio-behavioral qualities of the built environment', in ibid., p. 116.
114. Martin Coward, 'Against anthropocentrism: The destruction of the built environment as a distinct form of political violence', in *Review of International Studies* 32:3 (2006), pp 421–3.
115. Ferriter, *A Nation and Not a Rabble*, p. 187, quoting *Freeman's Journal*, 23 Jan. 1919.
116. Department of Agriculture and Technical Instruction to Chief Secretary, 20 Nov. 1919, NAI (92/2/337); *Freeman's Journal*, 6 Nov. 1919.
117. *The Nationalist* (Tipperary), 22 Nov. 1919.
118. James Dwyer to Under Secretary for Ireland, 3 Dec. 1919, NAI (92/2/337); 'The suppression of markets in many places has increased Ireland's economic troubles and inflicted serious injury, particularly upon the peasant population.' Report of the Labour Commission to Ireland, p. 55.
119. Mr G. de L. Willis to H. J. Barrie, Board of Agriculture, 18 Nov. 1919; statement adopted at a meeting held in Ennis, 4 Nov. 1919, NAI (92/2/337); 'The Clare protest', *Irish Independent*, 8 Dec. 1919.
120. Macardle, *Irish Republic*, p. 377.
121. James J. Kennelly, 'The "dawn of the practical": Horace Plunkett and the cooperative movement', in *New Hibernia Review* 12:1 (Spring 2008), p. 63; see also, Cyril Ehrlich, 'Sir Horace Plunkett and agricultural reform', in J. M. Goldstrom and L. A. Clarkson (eds), *Irish Population, Economy, and Society: Essays in Honour of the Late K. H. Connell* (Oxford, 1981), pp 274–6; see also, Crowley, Ó Drisceoil, Murphy (eds) and Borgonovo (associate ed.), *Atlas of the Irish Revolution*, p. 108.
122. Report of the Irish Agricultural Organisation Society for the year ending 31 March 1921 (Dublin: IAWS Printing Department, 1922), pp 52–69.
123. Andy Bielenberg, *Ireland and the Industrial Revolution: The Impact of the Industrial Revolution on Irish Industry, 1801–1922* (New York, 2009; 2014 edn), p. 75.
124. F. M. Carroll, 'The American Committee for Relief in Ireland, 1920–22', in *Irish Historical Studies* 23:89 (May 1982), p. 33.
125. Allen, 'National reconstruction', p. 128.
126. George Russell, 'AE', 'A plea for justice: Being a demand for a public enquiry into the attacks on co-operative societies in Ireland', in *The Irish Homestead* (Dublin, 1920), p. 2.
127. Reproduced in *The Nationalist* (Tipperary), 4 Dec. 1920.
128. *Irish Independent*, 10 Jan. 1921.
129. Proinnsias Breathnach, 'Creamery attacks', in Crowley, Ó Drisceoil, Murphy (eds) and Borgonovo (associate ed.), *Atlas of the Irish Revolution*, p. 555.
130. *Irish Homestead*, 28 Aug. 1920.
131. Cyril Ehrlich, 'Sir Horace Plunkett and agricultural reform', p. 281.
132. F. M. Carroll, 'The American Committee for Relief in Ireland, 1920–22', p. 33; see also, President's Address [Sir Horace Plunkett], 'Minutes of the Annual General Meeting of the Irish Agricultural Organisation Society, Limited', held 23 Mar. 1921, in *Report of the Irish Agricultural Organisation Society, Ltd. For the Year ending 31 March 1920* (Dublin: IAWS Printing Department, 1921), p. 46.
133. Ibid., p. 44.
134. *Evening Echo*, 22 Sept. 1920; *Belfast Newsletter*, 10 Sept. 1920; *Freeman's Journal*, 22 Sept. 1920; *Irish Independent*, 27 Sept. 1920.
135. *Belfast Newsletter*, 11 Sept. 1920.
136. Fitzpatrick, 'The price of Balbriggan', pp 75–101, and Ross O'Mahony, 'The sack of Balbriggan and tit-for-tat terror', in David Fitzpatrick (ed.), *Terror in Ireland* (Dublin, 2012), pp 58–74.
137. Gerard Noonan, *The IRA in Britain, 1919–1923: 'In the Heart of Enemy Lines'* (Liverpool, 2014), p. 139; O'Mahony, 'The sack of Balbriggan and tit-for-tat terror', p. 64.
138. Fitzpatrick, 'The price of Balbriggan', p. 85.
139. *Belfast Newsletter*, 22 Sept. 1920.

140. *Evening Echo*, 24 Sept. 1920.
141. *Drogheda Independent*, 2 Oct. 1920.
142. Ibid., 25 Sept. 1920; ibid., 16 Oct. 1920.
143. *Irish Independent*, 23 Sept. 1920.
144. Bennett, *The Black and Tans*, p. 94
145. 'The Bould Black an' Tans', n.d., Pamphlets, Songs and Ballads, 1914–1922, NLI (IR 82104 p1).
146. For American commission on conditions in Ireland on Balbriggan, see 'Destruction of a factory brings destitution', in Coyle, *Evidence on Conditions in Ireland*, pp 92–111.
147. Fitzpatrick, 'The price of Balbriggan', pp 79, 81.
148. *Offaly Independent*, 25 Sept. 1920; O'Mahony, 'The sack of Balbriggan and tit-for-tat terror', p. 58; Jon Lawrence, 'Forging a peaceable kingdom: War, violence, and fear of brutalization in post-First World War Britain', in *The Journal of Modern History* 75:3 (September, 2003), p. 577; 'The Balbriggan horrors!', *Drogheda Independent*, 25 Sept. 1920; *Irish Independent*, 30 Sept. 1920, which notes coverage of Balbriggan in the French press.
149. Crown forces responded to IRA activity in Cork, Meath and Wexford in late September. Following a raid on the barracks at Trim, Volunteers promised the residents there that they would protect the town from retaliation. However, when the police showed up in the wake of the raid, two men were shot and killed, and the police destroyed property valued at an estimated £50,000. See Dublin Castle outrage reports, TNA (CO 904/149); *Meath Chronicle*, 8 Jan. 1921; *Westmeath Independent*, 2 Oct. 1920; Noonan, *The IRA in Britain, 1919–1923*, p. 139.
150. John Dorney, 'The sack of Balbriggan and British reprisals in Ireland in Autumn 1920', *The Irish Story*, 14 Oct. 2020, https://www.theirishstory.com/2020/10/14/the-sack-of-balbriggan-and-british-reprisals-in-ireland-in-autumn-1920/, accessed 9 October 2022.
151. *Irish Independent*, 30 Sept. 1920.
152. *Freeman's Journal*, 11 Feb. 1924.
153. *Irish Independent*, 30 Sept. 1920.
154. *Irish Independent*, 30 Sept. 1920.
155. Macardle, *Irish Republic*, pp 377–8.
156. *Irish Independent*, 30 Sept. 1920.
157. Coyle, *Evidence on Conditions in Ireland*, p. 913. Dempsey described the Seventeenth Lancers as being 'like demons in the town. Those of us who remained in the town did not think that human nature could descend to the depths that they did that night.' Ibid., p. 512.
158. Ibid., p. 590.
159. *Cork Constitution*, 30 Sept. 1920; Donnelly, '"Unofficial" British reprisals and IRA provocations', p. 184.
160. Donnelly, '"Unofficial" British Reprisals and IRA Provocations', p. 182; Coyle, *Evidence on Conditions in Ireland*, p. 915; *Irish Independent*, 1 Oct. 1920.
161. Rev. M. D. Forrest, *Atrocities in Ireland: What an Australian Has Seen* (Sydney: The Irish Nationalist Association of New South Wales, 1920), p. 12.
162. Testimony of Miss Ellen C. Wilkinson, Coyle, *Evidence on Conditions in Ireland*, p, 590.
163. Statistics compiled from Dublin Castle outrage reports, TNA (CO 904/149–150).
164. Leeson, *Black and Tans*, pp 170–3.
165. *Freeman's Journal*, 2 Oct. 1920.
166. 'During the period Oct. 31 to Nov. 10 the aggregate loss in life and destruction of property far exceeds anything of a similar character for the same period in any other part of Ireland.' *Irish Independent*, 12 Nov. 1920.
167. *The Struggle of the Irish People: Address to the Congress of the United States, Adopted at the January Session of Dáil Éireann, 1921*, pp 15–18; Gerry White and Brendan O'Shea, *The Burning of Cork* (Cork, 2006), passim 68– 103; see also, 'Sabotage', *Irish Bulletin* summary for week ending 4 Dec. 1920, pp 11, 14.
168. John Borgonovo, *Spies, Informers and the 'Anti-Sinn Féin Society': The Intelligence War in Cork City 1920–1921* (Dublin, 2007), p. 37.
169. Cork enquiry: supplementary report by General Tudor, TNA (CO 904/150), pp 17–18.
170. 'Retrospect and Forecast', 'Jacques', *Irish Independent*, 18 Dec. 1920.
171. Reproduced in the *Irish Independent*, 13 Dec. 1920.

172. *Freeman's Journal*, 15 Dec. 1920.
173. 'Retrospect and forecast', 'Jacques', *Irish Independent*, 18 Dec. 1920.
174. Borgonovo, *Spies, Informers and the 'Anti-Sinn Féin Society'*, pp 37–8; Leeson, *Black and Tans*, p. 173; Ferriter, *A Nation and Not a Rabble*, p. 198.
175. *Evening Echo*, 13 Dec. 1920.
176. Reproduced in the *Irish Independent*, 14 Dec. 1920.
177. *Cork Examiner*, 29 Dec. 1920.
178. *Cork Examiner*, 18 Apr. 1921.
179. Leeson, 'The burning of Cork', in Crowley, Ó Drisceoil, Murphy (eds) and Borgonovo (associate ed.), *Atlas of the Irish Revolution*, p. 382.
180. Hopkinson, *The Irish War of Independence*, p. 93.
181. Strickland signed these Proclamations on 27 December 1920. *Freeman's Journal*, 4 Jan. 1921; 'Three proclamations', *Skibbereen Eagle*, 8 Jan. 1921.
182. 'A terrible expedient', *Irish Independent*, 5 Jan. 1921.
183. 'Only inflaming the wound', *Freeman's Journal*, 7 May 1921.
184. *Irish Independent*, 18 May 1921.

CHAPTER FIVE

CULTIVATING ENVIRONMENTAL VICTIMHOOD IN IRELAND AND ABROAD

INTRODUCTION

Preaching in Balham, London, in October 1920, Reverend Norbert Jones (CRL) paused his sermon to request prayers for Ireland. Jones, an Englishman, was a veteran prelate engaged in preserving the Church's social conservatism.[1] In 1908, he penned a stalwart defence of *Pascendi dominici gregis*, Pope Pius X's anti-modernist encyclical reproving progressivism and Catholic secularism.[2] He was assigned to Eltham in 1913, and would remain in the Diocese of Southwark, in south London, throughout the Great War.[3] Like most, Reverend Jones was daily exposed to the war's devastating impacts in some form or another. Intimately, through the thousands of Belgian refugees who were driven from their homes in autumn 1914 and resettled in London and beyond, and peripherally, through newspaper reports and government reports of 'alleged German outrages' that included destroyed homes and eviscerated landscapes throughout Belgium and France.[4] Such publicity, coupled with the Allies' orchestrated framing of 'Belgium' as 'shorthand for the moral issues of the war' between 1914 and 1918 – particularly as it pertained to the violation of neutrality and the atrocities committed against churches and civilians – may have prompted Reverend Jones to contextualise the Irish experience in 1920 as he did, and appeal for prayers.[5] 'The other day I was shown some pictures,' he told the parish,

> And [I] exclaimed 'The Hun in Belgium,' but, my God, when I looked closer, it was not Belgium – it was not the German Hun – but Ireland, and the work of the Black and Tans. Does it not make you ashamed that this is done by those bearing commission from the country in which we live?[6]

Jones' rhetorical question may have fallen upon a sympathetic congregation. The Irish Self-Determination League of Great Britain had a strong membership in south London, particularly the neighbourhoods of Balham, Tooting and Clapham.[7] His impression, however, resonated beyond a local autumn Mass. Irish dailies mobilised Jones' statement, which in turn echoed a litany of appraisals that articulated destruction, loss and civil distress in Ireland as akin to wartime Belgium's universally recognised suffering.[8]

Damaged landscapes were instrumental in articulating Ireland's unique victim narrative, which situated the Irish revolutionary experience within a broader Great War context. Alongside political arguments that identified the concept of self-determination as applicable to Ireland as it was to Poland, Schleswig and Alsace-Lorraine, Crown reprisals against Irish cities, small towns and individual homesteads between 1919 and 1921 produced Ireland's own *regions dévastées*, writ small.[9] Comparisons to war-torn Belgium and France underemphasised significantly disproportional levels of destruction. Still, terror in

Ireland presented a *moral* equivalent.[10] Headlines that read 'Ireland like Belgium in 1914' flipped a familiar narrative that had demonised German military conduct at the outbreak of the Great War.[11] Arousing memory of war atrocities in this way cultivated sympathy and charity for the Irish cause, as well as condemnation of Crown forces and the British Government.[12] Various sources presented analogies that paired revolutionary Ireland with wartime Belgium and occupied France, which featured individual observations, Great War veterans' evaluations, political committee reports and survey work performed by various relief societies. This chapter illustrates how familiar observations of the Great War communicated environmental destruction and displacement during the Irish Revolution. It shows that memorable narratives of German atrocities in Belgium governed the context and presentation of Crown force terror and reprisals in Ireland. This behaviour was widely documented and proportionately devastating, as the previous chapter showed. Its occurrence within a broader period framework of terror and barbarism cultivated emotional responses, amplified a sense of allied hypocrisy and bolstered the independence movement in Ireland and abroad.

Crafting Victimhood

The Great War provided context for Dubliners attempting to process the Easter Rising. Since August 1914, newspaper editorials, pictorials and propaganda had conveyed the experience of war and destruction, with the sinking of the *Lusitania* and the *Leinster*, the despoiling of small, Catholic Belgium and the murder of Edith Cavell serving as atrocity propaganda to aid recruiting efforts in Ireland.[13] Easter Week 1916 brought select experiences home, and comparisons with war-torn Europe began almost immediately. 'Soldiers amongst us who have served abroad,' James Stephens explained, 'say that the ruin of this quarter is more complete than anything they have seen at Ypres, than anything they have seen anywhere in France or Flanders.'[14] National newspapers that carried the Rising outside Dublin mirrored observations on the ground and exhibited the Capital, a young Frank O'Connor recalled, 'as they showed Belgian cities destroyed by the Germans, as smoking ruins inhabited by men with rifles and machine guns'.[15] The parallel carried beyond broken buildings. The British response was criticised as not merely reproducing the landscape of war-torn Belgium – a 'Louvain by the Liffey' – but of practising the very methods it had previously condemned as German barbarism.[16]

Nationalists applied several victim narratives to Ireland between 1916 and 1921, but two in particular illustrate the types of moral outrage that observers, propagandists and diplomats wished to ignite in readers, international audiences and foreign governments. First, the brief but concentrated destruction of Dublin in 1916 was widely compared to contemporary devastation in Europe. State-directed, large-scale damage to the urban built landscape resurfaced in Ireland in 1920, when both sanctioned and rogue reprisals against Irish guerrillas and civilians prompted a comparison with occupied Belgium and northern France and, in the eyes of many, British Army commanders with Prussian warlords.

The second approach gained momentum during the Great War and proceeded throughout the War of Independence. Post-war recognition and establishment of various autonomous, ethnic and cultural nation-states in eastern and central Europe, founded upon the Wilsonian peace settlement, contrasted Ireland's political and cultural bondage, seen as a violation of the concept of self-determination and the rights of small nations for which the war had been ostensibly fought. In this way, distinct themes of victimhood – environmental and political – aligned to more completely present Ireland's injustice within the framework of the Great War, its subjugation reminiscent of occupied France and Belgium. However, the delicate post-war Anglo-Franco-American relationship often complicated Irish nationalists' attempts to portray wartime destruction on the continent to counter-revolutionary persecution in Ireland. At times, Irish republican attacks on hallowed veterans and public figures and disruption of victory parades stalled, and even reversed, efforts to mobilise sympathy behind the Irish independence movement. Nevertheless, the extent of Ireland's damaged landscapes, corroborated by numerous witnesses and recorded in the minutes of various relief societies, positioned its persecution within the wider war narrative. This continued after the war, as formerly embedded wartime correspondents reflected on the previous years and reinforced the concept of German barbarism. Homer Folks, who organised and directed the Department of Civil Affairs of the American Red Cross in France, described the rebuilding process in Louvain: 'The walls of the great university stand, but there are nothing but walls.' Digression was unnecessary when describing the towns, cities and regions that many readers had come to know throughout the war. 'The ruins of Ypres have been made familiar to the entire world,' Folks continued. 'The regions of Messines, Wulerghem, Locre, Demmel, Dranoutre, names which the world read with a sinking heart in the spring of 1918, represent regions of complete destruction.'[17] Alternatively, the brief Russian occupation of east Prussia and the German civilians who suffered under it failed to offset perceptions of an exclusively German 'barbarism'. King Leopold II's brutal imperialism in the Congo, which Irish humanitarian Roger Casement exposed in 1904, also failed to challenge what the *Nation* and other newspapers portrayed as 'The rules of Huns and Bashi-Bazouks.'[18]

Far from a unique program, Irish nationalists essentially implemented the techniques of wartime propagandists and political cartoonists, such as the Dutch artist Louis Raemaekers, whose illustrations 'made intensely clear to the people the single issue upon which the war [was] joined'.[19] John Horne and Alan Kramer described the process more broadly:

> The [German] 'atrocities' permitted a sense of national victimhood to be derived from the fate of individual people and places in three ways. First was the exposure of women, children and families to the brutality of the invader. Second was the destruction of localities. Third was the need for remembrance of the invasion while the war was still in progress. All three dimensions provided ways of defining the national community in terms of suffering and outrage.[20]

Newspaper articles, parliamentary memos and relief commission reports identified and highlighted destruction and terror in Ireland as it occurred. However, press censorship and suppression in Ireland often limited distribution. From 1919, members of the separatist Sinn Féin Party and Dáil Eireann, the alternative Irish parliament formed in the wake of the 1918 General Election, pushed to counter British propaganda and to internationalise Ireland's suffering and claim to nationhood 'within the context of the emerging post-First World War world' through their own small newspaper, the *Irish Bulletin*.[21] Directed from Sinn Féin's Department of Propaganda, the *Irish Bulletin* synthesised various reports and editorials on the Irish situation, and habitually framed the British Army in Ireland within the context of the German Army in Belgium. Ian Kenneally presented the *Irish Bulletin*'s governing narrative more directly: 'The whole policy of the British Government was portrayed as one of destruction aimed at the Irish people.'[22]

This characterisation extended beyond narratives highlighting physical destruction to sensationalise the general militarisation of Irish society. For instance, following an unsuccessful attack on the Lord Lieutenant, Sir John French, in December 1920, the *Catholic Herald* explained French's role in Ireland as 'that of [General Moritz] von Bissing in Belgium or of the Germans in Alsace Lorraine or of the Turk in Armenia or of the Austrian in Poland'.[23] So infamous was von Bissing, the Governor-General of occupied Belgium during the war, that his name was synonymous with tyranny and oppression representative of the collective Central Powers. Comparisons to von Bissing appeared in Ireland as early as 1916, contributing to atrocity propaganda that presented the invasion of Belgium as defiling international sovereignty.[24] By 1920, martial law, incendiary reprisals, fines imposed on Irish civilians for dissent and the alleged use of human shields provided the *Evening Herald* and the *Irish Independent* with evidence that 'the South of Ireland' was 'being rapidly assimilated to that of Belgium during the German occupation' – suppression 'faithfully copied from the von Bissing precedent'.[25]

The press also reframed familiar wartime tragedies in order to amplify the destruction of Irish towns. Tuam was rechristened the Irish Aerschot, Balbriggan the Irish Louvain. The *Drogheda Independent* projected that at the current pace, 'Ireland will soon be a desolation as complete and terrible as the battle-plains of France and Belgium after five years of fearful war.'[26] British reprisals tipped Irish victimisation beyond equal comparison: while the Germans had 'only aimed at terrorism', one observer clarified, the Black and Tans destroyed 'for mere destructions sake'.[27] Britain's *Daily News* complemented the motif, compounding criticism that had been recently raised in both houses of Parliament. In November 1920, it published a soldier's account that described the deliberate persecution of Irish civilians, noting that 'Such a letter might almost be dated "Belgium, 1914".'[28] The following month, London's *Daily Telegraph* described Cork City, which had suffered large-scale damage in December, as 'an exact reproduction of the shattered towns in Flanders'.[29] Urbain Falaize went further. Writing for *L'Echo de la Loire*, a regional paper published in western France, he explained that Cork's experience had no parallel save in Germany's occupation during the war. A longer view showed Cork to have few parallels in contemporary French history:

> In 1870 the Germans did not burn the villages suspected of sheltering the *Francs-Tireurs*. They were careful, at least, to see that the individuals whom they made scape-goats underwent a semblance of a trial. In Ireland, the famous Black and Tans, the British auxiliary police, are not bound by any such scruples. When one of their men has been the victim of an Irish exploit, they attack the village or the city where it has taken place, and, like veritable bandits, they burn, pillage and kill.[30]

Irish destruction continued to be validated against the Great War, but some claimed it surpassed this standard. In October 1920, Arthur Griffith informed the House of Lords that 'terrorism and destruction' in Ireland was in *excess* of that experienced in Belgium.[31] The Rt Rev. Bishop Shannon, Rector at the Catholic University of America in Washington, DC, likened the burning of Cork City to pagan indulgence, an accusation of 'barbarism' in its own right. This 'saturnalia of murder and arson and loot', he told *New York World* readers, surpassed 'in grim horror and fierce injustice the crime of Louvain'.[32] The Lord Mayor of Cork, Donal O'Callaghan, habitually framed military and police outrages in Ireland as 'far more terrible and far more cruel' than those alleged against Germany in Belgium.[33] His ad hoc testimony to the American Commission on Conditions in Ireland – a body composed of influential American politicians, philanthropists, businessmen, journalists and religious authorities – were greatly editorialised. In January 1921, Michael Francis Doyle, a Philadelphia-born lawyer attached to the Commission, challenged O'Callaghan to demonstrate a claim that the number of Irish towns destroyed in a 12-month period (90) exceeded those wrecked in Belgium over a similar period of time.[34]

> Mr. Doyle: Have you tried to compare the campaign of the British authorities in Ireland with the campaign of the German military authorities in Belgium? For instance, the destruction of towns; second, the service of notice such as was served at Louvain; third, the killing of priests and the taking of bishops as hostages; then the destruction of large cities, and so on? Have you made that comparison, and have you prepared any data showing how they did apparently along the same line?
>
> A [O'Callaghan]: No, sir, I have not done anything of that kind. Of course, it seems to me, and I think it is perfectly clear, that very few people believe that all the crimes and atrocities alleged, and news of what was disseminated during the period, did take place. That I think is pretty universally doubted now.
>
> Q. Chairman [L. Hollingsworth] Wood: You have no personal method or special opportunity of making this comparison, have you?
>
> A. No, sir.[35]

Despite O'Callaghan's implausible evaluation, his testimony provided the Commission invaluable insights into Ireland's revolutionary experience. Less sensational assessments also held value. The American Society of Friends, which toured Ireland between 12 February and 31 March 1921, framed its report on distress and destruction in Ireland proportionately. 'The destruction of buildings in 150 towns in so small a country as Ireland,' it suggested, 'is relatively as serious as the destruction of buildings in 5,000 towns and villages would be in so large a country as the United States.'[36] With the exception of Serbia, Belgium's Great War experience was unequal even in a proportional sense, and claims to equivalent or excessive physical destruction in Ireland were gratuitous. On the whole, the Irish independence lobby mobilised Belgium as a moral parallel, which would invalidate prior sensationalism of German barbarism in Belgium unless it be similarly observed of Crown forces in Ireland.

It is unclear whether proponents of Irish-Belgian parity really believed their own claims. Journalists certainly positioned Ireland within the broader transnational experience of war damage and displacement with the knowledge that their words would travel beyond Ireland, aid fundraising and influence international recognition for Irish independence.[37] But Ireland's victim narrative also underlines a distinct post-Versailles attempt to highlight British hypocrisy towards the principle of self-determination of small nations and its condemnation of militarism throughout the war. Criticism of German, Austrian and Ottoman war methods, treatment of prisoners and management of occupied territory propped Britain's claim to have entered and conducted the war on higher moral grounds. However, opponents identified the coalition government as embodying the very militarism it had fought to destroy. Outbreaks in Thurles, Arklow, Fermoy, Tuam and Cork throughout 1920 appeared to invalidate the British Government's denunciations of 'the Louvain horror' as lip service.[38] 'When Belgian bishops and priests and people raised their voices against Prussian domination they were heroes in English eyes,' recalled the Most Rev. Dr O'Doherty, Bishop of Clonfert; 'anyone who protests against quite as brutal a domination here is regarded as a traitor.'[39] The issue risked eroding British political capital throughout the Empire and the world. This was particularly important in North America, where established bases of Irish nationalist activism had mobilised. British policy in Ireland was criticised in the mainstream American press, carried through localised metaphors. 'If Ireland is to be crushed down by the iron heel of British militarism,' *The Baltimore Sun* observed, 'the army should be strong enough to do its work according to the regular military code, and not according to the code of Mexican banditti.'[40] The *Manchester Guardian* predicted that Britain's draconian methods would embolden its enemies abroad and diminish its moral standing in the eyes of the world:

> While we have all been leading the world in talk about security for Armenians and freedom for little Belgium we have ourselves drifted into a position where our criminal failure to govern a conquered white people stinks in the nostrils of the world worse than any other contemporary scandal or misgovernment.[41]

In essence, conveying Ireland's subdual as that experienced in France and Belgium during the First World War made for powerful, if at times fanciful reporting.

Reporting Militarised Environments

Post-war editorials paired the destruction of Irish urban and rural landscapes within Belgian and French precedents, but everyday militarism had permeated into Irish life in other ways. This included emergency peacekeeping legislation, expanded home raids, reprisals, internment, reinforced barracks and commandeered buildings, and martial law. As observed in Chapter Two, nationalist political symbols and demonstrations also altered public space and the landscape it comprised. Crown force militarism sought to reclaim those spaces through methods that again recalled wartime tyranny.

The British Government expanded its military presence in Ireland without a formal declaration of war. This comprised an increase in personnel, equipment and military behaviour that effectively hybridised Irish environments as militarised civilian spaces.[42] The IRA's steady campaign of home invasion, ambush and assassination complemented this atmosphere to create and maintain tension and anxiety.[43] The same can be said of the IRA's attempts to superimpose republican security, finance and justice over existing British models.[44] In many places, the presence or absence of police and military forces communicated the degree to which an area had been militarised. Soldiers stationed in urban areas and concentrated in select rural districts removed any ambiguity of Britain's commitment to restore order. The process intensified in the late spring and throughout the summer of 1920. In her seminal work *The Irish Republic*, Dorothy Macardle described soldiers 'in war equipment' clustered at railway stations; throughout Dublin, there was an ever-present network of regular soldiers, Auxiliaries, Black and Tans, Dublin Metropolitan Policemen, plain clothes cops and G Division detectives.[45] The presence of war material and security barriers restricted space and reconstituted the urban environments into militarised landscapes. Sandbagged and barbed-wired buildings, commandeered houses,[46] curfew, checkpoints and ever-present soldiers formed impressions of 'militarism' in Ireland and populated its own reporting category within the *Irish Bulletin*. Subtle adornments, such as lattice wire installed in windows,[47] soon expanded to guileless assertions of military clout. Lorries full of imported soldiers replaced bicycle patrols by local police, shaking houses as they rumbled down the street.[48] 'Tanks and motor lorries are now the commonest sight on country roads,' the *Freeman's Journal* reported in February 1920, 'and Ireland is dragooned even more thoroughly than General von Bissing dragooned Belgium.'[49] Dublin-born Joseph Henry Longford, Emeritus Professor of Japanese Studies at the University of London, informed the *Fortnightly Review* in 1919: 'There is military domination in Ireland of which, to find a parallel, we must go to Alsace before the war – or even to Belgium under Prussian rule.'[50] Great War veterans deployed in Ireland also noted its increasingly militarised atmosphere. Soldiers stationed in Tipperary claimed to have observed greater militarism in Ireland during their time there 'than they had seen in Belgium during the German occupation'.[51] Major Henry Kelly assessed the Irish situation from his credibility as a Victoria Cross recipient. He informed a public meeting in Manchester that 'the state of affairs in Ireland was worse than the worst years of the German occupation in Belgium, and far worse than was in any part of Italy under the Austrians. [...] There was worse militarism in Ireland than there was in Belgium under the Germans.'[52]

Low-ranking active soldiers often provided more grounded impressions of daily militarism in Ireland. J. P. Swindlehurst, a private with the Lancashire Fusiliers, arrived in Dublin in January 1921. His diary records many of the ways the city had morphed into a militarised environment and its impact on civilians and soldiers. For instance, Swindlehurst noted that, when not walking around 'like miniature arsenals', the Black and Tans dashed about Dublin 'in cars with wirenetting covers at all hours of the day and night, bent on some raid, reprisal, or the capture of some Sinn Féiners'. Hundreds of social and precautionary formalities governed safety on patrol, he wrote. Soldiers were instructed to beware of Irish 'Colleens', who would attempt to distract, stall and mislead them; helmets were to be worn at all times to protect against projectiles, specifically empty Guinness bottles.

> We have a rumour going the rounds, that the favourite joke of the Irishmen, it's to get you to stand a bottle of Guinness, drink your health, and then crash you on the head with the empty bottle. We now know what the rifles and other warlike equipment which have been issued, are for.[53]

The presence of soldiers also modified civilian behaviour. Hands were to be held out of pockets in public, Swindlehurst recalled. 'It's a bad day for the one who doesn't or forgets, he most likely will find himself looking down a machine gun from the patrols or an automatic of the C.I.D. [Criminal Investigation Department].' Such an atmosphere disturbed Dublin in many ways, imposing individual and collective trauma amongst civilians. Swindlehurst saw anxiety in people's faces and uncertainty in their movements. 'We were on the main street when a lorry backfired,' he recalled, 'and instinctively people dodged into doorways, some stood still, but it just shows, that the greater part of the population are living in a reign of terror.'[54] Though fewer in number and generally imitative of other descriptions, veterans' assessments lent a certain element of validity to broader observations of militarism in Ireland, strengthened by their first-hand experience.

Reactionary, defensive measures were often taken to reinforce and protect conflict sites such as barracks, police stations and government offices, but Irish environments were also pre-emptively militarised in anticipation of conflict or civil disorder, at times with repurposed natural features. For instance, sand from Merrion Strand filled the bags that barricaded sections of Dublin, defensive fronts that manufactured 'suspense and anxiety for all law-abiding citizens as well as for the authorities' before the 1920 Easter holiday.[55] Soldiers fortified Dublin again the following year, observing 'military operations on a scale unprecedented since 1916'. A half-square-mile perimeter was established around the Four Courts area, with barricades, barbed wire and sentries effectively cutting off the area. Tanks and armoured cars patrolled surrounding streets, above which the military installed machine guns in the upper rooms of houses and atop their roofs. The *Irish Independent* described 'a wall of steel' around the inner city.[56]

Military barricades also deterred confrontation during the Orange Order marching season. Sandbagged gun positions and checkpoints were erected on approach to Armagh in July 1920, where soldiers interrogated travellers bound for Ulster.[57] Trenches, sandbag forts and troop huts constructed along the River Foyle in Londonderry suggested more permanent military presence within the walled city, which had recently experienced civil unrest.[58]

Critics observed Ireland's militarisation as wilfully ignorant of populist resistance throughout history.[59] The *Freeman's Journal* recommended that Coalition Prime Minister David Lloyd George and General Macready learn Napoleon's lesson, 'that above the individual, there is a nation'.[60] Nationalist sentiment aroused in Germany and Spain during the Napoleonic Wars, the House of Commons was reminded in June 1921, 'broke Napoleon, and it has broken already the Chief Secretary for Ireland'.[61] As one Great War veteran observed, Ireland was immune to the 'doctrines of Clauswitz' and incapable of being suppressed on the 'Prussian model' of collective punishment. Addressing the House of Commons as MP for Harrow, Oswald Mosely criticised the Chief Secretary for *inefficient* 'Prussianism', which permitted Irish guerrillas to continue to operate and move freely throughout the country. 'They are not living in villages,' Mosely observed, but on the land, 'on the bogs and in the hills, on the run'.[62] Terror as deterrent, he felt, only subsidised Sinn Féin propaganda in the United States, and evoked international 'indignation [that] eclipses the indignation felt against the Germans in regard to their action in Belgium'. But the long-term political and environmental costs were seldom inferred. The Marquis of Crewe questioned how the Irish population could reconcile with Britain after such violence:

> Suppose it becomes necessary, in a military sense, to reduce parts of the South and West of Ireland to the condition of Northern France? Suppose you make Limerick or Ennis into as close an imitation of the present condition of Ypres as circumstances will admit? You may [...] thus sweep away the rebellion. But, unless you exterminate the population altogether, where will you be then?[63]

News of militarised landscapes and public debate on how best to contain and counter rebel activity reached international audiences and prompted several relief societies, political delegations and non-partisan bodies to visit Ireland between 1920 and 1921. Envoys were often met with scenes that confirmed the reports that prompted their visits. But in some cases, destruction touched on the senses. Like in Dublin after the 1916 Easter Rising, distinct odours reconstituted Irish towns as warzones; the smell of fire and smoke, and asphyxiation that befell those unable to escape it, made for powerful reporting.[64] In September 1920, reprisals for an IRA ambush that killed Captain Alan Lendrum, former British Army Officer and local Resident Magistrate, severely damaged several towns and agricultural stock in County Clare. In particular, Lahinch, Ennistymon and Miltown Malbay were said to resemble 'Belgian towns after the Huns'.[65] Liam Haugh, who participated in the ambush, recalled that 'over twenty miles' of scorched earth 'smoked and smouldered for days afterwards'.[66] This was the scene that met Paul Furnas, John Henry Barlow and Roger Clark when they arrived in September to investigate on behalf of the Quaker Society of Friends in England.[67] 'On entering Ennistymon,' Furnas testified, 'the acrid smell of burning met us everywhere. Some of the ruins were still smoking, and here and there flame was flickering over the ashes.'[68] The Quakers' observations were not without context. The trio, operating under the title of the 'Meeting of Suffering', had earlier surveyed County Antrim, where the destruction of Lisburn offered them a primer for revolutionary and sectarian violence. 'House after house, shop after shop, burnt out completely, in some cases not even the walls left standing.'[69] Arnott Erskine Robinson and Ellen Wilkinson, representing the Women's International League (British section), also visited Lisburn around the same time and confirmed the extent of its destruction. The scene from the top of the main street 'was one of absolute devastation'. Destroyed houses, 'some of them [...] merely heaps of stone [...] reminded me,' Robinson recalled, 'of pictures I had seen of the northern district of France after the German invasion.'

Another Quaker-led body, the American Committee for Relief in Ireland (ACRI), visited nearly 100 damaged towns throughout Ireland over a 49-day tour between February and March 1921. Founded in New York on humanitarian grounds the previous December, its delegation included relief workers who had operated in France and Serbia during the war. While Irish-American organisations, such as the Ancient Order of Hibernians, Clan na Gael and The Friends of Irish Freedom (FOIF), openly advocated for Irish independence and fundraised on its behalf,[70] the American Committee was ostensibly apolitical and sought to relieve personal and economic distress that resulted from the Anglo-Irish War. Its appeal to the American public, which launched on St Patrick's Day, 1921, presented Ireland's condition in familiar terms. Terrorism and widespread destruction greatly impacted Irish non-combatants, who were 'drinking the dregs of human suffering to a still greater degree even than Belgium during the great war [sic]. [...] As America succored Belgium so will she come to the aid of stricken Ireland.'[71] Destroyed Irish homes and industries as well as destitute families – all of which had featured in the American press – featured prominently in the delegation's report.[72] The American Committee estimated that British forces inflicted material damage to Irish shops, factories, homes and creameries to the amount of roughly $20 million, or £5 million, affecting 25,000 families.[73] The report stated:

> In Ireland today, thousands of women and children have been driven to the pitiful refuge of the

fields and open country. Balbriggan, Granard, Tralee, Templemore, Trim, Tobercurry, Lisburn, Thurles, Mallow and numerous other towns and villages have been burned and are partly or wholly in ruins. In Cork alone acres of business buildings and homes have been wiped out by fire.[74]

Funds raised throughout New England were transferred to Ireland under the care of the Irish White Cross and its Honorary Treasurer, James Douglas, a Dublin-born merchant's son and member of the Society of Friends.[75] The White Cross operated throughout the Irish Civil War to restore homes and industry. By October 1922, its Reconstruction Commission distributed nearly a quarter-million pounds of aid.[76]

The British Labour Party also sent a delegation to Ireland. Its protest in the House of Commons against the use of physical force in governing Ireland was balanced by a desire to preserve and restore British honour and prestige that, it felt, the policy of repression and coercion had tarnished in the eyes of the international community.[77] The chairman of the Labour Commission to Ireland, Arthur Henderson, MP, confessed that it was 'difficult for him to exaggerate the deplorable conditions there'. His brief tour of greater Dublin included the recently disturbed cities of Balbriggan and Skerries, and a meeting with ranking political and military figures at Dublin Castle. Several days later he was in Lancashire, speaking to his constituents at Widnes. 'Normal life [in Ireland] has been made impossible,' he told them. 'Day by day the unhappy inhabitants were reminded that their country was under the heel of ruthless military occupation. It is actually true to say that life was safer in Brussels during the German occupation than it is now in Dublin, Cork or Derry.'[78] It's difficult to gauge the impact of the Labour Commission's report. Opposition politics made the Coalition Government a target in many respects, most visibly its handling of the Irish situation. However, socialists in nearby Yorkshire certainly saw parity in Ireland's war-torn regions and those that remained in France and Belgium. In June 1921, Bradford City Council heard a motion to reallocate a £5,000 loan raised to help the devastated French towns of Bailleul and Nieppe to Irish towns that had suffered damage due to revolutionary violence. Though it was defeated, the motion nevertheless contributed to an expanding international recognition of and sympathy towards the Irish situation, as well as mounting fundraising efforts towards Irish relief and condemnation of British governance in the light of post-war self-determination.[79]

Perfidious Albion?

Britain's wartime allies – particularly France, Italy and the United States – contextualised Irish victimhood with similar Great War hyperboles. France had been closely monitoring the Irish political situation for over 20 years. Prior to 1914, Ireland's strategic geographic location on Britain's western border, renewed agitation for Home Rule, and growing tensions in Europe spotlighted its place in the broader future of Anglo-French security.[80] The French Department of Interior Affairs continued to record Ireland's seditious activities throughout the war; Roger Casement's activities in Germany, the 1916 Easter Rising and the 1918 'German Plot' registered most prominently.[81] However, between November 1918 and June 1919 – from the commencement of the Armistice to the conclusion of the peace conference – Ireland barely featured in the French press.[82] Harsh reprisals and political suppression revived France's interest in Ireland, which certain French journalists and writers communicated in the context of Great War militarism.

Henri Béraud arrived in Dublin on a quiet Sunday in September 1920. Writing for *Le Petit Parisien*, he described the city as exhibiting a 'gloomy and mysterious air', where the revolution appeared as *l'émeute invisible*, an invisible riot. This was all the more apparent after he was unable to locate his republican contacts, and observed soldiers who, 'yawning, leaning on their carbines, and behind their curly barbed wire, seem to be expecting a movie director'.[83] The city and its citizens revealed the revolution in other ways. 'Throughout the day,' Béraud wrote, 'I walked the streets, the squares, the avenues of Dublin, meeting nothing but very peaceful people [...] hastening like shadows along the walls. Not a patrol, not a talk, not the smallest bit of a procession. And, however, the rebellion is brooding here, as in Cork and Belfast.'[84] The sack of Balbriggan a few days later presented Béraud and his readers a much different experience, one that exhibited militarism's excess at the expense of an increasingly incorporeal public, 'prostrate in shadows with clasped hands, which stood out against the wild decor of the crumbling walls and smoking ruins'.[85] Galway offered Béraud a similar scene the following month – 'Everywhere ruins. Old ruins, old riots, in front of recent ruins, still blackened by the smoke of the fires' – by which time he had made what sense he could of the pace and location of violence and material destruction in revolutionary Ireland. 'The revolution in Ireland is neither general nor localized,' he explained. 'It manifests itself successively on all points of the territory [and] it is useless to get around to "see the battle". The battle, already, is elsewhere.'[86] Another French journalist, most likely Joseph Kessel, also witnessed Balbriggan's destruction, which he said resembled French villages at the Front during the war. His observations, first published in the newspaper *Le Liberté* and subsequently reprinted in the book *L'ame de l'Irlande*, identify Balbriggan as home to destruction, trauma and death:

> I saw men livid with anguish. I saw a factory employing hundreds of workers who had been ransacked, the soldiers having burned raw materials worth several million francs. I have seen little girls that neighbours have to dress because all their clothes had disappeared in the fire. I saw a big guy, strong and smart, mumbling foolish words. I finally saw the corpses of the two traders killed, riddled with bayonets and atrociously mutilated.[87]

The Chief Secretary for Ireland, Sir Hamar Greenwood, denounced comparison between Balbriggan and Belgian frontline towns.[88] But the impression left upon embedded French journalists and their readers favoured the sentiment. Simone Tèry, who wrote for *L'Oeuvre* during the period and published her broader impressions in *En Irlande* after the civil war, summarised terror as the author of local memory. 'Each village had its victims; each hamlet, its arson,' she wrote. 'Like our own French villages after the War of 1870, or the last war, each Irish village has its memories of the War of Independence, of the reign of terror of the soldiers and police.'[89]

The French nationalist and radical press were appalled at Britain's Irish policy and wrote in much less reserved tones.[90] *Le Lanterne* identified that since 1916, Ireland had 'reclaimed for itself the justice for which it fought in Belgium, in France and elsewhere', yet had simultaneously experienced 'a system of brutality hardly credible, worse than the German regime in Belgium and the north of France'.[91] Writing for *Floreal*, a short-lived French socialist paper, 'John Reader' positioned Ireland within the broader post-war landscape but outside the free nations that had emerged from fallen empires. 'The World War has awakened the principle of nationalities throughout the world,' he wrote in February 1920:

> But victorious England, which pretended to defend the right of peoples to self-determination on the Continent, persists in violating that sacred right at home, and refusing independence to neighbouring Ireland. It proclaimed a hundred times that the independence of Poland was necessary for the pacification of Europe. It stated no less frequently that the Polish problem was an international problem. Regardless of the blatant contradiction between its principles and its actions, the London cabinet resists by all means, including arms, to the Irish independent movement, and does not want to admit any external intervention in this secular conflict that puts England with the rebel island. [...] The oppression of a people interests all the peoples of the world. England must obey the will twice expressed by Ireland. Otherwise, it will incur universal reprobation and ban itself from the League of Nations.[92]

Like *Floreal*, other journalists and observers internationalised the Irish case against wider post-war European political reconstruction. However, 'Irish Louvain', a label pinned to separate reprisals throughout 1920, extended its apparent meaning beyond ruined cities.[93] Britain was criticised for physical destruction in Ireland, but more expressly for employing harsh methods it previously denounced and for failing to recognise its own duplicity in doing so. Both were eroding its moral authority in the world, it was stated, while advancing sympathy and international recognition for Ireland amongst Britain's wartime allies. This was not merely fodder for fundraisers and propagandists. Well-known and influential English literary and religious figures also criticised the counter-insurgency as antithetical to British values. 'The good name of England is suffering throughout the world,' recorded the Anglican Bishop of Southwark, Dr Cyril Garbett, in a 1921 pastoral letter; 'we dare not tolerate in Ireland actions and methods which were condemned unsparingly when employed by the Germans in Belgium.'[94] Likewise, prolific writer and critic G. K. Chesterton explained that Germany had crossed a line in Belgium, 'the boundary between Christendom and the barbarians', which Britain had repeatedly emphasised to the international community throughout the war. Writing for the Peace with Ireland Council, Chesterton held that Britain had crossed the same line in Ireland, and 'the whole world has seen them do it.'[95] Fellow Council member and outspoken parliamentarian Lord Henry Bentinck likewise denounced military policy as 'a disgrace to civilization'.[96] Mo Moulton examined this issue in greater depth, illustrating that individual advocates and anti-reprisal campaigns saw reprisals as negating Britain's moral leadership in the post-war world.[97] During the broader Great War and Irish Revolution period, as David Fitzpatrick noted, 'the Irish conflict was internationalized as never before. [...] The post-war peace conference and carving up of defeated empires encouraged republicans to extend their appeal to a global audience.'[98] In addition to these efforts, foreign journalists verified both the extent of violent revolution in Ireland and comparison with war-torn Belgian and French villages.

Irish expatriate and diaspora communities also worked to expose Ireland's plight to the international community. *The Irish Exile*, a journal focused on Irish interests in and around London and the activities of the Irish Self-Determination League of Great Britain, reported assaults on Irish women, terror, and murder through the lens of wartime atrocity.[99] Beyond its fundraising activities, the FOIF newsletter incorporated international coverage of Irish affairs and reprinted foreign opinion, which often spotlighted reports on British brutality in Ireland as well as editorials critical of Ireland's exclusion from the community of independent nation-states recognised after the war. Though foreign governments did not officially recognise Dáil Éireann, its envoys and publicity department nevertheless ensured foreign audiences were kept informed through translation and distribution of the *Irish Bulletin* and other works.[100] George Gavan Duffy and Seán T. O'Kelly worked diligently in France and beyond.[101] In Spain, Marie O'Brien and a dedicated corps of student volunteers translated, published and distributed Irish political bulletins, news of IRA assaults and British atrocities, and a collected volume of essays by Erskine Childers and Darrell Figgis entitled *La Tragedia de Irlanda*.[102] Translation and distribution ran both ways. Irish affairs that appeared in the Spanish and Continental press were collected and forwarded back to Dublin, part of the 'Trojan work' performed by O'Brien and her staff meant to demonstrate the revolution's transnational legitimacy.[103] They and others succeeded to great effect. Writing for the *Observer* in France, Stephen Gwynn contributed that there was 'no use in trying to persuade France – and I expect that the same is true of all European countries – that the Irish question is a domestic affair for Great Britain. In the eyes of France, at all events, it is no more a domestic affair than was Italy under the Austrians.'[104]

Catholic solidarity also guided public outcry, and Britain's wartime allies were not silent on the issue. Italian support resonated in the Irish press, through which Signor Angelo Mauri, Professor of the Catholic University and the Popular Party's Deputy for Milan, framed Ireland's struggle in the language of the Great War, as one of 'self-determination'.[105] In a widely circulated article, he observed Ireland's subjugation to be 'no less inhuman' than the German invasion of Belgium and the devastation of Louvain. He continued, incorporating other common elements:

> It is to be all the more reprobated since it is inspired and commanded [...] by a Government which loves to parade itself as the champion of liberty of other peoples, and this, in an historic period in which the brotherhood of peoples and the respect of nationalities have been reasserted as the very basis of human society.[106]

Mauri carried the point into December. During the Deputies' debate on the Treaty of Rapallo (1920), through which Italy and newly formed Yugoslavia sought to resolve territorial disputes in the region, he asked the chamber, 'liberty should be for all countries without exception [...]. What about martyred Ireland?'[107]

A narrower view implies Catholicism, rather than nationalism, negotiated Irish-Italian solidarity. The Vatican refused to explicitly condemn Sinn Féin lest it alienate the party's Catholic core.[108] It carefully navigated the Irish independence movement's moral and political minefield throughout the period, which the Irish hierarchy correspondingly followed in order to avoid nationalist backlash at home. Grappling with the moral issues of guerrilla war was one of the 'new challenges' the Church faced; as Ferriter notes, to condemn the revolution was to risk alienating its overwhelmingly Catholic adherents, as well as sympathisers abroad. As such, inter-European Catholic camaraderie condemned unconventional violence in Ireland – particularly arson and the destruction of property – in humanitarian tones that played at broader post-war desires for peace and war relief. Further, Pope Benedict, Belgium's Cardinal Mercier, and the Bishops of Liege, Bruges,

Namur, Tournai and Ghent subscribed substantial funds towards relief in December 1920, to be distributed via the Irish White Cross.[109]

International sympathy was not universal, and support for Irish independence certainly had its dissenters. Anti-Irish groups, Great War veterans and Wilsonian internationalists joined political and military voices within the British Government to denounce Irish republicanism. More specifically, they levelled accusations that, in vilifying Britain, Irish expatriate and diaspora communities threatened the peace settlement as well as the future of the Anglo-Franco-American alliance. Numerous voices assessed the efficacy of Irish influence abroad in this way. Despite support from radical corners, Dáil Éireann's Minister for Foreign Affairs, George Noble Plunkett, determined the mainstream French press to be overall conservative 'and anxious to do nothing to offend Great Britain'.[110]

Several French papers viewed demands for Irish independence as undermining the allied cause. This included those traditionally opposed to Sinn Féin, *L'Echo de Paris* and *L'Action Française*, as well as *Le Temps* and *La Croix*, which resisted prioritising sympathy towards Ireland above allied solidarity.[111] Conveying his opinion on American views towards Ireland in March 1920, Sir Horace Plunkett perceived Americans as hopeful for a degree of Irish self-government compatible with the Empire's security, 'which many [...] believe they are as much concerned as the British'.[112] Sir John Simon, a seasoned government servant who held a variety of senior posts throughout the war and had journalism experience, attacked rhetoric of British brutality in Ireland as he felt it was 'poisoning the relations of England with America'. Speaking at Streatham, south London, in January 1921, he argued that Ireland had deliberately demonised England in the eyes of the world in an attempt to make its devotion 'to protect a small country like Belgium seem futile.'[113] The Protestant Bishop in Birmingham further qualified that the Irish situation encouraged Germany, frustrated Anglo-American friendship and made France 'doubtful of England's love of freedom'.[114] Though anti-Irish sentiment had deep historical roots, pushback against Irish nationalism in the immediate post-war period was wed to larger desires to nurture bonds between France, Britain and the United States, in order to 'preserve the victory'. This was particularly true in the United States, where various immigrant communities diverged over religious tradition, political sentiment and the implications of the allied victory. Two New England-based groups, New York's Allied Loyalty League and Boston's Loyal Coalition, demonstrated efforts to prevent the Irish nationalist victim narrative from damaging post-war relations.

Founded on an anti-Bolshevist platform in the summer of 1919, the Allied Loyalty League originally sought to root out destructive propaganda and to promote unity and friendship between the United States and its wartime allies.[115] Its first president, Maurice Egan, later refined the League's duty to combat elements that 'may gradually undermine that understanding on which the future peace of the world depends'.[116] James M. Beck, who succeeded Egan as president, described the organisation as a 'League of Remembrance' that sought to perpetuate 'the tender memories and noble affections of the Great Alliance'. The Allied Loyalty League came to identify Sinn Féin and Irish nationalism, generally, as obstacles to European peace and effective American foreign policy, and it attempted to remove and prohibit pro-Irish media in public spaces, notably motion picture houses.[117]

The League reinforced its views throughout 1920 as Americans received news of British reprisals, terror and destruction in Ireland. Locally, it attempted to exploit an attack on the

Union League Club on 25 November 1920, Thanksgiving Day, as evidence of orchestrated Irish divisiveness. The accused had come from a memorial Mass for Terence MacSwiney at St Patrick's Cathedral, reports noted, and were incensed at the sight of the Union Jack flag suspended outside the building. League officers registered a formal protest with New York City Mayor John Francis Hylan, though nothing came of it. The mayor's recent ceremonial gestures perhaps better demonstrated his outlook towards the Irish. Hylan bestowed the freedom of the city on the vocal Irish-Australian nationalist Archbishop Daniel Mannix the previous July; in December he presented it to Terence MacSwiney's widow, Muriel, the first woman to receive the honour.[118] Regardless, the Allied Loyalty League carried forward and continued its society page proceedings, hosting luncheons recognising America's wartime allies and protesting Irish influence on American politics.[119] It specifically targeted the American Commission on Conditions in Ireland that sat in Washington, DC, between December 1920 and January 1921. The Commission collected evidence and heard testimony regarding British conduct in Ireland, which numerous eyewitnesses provided with license, often helping to influence American views towards the Irish Revolution. League president James M. Beck labelled the Lord Mayor of Cork, Donal O'Callaghan, 'a propagandist for Sinn Féin', and protested his entering the United States.[120] Further, the American Commission was itself criticised for wielding 'insidious influence' against the Anglo-American relationship. 'Is it not time to protest against an Irish commission,' Mrs. R. Lester Fleming asked *The New York Times*, 'misnamed "American", with headquarters in Washington, evidently with the intention of giving it a national character it does not possess?'[121]

The Allied Loyalty League reflected broader trends in resurgent, progressive-era American nativism.[122] Niche xenophobia, including anti-radical and anti-Catholic sentiment, swelled in the years immediately prior to the First World War,[123] while post-war desires for stability recast nationalist, socialist and labour agitation as un-American. Boston's Loyal Coalition carried this message from its inception in March 1920. Its members believed that there was 'too much Ireland in America',[124] and openly criticised Sinn Féin supporters in New England as 'alien propagandists' who, in un-American fashion, only thought of 'themselves alone'.[125] The group petitioned various American political officials, including President Harding and Attorney General Mitchell Palmer, to dissuade public support for Ireland and outlaw Irish publicity and fundraising in the United States.[126] Like the Allied Loyalty League, the Loyal Coalition believed that the Irish situation threatened wartime alliances, and that rebel Ireland's informal partnership with Imperial Germany leading up to the Easter Rising precluded American support towards its independence. Coalition leadership informed US Secretary of State Bainbridge Colby that America's recognition of an Irish republic would antagonise Britain, dilute American identity and further encourage the 'hyphen menace',[127] which one contemporary supporter observed in 'those who masquerade as American citizens but actually place the interests of an alien racial group or nation before our own honor and welfare'.[128] Rear Admiral William Sims, Head of the Naval War College who commanded the American Fleet during the war, habitually slated Irish influence in the United States as an obstacle to long-term peace and national unity.[129] Addressing a meeting of the English Speaking Union in London in June 1921, Sims explained:

> There are many in our country who, technically, are Americans, naturalized or born here, but none of them Americans at all. They are Americans when they want money but Sinn Féin on the platform. [...] The simple truth is that they have blood of English and American boys on their hands. They are like zebras, neither black horses with white stripes or white horses with black stripes, but we know that they are not horses, they are asses.[130]

Both the Allied Loyalty League and the Loyal Coalition publicly defended Sims' viewpoint, while a local council of the American Association for Recognition of the Irish Republic in New York arranged a satirical welcome party on his return from London, complete with a donkey, as thanks for bringing further attention to the Irish cause.[131]

Sensationalised episodes such as these may help to explain why, unlike the Allied Loyalty League, the Loyal Coalition enjoyed much wider press coverage, though its membership and fundraising was never as respectable.[132] Confrontational opposition to Irish interests in defence of Anglo-American friendship made for charged reading and public spectacle. The Coalition raucously denounced sympathy for Ireland and recognition of the Irish republic at the Democratic Party platform convention in San Francisco in June 1920, which carried to newspapers in South Carolina, Montana and Nebraska.[133] Later that autumn, Loyal Coalition president Demarest Lloyd appraised Terence MacSwiney's hunger strike as self-induced starvation, and argued that it was of no concern to the United States Government.[134] His comments were translated into Slovakian for Cleveland, Ohio's *Svĕt*, 'The "World" Independent Bohemian Daily Newspaper.'[135] Both societies ostensibly preached peace and co-operation between the United States and its wartime allies, though in vehemently anti-Irish tones. In many ways, American nativists and imperialists viewed Irish nationalism as a threat to American unity and the new world order it would direct. Unlike bolshevism's 'Red Spectre', however, the imaged green *púca* matured from a nineteenth-century apparition of poverty and social burden to command significant political influence and public opinion in the United States.

Conclusion

Irish landscapes endured diverse destruction, contamination and militarisation throughout the War of Independence. This accelerated in scope and scale after the Armistice and, within the war's moral tone of self-determination and the rights of small nations, implicated the international community. Journalists and observers sympathetic to the republican movement communicated Ireland's ruin through the template of First World War atrocity propaganda, which had been cultivated by Britain and the Allies as a means of cultural mobilisation between 1914 and 1918. Two distinctions further aligned the Irish independence movement to the First World War in this regard. The first distinction was that the destruction of Irish towns and the suppression of Irish civilians drew comparison to occupied Belgium and France, and British military governance to Prussian barbarism. The second questioned Ireland's exclusion from the community of free nations created after the war in accordance with Woodrow Wilson's Fourteen Points, in which some critics viewed the Allied victory as incomplete.[136]

The international community turned its attention to Ireland following the Paris peace settlements. Aid committees, relief societies and elements of the foreign press reported their experiences and findings to international readers. Equally, Irish witnesses travelled abroad and shared their experiences. While this exposure helped to rally many in Europe and the United Stated to the Irish cause, others viewed its divisive subtlety as a threat to post-war peace and a means to draw war-weary nations into diplomatic conflict or icy relations. The nature of the Irish Revolution, coupled with its exposition as a continuum of wartime atrocity, placed it beyond a merely domestic political affair. Diverse voices throughout the European community echoed the observation of Albert Coyle, Reporter to the American Commission on Conditions in Ireland, in 1921:

> Our boys died in France to prevent forever the repetition of such atrocities, and to guarantee to small nations everywhere the right to a free and democratic government of their own choosing. Persistent reports which continue to come to this country indicate that the worst atrocities alleged against the German army of occupation in Belgium are being perpetrated on even a more ruthless scale in Ireland today. For these reasons the situation in Ireland, no less than that which existed in Belgium, cannot be regarded by any civilized nation as merely a domestic affair. It is a matter of grave international concern.[137]

While the Great War certainly established new standards for destruction, displacement and civilian abuse, crafting its atrocity narratives as basely polemic simplified the conflict's moral dimensions. Irish nationalists and their supporters exploited this reality, articulating Ireland's victimhood as akin to occupied Belgium and France, and around a reconstructed wartime framework highlighting disproportionate and unwarranted destruction and abuse.

NOTES

1. *The Official Catholic Directory and Clergy List for the Year of Our Lord 1909* XXIV (New York, 1909), p. 50.
2. *The Tablet* praised the Pope's encyclical though English Catholics generally criticised it. Lawrence Barmann, 'The Pope and the English modernists', in *U.S. Catholic Historian* 25:1 (Winter 2007), pp 49–51.
3. Additional sources verify Jones' appointments. Christchurch Priory, Eltham, *The Catholic Directory: Ecclesiastical Register and Almanac for the Year of our Lord 1913* (London, 1913), p. 540.
4. Sidmouth's convent received several Belgian refugees shortly after the outbreak of the war, specifically girls and young women, while numerous aid appeals, rallies and receptions transformed parts of London. *The Times* referred to the Bloomsbury Hotel as 'a Belgium in London', with French and Flemish heard as commonly as English in the museum district. For sources and scholarship on Belgian refugees in the United Kingdom, see *Report of the Committee on Alleged German Outrages*, presided over by The Right Hon. Viscount Byrne (New York, 1915); *The Times*, 15 Oct. 1914; Commandant de Gerlache de Gomery, *Belgium in War Time* (New York, 1916); Catriona Pennell, 'Going to war', in John Horne (ed.), *Our War*, p. 42; Pierre Purseigle, '"A wave on to our shores": The exile and resettlement of refugees from the Western Front, 1914–1918', in *Contemporary European History* 16:4 (November 2007), pp 428, 431; James Morgan Read, *Atrocity Propaganda 1914–1919* (New York, 1972), p. 206; Trevor Wilson, *The Myriad of Faces of War: Britain and the Great War, 1914–1918* (Cambridge: Polity Press, 1986), p. 158; Tammy M. Proctor, *Civilians in a World at War 1914–1918* (New York, 2010), pp 119, 140–1.
5. Sophie de Schaepdrijver, 'Occupation, propaganda and the idea of Belgium', in Aviel Roshwald and Richard Stites (eds), *European Culture in the Great War: The Arts, Entertainment, and Propaganda, 1914–1918* (Cambridge, 1999; 2002), p. 268; John Horne, 'Our war, our history', in Horne (ed.), *Our War*, pp 7–8.
6. 'The English Huns', *Limerick Leader*, 18 Oct. 1920; *Fermanagh Herald*, 23 Oct. 1920; *Ulster Herald*, 23 Oct. 1920; *Donegal News*, 23 Oct. 1920.
7. By October 1919 the neighbourhoods of Central, Willesden, Balham and Tooting, Clapham, Peckham, Paddington, Highbury, Fulham, St Pancras, Woolwich, Poplar, St Anne's, Underwood St, Tottenham and Bermondsey boasted active branches of the Irish Self-Determination League of Great Britain (*Irish Independent*, 27 Oct. 1919). In April 1920, the Balham and Tooting branch of the ISDL of Great Britain hosted over 350 people attending Máire Ní Mhainín's lecture on the '67 movement. (*Irish Independent*, 10 Apr. 1920). The Women's Section of the Balham and Tooting Labour Party offered condolences after Terence MacSwiney's death and were particularly appreciative of 'the late Lord Mayor of Cork's devotion to principle'. *Freeman's Journal*, 13 Nov. 1920.
8. Sophie de Schaepdrijver notes that, 'this being the age of total war, the Belgian question was being fought out internationally with exactly those "tricks of political propaganda", and this largely without consulting the Belgians themselves.' 'Occupation, propaganda and the idea of Belgium', p. 268.
9. *Donegal News*, 23 Apr. 1921, reprinted story from *The Chicago Tribune*; 'Report of conditions in Ireland made by the Women's International League', in Albert Coyle, *Evidence on Conditions in Ireland Comprising the Complete Testimony, Affidavits and Exhibits Presented Before the American Commission on Conditions in Ireland* (Washington, DC, 1921), p. 622.
10. John Horne and Alan Kramer, *German Atrocities, 1914: A History of Denial* (New Haven: Yale University Press, 2001), pp 292–5, 371.
11. Ian Kenneally, *The Paper Wall: Newspapers and Propaganda in Ireland 1919–1921* (Cork, 2008), p. 166. Equally flipped, or ignored, were the atrocities committed in the Belgian Congo. Horne and Kramer, *German Atrocities*, p 423.
12. *Irish Independent*, 19 Nov. 1920; *Fermanagh Herald*, 27 Nov. 1920; *Ulster Herald*, 27 Nov. 1920; *Donegal News*, 27 Nov. 1920.
13. Ben Novick, *Irish Nationalist Propaganda During the First World War*, pp 72–81; Edward Madigan, '"An Irish Louvain": Memories of 1914 and the moral climate in Britain during the Irish War of Independence', in *Irish Historical Studies* 44:165 (2020), p. 97.
14. Stephens, *Insurrection in Dublin*, p. 75.
15. As Ferriter put it: 'How could a boy with a cultural diet of English public school comic books be expected to identify with the scenes at the GPO?' *Transformation of Ireland*, pp 149–50. France had

rapidly mobilised war damage in the national press, showing the destruction of Visé in August 1914. Emmanuelle Danchin, *Le temps des ruines 1914–1921* (Rennes, 2015), p. 45.
16. Novick, *Irish Nationalist Propaganda During the First World War*, pp 83–6, idem Chapter 2.
17. Homer Folks, *The Human Costs of the War* (New York, May 1920), pp 102–3.
18. Article pertains to British rule in Ireland and Lloyd George's defence of it. *Freeman's Journal*, 16 Nov. 1920; 'The rules of the Huns', excerpt cited from *Nation* in *Tuam Herald*, 11 Nov. 1922.
19. J. Murray Allison (compiler, editor), 'Forward', in *Raemaekers' Cartoon History of the War, Volume One: The First Twelve Months of War* (New York: The Century Co., 1918), p. v.
20. Horne and Kramer, *German Atrocities 1914*, p. 302.
21. Kenneally, *The Paper Wall*, p. 44.
22. Kenneally, *The Paper Wall*, p. 49.
23. 'If Lord French were a German' (reprinted from the *Catholic Herald*, London, 27 Dec. 1919), *Irish Bulletin* 1, 12 July 1919–1 May 1920, p. 158. Also, Dr Garbett, Protestant Bishop of Southwark, in a pastoral letter, said such actions only perpetuate throughout Europe and America the belief that 'we are treating Ireland in much the same way as the Austrians treated Italy, or the Russians suppressed the attempts of the Poles to regain independence.' *Cork Examiner*, 6 Apr. 1921.
24. 'Scathing rebuke for Von Bissing' is the *Cork Echo* heading; statement of Liam de Róiste, BMH, WS 1698, pp 306–7. Sophie de Schaepdrijver, 'Occupation, propaganda and the idea of Belgium', p. 268; Becker, *France at War in the Twentieth Century*, p. 16; rebuke for difference of coverage in conditions, Coyle, *Evidence on the Conditions in Ireland*, p. 785.
25. 'Copying von Bissing; Ireland becomes like Belgium', *Irish Independent*, 5 Jan. 1921.
26. *Freeman's Journal*, 21 July 1920; *Drogheda Independent*, 9 Oct. 1920.
27. Kodak, 'Snapshots', *Drogheda Independent*, 9 Oct. 1920.
28. Reprinted in *Irish Independent*, 19 Nov. 1920; *Fermanagh Herald*, 27 Nov. 1920; *Ulster Herald*, 27 Nov. 1920; *Donegal News*, 27 Nov. 1920
29. Reprinted in the *Irish Independent*, 15 Dec. 1920.
30. Falaize, American Irish Historical Society, New York, Friends of Irish Freedom Records (Box 5, Folder 1: newsletters of FOIF, II:30, 22 Jan. 1921, p. 4).
31. *Evening Herald*, 22 Oct. 1920.
32. 'Relief for Irish sufferers', *Irish Independent*, 29 Dec. 1920. Hamar Greenwood dismissed the comparison on grounds of intension and nuance. *Skibbereen Eagle*, 18 Dec. 1920.
33. Coyle, *Evidence on Conditions in Ireland*, p. 771.
34. Ibid., pp 822–3.
35. 'No personal comparisons with Belgian atrocities', in *Evidence on Conditions in Ireland*, p. 827.
36. 'Report on distress in Ireland: A survey by the American Unit under the auspices of the American Committee for Relief in Ireland 1921', in J. Anthony Gaughan (ed.), *Memoirs of Senator James G. Douglas (1887–1954): Concerned Citizen* (Dublin, 1998), p. 138.
37. In many ways this was successful. See 'Relief for Irish sufferers', *Irish Independent*, 29 Dec. 1920.
38. 'Read their war speeches,' the *Irish Independent* urged. 'They were all out to kill Prussian militarism. It was arrogant and antagonistic to constitutional liberties. […] German militarism in Belgium during the period of occupation was not worse than the present hateful regime in Ireland.' *Irish Independent*, 27 Jan 1921; 'An Irish Louvain', *Freeman's Journal*, 21 July 1920; *Irish Independent*, 6 Jan. 1921.
39. *Freeman's Journal*, 16 Feb. 1920.
40. 'What America thinks of Britain: Lesson of Cork burnings', *Irish Independent*, 6 Jan. 1921.
41. *Drogheda Independent* (quoting *Manchester Guardian*), 9 Oct. 1920.
42. Rachel Woodward, *Military Geographies* (Malden, MA, 2004), p. 73.
43. Chris Pearson, *Mobilizing Nature: The Environmental History of War and Militarization in Modern France* (Manchester, 2012), p. 112.
44. Statement of John O'Driscoll, BMH, WS 1250.
45. Dorothy Macardle, *The Irish Republic*, (Dublin, 1965 edn), pp 347, 355.
46. *Nenagh Guardian*, 12 Nov. 1921.
47. *Kilkenny People*, 27 Sept. 1919; see also, *Freeman's Journal*, 19 Aug. 1919; *Belfast Newsletter*, 3 Mar. 1920; *Irish independent*, 3 Mar. 1920.
48. Macardle, *The Irish Republic*, p. 355.

49. *Freeman's Journal*, 6 Feb. 1920; *Irish Bulletin* 1, 12 July 1919–1 May 1920, p. 255; Kenneally, *The Paper Wall*, p. 82; statement of John O'Driscoll, BMH, WS 1250, p. 5.
50. *Irish Bulletin* 1, 12 July 1919–1 May 1920, p. 78.
51. Ibid., 30 July 1919, p. 21.
52. *Waterford News*, 23 Apr. 1920.
53. Swindlehurst diary, 7 Jan. 1921, Imperial War Museum (P538).
54. Ibid.
55. *Belfast Newsletter*, 1 Apr.1920.
56. *Irish Independent*, 17 Jan. 1921.
57. *Belfast Newsletter*, 12 July 1920.
58. *Belfast Newsletter*, 5 July 1920.
59. Ben Novick similarly notes the use of Irish history in nationalist propaganda during the Great War. Particularly, the conduct of British soldiers and military systems since 1798. See Novick, *Conceiving Revolution*, pp 90–102.
60. 'What Napoleon forgot', *Freeman's Journal*, 10 May 1921.
61. Oswald Mosely, Military Operations, Ireland, H. C. Deb. (1 June 1921), vol. 142, cc 1153–98.
62. Ibid.
63. The Government of Ireland, H. L. Deb. (21 June 1921), vol. 45, cc 702–3.
64. In May 1920, a false-flag operation in Thurles, County Tipperary, aimed at cultivating hostility towards Sinn Féin and the IRA, targeted the McCarthy family, whose house on Fianna Road was bombed and burned in an attack described as 'Worse Than Prussian'. Ushering his family out of their home, Mr McCarthy recalled that 'the odour was suffocating [...]. Our faces and hands and nostrils [...] were coated with this dust, and it took us a considerable time to wash it off.' The next day, a local Great War veteran gave his assessment: 'The man who used the explosion,' he stated, 'must have been an expert at the business.' *Freeman's Journal*, 15 May 1920.
65. *Irish Independent*, 24 Sept. 1920
66. Statement of Liam Haugh, BMH, WS 474, p. 19. 'Over twenty miles smoked and smouldered for days afterwards; dwellings and business premises in the above-mentioned towns [Lahinch and Miltown Malbay], and almost the entire hay and corn harvest thence to Kilkee.' See also, Coyle, *Evidence on Conditions in Ireland*, pp 602–3.
67. *Irish Independent*, 10 Dec. 1920.
68. Coyle, *Evidence on Conditions in Ireland*, p. 520.
69. Coyle, *Evidence on Conditions in Ireland*, p. 520; 'Report on distress in Ireland: A survey by the American Unit under the auspices of the American Committee for Relief in Ireland 1921', in J. Anthony Caughan (ed.), *Memoirs of Senator James G. Douglas*, p. 138.
70. Michael Doorley, 'The friends of Irish freedom: A case-study in Irish-American nationalism, 1916–21', in *History Ireland* 16:2 (March–April 2008), pp 22–7.
71. ACRI Report, Section III, NLI (IR94109 p63), p. 50; Irish White Cross Report, NLI (IR94109 p63), pp 16–18.
72. ACRI Report, Section III, 'Origin and History of ACRI', NLI (IR94109 p63), p. 48.
73. ACRI Report, NLI (IR94109 p63), p. 63.
74. NLI, James G. Douglas papers (Ms 49,581/56 folder 6).
75. Statement of James Brendan Connolly, Boston, MA, Commissioner for the American Committee for the Relief in Ireland, 1921. BMH, WS 849, p. 11.
76. Irish White Cross Report, Appendix E, NLI (IR94109 p63), p. 140; Áine Ceannt, *The Story of the Irish White Cross, 1920–1947: The Story of its Work* (Dublin, 1947). By autumn 1921, the prospect of peace prompted a shift in the Irish White Cross policy of reconstruction. Memo by James G. Douglas from meeting of ACRI Executive Committee, 31 Oct. 1921, NLI, Douglas papers (MS 49,581/56 folder 1).
77. Report of the Labour Commission to Ireland, p. 1; Horne and Kramer, *German Atrocities*, p. 371.
78. *Irish Independent*, 10 Dec. 1920
79. *The Times*, 15 June 1921, p. 12
80. Jérôme aan de Wiel, 'The long rupture, 1870–1970: The darker side of Franco-Irish relations', in *The International History Review*, 37:2 (2015), p. 208. Such works included Louis Paul-Dubois, *L'Irlande Contemporaine et la Question Irlandaise* (1907); and Louis Maisonnier and Georges Lecarpentier, *L'Irlande et le Home Rule* (1912).

81. Bernard Ducret, 'La France et l'Irlande (1914–1923)', in *Etudes irlandaises* 9 (1984), pp 191–97; NLI (Ministere des Affaires étrangeres – Archives Diplomatique Irlande, no. 1, Z-282-1.1a2-7-18-20. Affaires interieures, I. Juin 1918–Mars 1922).
82. Bernard Ducret, 'La France et l'Irlande (1914–1923)', in *Etudes Irlandaises* 9 (1984), pp 197–8.
83. The quote is: 'Il faut aller jusqu'aux portes de la ville pour trouver quelques postes de *soldiers*, qui baillent, appuyés sur leur carabines, et qui, derrière leurs chevaux de frisé en barbelé tout neuf, ont l'air d'attendre un opérateur de cinéma.'
84. 'Un dimanche à Dublin: L'émeute invisible', *Le Petit Parsien*, 16 Sept. 1920.
85. 'Le drame Irlandais: Vision de Guerre Civile', *Le Petit Parisien*, 28 Sept. 1920.
86. *Le Petit Parisien*, 7 Oct. 1920.
87. *La Liberté*, 28 Sept. 1920; Xavier Moisant, *L'ame de l'Irlande*, pp 128–31.
88. For debate on comparisons of Balbriggan to Belgian front-line towns, see Vote of Censure Proposed, H. C. Deb. (20 Oct. 1920), vol. 133, cc 925–1039; see also, Madigan, '"An Irish Louvain"', p. 101.
89. Simone Tèry (trans. Marilyn Gaddis Rose), 'Raids and reprisals: Ireland: Eye-witness (1923)', p. 35.
90. Kenneally, *The Paper Wall*, p. 46.
91. *Le Lanterne*, 20 Sept. 1920; see also, Mr Howe speaking at a campaign rally: 'There was a country at our very doors ruled as Germany never oppressed Alsace-Lorraine, as Austria never oppressed Serbia, as Russia oppressed Poland.' *Sunday Independent*, 18 Apr. 1920.
92. John Reader, 'L'Irlande veut l'Independence', *Floreal*, 14 Feb. 1920; NLI, French Pamphlets (ILB 04 p9).
93. 'An Irish Louvain', *Freeman's Journal*, 21 July 1920.
94. 'Condemns Irish reprisals', *Cork Examiner*, 6 Apr. 1921.
95. G. K. Chesterton, 'What are reprisals?' Peace with Ireland Council, London, 1921, NLI (IR 94109 p1); 'An Irish Louvain', *Manchester Guardian*, reprinted in *Drogheda Independent*, 9 Oct. 1920. For another question of Ireland being the only white race ruled, see *Irish Exile* 1:5, July 1921; see also, AIHS, New York, Friends of Irish Freedom Records (Box 5, Folder 1: newsletter of the Friends of Irish Freedom II:13, 25 Sept. 1920).
96. 'Lord Henry Bentinck denounces military rule in Erin – closing down of Tralee', *Catholic News Service*, 6 Dec. 1920.
97. Mo Moulton, *Ireland and the Irish in Interwar England* (Cambridge, 2014), pp 80–8.
98. David Fitzpatrick, 'Historians and the commemoration of Irish conflicts, 1912–23', in John Horn and Edward Madigan (eds), *Towards Commemoration: Ireland in War and Revolution 1912–1923* (Dublin, 2013), p. 129.
99. *The Irish Exile: An Organ of Irish Movements in and around London*, various issues April 1921–June 1922, NLI, Joseph Fowler collection (Ms 27,097).
100. Dermot Keogh, *Ireland & Europe 1919–1948*, pp 6–7, 10.
101. University College Dublin Archives, George Gavan Duffy papers (P152).
102. Military service pension application of Marie O'Brien, Spain, Irish Military Archives, Military Service Pensions Collection (MSP34REF59976). These essays were, according to Darrell Figgis, 'The historic case for Irish independence', and 'The economic case for Irish independence'; Erskine Childers, 'The military terror in Ireland', *La tragedia de Irlanda: Sus origenes, su desarrollo historico, su fase actual*, translated by A. Ruis y Pablo (Barcelona: Inustrias Graficas Seix & Barral Herms, SA, 1921).
103. Under Secretary for Foreign Affairs (Robert Brennan) to Miss O'Brien, 28 June 1921, Military service pension application of Marie O'Brien, Spain (MSP34REF59976); Robert Brennan, *Allegiance* (Dublin, 1950), p. 324.
104. 'Feeling in France', *Donegal News*, 23 Oct. 1920; 'Denial of Ireland's claim a world danger', Erskine Childers in *The Irish Standard* (Minneapolis), 27 Sept. 1919.
105. *The Kerryman*, 6, 13 and 20 Nov. 1920; *Cork Examiner*, 15 Nov. 1920.
106. Letter of 5 November 1920; statement of Right Rev. Monsignor M. Curran, PP, BMH, WS 687, pp 481–3; he used similar language in late November 1920, when he addressed a large gathering in Milan in support of Irish independence. *Catholic News Service*, 29 Nov. 1920; for further coverage of the Milan meeting, see newsletter of the Friends of Irish Freedom II:23, National Bureau of Information (4 Dec. 1920).

107. *Irish Independent*, 7 Dec. 1920. Other Popular Party members supported Mauri who, along with the Catholic Young Men's Society, orchestrated meetings and rallies. A meeting attended by 6,000 in Milan. *Irish Independent*, 7 Dec. 1920; *Fermanagh Herald*, 8 Jan. 1921; *Meath Chronicle*, 1 Jan. 1921.
108. Aisling Walsh, 'Michael Cardinal Logue 1840–1923', in *Seancas Ardmhacha: Journal of the Armagh Diocesan Historical Society* 18:1 (1999/2000), p. 188; Ferriter, *A Nation and not a Rabble*, pp 87, 188.
109. Newsfeeds, *Catholic News Service*, 20 Dec. 1920. 'Bishops of Belgium send sympathy to Irish hierarchy', *Catholic News Service*, 13 June 1921; *The Catholic News Sheet* (issued by the National Catholic Welfare Council), 27 Sept. 1920.
110. Kenneally, *The Paper Wall*, p. 45; *The Times*, 7 July 1919.
111. Bernard Ducret, 'La Frace et l'Irlande (1914–1923)', in *Etudes Irlandaises* 9 (1984), p. 198.
112. *New York Times*, 5 Mar. 1920. He had previously commented that to counter Sinn Féin extremism, 'civil management must be substituted for Prussian militarism.' W. Alison Phillips, *The Revolution in Ireland, 1906–1923* (London, 1923), p. 170. Phillips directly cites Plunkett from a speech he delivered at the National Liberal Club on 30 October 1919.
113. *Irish Independent*, 24 Jan. 1921.
114. 'Ireland bars the way', *Fermanagh Herald*, 9 Apr. 1921. His Diocesan letter concluded with a hope that Irishmen 'could be won', which would only happen 'by an England that understands them'.
115. *New York Times*, 27 July, 31 Aug. 1919.
116. James M. Beck succeeded Egan at this time, though the latter was cited as president. *New York Herald*, 19 Jan. 1920; *The Sun and New York Herald*, 1 Feb. 1920.
117. 'If you could get theatres […] to refuse to show these Anti-British pictures, you would accomplish more than I can say.' Frank L. Stratton to John Magee, 20 Jan. 1921, New York Public Library, Schwartzman Building (Allied Loyalty League Records, Folder: Allied Loyalty League: Correspondence, 1919–1922: R–S).
118. *New York Tribune*, 28 Nov. 1920.
119. *Washington Herald*, 8 Jan. 1921; *New York Tribune*, 16 Jan. 1921; *New York Herald*, 16 Jan 1921.
120. For contrast with Duffy's ejection from Paris on the same grounds, see *The Sun* and the *New York Herald*, 5 Sept. 1920. Further, O'Callaghan was denied application for political asylum. *Evening Public Ledger*, 30 Mar.1921; Loyal Coalition of Boston wrote to President Harding, Secretary of Labor Davis and Attorney General Daugherty, calling for O'Callaghan to be removed from the US. *Carroll County Democrat*, Huntington, Tennessee, n.d.
121. Mrs R. Lester Fleming to the editor of *The New York Times*, 12 Jan. 1921.
122. John Higham, *Strangers in the Land: Patterns of American Nativism 1860–1925* (New York: Atheneum, 1963), p. 158.
123. Ibid., pp 176, 178–81.
124. Demarest Lloyd, Arthur W. Joslin and George W. Solley, 'The loyal coalition', 12 Sept. 1920, New York Public Library, Schwartzman Building (Allied Loyalty League Records, Folder: Allied Loyalty League: Printed Material and Clippings).
125. *New York Herald*, 4 Oct. 1920.
126. 'Loyal coalition demands US stop Irish bond drive', *New York Tribune*, 25 May 1920; *Tulsa World*, 3 Sept. 1920. This petition occurred alongside de Valera's tour of America for bond drive and recognition of the Irish republic.
127. *The Washington Times*, 20 Apr. 1920; *New York Herald*, 4 Oct. 1920.
128. James C. M'Mullin to the editor of the *New York Tribune*, 6 May 1920; *New York Tribune*, 11 May 1920; Higham, *Strangers in the Land*, p. 199.
129. 'Mrs. Paul FitzSimmons, formerly Mrs. French Vanderbilt, who has startled Newport by starting a campaign against recognition of the Irish Republic in the United States.' *The Urbana Daily Courier*, 28 July 1920.
130. *The Great Falls Tribune*, 26 Jan. 1921; see also, *The Ogden Standard Examiner*, 26 Jan. 1921; *DeKalb Daily Chronicle*, 9 June, 10 June 1921; *The New York Times*, 18 June 1921; *Monmouth Daily Atlas*, 10 June 1921; *New York Tribune*, 30 June 1921.
131. *New York Tribune*, 22 June 1921.
132. *Kentucky Irish American*, 30 Apr. 1921.
133. *The Manning Times*, South Carolina, 30 June 1920; see also, *The Butte Daily Bulletin*, 30 June 1920, *The Washington Times*, 27 June 1920; *The Bee: Omaha*, 30 June 1920.

134. *Tulsa World*, 3 Sept. 1920.
135. *Svĕt*, 3 Sept. 1920. *Thanks to Samantha Simpson, MA, for translating.*
136. Marc Sangier, 'Pour l'Irlande Libre', 28 June 1920, NLI (Ir94109 p. 44).
137. Albert Coyle, 'Preface', in *Evidence on Conditions in Ireland* (May 1921), p. ix.

CHAPTER 6

DESTRUCTION IN THE FOG OF WAR

INTRODUCTION

The IRA's guerrilla campaign to frustrate British rule in Ireland effectively aligned environmental damage to the nationalist cause. Fallen trees, trenched roads, charred police barracks and broken communication lines evidenced rebel activity in any given area, eroded state control, and aided ambushes and interpersonal violence. Retaliatory Crown force destruction, which occurred on a scale between broken panes of glass to the discriminate devastation of entire towns, also served the Irish cause in that it afforded rebel propaganda many examples of the British counter-insurgency's indiscipline and resulting material destruction and human displacement. Generally, environmental destruction during the Irish revolution was politically motivated and was the result of either rebel or Crown force actions.

Other instances of environmental damage are more difficult to categorise as their motivations either fell outside a simple political dichotomy and reflected deeper, often long-held social tensions, or were, in the case of the Irish Civil War, part of the everyday violence and destruction of the period. This chapter examines agrarian-based damage as one aspect of environmental damage that transcended the broader political revolution. In essence, wartime pressure to produce agricultural goods, an ill-defined association with Sinn Féin, and the ebb and flow of security and control all presented opportunities for pre-revolution agrarian grievances to re-emerge. Agrarian sabotage occurred throughout 'the transition to independence' as local rivalries, land-grabbing and anti-grazier sentiment resulted in the destruction of fences, walls and earthen boundaries, cattle-maiming, and the burning of fields, crops, turf and farming implements.[1] Animosity aimed at the grazier and landlord class also inspired violence against the Anglo-Irish 'Big House', its owners and caretakers, and the demesne lands on which they stood; acts that transcended the War of Independence and civil war periods. This chapter also surveys each of the revolution's preceding categories of environmental destruction as they featured during the Irish Civil War. However, their direct and indirect impacts on both active combatants and civilians often amplified the destruction. Many endured ruined landscapes and infrastructure that impeded their livelihoods and complicated independent Ireland's emergence into statehood. This chapter offers a brief overview of the ways environmental destruction had come to personify guerrilla conflict in Ireland, often irrespective of motivation or enemy.

AGRARIAN DAMAGE

Successive British legislation from the 1870s onward attempted to address the Irish land question from a native perspective. The aim was to ease the tension between landlords and tenants, fund the sale and transfer of land, and in doing so downplay the appeal of agrarianism and Fenianism.[2] At the same time, the Home Rule movement effectively allied land reform with nationalism; the restoration of a native and independent Irish parliament was often linked to the restoration of land to native holders, albeit through land purchase agreements.[3] Nationalist reaction upheld graziers as those who had done well out of the Famine, vilifying this agricultural class while positioning tenants' propriety and tillage as natural complements to Ireland's rural economy and traditional character.[4] The United Irish League, an agrarian body aligned to the demands of agricultural laborers, led calls for the division of grazing lands at the turn of the twentieth century, reaffirming land tenure as Ireland's binding political issue.[5] Its founder, William O'Brien, called for an end of landlordism and generally criticised graziers, whom nationalists broadly associated with the Ascendancy.[6] Anti-grazier agitation proceeded throughout the 'Ranch War' between 1906 and 1909, during which smallholders drove cattle and boycotted and intimidated landlords who had yet to sell out.[7] Division amongst Ireland's farming class thus exposed a nationalist contradiction: while small farmers represented the type of back-to-the-land economic autonomy popular amongst Home Rule advocates and co-operative societies of the early twentieth century, nationalism required the support of graziers and well-to-do farmers in order to appear legitimate.[8] In a similar way, critique of the grazing class and ascendency landowners helped establish Sinn Féin as the political party for landless men and small farmers.

Despite extensive land transfers completed under the Wyndham Act (1903) and Birrell Act (1909), tension amongst small farmers persisted. But as Paul Bew noted, successful land purchase 'was perfectly compatible with the continuation of other tensions'.[9] In western counties, for instance, land purchase tended to stimulate further demand amongst both tenant proprietors and landless men.[10] Pressure on the land increased during the pre-independence years as Congested Districts Board (CDB) purchasing funds were frozen, the number of farms was reduced to prevent uneconomic holdings, and a wartime halt to emigration kept men on the land.[11] 'The result,' Rumpf explained, 'was greatly increasing pressure on the land at a time when agrarian reform was forced to come to an almost complete standstill.'[12] The Great War contributed to this pressure. While the conflict brought an agricultural boom to Ireland, its dividends were not evenly allocated; the gain enjoyed by producers was disproportionate to the pain felt by consumers.

Food shortages after 1916 impelled the government to call for expanded tillage. Sinn Féin initially promoted this measure as a means of satisfying land-hungry tenants who had been frozen out of purchase during the war.[13] Local cumann often orchestrated land division, escorting 'congested' men to the fields behind ploughs, bands and tri-colour flags.[14] Further calls for expanded tillage for food export quickly animated accusations of exploitation and British misrule, which piled onto existing anti-war sentiment and triggered anxiety of potential famine in Ireland.[15] Sinn Féin urged Dubliners to purchase directly from farmers, for farmers to sell their produce for consumption in Ireland, and for workers to refuse to handle food for export.[16] The party executive ordered special markets to be established in the rural districts of Cork, Kerry, Clare, Mayo, Wexford and Tyrone to ensure food was available for the poor.[17] As Terence Dooley observed, 'agrarian grievance, political resentment and land hunger became enmeshed.'[18]

Anti-grazing sentiments skewered broader political issues, present in Sinn Féin speeches throughout the 1917 by-elections. Canvassing for Count Noble Plunkett, long-time agrarian activist Laurence Ginnell told a gathering at Elphin in County Roscommon – one of the most agriculturally disturbed counties in Ireland at the time – that:

> As a result of Mr. Redmond's action thousands of Irishmen are buried today at the bottom of the Dardanelles, in Sulva Bay, and in the trenches of Flanders who ought to be at home breaking up the ranches of Roscommon. [...] We want you to seize the present opportunity to have every sod of ranch land broken up and force the Government to send down steam ploughs, turn them up, and divide them into holdings [...]. [19]

Éamon de Valera also spoke at Elphin in February 1918, where he advocated for Volunteer companies to be formed in alignment with every Sinn Féin club, whose duty it would be to prevent conscription and 'to help divide the land evenly'.[20] Other Sinn Féin agents resurrected memory of the Famine in calls for land division and framed successive Land Acts since the nineteenth-century as the fruit of land agitation and agrarian violence.[21] For instance, Joseph Stanley, printer, cinema operator and republican publicist, explained the Land Acts to have been the result of 'rioting, cattle-driving, boycotting, and moonlighting'; 'the only way to get anything,' he told a Drogheda political gathering, 'was to have the head of a landlord in one hand and the tail of a cow in the other.'[22]

Land division and redistribution quickly took on a life of its own, animated by land-hungry and food-hungry men whom the wartime agricultural boom had left behind. Antagonists operated at the intersection of nationalism and moonlighting where, Fitzpatrick noted, 'the same assailant was often Volunteer, Sinn Féiner and uneconomic holder or landless younger son.'[23] Newspaper reports, criminal injury claims and recollections thereafter recorded the varieties of damage. Applications for compensation from counties Clare, Cork and Limerick in 1917 and 1918, for instance, all cite broken or thrown-down walls of various length and material, as well as the removal or destruction of gates and other property boundaries.[24] This destruction may be categorised as 'scattered attacks' within what Charles Tilly observed as being decentralised and indirectly political destruction.[25] However, such a label lends as much clarity to the nature and extent of agrarian violence as the contemporary term 'outrage'.[26] Moreover, displacing boundaries, clearing grazing land and claiming and distributing plots held a deeper cultural meaning. The destruction of boundary markers and the sabotage of grazing space also functioned as acts of decolonialisation; resistance which, in 1917 and 1918, had the support (or at the very least non-intervention) of Sinn Féin. Increasingly, the satisfactory response to the land question was to reconcile the Irish people to Irish soil and to address the inequities of a grazing system through which 'cattle [had] displaced human beings.'[27]

Land agitation and environmental damage connect the revolutionary period to previous eras of agrarian disturbance. This continuity distinguished agrarian agitation as a constant against the more recent political challenge of Sinn Féin. Agrarian actors stepped into the gaps in security and order to sabotage graziers, clear plots and redistribute land.[28] The 'men of no property' underscored the dichotomy between priorities at the periphery and attitudes at the political centre.[29] Thus, while it was often appropriated to support aspects of the independence movement, land agitation remained a movement unto itself.[30]

A second wave of land agitation materialised in the west of Ireland in the spring of 1920. Fergus Campbell identifies that the issues of the previous agitation of 1917–18 – congestion, hiatus on emigration, agricultural price inflation and the CDB's pause in purchase financing – remained motivating factors for land seizure in 1920.[31] Several additional factors intensified the situation: a particularly wet spring growing season that spread fear of a potentially poor harvest, protest over the 11-month conacre leases set to begin in May, and the erosion of state security as the RIC was withdrawn from many remote rural regions in the face of IRA attacks.[32] The RIC Inspector General identified the latter point in his report on County Clare, citing 'the lawless element which took advantage of the state of things to gratify private spleen and obtain land.'[33] Kevin O'Shiel, who served as a special judicial commissioner on behalf of Dáil Éireann, recalled that land agitation throughout the bordering province of Connacht spared 'neither great ranch nor medium farm and inflict[ed] in its headlong course, sad havoc on man, beast, and property.'[34]

Agrarian outrages affecting property and 'the public peace' show the extent and severity of intimidation, displacement, injury to animals and damage to the agricultural environment that occurred alongside the Sinn Féin political revolution. Intimidation typically took the form of threatening letters or a menacing delegation of landless men who induced landowners to clear, portion and sell their land, often at a deflated price. The RIC reported 329 instances of intimidation to have occurred between 1 January and 19 May 1920, the majority of which took the form of threatening letters and notices.[35] Destruction of hay, turf and farm equipment, demolition of boundary walls and fences, field spiking, cattle driving and arson also conveyed the desire for grazing land to be cleared for occupation or given up for division amongst congested tenants, uneconomic holders and landless labourers.[36] After being cleared from the land, animals were often repurposed as a means of compounding protest, frequently pushed up to the landlord's house, maimed or driven to exhaustion in order to devalue the stock.[37] In one instance, cattle were recovered with a placard skewered on their horns that read 'The land for the people, and the road for these', showing further disdain towards grazing's displacement of farmers.[38] At times, the land itself was prepared as an agent of intimidation. For example, a turf field outside Cashel, Tipperary, was intentionally flooded in May 1920 as a warning to competing interests to cease their cultivation.[39] On the Fitzherbert estate in Navan, Meath, 'nocturnal raiders' attacked farm land as well as grazing land, driving cattle and sheep and folding freshly ploughed sod back into the earth.[40] Death threats and imitation graves prepared outside the homes of obstinate proprietors – 'a mute but eloquent gesture' that occurred throughout disturbed counties – proved more explicit intimidation tactics.[41]

Ireland witnessed more agrarian outrages in 1920 than any year since 1882, the apex of the first Land War. Injury to property in its various forms was the primary feature of these outrages.[42] Examining the daily returns for agrarian outrages from May to September 1920, when Dáil Éireann's emergency arbitration courts were in operation, reveals steady returns for agrarian-related intimidation and destruction of property. What is perhaps more revealing about the scale of agrarian outrages in 1920 is its astonishing increase from the previous year. Statistics for agrarian outrages reported to the RIC Inspector General tallied the total number of offences that had occurred up to that day since the first of January. If a percentage change formula is applied to the number of outrages that occurred to date in 1919 and again for that same period in 1920, and that change is averaged against the number of days in which data was reported for a given month, then a clearer picture emerges as to the exponential increase in threatening activity and injury to property that created truly chaotic circumstances in agrarian communities in Ireland in the spring and summer of 1920.

Month, Year, and Number of Days Reported	Monthly Average of Returns and Percentage Change Between 1919 and 1920					
	Threatening Letters and Notices	Percentage Change	Otherwise (Intimidation)	Percentage Change	Injury to Property	Percentage Change
May 1919 (8 days recorded)	73	+265%	14	+459%	26.25	+736%
May 1920 (8 days recorded)	266.3		78.25		219.25	
June 1919 (20 days recorded)	86.8	+246%	15.85	+533%	33.15	+691%
June 1920 (20 days recorded)	300.4		100.25		262.1	
July 1919 (17 days recorded)	103.4	+210%	18.94	+484%	41.23	+600%
July 1920 (17 days recorded)	319.5		110.5		288.52	
August 1919 (14 days recorded)	121.9	+173%	23.4	+390%	47.9	+539%
August 1920 (14 days recorded)	332.7		114.3		304.3	
September 1919 (11 days recorded)	131.1	+156%	26.1	+341%	60.2	+412%
September 1920 (11 days recorded)	336.1		115		308	

[43]

The overall gap between 1919 and 1920 for each offence closed as the summer progressed, but this is not to suggest that activity for 1920 was anything less than overwhelming when compared to the previous year.

The widespread campaign of agrarian violence and land seizure in 1920 threatened to undermine the nationalist movement and alienate large farmers, an important base of support for Sinn Féin. The nature and extent of land seizure was chaotic and had become embarrassing to a political apparatus seeking to exude legitimacy and order.[44] Previous Sinn Féin policy had forbidden cattle driving without the sanction of the local executive, protocol often overlooked or simply ignored.[45] By 1920, the party sought to distance itself entirely; its standing committee ordered that the labels of Sinn Féin and Dáil Éireann 'not be used in connection with land seizures',[46] and decreed that the people's energies be directed towards 'clearing out – not the occupier of this or that piece of land – but the foreign invader of our country.'[47]

Republican leadership certainly sought to redress inequity, but on its own terms. Arbitration courts emerged as a conservative tool to uphold property rights, but the sheer volume of agrarian disputes quickly necessitated distinct land courts.[48] The Dáil Land Commission replaced the emergency tribunal scheme in September 1920, while a National Land Bank, Banc na Talmhan, operated from April 1920, through which Dáil Éireann financed loans for land purchase on a co-operative basis.[49] Kevin O'Shiel recalled that while the land commission and courts did not solve Ireland's agrarian problem – 'the most combustible subject in Ireland' – they nevertheless 'checked a grave menace to property and life at a time of violent revolutionary turmoil in the country'.[50] Through a more critical lens, it might be said that Dáil Éireann managed agrarian agitation in a way that permitted an appearance of control over the situation, while moving towards resolution of land inequity. Legislation did not abate land hunger, and civil conflict continued to provide a pretext for continued seizure and destruction.[51] Nowhere was this more acutely realised than in the experience of the Anglo-Irish Big House.

Country mansions and estates, the Anglo-Irish 'Big Houses' of the landed elite, were targeted for division and destruction throughout the Irish Revolution under the pretext of agrarian grievance and security concerns, and because they symbolised 'the footprint of the coloniser'.[52] Though its influence had declined steadily in the decades preceding the First World War, the Big House and its associated family continued to embody local power, military tradition and social elitism, which in turn fostered resentment and a sense of injustice amongst dispossessed nationalists.[53] The incentive for burning mansions had complex social roots, which often existed outside immediate religious contexts.[54] Burning the Big House could be both practical and patriotic. Terence Dooley argues that their destruction was part of the IRA's active campaign against British authority in Ireland, as opposed to being simply a derivative by-product of revolutionary violence; that is, Big Houses were not collateral damage but intentional targets.[55]

The RIC's withdrawal from remote barracks disconnected Big Houses from their principal means of protection. Houses located near vacated or destroyed police barracks were often attacked as an extension of the campaign against state authority, as it was anticipated that a previously abandoned patrol area might be reconstituted or reinforced from the Big House. Annesgrove House (County Cork), Killester House (County Dublin), Gaulstown Mansion (County Westmeath) and Curraghboola House (County Longford), for example, were all burned in May and June 1920 in anticipation of their being occupied by the police or military. Cork (East Riding district) 'maintained its reputation as about the worst county in Ireland' in July 1920, after Rochesfordtown House was destroyed along with eight vacated barracks, a courthouse and an abandoned military barracks at Catford. All were burned, reports claimed, to prevent them being reopened and to prevent police from returning to the area.[56] Proximity to the spiralling violence between the IRA and Crown forces also claimed Big Houses, which were burned as revenge for Black and Tan and Auxiliary police reprisals.[57] As James S. Donnelly argues, selecting Big House targets was both circumstantial and systematic, and was orchestrated to offset and deter reprisals in select areas. Revenge was, therefore, another motivating factor. In late May 1921, Christopher O'Connell helped burn Dunboy Castle in County Cork as a reprisal for IRA men's homes being burned, namely those of Liam O'Dwyer and Jeremiah O'Connor (Ardgroom, 25 May 1921), and Micheal Og O'Sullivan and Tim Spillane (Rossmacowen, 26 May 1921).

Perpetrators infrequently provided greater details as to their motivations to destroy Big Houses, even in hindsight. When in 1935 an interviewer pressed Waterford Volunteer John Brazil on the nature of his military service, specifically the burning of Lord Ashtown's (Frederick Oliver Trench) estate, Glenahiery House, he simply replied that it had been ordered by the brigade as 'Tans or military of some description [were] going to stay there.'[58] However, deeper motives were often at play. For Glenahiery House, these included Lord Ashtown's refusal to sell any estate lands under the 1903 Wyndham Land Act as well as his viciously anti-nationalist attitude, which the self-financed monthly periodical *Grievances from Ireland* transmitted from 1906 to 1910.[59] Guerrillas also navigated the revolutionary period with a heightened awareness of the historic 'landlord-tenant dichotomy', which identified landowners as alien to wider Irish society and thus legitimate targets.[60] Like barracks, coast guard stations and court houses, Anglo-Irish Big Houses represented the cultural and political authority republicans sought to overthrow and ultimately erase.[61] Lord Ashtown claimed £15,000 for the destruction of Glenahiery House, which, along with the eradication of Ballymacarbery, Ballinamult and Kilmanahan RIC Barracks nearby, significantly limited enemy presence and friendly quarter for Crown forces in the region.[62] However, the Baron's losses extended far beyond his scenic lodge on the River Suir. Dungarvan Quarter Sessions heard of the estate's 'wholesale destruction': over 1,000 trees had been either uprooted, cut and carried away, or maliciously snapped in half; the gates and fences surrounding the property were knocked down and broken; Kilronan Church, the family's private chapel, was damaged; and Woodbine Cottage, an adjoining property, was again damaged after suffering a previous attack.[63]

Politicising the Irish landscape had changed the meaning of the Big House, a process that began long before the Irish Revolution, with mansions, demesne land and territorial boundaries of possession contrasting uneconomic holdings, land hunger and dispossession.[64] Their destruction, therefore, eliminated potential billets (military dimension), punished perceived class enemies and checked 'anti-Irish' behaviour (social and political dimension), but also acted to rectify what many nationalists viewed as a historically unjust cultural landscape (colonial dimension). Gemma Clark also sees Big House destruction as symbolic, an 'uncivilized end' to the broader 'process of Plantation' and a 'direct challenge to their social and economic standing in the local community – and to their outmoded way of life'.[65] Suitably, F. S. L. Lyons observed that 'it seemed by the end of 1923 as if the Anglo-Irish tradition was destined to end in fire and ruin.'[66] The

Irish Civil War quickened this ruin in that it provided pretense for 'everyday violence' to function more broadly together with prevailing political violence.[67]

Big House burnings during the opening phase of the Irish Civil War – between August and October 1922 – occurred in what the Ministry of Agriculture observed to be an unusual time for land agitation:

> The Land War is very widespread and very serious even at present. In the past, even when it developed into large proportions, it always began in Spring. On this occasion there is a change; lands have been seized in Autumn, and there are all the signs of very serious trouble developing in the months of January and February.[68]

Lord Landsdowne's 'much loved Irish home' at Derreen, Cork, was one such residence.[69] His estate agent accounted the looting and violence that took place in September 1922, destruction that appeared to transcend simple political or sectarian motives:

> On arrival at Derreen the scene that met our eyes beggars [sic] description, crowds of every description round the house, men, women and children, pulling, hauling, fighting for what they could take. The house is absolutely destroyed, doors all smashed, every particle of furniture taken. [...] they got at the cellars and the men were all half drunk, fighting and revolver shots going off. [...] regret to say everything is gone, all the windows, doors, flooring, etc., have been taken, motor garage gone. [...] all outbuildings either removed or burnt, green house smashed up. [...] In fact there is nothing left of Derreen or its surroundings.[70]

President W. T. Cosgrave explained the destruction of Derreen and other landed estates as 'symptoms of the demoralization which has already seized the whole social fabric when we took over the administration of government'. Cosgrave assured Winston Churchill that the Provisional Government were 'grappling with the monster with all our might'.[71]

The majority of Big House burnings occurred during the Irish Civil War alongside escalations in land seizure and general damage to property, the by-product of the anti-Treaty military campaign against Provisional Government and later Free State forces.[72] As such, 'land for the people' and 'in the name of the Republic' were at times transposable motives where, in the fog of war, 'almost as many abuses could be perpetrated under one pretext as the other.'[73]

Civil War Damage

Environmental destruction in Ireland had become codified by the outbreak of the civil war. The IRA split of spring 1922 demonstrated the depths of anti-Treaty recalcitrance and its views towards the immediate future, as defensive posts were established and raids on post offices and bank robberies abounded in an effort to maintain the republic and secure vital funds towards its function. Both Provisional Government and anti-Treaty forces fortified positions in the Capital – Beggar's Bush Barracks acted as the pro-Treaty military headquarters while the republican IRA forces occupied the Four Courts – a 'startling and sensational move' that definitively alienated pro- and anti-Treaty IRA factions.[74] The Four Courts were a problematic headquarters, dislocated from other republican garrisons in the city whose occupation seemed to represent 'intransigence and protest' rather than any coherent military strategy.[75] Ernie O'Malley later lamented the absence of any 'clear-cut policy' and 'a haphazard pattern of war'.[76] But some, like Sean Prendergast, an officer commanding C Company in the Dublin Brigade, saw the Four Courts as sacred ground in the establishment of the republic in 1916 and in its defence in 1922.[77] Regionalism outside the Capital saw both IRA factions scramble to capture evacuated RIC barracks throughout the country.[78] Confrontation over control of towns frequently provoked republican evacuation and the burning of their evacuated barracks, strategic withdrawal that complicated logistics and operational control for Provisional Government forces and portrayed its government as incapable.[79]

National events progressed quickly throughout June 1922. The results of the Pact Election certified pro-Treaty Sinn Féin candidates on the grounds of national stability and endorsed the Constitution of the Irish Free State, published on polling day. The assassination of Sir Henry Wilson, former Chief of the Imperial General Staff, Unionist MP for North Down, and at the time military advisor to the Northern Ireland government, in London on 22 June upset already delicate relations between the Provisional Government and the British Cabinet, and 'brought the focus back to the Four Courts'.[80] The question facing the Provisional Government was whether it or the British military would unseat republican strongholds throughout Dublin, the latter option having the possibility of unifying the IRA at the cost of the Treaty settlement. '[B]owing to immediate circumstances' and entrenched against the IRA's kidnapping of J. J. O'Connell (National Army Deputy Chief of Staff), the Provisional Government began shelling the Four Courts on 28 June 1922 in order to establish itself as the sole military authority in the country.[81]

Observational reports from British Army personnel who remained in Dublin detail the progression of the Provisional Government's assault on the Four Courts and general fighting in neighbouring areas, much of which replayed the scenes of Easter 1916. Republican sniping and guerrilla operations coagulated around Rutland Square (Parnell Square), while ambushes occurred around the Camden Street–Harcourt Street and Leeson Street–Baggot Street areas as anti-Treaty forces manoeuvred to Dublin's southern neighbourhoods. After roughly two days' fighting, the anti-Treaty front was confined to rows of houses that extended from Prussia Street to Lower Gardiner Street north of the River Liffey, and between Beggar's Bush and Rathmines bordering the Grand Canal.[82] Shattered masonry and debris reinforced barricades within the Four Courts, around which mines and barbed wire had been laid. Sections of the building had caught fire, including the main munitions cache located in the west end of the 'headquarters block'. While the Land Registry Office, the Treasury portion of the Public Records Office and the law courts shielded it from direct artillery fire, heat from encroaching fires reached a critical level and ignited stored explosives.[83] The British Army situation report simply read: 'a mine was exploded in the Four Courts, location unknown. The situation in the Four Courts is thus obscure.'[84] Inside the Four Courts, the scene was more expressive, and to some poetic. The explosion incited duelling orchestras of crashing stone and singing flame, O'Malley recalled.[85] Sean Prendergast, who had been reassigned to Great Brunswick Street (now Pearse Street), concluded, 'as far as one could judge the position the fall of the Four Courts presaged that stone and mortar were not invulnerable to attack then any more than they were in 1916.'[86] Although the explosion claimed no human casualties, the resulting architectural ruin of the law courts and subsequent obliteration of centuries of records – in addition to the fact that neither Provisional Government nor anti-Treaty republican forces took care to avoid their destruction – amounted to what John Regan termed 'cultural vandalism'.[87]

Damage to republican-held buildings in north-eastern Sackville Street, adjacent to the structures damaged in 1916, were also 'an ugly reminder of both business and civilian losses'.[88] Annie Farrington witnessed the battle for Dublin unfold from the nearby Barry's Hotel on Great Denmark Street, which she had purchased in July 1921. Soldiers evicted guests in order to utilise their rooms as defensive posts. They smashed windows, erected barricades and 'loopholed' tunnels between the hotel and adjoint buildings; a makeshift republican headquarters was established in the dining room.[89] A 'distraught' Farrington remained to supervise the occupation and protect her property, a stressful experience that caused her to develop neurotic rheumatism. 'I was half out of my mind thinking of all the money I owed the bank which financed the purchase of the hotel and I now saw the possibility of the whole place going up in smoke. [...] They had the doors barricaded with my good tables and furniture.'[90] As republican resistance in the area eroded, she convinced withdrawing engineers to spare the building by disarming mines that had been laid under the front door and within the roof. While the incursion was short-lived, it was nevertheless costly. In 1924, the hotel's manager, Miss Keogh, lodged a claim for over £2,000 for damage and consequential losses.[91]

Neighbouring hotels and businesses on the east side of O'Connell Street, such as the Gresham, Granville and Hammam hotels, were also destroyed in the fighting, depriving Dublin of its most 'commodious hotels' ahead of the August horse show, reported the *Westmeath Independent*.[92] Fire had quickly spread between tunnels that had been cut amidst the buildings stretching between Findlater Place and Cathedral Street, which were hit with artillery and machine-gun fire, whose injury was estimated at between £3 and £4 million.[93] Like in the aftermath of the 1916 Easter Rising, many buildings' integrity had been compromised. Collapsing masonry required demolition in the weeks that followed.[94] The *Freeman's Journal* provided a view of Dublin's main thoroughfare that went beyond simple material damage to assess the value of architectural and cultural loss:

> It now only remains to destroy the 'Old House at Home' and the west front of Trinity College and all the unique architectural grandeur that made Dublin one of the choice art centres of the world will have perished. Everything distinctive that was Dublin's own, except Trinity and the Bank, has gone into ruins.[95]

Republican surrender and withdrawal released Dublin as an active military theatre. By early July, banks and shops had reopened amidst 'The New Ruins' of O'Connell Street and tramlines resumed carrying passengers throughout the city.[96] British situational observations for 6 July noted that 'the nearest republican post to Dublin was at Saggart.'[97] Overall, the battle of Dublin showed the anti-Treaty position to have elevated symbolism over a coherent military strategy.[98]

As the IRA decentralised, it retreated into local skirmishes and guerrilla warfare. Intelligence reports show a return to landscape manipulation and sabotage.[99] Dan Breen's second statement to the Bureau of Military History, which recounts the civil war period, explained such priorities as indispensable to any guerrilla army engaging a better-equipped enemy, an outlook the IRA had adopted and developed during its previous engagement with British Crown forces.[100] IRA Department of Engineering orders illustrated how anti-Treaty forces planned to engage their former comrades, and what modifications or improvements were required given that many Provisional Government troops, and in particular their leadership, were schooled in the same military doctrine of guerrilla warfare.

Engineering notes show that road obstruction during the civil war extended beyond basic trenching. A road's proximity to water, adjacent to a stream or within boggy territory, meant a softer, easier dig. It was also suggested that if water could be 'temporarily diverted through any trench cut in the road it will help to keep the bottom soft'.[101] Trees, stones and traps comprised further barriers, with foresight towards their repair or removal modifying procedures for obstruction in some cases. For instance, it was instructed that large stones and boulders, big enough to require removal by drilling or blasting (approximately 27 cubic feet), were to be placed in a 'zig-zag form' along roads that ran through glens and valleys. To prevent clearing, all available sledgehammers and drills within a three-mile radius from the site of obstruction were ordered to be removed and stored offsite.[102]

Deception was also encouraged. One 'temporary and urgent' road obstruction technique called for whitethorn and furze shrubs to be placed at intervals along with smaller stones and broken branches to give the impression that mines had been recently set. This, in addition to the detonation of a small mine, 'would probably frighten the enemy and make him turn back'.[103] Baited traps were not uncommon, giving obstructions an air of danger in their own right.[104]

Captured documents from July 1922 show that the IRA again prioritised a knowledge of the landscape. It requested divisional area commanders be supplied survey maps to identify the location and certain advantages of roads ('Positions for ambushing, obstructions, pits'), railways ('Position of curves, distances from nearest stations, suitability for ambushing [and] derailing'), bridges ('The destruction of one bridge will often render several routes impassable') and rivers ('Positions for crossing or fording, depth of water at various times, natural advantages for retreating').[105] Situational awareness also considered the human landscape and civilians' needs to interact with their environment and go about their daily lives. Where enemy movement was to be entirely cut off, 'it must be remembered that the travelling public are to get all reasonable facilities for carrying on their ordinary work.'[106] Such thoughtfulness no doubt aimed to win hearts and minds towards the republic, or at least to avoid alienating civilians from it. This proved difficult as widespread train derailing and damage to lines threatened food supplies in the west, generally disrupted traffic and, where viaduct bridges had been destroyed, flooded adjacent lands. The destruction of the railway viaduct over the River Blackwater at Mallow in August 1922, for instance, severed communications between Dublin and Cork, while debris blocked the flow of the river and flooded and destroyed surrounding bridges, fences and lands.[107] 'The damage done in practically every direction is so serious,' reported the *Cork Examiner*, 'that in some cases years must elapse before a complete service is attempted.'[108]

County Limerick provides some further examples of the war's infringement on private life. Limerick acted as a thoroughfare for anti-Treaty republican forces, which withdrew south from Limerick City ahead of Provisional Government reinforcements in July 1922. Michael Hopkinson noted the city's importance: 'Even before the fighting in Dublin was over it became clear that Limerick City would become the next crucial centre for concern. In retrospect, both Republican and pro-Treaty participants held that the struggle for control of the city decided the war.'[109] A small sample of 25 incidents from Limerick for June, July and August 1922 illustrates the diversity of damage and how it affected the land and its inhabitants. These include the destruction of bridges, knocking of walls and fences, felling of trees, digging of trenches and formation of barricades across roads.[110] By late August 1922, compensation claims arising out of disturbances in Limerick already totalled £176,000, the *Cork Examiner* reported.[111] This small but representative sample only contributed £1,500 to that figure – not even one per cent of the total.

Destruction stemming from communal tensions, such as cattle driving and land occupation, were not as prevalent in Limerick at this time; damage was almost exclusively linked to military manoeuvres. However, while overtly linked to military strategy, the destruction of trees, roads, bridges and walls produced unforeseen costs, and perhaps unintended damage – consequential damage we often fail to categorise. Several claims illustrate this point. Both the republican IRA and Free State National Forces destroyed a number of bridges between June and August. Specifically, Coolavehy Bridge south of Ardpatrick, two bridges spanning the River Awbeg that connected Mountrussell, Jamestown, Ballymacshaneboy and Newpark Cross south of Kilmallock, a bridge that covered the rail line at Garrienderk, and further north, a bridge between the town lands of Drombane and Castle Erken. Although demolished to impede troop movement, the destruction of these bridges led to further landscape deformation. Thomas Hickey and John Blackwell claimed that flooding following the destruction of the bridge between Drombane and Castle Erken by National Troops in early July had seriously damaged their lands, ruining five and seven acres of grassland and produce, respectively. The fences marking James Quane's property were torn down and his land was transformed into a makeshift road after Coolavehy Bridge was destroyed. Similarly, traffic was diverted through the farms of David Coleman and David Roche near Jamestown, where trespass continued until 1924. In his compensation application, Roche claimed: 'as each passage became too cut up for traffic, fresh passages were cut away from fields […] [leaving them] torn up and useless.' One field under tillage had to be continually guarded, he stated, to prevent cattle from destroying his crops. While initial destruction of property shows the flow of military pursuit, its consequent impact highlights important but often-unseen aspects of the Irish Civil War: the banal experience of everyday life. The road adjacent to Roche's farm (south) was the only route to the local creamery. In reality, his land was rutted, churned and disrupted more by his neighbours than any military force; people from the community who, like himself, had to 'draw home hay and turf' and continue with their lives in spite of a wrecked bridge.

As retreating republicans destroyed bridges, sabotaged roads and uprooted railways, the Provisional Government entrenched itself behind the narrative of majority rule and democratic legitimacy and publicised environmental ruin – at least that caused by the 'Irregulars' – as a war on the Irish people.[112] Propaganda aimed to 'rouse public feeling against interference with the railway' and to infuse 'a proper civic spirit' would, it believed, cause destructive activities to cease outside active military areas.[113] In a memorandum distributed to Local Government authorities, W. T. Cosgrave outlined how republican operations were 'assuming more distinctly the character of a war upon the economic life of Irish people' and urged 'all clergy and public men', i.e. those of influence, to take an active part in the 'establishment of order and public security' by clearing blocked roads and repairing bridges and railways. 'The best way to stop the campaign of outrage and destruction is to let it be seen that it is arousing the people to opposition, and that it is, therefore, futile.'[114] The *Irish Independent* carried the government's position: 'The whole economic life of the country is threatened. The safety and future welfare of the nation depend upon the power of the irregulars being broken. It is the duty of all to stand solidly together to establish that the will of the people shall prevail.'[115]

Various newspapers reinforced the view that republicans were cutting a 'trail of destruction', a headline that was reproduced verbatim throughout July 1922,[116] but it was *Truth*, a short-lived government mouthpiece, that encapsulated the message in its simplest form: 'The Country is in danger. The trail of the Irregulars is a trail of fire and destruction. The cost will be paid by the Irish people. It will run into millions.'[117]

It is difficult to assess the 'cost' of the Irish Civil War in any conclusive form. Like the conflict's political and social legacy, the cost of compensation and rebuilding lingered in Irish society for many years. Michael Hopkinson places material damage at over £30 million, overheads that remained a fixture in Ernest Blythe's budget proposals throughout his tenure as Finance Minister.[118] Campaigning in 1927, W. T. Cosgrave told a Kilkenny crowd that approximately £10,000 a year were levied on top of county rates to address Damage to Property Compensation Act claims.[119] That same year, The *Irish Statesman* dissected the Free State budget for its readers, listing compensation as one of the state's enduring budgetary 'abnormalities'.[120]

Conclusion

Numerous acts of environmental manipulation and destruction occurred in Ireland throughout the revolution, to which it is difficult to categorise or assign definitive political motives. Land seizure and anti-grazier movements reflected long-standing agrarian concerns that were resurrected amidst wartime discontent and Sinn Féin's political ascent in order to challenge calls for expanded tillage, occupy contested land and sabotage agricultural holdings. This activity greatly expanded under a fog of war that occupied the attention of state security forces, primarily the RIC. The destruction of Anglo-Irish 'Big Houses' also occurred throughout the revolution. Their elimination served several ends; their destruction was deemed essential to controlling territory and eliminating potential enemy billets, while at the same time uprooting sections of the landed gentry.

The Irish Civil War's opening phase again demonstrated the disadvantages and consequences of attempting to hold static, disconnected buildings as strongholds against superior firepower, as had been the case in 1916. The conflict quickly pivoted towards guerrilla warfare and featured methods familiar to both the republican IRA and Provisional Government forces, former comrades who had previously engaged the British forces on the same model. Resulting environmental damage demonstrated the extent to which destroyed bridges and obstructed roads impacted local communities, and permitted the Provisional Government to claim the moral high ground over 'Irregulars', who were accused of plunging the country into ruin.

NOTES

1. David Jones uses the phrase 'the transition to independence' to refer to the 1919–1923 period while reflecting on his book, *Graziers, Land Reform and Political Conflict in Ireland*. David Jones, 'The issue of land distribution: Revisiting *Graziers, Land Reform and Political Conflict in Ireland*', in Fergus Campbell and Tony Varley (eds), *Land Questions in Modern Ireland* (Manchester, 2013), pp 117–48.
2. Philip Bull, *Land, Politics and Nationalism: A Study of the Irish Land Question* (Dublin, 1996), pp 54, 60.
3. Ibid., p. 67.
4. Jones, 'The issue of land distribution', pp 138–9, 141. On stereotypical views toward the Anglo-Irish landlord, see F. S. L. Lyons, *Culture and Anarchy in Ireland 1890–1939* (Oxford, 1979), pp 22–3.
5. Diarmaid Ferriter, *The Transformation of Ireland 1900–2000* (London, 2005 edn), pp 30, 43.
6. Jones, 'The issue of land distribution', p. 139.
7. Ibid., p. 122; Ferriter, *The Transformation of Ireland*, p. 69.
8. Paul Bew, 'Sinn Féin agrarian radicalism and the War of Independence, 1919–1921', in D. G. Boyce (ed.), *The Revolution in Ireland, 1879–1923* (MacMillan Education Ltd, 1988), pp 219–20.
9. Ibid., p. 224.
10. Erhard Rumpf and A. C. Hepburn, *Nationalism and Socialism in Twentieth-Century Ireland* (New York, 1977), pp 50–1.
11. Rumpf and Hepburn, *Nationalism and Socialism*, p. 53; Michael Laffan, *The Resurrection of Ireland: The Sinn Féin Party* (Cambridge, 1999), p. 310; Terence Dooley, *Burning the Big House: The Story of the Irish Country House in a Time of War and Revolution* (London, 2022), pp 79–82.
12. Rumpf and Hepburn, *Nationalism and Socialism*, p. 53; see also, Kevin O'Shiel, 'Some recent phases of the Irish land question', *Manchester Guardian*, 10 May 1923.
13. David Fitzpatrick, *Politics and Irish Life*, pp 61–2, 65.
14. Dorothy Macardle, *The Irish Republic*, pp 240–1; see also, Fitzpatrick, *Politics and Irish Life*, p. 130; Inspector General's monthly report for February 1918, Inspector General (Byrne) to Under Secretary, 15 Mar. 1918, TNA (CO 904/105).
15. Inspector General's monthly report for January 1917, Assistant Inspector General RIC to Under Secretary, 13 Feb. 1917, TNA (CO 904/102).
16. Inspector General's monthly report for December 1917, Inspector General RIC to Under Secretary, 12 Jan. 1918, TNA (CO 904/104); see also, Ferriter, *A Nation and Not a Rabble: The Irish Revolution 1913–1923* (London: Profile Books, 2015), p. 178.
17. Inspector General's monthly report for March 1918, Inspector General RIC to Under Secretary, 13 Apr. 1918, TNA (CO 904/105).
18. Dooley, *Burning the Big House*, p. 82.
19. Meeting at Elphin, County Roscommon, 28 Jan. 1917, Sinn Féin meetings and speeches, TNA (CO 904/23/3); Laffan, *The Resurrection of Ireland: The Sinn Féin Party*, p. 78.
20. Inspector General's monthly report for February 1918, Inspector General (Byrne) to Under Secretary, 15 Mar. 1918, TNA (CO 904/105).
21. Speech by D. McCarthy, meeting at Callan, County Kilkenny, on 5 Aug. 1917; speech by Éamon de Valera, meeting at Enniscorthy, County Wexford, 13 Aug. 1917, Sinn Féin meetings and speeches, TNA (CO 904/23/3).
22. Speeches by Joseph Stanley, meeting at Drogheda, 19 Aug. 1917, meeting at Tullyallen, Louth, 19 Aug. 1917, Sinn Féin meetings and speeches, TNA (CO 904/23/3).
23. Fitzpatrick, *Politics and Irish Life*, pp 43, 65; Bew, 'Sinn Féin agrarian radicalism and the War of Independence, 1919–1921', p. 222. See also, Laffan, *The Resurrection of Ireland*, p. 188.
24. Criminal Injury Books, Clare, 1912–1920, NAI (1D/40/1); Criminal Injury Books, Clare, 1907–1919, NAI (1D/34/12); Criminal Injury Books, Cork (East Riding), April 1909–February 1918, NAI (1D/37/162).
25. Charles Tilly, *The Politics of Collective Violence* (New York, 2006 edn), p. 171.
26. Conor McNamara, *War and Revolution in the West of Ireland: Galway 1913–1922* (Kildare, 2018), p. 21.
27. Terry Dunne, '"Cattle drivers, marauders, terrorists and hooligans": The agrarian movement of 1920', in *History Ireland* 28:4 (July/August 2020), p. 30; Testimony of Frank Dempsey, Chairman, Mallow Urban Council, 19 Jan. 1921; Albert Coyle, *American Commission on Conditions in Ireland*

Comprising the Complete Testimony, Affidavits and Exhibits Presented Before the American Commission on Conditions in Ireland (Washington, DC, 1921), pp 936, 941. On the inequities of the peripheral agrarian economy, see Michael Hechter, *Internal Colonialism: The Celtic Fringe in British National Development, 1536–1966* (Berkeley and Los Angeles, 1975; 1977 edn), p.143.

28. Laffan, *The Resurrection of Ireland*, p. 310.
29. Michael Hopkinson, *Green Against Green: The Irish Civil War* (Dublin, 1988), p. 46.
30. Francis Costello, 'Labour, Irish republicanism, and the social order during the Anglo-Irish War', in *The Canadian Journal of Irish Studies* 172 (December 1991), pp 1–2.
31. Fergus Campbell and Kevin O'Shiel, 'The last land war? Kevin O'Shiel's memoir of the Irish Revolution (1916–21)', in *Archivium Hibernicum* 57 (2003), pp 161–2.
32. The rain table for January 1920 showed rainfall as 151 per cent of the historic average (1875–1909). In March, upwards of six inches of rain fell in the west of Ireland, though overall rainfall was only 89 per cent of the historic average. *The Meteological Magazine* 55 (January 1920), p. 16; (March 1920), p. 36; Arthur Mitchell, *Revolutionary Government in Ireland: Dáil Éireann 1919–22* (Dublin, 1995), p. 130.
33. Inspector General's monthly report for June 1920, TNA (CO 904/112).
34. Kevin O'Shiel, 'The last land war', *Irish Times*, 22 Nov. 1966; see also, Fergus Campbell and Kevin O'Shiel, 'The last land war?', p. 195
35. Return of agrarian outrages reported to the Inspector General of Royal Irish Constabulary on 19 May 1920, TNA (CO 904/121), p. 195.
36. Fergus Campbell, 'The last land war?', pp 163–4.
37. Ibid., p. 164.
38. *Connacht Tribune*, 11 June 1921.
39. Return of agrarian outrages reported to the Inspector General of Royal Irish Constabulary on 4 June 1920, TNA (CO 904/121), p. 211.
40. *Belfast Newsletter*, 10 Mar. 1920.
41. Kevin O'Shiel, 'The last land war?', *Irish Times*, 22 Nov. 1966; see also, Fergus Campbell and Kevin O'Shiel, 'The last land war?', p. 195.
42. Terry Dunne, '"Cattle drivers, marauders, terrorists and hooligans"', p. 30.
43. Return of agrarian outrages reported to the Inspector General of Royal Irish Constabulary, 19 May 1920–29 September 1920, TNA (CO 904/121), pp. 195–337. Change in percentage found using ($\sqrt{2} - \sqrt{1})/\sqrt{1} \times 100$.
44. Ferriter, *A Nation and Not a Rabble*, p. 231.
45. Arthur Mitchell, *Revolutionary Government in Ireland*, p. 131.
46. Laffan, *The Resurrection of Ireland*, pp 310–11, 315; Tony Varley, 'Land, revolution and counter-revolution in the west', in *Atlas of the Irish Revolution*, p. 496.
47. Erskine Childers, *The Constructive Work of Dáil Éireann* 1 (1921), p. 18; Dooley, *Burning the Big House*, pp 141–2.
48. Hopkinson, *Green Against Green*, p. 45; David Fitzpatrick, 'Class, family and rural unrest in nineteenth-century Ireland', p. 41; Ferriter, *A Nation and Not a Rabble*, p. 179; Campbell and O'Shiel, 'The last land war?', p. 161; Mitchell, *Revolutionary Government*, p. 136.
49. Mitchell, *Revolutionary Government*, pp 85–7.
50. Kevin O'Shiel, 'The Dáil land courts', *Irish Times*, 14 Nov. 1966; 'Fellow travellers', *Irish Times*, 17 Nov. 1966; see also, Campbell and O'Shiel, 'The last land war?', pp 180, 186.
51. Stathis N. Kalyvas, *The Logic of Violence in Civil War* (Cambridge, 2006; 2013 edn), p. 380; Dooley, *Burning the Big House*, pp 134, 142.
52. Dooley, *Burning the Big House*, p. 97.
53. Dooley, *Burning the Big House*, p. 168; Gearoid O Tuathaigh, 'Irish land questions in the state of the Union', in Fergus Campbell and Tony Varley (eds), *Land Questions in Modern Ireland* (Manchester, 2013), pp 14–15.
54. Donnelly concludes, 'The examination of Big House burnings in 1920–21 does not offer any significant support to the view that members of the embattled Protestant landed elite of Cork were victimized because of their religion.' James S. Donnelly, Jr, 'Big House burnings in County Cork during the Irish Revolution, 1920–21', in *Éire-Ireland* 47:3–4 (Fall/Winter 2012), p. 195; Peter Martin, 'Unionism: The Irish nobility and the revolution 1919–23' in Joost Augustein (ed.), *The Irish Revolution* (Palgrave, 2002), pp 152–3, 156–7.

55. Dooley, *Burning the Big House*, p. 100; Ferriter, *A Nation not a Rabble*, p. 290, quoting Dooley, *The Decline of the Big House in Ireland: A Study of Irish Landed Families, 1860–1960* (Dublin, 2001) p. 171ff; Dooley, *Burning the Big House*, p. 168.
56. Inspector General's report for July 1920, TNA (CO 904/112).
57. Dooley, *Burning the Big House*, pp 101, 112.
58. Sworn statement by John Brazil given before the pensions advisory committee, 13 Nov. 1935, Irish Military Archives, Military Service Pensions Collection (MSP34 REF 3883).
59. 'The mansions left to fall into decay', *Irish Times*, 1 Nov. 2012; statement of Henry O'Keefe BMH, WS 1315, p. 3.
60. Ciarán O Murchadha, *The Great Famine: Ireland's Agony 1845–1852* (New York, 2013), p. 11.
61. In some instances, landlords also owned local barracks, compounding the connection between landed elitism, military tradition, landlordism and State authority. See cases of Bowen-Colthurst family, Inspector General's Report for June 1920, TNA (CO 904/112); Donnelly, *Burning the Big House*, pp 146, 150; *Kerry News*, 5 Jan. 1920; *Irish Examiner*, 4 Oct. 1921.
62. Statements of Patrick Ryan, BMH, WS 1314, p. 4; and Henry O'Keefe, BMH, WS 1315, p. 3.
63. Glenahiery's servants were compelled to quit under threat of death. The steward abandoned the estate after being shot at. *Munster Express*, 15 Jan., 9 Apr. 1921.
64. Brian Graham, 'Ireland and Irishness: Place, culture and identity', in Brian Graham (ed.), *In Search of Ireland: A Cultural Geography* (New York, 1997), p. 4; Dooley, *Burning the Big House*, pp 161, 168–70; ibid., pp 14–17; on Big House as embodying 'anti-Irish' behaviour, see Florence O'Donoghue, *No Other Law* (Kerry, 1986), p. 154–5 fn 94.
65. Gemma Clark, *Everyday Violence in the Irish Civil War* (Cambridge, 2014), pp 74–5.
66. F. S. L. Lyons, *Culture and Anarchy in Ireland 1890–1939* (Oxford, 1979), pp 101–2, 105; Martin, 'Unionism', p. 160.
67. Clark, *Everyday Violence in the Irish Civil War*, pp 14–15.
68. Memo from the Ministry of Agriculture, Agriculture: Seizure of land, signed 22 Dec. 1922, received 10 Jan. 1923, NAI (TAOIS/S1943).
69. Landsdowne to Churchill, 20 Sept. 1922, NAI (TAOIS/S1940).
70. Unknown to Lord Landsdowne, 3, 5 September 1922, NAI (TAOIS/S1940).
71. Cosgrave to Churchill, 23 Oct. 1922, NAI (TAOIS/S1940).
72. John Dorney, 'The burning of the Big Houses revisited 1920–23', in *The Irish Story* (6 Nov. 2015), https://www.theirishstory.com/2015/11/06/the-burning-of-the-big-houses-revisited-1920-23/, accessed 9 October 2022.
73. Memo from the Ministry of Agriculture, Agriculture: Seizure of land, signed 22 Dec. 1922, received 10 Jan. 1923, NAI (TAOIS/S1943). Further, extracts from the minutes of the Executive Council meetings from 10 January and 23 April 1923 juxtapose 'incendiary activities of the Irregulars' with 'agrarian outrages'. Irregulars: Incendiary activities, NAI (TAOIS/S1940).
74. Statement of Sean Prendergast, BMH, WS 755 p. 588.
75. Michael Hopkinson, *Green Against Green*, p. 122.
76. Ernie O'Malley, *The Singing Flame* (Dublin, 1979 edn), pp 75, 102.
77. Statement of Sean Prendergast, BMH, WS 802, p. 13
78. Hopkinson, *Green Against Green*, pp 58, 129.
79. Clark, *Everyday Violence*, p. 64; see also, Hopkinson, *Green Against Green*, p. 129; Hopkinson, 'Civil war: The opening phase', in *Atlas of the Irish Revolution*, p. 681.
80. Diarmaid Ferriter, *Between Two Hells: The Irish Civil War* (London, 2021), p. 42. Hopkinson, *Green Against Green*, p. 114.
81. Hopkinson, *Green Against Green*, p. 118.
82. Daily reports on Four Courts garrison, 29 June 1922: 1800 hours, 30 June 1922: 10.00 hours, TNA (WO 35/92).
83. Michael Fewer, 'The battle of the Four Courts, 28–30 June 1922', in *History Ireland* 27:4 (July/August 2019), https://www.historyireland.com/the-battle-of-the-four-courts-28-30-june-1922/, accessed 9 October 2022.
84. Daily reports on Four Courts garrison, 30 June 1922: situation report 1300 hours, TNA (WO 35/92).
85. Ernie O'Malley, *The Singing Flame*, pp 114–15.
86. Statement of Sean Prendergast, BMH, WS 802, p. 23.

87. Ferriter, *Between Two Hells*, p. 46, citing John M. Regan, 'Kindling the singing flame: The destruction of the Public Record Office (30 June 1922) as a historical problem', in Cormac K. H. O'Malley (ed.), *Modern Ireland and Revolution: Ernie O'Malley in Context* (Kildare, 2016), pp 107–24.
88. Ferriter, *Between Two Hells*, p. 47.
89. Farrington had previously managed the neighbouring Crown Hotel, where she observed the comings and goings of IRA staff, Auxiliaries, and Black and Tans throughout the War of Independence period. Statement of Annie Farrington, BMH, WS 749, p. 6.
90. Ibid., p. 7.
91. See also, Damage to Property (Compensation) Act 1923, Annie Farrington (FIN/COMP/2/28/1740).
92. *Westmeath Independent*, 15 July 1922.
93. Hopkinson, *Atlas of the Irish Revolution*, p. 684; Hopkinson, *Green Against Green*, p. 124.
94. *Irish Independent*, 8 July 1922.
95. 'Architectural masterpieces in ashes', *Freeman's Journal*, 7 July 1922.
96. 'The new ruins', *Evening Herald*, 17 July 1922.
97. Daily reports on Four Courts garrison, 6 July 1922: situation report 10.00 hours, TNA (WO 35/92).
98. Eunan O'Halpin, *Defending Ireland: The Irish State and its Enemies since 1922* (Oxford 1999; 2000 paperback edn), pp 26–7.
99. Fergus Campbell, 'Land and Revolution revisited', in Campbell and Varley (eds), *Land Questions in Modern Ireland* (Manchester, 2013), p. 164.
100. Statement of Dan Breen, BMH, WS 1763, pp 103–4.
101. Road obstructions, 27 July 1922, Irish Military Archives (Captured Documents, Lot 229).
102. Road obstructions, 27 July 1922, IMA (Captured Documents, Lot 229); Third Tipperary Brigade, Dept. Org. ref. 76 to all Battalion O/Cs, 23 Jan. 1923, IMA (Captured Documents, Lot 110).
103. Road obstructions, 27 July 1922 (IMA, Captured Documents, Lot 229); Simon Donnelly concealed trenches with small brush and dirt to give the impression of safe passage. Statement of Simon Donnelly, BMH, WS 481, p. 26; see also, *Belfast Newsletter*, 29 Nov. 1920.
104. Weekly report of operations, south-west area, week ended 8 December [1922], IMA (CS/OPS/04/17).
105. Engineering order no. 2, 8 July 1922, IMA (Captured Documents, Lot 229); Destruction of masonry bridges and walls, Engineering Circular no. 26, Fermoy, 1 Aug. 1922, IMA (Captured Documents, Lot 229).
106. Road obstructions, 27 July 1922, IMA (Captured Documents, Lot 229).
107. NAI (FIN/COMP/2/4/1322, FIN/COMP/2/4/2475); *Irish Independent*, 15 Aug. 1922.
108. 'War on the railways: Years to repair damage', *Irish Independent*, 22 Sept. 1922, quoted from *Cork Examiner*.
109. Hopkinson, *Green Against Green*, p. 146.
110. I purposefully excluded arson and the destruction and commandeering of property due to their volume and frequency at this time.
111. *Irish Examiner*, 23 Aug. 1922.
112. Hopkinson, *Green Against Green*, p. 111; Meeting of the Provisional Government, 8 July 1922, NAI (TSCH/1/1/2/1 Provisional Government Minutes, 29 June–30 July 1922, P.G.54).
113. Meeting of the Provisional Government, 10, 11 July, 1922, NAI (TSCH/1/1/2/1 Provisional Government Minutes, 29 June–30 July 1922, P.G.55, 56).
114. Government Memorandum, W. T. Cosgrave, c. July 1922, NAI (TAOIS /s1602).
115. 'Laying the country waste', *Irish Independent*, 20 July 1922
116. See, for example, *Evening Herald*, 14 July 1922; *Irish Independent*, 22 July 1922; *Freeman's Journal*, 27 July 1922; *Derry Journal*, 28 July 1922; *Sligo Champion*, 29 July 1922; *Westmeath Independent*, 29 July 1922.
117. *Truth*, 18 July 1922.
118. Hopkinson, *Green Against Green*, p. 273.
119. *Irish Independent*, 12 Sept. 1927.
120. *The Irish Statesmen*, 30 Apr. 1927.

Conclusion

The Irish Revolution produced significant environmental change, altering physical landscapes and often the meaning attached to them. This transformation demonstrated the devastating effects of rebellion and revolutionary violence, and the displacement experienced by those who endured it. Modifications to space challenged existing political boundaries, renegotiated military control and redefined social identities. Landscapes were enlisted as tools of war in various contexts: as stages for rebellion, weapons factories and caches, and ambush sites. Crown force reprisals effectively punished Irish environments as an extension of the people who lived within them. The resulting destruction helped to articulate a victim narrative that mobilised international judgment of the Irish independence movement. However, moral rulings often failed to capture the nuance of other types of destruction that occurred in the background of revolution, such as agrarian violence. In addition, while the Irish Civil War showed that guerrilla methods held their value, it redoubled many of the lessons of the preceding years, with Irishmen and women enduring ruin that disrupted their lives and left indelible scars on the Irish landscape for years to come.

How does an environmental view develop our understanding of the Irish Revolution? In many ways, it emphasises the reciprocal relationship between people and the environments in which they lived. On an interpretive scale, it shows the extent to which damage or destruction of those environments displaced communities and economies, as well as individual and collective psychologies.[1] In addition, repositioning the revolution along an environmental timeline invariably exposes the incompatibility of the traditional political chronology with the environmental chronology. This might extend in both directions beyond 1912–1923, to better incorporate pre-revolutionary elements such as agrarian unrest, politicised spaces and articulations of Irish resources surrounding the Home Rule debate on one end, and the Irish Free State's rebuilding and restoration efforts, property compensation priorities and the politics of indemnity, national afforestation and improvement projects, as well as the environment's role in the reimagining of Ireland's post-colonial identity, on the other.

As this is the first book to examine the environmental processes of the revolutionary period, it is in many ways incomplete. While it has explored episodes of environmental destruction associated with the broader political revolution and its military wing, it overlooks several others that deserve focused study going forward. Principle amongst these is the exploration of the pre-Rising years and the militarisation of Irish landscapes and the public sphere by the Irish Citizen Army, Na Fianna Éireann, the Ulster Volunteer Force, the Irish Volunteers and Cumann na mBan. The destruction of goods and disrupted economies that resulted from the Belfast Boycott, and environmental ruin and displacement that accompanied sectarian violence in Northern Ireland between 1920 and 1922, also require dedicated space. Additionally, further study remains to be conducted beyond the environmental history of the political revolution. In particular, the debate over the cultivation and application of natural resources in an independent Ireland, which was present in the Home Rule debate decades before the Easter Rising and remained the focus of national reconstruction discussions throughout the revolutionary period.

Compensation and reconstruction are perhaps the most daunting categories for further study due to the sheer volume of material they represent and the content's minutia. Fortunately, the ongoing cataloguing and release of Damage to Property (Compensation) Act 1923 files at the National Archives of Ireland mean that broader studies of the environmental destruction that occurred during the Irish Civil War may be conducted beyond the single-county model. Treasury and Department of Finance files (for both the UK and Ireland) complement this collection, as well as Criminal Injury and Indemnity files for the War of Independence period and the records of the Office of Public Works. Furthermore, reassessing the Cumman na nGaedheal government at the centenary of its ascension to power will certainly require further comment on how it prioritised compensation and reconstruction.

The environmental history of the Irish Revolution exists at the intersection of political change, altered spaces, violence and material ruin, displacement, compensation, and natural and physical restoration. This book has offered a view to these processes in Ireland between 1916 and 1923, one that presents some familiar topics anew while stimulating discussion on further reinterpretations of the period.

NOTES

1. Chris Pearson, 'Researching militarized landscapes: A literature review on war and the militarization of the environment', in *Landscape Research* 37:1 (February 2012), p. 116, citing Rachel Woodward, *Military Geographies* (Oxford, 2004), p. 3; see also, J. Schofield, *Combat Archaeology: Material Culture and Modern Conflict* (London, 2005), p. 44.

Bibliography

Archives

American Irish Historical Society, New York
Friends of Irish Freedom Records

Dublin City Archives, Dublin
City Council Minutes, 1916

Imperial War Museum, London
Anthony Mildmay Jameson papers
Diary of J. P. Swindlehurst
Major General L. A. Hawes memoir
Sir Peter Strickland papers

Irish Military Archives, Dublin
A-Series files
Bureau of Military History Witness Statements
Civil War Captured Documents Collection
Civil War Operations and Intelligence Reports Collection
Military Service Pensions Collection

Irish Railway Records Society, Dublin
Sinn Féin Rebellion files

National Archives of Ireland, Dublin
Criminal Injury Books, Clare
Criminal Injury Books, Cork (East Riding)
Criminal Injury Books, Limerick
Dáil Éireann Ministry and Cabinet Minutes
Department of Finance
Department of the Taoiseach
Office of Public Works
Property Losses (Ireland) Committee, 1916
Provisional Government papers

The National Archives, Kew, London
Cabinet minutes
Colonial Office records
Home Office records
Treasury records
War Office records

National Library of Ireland, Dublin
Archives Diplomatique Irlande
Art Ó Briain papers
Joseph Brennan papers
Joseph Fowler papers
French Pamphlets
James G. Douglas papers
John Redmond papers

New York Public Library, New York
Allied Loyalty League Records
Maloney Collection of Irish Historical Papers, 1857–1965

Public Records Office Northern Ireland, Belfast
Finance records

University College Dublin Archives, Belfield, Dublin
George Gavan Duffy papers

Contemporaneous Published Material

Bolton, Albert D., 'Damage to Property (Compensation) Act, 1923 and the Damage to Property (Amendment) Act, 1923 together with all recent regulations relating to the payment of compensation' (Dublin: John Falconer, 1923).
Breen, Dan, *My Fight for Irish Freedom* (Dublin: Talbot Press, 1924).
British Meteorological and Magnetic Year Book [1917–22] (London: Meteorological Office, 1918–1923).
Chesterton, G. K., *What Are Reprisals?* (London: Peace with Ireland Council, 1921).
Childers, Erskine, *Military Rule in Ireland: A Series of Eight Articles Contributed to The Daily News March–May 1920* (Dublin, 1920).
Childers, Erskine, *The Constructive Work of Dáil Éireann* (1921).
Commandant de Gerlache de Gomery, 'Belgium in war time' (New York: George H. Doran Company, 1916)
Coyle, Albert (transcriber and annotator), *Evidence on Conditions in Ireland Comprising the Complete Testimony, Affidavits and Exhibits Presented Before the American Commission on Conditions in Ireland* (Washington, DC, 1921).
Delany, J. F., 'The tarring of roads', in *Transactions of the Institution of Civil Engineers of Ireland*, 41–2, 3 January 1916.
Desmond, Shaw, *The Drama of Sinn Féin* (New York: C. Scribner's Sons, 1923).
Fletcher, George, *Connaught* (Cambridge: Cambridge University Press, 1922).
Folks, Homer, *The Human Costs of the War* (New York: Harper & Brothers Publishers, May 1920).
Forrest, Rev. M. D., *Atrocities in Ireland: What an Australian Has Seen* (Sydney: The Irish Nationalist Association of New South Wales, 1920).
Labour Party, *Report of The Labour Commission to Ireland* (London: Caledonian Press Ltd, 1921).
Lynd, Robert, '"Hellish reprisals" in Ireland' (London: Liberal Publication Department; Roberts and Leete, Ltd, October 1920).
Maisonnier, Louis, and Lecarpentier, Georges, *L'Irlande et le Home Rule* (Paris: Librairie des sciences politiques *et* sociales, 1912).
Moisant, Xavier, *L'ame de l'Irlande* (Paris: G. Beauchesne, 1920).
Murray, Allison J. (compiler, editor), *Raemaekers' Cartoon History of the War, Volume One: The First Twelve Months of War* (New York: The Century Co., 1918).
O'Duffy, Eimer, *The Wasted Island* (Miami: Hardpress Publishing, 2013; reprinted from Dublin: Martin Lester, Ltd, 1919).
Pablo, A. Ruis y (translator), *La tragedia de Irlanda: Sus origenes, su desarrollo historico, su fase actual* (Barcelona: Inustrias Graficas Seix & Barral Herms, SA, 1921).
Paul-Dubois, Louis, *L'Irlande Contemporaine et la Question Irlandaise* (Paris: Perrin, 1907).
Phillips, Alison W., *The Revolution in Ireland, 1906–1923* (London: Longmans, Green and Co., 1923).
Piggott, Horace and Finch, Robert J., *Dent's Historical and Economic Geographies: Great Britain and Ireland* (London: J. M. Dent & Sons Ltd, 1922).
Public Works, Ireland, *Eighty-Ninth Annual Report of the Commissioners of Public Works in Ireland: With Appendices for the Year Ending 31 March, 1921* (Dublin: His Majesty's Stationary Office, 1921).
Report of the Committee on Alleged German Outrages, presided over by The Right Hon. Viscount Byrne (New York: MacMillan and Company, 1915).
Russell, George ('Æ'), 'A plea for justice: Being a demand for a public enquiry into the attacks on co-operative societies in Ireland by the Irish homestead' (Dublin, 1920).

Sangnier, Marc, *Pour l'Irlande libre: Discours prononcé à Paris le 28 juin 1920 et précédé d'une allocution de M. Gavan Duffy, délégué du Gouvernement élu de la République irlandaise* (Paris: La Démocratie, 1920).
Stephens, James, *The Insurrection in Dublin* (Dublin, 1916).
Street, C. J. C., *The Administration of Ireland, 1920* (London: Philip Allan & Col, 1921).
Tales of the R.I.C. (Edinburgh and London: William Blackwood and Sons, 1921).
Tèry, Simone (trans. Marilyn Gaddis Rose), 'Raids and reprisals: Ireland: Eye-witness (1923)'.
The Sinn Féin Rebellion Handbook: A Complete and Connected Narrative of the Rising, With Detailed Accounts of the Fighting at All Points (Compiled by the *Weekly Irish Times*, Dublin, 1917 edn).
The Struggle of the Irish People: Address to the Congress of the United States, Adopted at the January Session of Dáil Éireann, 1921 (Washington: Government Printing Office, 1921).

Newspapers

Anglo-Celt
Belfast Newsletter
Connaught Telegraph
Cork Constitution
Derry Journal
Donegal News
Drogheda Independent
Dundalk Democrat
Evening Herald
Evening Public Ledger
Fermanagh Herald
Freeman's Journal
Gaelic American
Great Falls Tribune
Irish Examiner
Irish Independent
Kentucky Irish American
Kerry Advocate
Kerry Press
Kerry Sentinel
Kerry Weekly Reporter
Kilkenny People
Killarney Echo and South Kerry Chronicle
Liberator (Tralee)
La Liberté
Le Figaro
Le Lanterne
Le Petit Parsien
Leitrim Observer
Leinster Express
Limerick Leader
Manchester Guardian News Bulletin
Meath Chronicle
Munster Express
Nationalist (Tipperary)
Nationalist and Leinster Times
Nenagh Guardian
New York Herald
New York Times
New York Tribune
Northampton Chronicle

Offaly Independent
Skibbereen Eagle
Sunday Independent
Strabane Chronicle
Times (London)
Truth
Sun
Ulster Herald
Washington Herald
Washington Times
Western People
Westmeath Independent

Periodicals, magazines and journals

An t-Óglach
Capuchin Annual
Catholic News Service
Constabulary Gazette
Éire-Ireland
Floréal
History Ireland
Irish Builder and Engineer
Irish Bulletin
Irish Exile: An Organ of Irish Movements in and around London
Irish Historical Studies
Irish Homestead
Irish Sword
Liberal Magazine
Meteorological magazine
New Hibernia Review
News Letter of the Friends of Irish Freedom National Bureau of Information
Tablet
Weekly Summary

Websites & web-based articles

Andrews, Kernan, 'The Galway MP who got thrown in the river', *Galway Advertiser*, 5 Sept. 2017 (https://www.advertiser.ie/galway/article/94889/the-galway-mp-who-got-thrown-in-the-river), accessed 9 Oct. 2022.

'Bomb factory discovered after Cork house explosion', in *Century Ireland* (https://www.rte.ie/centuryireland/index.php/articles/bomb-factory-discovered-after-cork-house-explosion), accessed 9 Oct. 2022.

Borgonovo, John and Doherty, Gabriel, 'Smoking gun? British government policy and RIC reprisals, summer 1920', in *History Ireland*, 17:2, March/April 2009 (https://www.historyireland.com/smoking-gun-british-government-policy-and-ric-reprisals-summer-1920/), accessed 9 Oct. 2022.

Dorney, John, 'The North King Street massacre, Dublin 1916', *The Irish Story*, 13 Apr. 2012 (https://www.theirishstory.com/2012/04/13/the-north-king-street-massacre-dublin-1916/#.YrnDbZDMJsY), accessed 9 Oct. 2022.

Duncan, Mark, 'Between armed rebellion and democratic revolution: the Irish Question in 1917', in *Century Ireland* (https://www.rte.ie/centuryireland/index.php/articles/between-armed-rebellion-and-democratic-revolution), accessed 9 Oct. 2022.

Ferriter, Diarmaid, 'The 1916 prisoners released on Christmas Eve', *Irish Times*, 24 Dec. 2016. (https://www.irishtimes.com/opinion/diarmaid-ferriter-the-1916-prisoners-released-on-christmas-eve-1.2915580), accessed 9 Oct. 2022.

Fewer, Michael, 'The Battle of the Four Courts, 28–30 June 1922', in *History Ireland*, 27:4, July/August 2019 (https://www.historyireland.com/the-battle-of-the-four-courts-28-30-june-1922/), accessed 9 Oct. 1922.

'Gravediggers on strike at Glasnevin', in *Century Ireland* (http://www.rte.ie/centuryireland/index.php/articles/gravediggers-on-strike-at-glasnevin).

Irish-Police.com, 'Easter Rising – DMP & RIC Casualties (http://irish-police.com/easter-rising-1916), accessed 9 Oct. 2022.

Kennerk, Barry, 'Compensating for the Rising: the papers of the Property Losses (Ireland) Committee, 1916,' in *History Ireland*, 21:2, March/April 2013 (http://www.historyireland.com/20th-century-contemporary-history/compensating-for-the-rising-the-papers-of-the-property-losses-ireland-committee-1916/), accessed 9 Oct. 2022.

McGreevy, Ronan, 'Home for Christmas – An Irishman's diary on the release of republican prisoners from Frongoch in 1916', *Irish Times*, 19 Dec. 2016. (https://www.irishtimes.com/opinion/home-for-christmas-an-irishman-s-diary-on-the-release-of-republican-prisoners-from-frongoch-in-1916-1.2910274), accessed 9 Oct. 2022.

Murphy, Eamon, 'The Raid on the Magazine Fort, Phoenix Park, Easter Monday 1916', in *The History of Na Fianna Éireann* (https://fiannaeireannhistory.wordpress.com), accessed 9 Oct. 2022.

O'Fallon, Donal, 'The "denizens of the slums" and looting during the Easter Rising', *Come here to me!*, 4 Oct. 2015 (https://comeheretome.com/2015/10/04/the-denizens-of-the-slums-and-looting-during-the-easter-rising/), accessed 9 Oct. 2022.

O'Fallon, Donal, 'The striking gravediggers', *Come Here to Me!*, 25 Apr. 2016 (https://comeheretome.com/2016/04/25/the-striking-gravediggers/), accessed 9 Oct. 2022.

O'Gorman, Ronnie, 'Woodford stood up to the power of Lord Clanricarde', *Galway Advertiser*, 6 May 2010 (https://www.advertiser.ie/Galway/article/25789/woodford-stood-up-to-the-power-of-lord-clanricarde), accessed 9 Oct. 2022.

Rouse, Paul, 'How Leix won the All-Ireland Hurling Championship of 1915', in *Century Ireland* (http://www.rte.ie/centuryireland/index.php/articles/how-leix-won-the-all-ireland-hurling-championship-of-1915/), accessed 9 Oct. 2022.

Theses

Butler, Benjamin Laurence, 'The British Army in Ireland 1916–1921: A social and cultural history', unpublished PhD thesis (University of Hull, 2007).

Hanon, Charles, 'The Irish Volunteers and the concepts of military service and defence 1913–1924', unpublished PhD thesis (University College Dublin, 1989).

Books, articles and chapters

Aalen, F. H. A., Kevin Whelan and Matthew Stout, eds, *Atlas of the Irish Rural Landscape* (Toronto: University of Toronto Press, 2011).

Aalen, F. H. A., 'Public housing in Ireland, 1800-1921', in *Planning Perspectives*, 2:2, 1987, pp 175–93.

aan de Wiel, Jérôme, *The Irish Factor 1899–1919: Ireland's Strategic and Diplomatic Importance for Foreign Powers* (Dublin: Irish Academic Press, 2011).

aan de Wiel, Jérôme, 'The long rupture, 1870–1970: The darker side of Franco-Irish relations', in *The International History Review*, 37:2, 2015, pp 201–18.

Abbott, Richard, *Police Casualties in Ireland* (Cork: Mercier Press, 2000).

Ahrentzen, Sherry, 'Socio-behavioral qualities of the built environment', in Riley E. Dunlap and William Michelson, eds, *Handbook of Environmental Sociology* (Westport, Connecticut: Greenwood Press, 2002), pp 96–136.

Ainsworth, John, 'British security policy in Ireland, 1920–1921', in *The Australian Journal of Irish Studies*, 2001, pp 176–90.

Andrews, C. S., *Dublin Made Me* (Dublin: Mercier Press, 1979).

Arrington, Lauren, 'Socialist republican discourse and the 1916 Easter Rising: The occupation of Jacob's Biscuit Factory and the South Dublin Union Explained', in *Journal of British Studies*, 53:4, October 2014, pp 992–1010.

Augusteijn, Joost, 'Accounting for the emergence of violent activism among Irish revolutionaries, 1919–21', in *Irish Historical Studies*, 35:139, May 2007, pp 327–44.

Augusteijn, Joost, *From Public Defiance to Guerilla Warfare: The Experience of Ordinary Volunteers in the Irish War of Independence, 1916–1921* (Kildare: Irish Academic Press, 1996).

Augusteijn, Joost, 'Military conflict in the War of Independence', in John Crowley, Donal Ó Drisceoil, Mike Murphy, eds, and John Borgonovo, associate ed., *Atlas of the Irish Revolution* (Cork: Cork University Press, 2017), pp 348–57.

Augusteijn, Joost, ed., *The Irish Revolution, 1913–23* (Basingstoke: Palgrave Macmillan, 2002).

Bailliet, Cecilia M., '"War in the home": An exposition of protection issues pertaining to the use of house raids in counterinsurgency operations', in *Journal of Military Ethics*, 6:3, 2007, pp 173–97.

Ballinger, W. A., *Rebellion* (London: Mayflower Books Limited, 1966).

Barmann, Lawrence, 'The Pope and the English modernists', in *U.S. Catholic Historian*, 25:1, Winter 2007, pp 31–54.

Barry, Tom, *Guerilla Days in Ireland* (Dublin: Anvil Books, 1995 edn).

Beatty, Aidan, 'The Gaelic League and the spatial logics of Irish nationalism', in *Irish Historical Studies*, 43:163, 2019, pp 55–72.

Bennett, Judith A., 'Pests and disease in the Pacific War: Crossing the line', in Richard P. Tucker and Edmund Russell, eds, *Natural Enemy, Natural Ally: Toward an Environmental History of War* (Corvallis: Oregon State University Press, 2004), pp 217–52.

Bennett, Richard, *The Black and Tans* (New York: Barnes and Noble, 1959, 1995 edn).

Bew, Paul, 'Sinn Féin agrarian radicalism and the War of Independence, 1919–1921', in D. G. Boyce, ed., *The Revolution in Ireland, 1879–1923* (London: MacMillan Education Ltd, 1988), pp 217–34.

Bielenberg, Andy, *Ireland and the Industrial Revolution: The Impact of the Industrial Revolution on Irish Industry, 1801–1922* (New York, 2009, 2014 edn).

Birdsall, Carolyn, *Nazi Soundscapes: Sound, Technology and Urban Space in Germany, 1933–1945* (Amsterdam: Amsterdam University Press, 2012).

Black, Jeremy, 'Geographies of war: The recent historical background', in Colin Flint, ed., *The Geography of War and Peace: From Death Camps to Diplomats* (New York: Oxford University Press, 2005), pp 19–25.

Bolton, Jonathan, *Blighted Beginnings* (Lewisburg: Bucknell University Press, 2010).

Borgonovo, John, *Spies, Informers and the 'Anti-Sinn Féin Society': The Intelligence War in Cork City 1920–1921* (Dublin & Portland: Irish Academic Press, 2007).

Bourke, Angela et. al., eds, *The Field Day Anthology of Irish Writing V, Irish Women's Writing and Traditions* (New York: New York University Press, 2002).

Boyce, D. George, *Nationalism in Ireland* (London: Croom Helm Ltd, 1982).

Brantz, Dorothee, 'Environments of death: Trench warfare on the Western Front, 1914–18', in Charles E. Closmann, ed., *War and the Environment: Military Destruction in the Modern Age* (College Station: Texas A&M University Press, 2009), pp 68–91.

Breathnach, Proinnsias, 'Creamery attacks', in John Crowley, Donal Ó Drisceoil, Mike Murphy, eds, and John Borgonovo, associate ed., *Atlas of the Irish Revolution* (Cork: Cork University Press, 2017), pp 555–7.

Brennan, Robert, *Allegiance* (Dublin: Browne and Nolan Limited, The Richview Press, 1950).

Brickell, Katherine, 'Geopolitics of home', in *Geography Compass*, 6:10, October 2012, pp 575–88.

Brun, Catherine, 'Reterritorializing the relationship between people and place in refugee studies', in *Geografiska Annaler: Series B, Human Geography*, 83:1, 2001, pp 15–25.

Bull, Philip, *Land, Politics and Nationalism: A Study of the Irish Land Question* (Dublin, 1996).

Callan, Patrick, 'Recruiting for the British Army in Ireland during the First World War', in *Irish Sword*, 17, Summer 1987, pp 42–56.

Campbell, Colm, *Emergency Law in Ireland, 1918–1925* (New York: Oxford University Press, 1994).

Campbell, Fergus, *'Land and Revolution* revisited', in Fergus Campbell and Tony Varley, eds, *Land Questions in Modern Ireland* (Manchester: Manchester University Press, 2013), pp 149–72.

Campbell, Fergus and O'Shiel, Kevin, 'The last land war? Kevin O'Shiel's memoir of the Irish Revolution (1916–21)', in *Archivium Hibernicum*, 57, 2003, pp 155–200.

Campbell, Fergus and Tony Varley, eds, *Land Questions in Modern Ireland* (Manchester: Manchester University Press, 2013).

Carroll, F. M., 'The American Committee for Relief in Ireland, 1920–22', in *Irish Historical Studies*, 23:89, May 1982, pp 30–49.
Ceannt, Áine, *The Story of the Irish White Cross, 1920–1947: The Story of Its Work* (Dublin: At the Sign of the Three Candles Publishing, 1947).
Clark, Gemma, *Everyday Violence in the Irish Civil War* (Cambridge: Cambridge University Press, 2014).
Clark, Gemma, 'Violence against women in the Irish Civil War, 1922–3: Gender-based harm in global perspective', in *Irish Historical Studies*, 44:165, 2020, pp 75–90.
Clear, Caitriona, *Social Change and Everyday Life in Ireland, 1850–1922* (Manchester: Manchester University Press, 2007).
Closmann, Charles E., 'Introduction: Landscapes of peace, environments of war', in Charles E. Closmann, ed., *War and the Environment: Military Destruction in the Modern Age* (College Station: Texas A&M University Press, 2009), pp 1–9.
Colbert, Evelyn (Speyer), *Retaliation in International Law* (New York: King's Crown Press, 1948).
Coleman, Marie, *The Irish Revolution, 1916–1923* (New York: Routledge, 2013).
Connolly, Linda, 'Towards a further understanding of the sexual and gender-based violence women experienced in the Irish Revolution', in Linda Connolly, ed., *Women and the Irish Revolution: Feminism, Activism, Violence* (Kildare: Irish Academic Press, 2020), pp 103–28.
Cooper, Jillym, *Animals in War* (London: William Heinemann Let, 1983).
Costello, Francis, 'Labour, Irish republicanism, and the social order during the Anglo-Irish War', in *The Canadian Journal of Irish Studies*, 17:2, December 1991, pp 1–22.
Costello, Francis, *The Irish Revolution and Its Aftermath 1916–1923* (Dublin: Irish Academic Press, 2003).
Coward, Martin, 'Against anthropocentrism: The destruction of the built environment as a distinct form of political violence', in *Review of International Studies*, 32:3, 2006, pp 419–37.
Crowley, Ethel, *Land Matters: Power Struggles in Rural Ireland* (Dublin: The Lilliput Press, 2006).
Cullen, Fintan, 'Marketing national sentiment: Lantern slides of evictions in late nineteenth-century Ireland', in *History Workshop Journal*, 54, Autumn 2002, pp 162–179.
Danchin, Emmanuelle, *Les Temps des Ruines 1914–1921* (Rennes: Presses Universitaires de Rennes, 2015).
Dolan, Anne, *Commemorating the Irish Civil War: History and Memory, 1923–2000* (Cambridge: Cambridge University Press, 2003).
Donnelly Jr and James S., 'Big House burnings in County Cork during the Irish Revolution, 1920–21', in *Éire-Ireland*, 47:3&4, Fall/Winter 2012, pp 141–97.
Donnelly, Jr and James S., '"Unofficial" British reprisals and IRA provocations, 1919–20: The cases of three Cork towns', in *Éire-Ireland*, 45:1&2, Spring/Summer 2010, pp 152–97.
Dooley, Terence, *Burning the Big House: The Story of the Irish Country House in a Time of War and Revolution* (London: Yale University Press, 2022).
Dooley, Terence, *The Decline of the Big House in Ireland: A Study of Irish Landed Families, 1860–1960* (Dublin: Wolfhound Press, 2001).
Doorley, Michael, 'The Friends of Irish Freedom: A case-study in Irish-American nationalism, 1916–21', in *History Ireland*, 16:2, March/April 2008, pp 22–27.
Ducret, Bernard, 'La France et l'Irlande (1914-1923)', in *Etudes irlandaises*, 9, 1984, pp 189–204.
Duffy, Patrick J., *Exploring the History and Heritage of Irish Landscapes* (Dublin: Four Courts Press, 2007).
Dunlap, Riley E. and William Michelson, eds, *Handbook of Environmental Sociology* (Westport, Connecticut: Greenwood Press, 2002).
Dunne, Terry, '"Cattle drivers, marauders, terrorists and hooligans": The agrarian movement of 1920', in *History Ireland*, 28:4, July/August 2020, pp 30–3.
Earner-Byrne, Lindsey and Urquhart, Diane, 'Gender roles in Ireland since 1740', in Eugenio F. Biagini and Mary E. Daly, eds, *The Cambridge Social History of Modern Ireland* (Cambridge: Cambridge University Press, 2017), pp 312–26.
Ehrlich, Cyril, 'Sir Horace Plunkett and agricultural reform', in J. M. Goldstrom and L. A. Clarkson, eds, *Irish Population, Economy, and Society. Essays in Honour of the Late K. H. Connell* (Oxford: Clarendon Press, 1981).
Ellis, Alan J., *The Burning of Cork* (Cork: Aubane Historical Society, 2004).

Everett, Nigel, *The Woods of Ireland* (Dublin: Four Courts Press, 2015 paperback edn).
Farry, Michael, *The Aftermath of Revolution: Sligo, 1921–23* (Dublin: University College Dublin Press, 2000).
Fedorowich, Kent, 'The problems of disbandment: The Royal Irish Constabulary and Imperial Migration, 1919–29', in *Irish Historical Studies*, 30:117, May 1996, pp 88–110.
Ferriter, Diarmaid, *A Nation and Not a Rabble: The Irish Revolution 1913–1923* (London: Profile Books, 2015).
Ferriter, Diarmaid, *Between Two Hells: The Irish Civil War* (London: Profile Books, 2021).
Ferriter, Diarmaid, *The Transformation of Ireland 1900–2000* (London: Profile Books, 2005).
Fitzgerald, Desmond, *Desmond's Rising: Memoirs 1913 to Easter 1916* (Dublin: Liberties Press, 1968, 2006).
Fitzpatrick, David, 'Class, family and rural unrest in nineteenth-century Ireland', in P. J. Drudy, ed., *Ireland: Land, Politics and People* (Cambridge: Cambridge University Press, 1982), pp 37–75.
Fitzpatrick, David, 'Historians and the commemoration of Irish conflicts, 1912–23', in John Horn and Edward Madigan, eds, *Towards Commemoration: Ireland in War and Revolution 1912–1923* (Dublin: Royal Irish Academy, 2013), pp 126–33.
Fitzpatrick, David, 'Home front and everyday life', in John Horne, ed., *Our War: Ireland and the Great War* (Dublin: Royal Irish Academy, 2008), pp 131–56.
Fitzpatrick, David, *Politics and Irish Life 1913–1921: Provincial Experiences of War and Revolution* (Cork: Cork University Press, 1977, 1998 edn).
Fitzpatrick, David, 'The geography of Irish nationalism 1910–1921', in *Past & Present*, 78, February 1978, pp 113–44.
Fitzpatrick, David, 'The logic of collective sacrifice: Ireland and the British Army, 1914–1918', in *The Historical Journal*, 38:4, 1995, pp 1017–30.
Fitzpatrick, David, 'The price of Balbriggan', in David Fitzpatrick, ed, *Terror in Ireland* (Dublin: The Lilliput Press, 2012), pp 75–101.
Fitzpatrick, David, *The Two Irelands: 1912–1939* (Oxford: Oxford University Press, 1998).
Flanagan, Frances, 'Against insurrection: Eimar O'Duffy and the memory of the 1916 Rising', in Brian Griffin and Ellen McWilliams, eds, *Irish Studies in Britain: New Perspectives on History and Literature* (Newcastle upon Tyne: Cambridge Scholars Publishing, 2010), pp 108–20.
Flint, Colin, 'Introduction', in Colin Flint, ed., *The Geography of War and Peace: From Death Camps to Diplomats* (New York: Oxford University Press, 2005), pp 3–18.
Foster, R. F., *Modern Ireland 1600–1972* (London: Penguin Press, 1988).
Foster, R. F., *Vivid Faces: The Revolutionary Generation in Ireland 1890–1923* (New York: W. W. Norton & Company, Inc., 2015).
Freeman, T. W., *Ireland: Its Physical, Historical, Social and Economic Geography* (New York: E. P. Dutton & Co. Inc., 1942).
Garvin, Tom, *The Evolution of Irish Nationalist Politics* (Dublin: Gill & Macmillan, 1981).
Gaughan, J. Anthony, ed., *Memoirs of Senator James G. Douglas (1887–1954): Concerned Citizen* (Dublin: University College Dublin Press, 1998).
Geraghty, Tom and Whitehead, Trevor, *The Dublin Fire Brigade: A History of the Brigade and the Emergencies* (Dublin: Four Courts Press, 2004).
Gladwin, Derek, *Contentious Terrains: Boglands, Ireland, Postcolonial Gothic* (Cork: Cork University Press, 2016).
Gladwin, Derek, 'Topobiographical inquiry: Lived spaces, place-based experiences, and ecologies', in Justin Dolan Stover and Kelly Sullivan, eds, *Éire-Ireland: An Interdicsiplinary Journal of Irish Studies*, Special Issue: Ireland and the Environment, 55:3&4, Fall/Winter 2020, pp 129–49.
Graham, Brian, 'The imagining of place: Representation and identity in contemporary Ireland', in Brian Graham, ed., *In Search of Ireland: A Cultural Geography* (New York: Routledge, 1997), pp 192–212.
Harker, Christopher, 'Spacing Palestine through the home', in *Transactions of the Institute of British Geographers*, 34:3, July 2009, pp 320–32.
Harnett, Mossie (ed. James H. Joy), *Victory and Woe: The West Limerick Brigade in the War of Independence* (Dublin: University College Dublin Press, 2002).
Hart, Peter, 'The geography of revolution in Ireland 1917–1923', in *Past & Present*, 155:1, May 1997, pp 142–76.

Hart, Peter, *The I.R.A. at War 1916–1923* (Oxford University Press, 2003, 2005).
Hart, Peter, *The I.R.A. & Its Enemies: Violence and Community in Cork 1916–1923* (Oxford: Oxford University Press, 1998).
Hechter, Michael, *Internal Colonialism: The Celtic Fringe in British National Development, 1536–1966* (Berkeley and Los Angeles: University of California Press, 1975, 1977 edn).
Henry, William, *Blood for Blood: The Black and Tan War in Galway* (Cork: Mercier Press, 2012).
Hepburn, A. C., *The Conflict of Nationality in Modern Ireland* (New York: St Martin's Press, 1980).
Higham, John, *Strangers in the Land: Patters of American Nativism 1860–1925* (New York: Atheneum, 1963).
Hopkinson, Michael, *Green Against Green: The Irish Civil War* (Dublin: Gill & Macmillan, 1998).
Hopkinson, Michael, *The Irish War of Independence* (Dublin: Gill & Macmillan, 2004).
Horne, John, 'Our war, our history', in John Horne, ed., *Our War: Ireland and the Great War* (Dublin: Royal Irish Academy, 2008), pp 1–34.
Horne, John and Gerwarth, Robert, *War in Peace: Paramilitary Violence in Europe after the Great War* (Oxford: Oxford University Press, 2012).
Hughes, Brian, *Defying the IRA? Intimidation, Coercion, and Communities During the Irish Revolution* (Liverpool: Liverpool University Press, 2016).
Hupy, Joseph P., 'The environmental footprint of war', in *Environment and History*, 14, 2008, pp 405–21.
Jeffery, Keith, 'Forward', in W. H. Kautt, *Ambushes and Armour: The Irish Rebellion, 1919–1921* (Dublin: Irish Academic Press, 2010).
Jeffery, Keith, 'The British Army and internal security 1919–1939', in *The Historical Journal*, 24:2, 1981, pp 377–97.
Johnson, James H., *The Human Geography of Ireland* (Chichester: John Wiley & Sons Ltd, 1994).
Johnson, Nuala, *Ireland, the Great War and the Geography of Remembrance* (Cambridge: Cambridge University Press, 2003).
Johnson, Nuala, 'Mapping monuments: The shaping of public space and cultural identities', in *Visual Communication*, 1:3, October 2002, pp 293–8.
Jones, David, 'The issue of land distribution: Revisiting *Graziers, Land Reform and Political Conflict in Ireland*', in Fergus Campbell and Tony Varley, eds, *Land Questions in Modern Ireland* (Manchester: Manchester University Press, 2013), pp 117–48.
Kalyvas, Stathis N., *The Logic of Violence in Civil War* (Cambridge, 2006, 2013 edn).
Katz, Cindi, 'Banal terrorism: Spatial fetishism and everyday insecurity', in Derek Gregory and Allan Pred, eds, *Violent Geographies: Fear, Terror, and Political Violence* (New York: Routledge, 2007), pp 349–61.
Kautt, W. H., *Ambushes and Armour: The Irish Rebellion 1919–1921* (Dublin: Irish Academic Press, 2010).
Kautt, W. H., ed., *Ground Truths: British Army Operations in the Irish War of Independence* (Kildare: Irish Academic Press, 2014).
Keane, Ronan, 'A mass of crumbling ruins: The destruction of the Four Courts in June 1922', in Caroline Costello, ed., *The Four Courts: 200 Years: Essays to Commemorate the Bicentenary of the Four Courts* (Dublin: Incorporated Council of Law Reporting for Ireland, 1996), pp 159–68.
Keizer, Garret, *The Unwanted Sound of Everything We Want: A Book About Noise* (New York: PublicAffairs, 2010).
Kenneally, Ian, *The Paper Wall: Newspapers and Propaganda in Ireland 1919–1921* (Cork: The Collins Press, 2008).
Kennelly, James J., 'The "dawn of the practical": Horace Plunkett and the cooperative movement', in *New Hibernia Review*, 12:1, Spring 2008, pp 62–81.
Kent, Susan Kingsley, *Aftershocks: Politics and Trauma in Britain, 1918–1931* (New York, 2009).
Keogh, Dermot, *Ireland & Europe 1919–1948* (Dublin: Gill & Macmillan, 1998).
Laffan, Michael, *The Resurrection of Ireland: The Sinn Féin Party* (Cambridge: Cambridge University Press, 1999).
Lawrence, Jon, 'Forging a peaceable kingdom: War, violence, and fear of brutalization in post-First World War Britain', in *The Journal of Modern History*, 75:3, September 2003, pp 557–89.
Lee, J. J., *Ireland, 1912–1985: Politics and Society* (Cambridge: Cambridge University Press, 1989).

Leeson, David, *The Black and Tans: British Police and Auxiliaries in the Irish War of Independence, 1920–1921* (New York: Oxford University Press, 2011).
Leeson, David M., 'The Royal Irish Constabulary, Black and Tans and Auxiliaries', in John Crowley, Donal Ó Drisceoil, Mike Murphy, eds, and John Borgonovo, associate ed., *Atlas of the Irish Revolution* (Cork: Cork University Press, 2017), pp 371–83.
Leeson, David, 'The "scum of London's underworld"? British recruits for the Royal Irish Constabulary, 1920–21', in *Contemporary British History*, 17:1, 2003, pp 1–38.
Lowe, W. J., 'The war against the R.I.C., 1919–21', in *Éire-Ireland*, 37:3&4, Fall/Winter 2002, pp 79–117.
Lowler, Lorraine, 'Amazonian landscapes: Gender, war, and historical repetition', in Colin Flint, ed, *The Geography of War and Peace: From Death Camps to Diplomats* (Oxford: Oxford University Press, 2005), pp 133–48.
Lyons, F. S. L., *Culture and Anarchy in Ireland 1890–1939* (Oxford, 1979).
Lyons, F. S. L., *Ireland Since the Famine* (London, 1985 edn).
Macardle, Dorothy, *The Irish Republic* (Dublin: Farrar Straus & Giroux, 1965 edn).
Madigan, Edward, '"An Irish Louvain": Memories of 1914 and the moral climate in Britain during the Irish War of Independence', in *Irish Historical Studies*, 44:165, 2020, pp 91–105.
Malcolm, Elizabeth, *The Irish Policeman, 1822–1922: A Life* (Dublin: Four Courts Press, 2006).
Malešević, Siniša, *The Sociology of War and Violence* (Cambridge: Cambridge University Press, 2010).
McGarry, Fearghal, *The Rising: Ireland, Easter 1916* (New York: Oxford University Press, 2011).
McKenna, Joseph, *Guerrilla Warfare in the Irish War of Independence, 1919–1921* (United States: McFarland, Incorporated, 2011).
McMahon, Timothy G., *Grand Opportunity: The Gaelic Revival and Irish Society, 1893–1910* (Syracuse: Syracuse University Press, 2008).
McManus, Ruth, 'Taking the urban housing problem in the Irish Free State, 1922–1940', in *Urban History*, 46:1, 2019, pp 62–81.
McNamara, Conor, *War and Revolution in the West of Ireland: Galway 1913–1922* (Kildare: Irish Academic Press, 2018).
McNeill, J. R., 'Woods and warfare in world history', in *Environmental History*, 9:3, 2004, pp 388–410.
Michelson, William, and van Vliet, Willem, 'Theory and the sociological study of the built environment', in Riley E. Dunlap and William Michelson, eds, *Handbook of Environmental Sociology* (Westport, Connecticut: Greenwood Press, 2002), pp 70–95.
Mikesell, Marvin and Phillip Wagner, eds, *Readings in Cultural Geography* (Chicago: University of Chicago Press, 1962).
Mitchell, Arthur, *Revolutionary Government in Ireland: Dáil Éireann 1919–22* (Dublin: Gill & Macmillan, 1995).
Mitchell, Frank and Ryan, Michael, *Reading the Irish Landscape* (Dublin: Town House and Country House, 1997 edn).
Molyneux, Derek and Kelly, Darren, *When the Clock Struck in 1916: Close-Quarter Combat in the Easter Rising* (Cork: The Collins Press, 2015).
Mommsen, Wolfgang J., 'Non-legal violence and terrorism in western industrial societies: An historical analysis', in Wolfgang J. Mommsen and Gerhard Hirschfeld, eds, *Social Protest, Violence, and Terror in Nineteenth- and Twentieth-Century Europe* (Palgrave Macmillan, 1982), pp 384–403.
Morris, Leslie, 'The sound of memory', in *The German Quarterly*, 74:4, Autumn 2001, pp 368–78.
Moulton, Mo, *Ireland and the Irish in Interwar England* (Cambridge: Cambridge University Press, 2014).
Mulcahy, Richard, 'Conscription and the General Headquarters' staff', in *Capuchin Annual*, 1968, pp 386–7.
Murphy, Alexander B. and Johnson, Douglas L., 'Introduction: Encounters with environment and place', in Alexander B. Murphy and Douglas L. Johnson, eds, *Cultural Encounters with the Environment: Enduring and Evolving Geographic Themes* (Lanham: Rowman & Littlefield, 2000), pp 1–16.
Murphy, William, *Political Imprisonment and the Irish, 1912–1921* (Oxford: Oxford University Press, 2014).
Murray, Christopher, 'Padraic Colum's "The land" and cultural nationalism', in *Hungarian Journal of English and American Studies (HJEAS)*, 2:2, 1996, pp 5–15.

Neeson, Eoin, 'Woodland in history and culture', in John Wilson Foster, ed., *Nature in Ireland: A Scientific and Cultural History* (Montreal: McGill-Queen's University Press, 1997), pp 133–56.

Noonan, Gerald, *The IRA in Britain, 1919–1923: In the Heart of Enemy Lines* (Liverpool: Liverpool University Press, 2014).

Noone, Simon et. al., 'Homogenization and analysis of an expanded long-term monthly rainfall network for the island of Ireland (1850–2010)', in *International Journal of Climatology*, 36:8, 2015, pp 2837–53.

Novick, Ben, *Conceiving Revolution: Irish Nationalist Propaganda During the First World War* (Dublin: Four Courts Press, 2001).

Novick, Ben, 'The arming of Ireland: Gun-running and the Great War, 1915–16', in Adrian Gregory and Senia Paseta, eds, *Ireland and the Great War: 'A War to Unite Us All'?* (Manchester: Manchester University Press, 2002), pp 94–112.

O'Brien, Joseph V., *Dear, Dirty Dublin: A City in Distress, 1899–1916* (California: University of California Press, 1982).

Ó Conchubhair, Brian, ed., *Rebel Cork's Fighting Story 1916–21: Told By the Men Who Made It* (Dublin: Mercier Press, 2009).

Ó Corráin, Daithí, '"They blew up the best portion of our city and ... it is their duty to replace it": Compensation and reconstruction in the aftermath of the 1916 Rising', in *Irish Historical Studies*, 39:154, November 2014, pp 272–95.

O'Donoghue, Florence, *No Other Law (The Story of Liam Lynch and the Irish Republican Army, 1916–1923)* (Kerry: Anvil Books, 1986).

O'Donoghue, Florence, 'Volunteer "actions" in 1918', in *Capuchin Annual*, 1968, pp 340–4.

Ó Faoláin, Seán, *Vive Moi* (Boston/Toronto: Little, Brown and Company, 1963).

O'Halpin, Eunan, *Defending Ireland: The Irish State and Its Enemies since 1922* (Oxford: Oxford University Press, 1999).

O'Halpin, Eunan, 'Historical revision XX: H. E. Duke and the Irish Administration, 1916–18', in *Irish Historical Studies*, 22:88, September 1981, pp 362–76.

O'Mahony, Ross, 'The sack of Balbriggan and tit-for-tat terror', in David Fitzpatrick, ed., *Terror in Ireland* (Dublin: The Lilliput Press, 2012), pp 58–74.

O'Malley, Ernie, *Army Without Banners: The Adventures of an Irish Volunteer* (Cambridge, Massachusetts: The Riverside Press, 1937).

O'Malley, Ernie, *On Another Man's Wound* (Dublin: Anvil Books, 1936).

O'Malley, Ernie, *The Singing Flame* (Dublin: Anvil Books, 1978).

Ó Murchadha, Ciarán, *The Great Famine: Ireland's Agony 1845–1852* (New York: Bloomsbury, 2013).

Oppenheimer, Martin, *The Urban Guerrilla* (Chicago: Quadrangle Books, 1969).

Ó Súilleabháin, Mícheál, *Where Mountainy Men Have Sown* (Tralee: Anvil Books, 1965).

Pattison, Gordon, 'The British Army's effectiveness in the Irish campaign 1919–1921 and the lessons for modern counterinsurgency operations, with special reference to C31 aspects', in *Cornwallis XIV: Analysis of Societal Conflict and Counter-Insurgency Workshop* (Vienna, 2009), pp 88–103.

Pearson, Chris, *Mobilizing Nature: The Environmental History of War and Militarization in Modern France* (Manchester: Manchester University Press, 2012).

Pearson, Chris, 'Researching militarized landscapes: A literature review on war and the militarization of the environment', in *Landscape Research*, 37:1, February 2012, pp 115–33.

Pennell, Catriona, 'Going to war', in John Horne, ed., *Our War: Ireland and the Great War* (Dublin: Royal Irish Academy, 2008), pp 35–62.

Pile, Steve, 'Introduction: Opposition, political identities, and spaces of resistance', in *Geographies of Resistance* (New York: Routledge, 1997), pp 1–32.

Pinkman, John A. (ed. Francis E. Maguire), *In the Legion of the Vanguard* (Dublin: Mercier Press, 1998).

Plamper, Jan, *The History of Emotions* (Oxford: Oxford University Press, 2017 edn).

Porteous, J. D. and Smith, S., *Domicide: The Global Destruction of Home* (Montreal: McGill Queens University Press, 2001).

Price, Dominic, *The Flame and the Candle* (Cork: The Collins Press, 2012).

Proctor, Tammy M., *Civilians in a World at War 1914–1918* (New York: New York University Press, 2010).

Purseigle, Pierre, '"A wave on to our shores": The exile and resettlement of refugees from the Western Front, 1914–1918', in *Contemporary European History*, 16:4, November 2007, pp 427–44.
Read, James Morgan, *Atrocity Propaganda 1914–1919* (New York: Arno Press, 1972).
Reinarz, Jonathan, *Past Scents: Historical Perspectives on Smell* (Urbana, Chicago, and Springfield: University of Illinois Press, 2014).
Rowley, Ellen, ed., *More Than Concrete Blocks: Dublin City's Twentieth-Century Buildings and Their Stories – Volume 1: 1900–1940* (Dublin: Dublin City Council with University College Dublin and Four Courts Press, 2016).
Rumpf, Erhard and Hepburn, A. C., *Nationalism and Socialism in Twentieth-Century Ireland* (Liverpool: Liverpool University Press, 1977).
de Schaepdrijver, Sophie, 'Occupation, propaganda and the idea of Belgium', in Aviel Roshwald and Richard Stites, eds, *European Culture in the Great War: The Arts, Entertainment, and Propaganda, 1914–1918* (Cambridge: Cambridge University Press, 1999, 2002), pp 267–94.
Schmitt, Carl (trans. C. J. Miller), *Theory of the Partisan* (1962).
Schofield, J., *Combat Archaeology: Material Culture and Modern Conflict* (London: Duckworth, 2005).
Sheehan, William, *A Hard Local War: The British Army and the Guerrilla War in Cork 1919–1921* (Dublin: The History Press Ireland, 2011, 2017 edn).
Sheehan, William, *Hearts & Mines: The British 5th Division, Ireland, 1920–1922* (Cork: The Collins Press, 2009).
Smyth, William J., 'A Plurality of Irelands: Regions, Societies, and Mentalities', in Brian Graham, ed., *In Search of Ireland: A Cultural Geography* (New York: Routledge, 1998 edn).
Solow, Barbara L., 'The Irish land question in a wider context', in Fergus Campbell and Tony Varley, eds, *Land Questions in Modern Ireland* (Manchester: Manchester University Press, 2013), pp 3–24.
Spillane, Sandra, 'Weather Easter 1916, Sunday 23 to Saturday 29 April 1916', in *Met Eireann Historical Note*, 7, 12 April 2016.
Stigger, Phillip, '1668: Numerous matters relating to grenades', in *Journal of the Society for Army Historical Research*, 81:326, Summer 2003, pp 168–77.
Stover, Justin Dolan, 'Families, vulnerability and sexual violence during the Irish Revolution', in Jennifer Evans and Ciara Meehan, eds, *Perceptions of Pregnancy from the Seventeenth to the Twentieth Century* (Switzerland, 2017), pp 57–75.
Stover, Justin Dolan, 'Modern Celtic nationalism in the period of the Great War: Establishing transnational connections', in Deborah Furchtgott, Georgia Henley and Matthew Holmberg, eds, *Proceedings of the Harvard Celtic Colloquium*, XXXII, 2012, pp 286–301.
Stover, Justin Dolan, 'Periphery of war or first line of defence? Ireland prepares for invasion (1900–1915)', in *Francia: Forschungen zur Westeuropäischen Geschichte*, 40, 2013, pp 385–96.
Taillon, Ruth, *When History Was Made: The Women of 1916* (Belfast: Beyond the Pale Publications, 1999).
Tilly, Charles, *The Politics of Collective Violence* (New York: Cambridge University Press, 2003).
Townshend, Charles, *Easter 1916: The Irish Rebellion* (London: Penguin Books, 2006).
Townshend, Charles, *Political Violence in Ireland Since 1848* (New York: Oxford University Press, 1984).
Townshend, Charles, *The British Campaign in Ireland 1919–1921: The Development of Political and Military Policies* (Oxford: Oxford University Press, 1975).
Townshend, Charles, 'The Irish Railway Strike of 1920: Industrial action and civil resistance in the struggle for independence', in *Irish Historical Studies*, 22:83, 1979, pp 265–82.
Townshend, Charles, 'The Irish Republican Army and the development of guerrilla warfare, 1916–1921', in *The English Historical Review*, 94:371, 1979, pp 318–45.
Townshend, Charles, *The Republic: The Fight for Irish Independence, 1918–1923* (London: Penguin Books, 2013).
Tucker, Richard P., 'The impact of warfare on the natural world: A historical survey', in Richard P. Tucker and Edmund Russell, eds, *Natural Enemy, Natural Ally: Toward An Environmental History of War* (Corvallis: Oregon State University Press, 2004), pp 15–41.
Vaughan, W. E., *Landlords and Tenants in Mid-Victorian Ireland* (Oxford: Oxford University Press, 1994).
Walsh, Aisling, 'Michael Cardinal Logue 1840–1924', in *Seancas Ardmhacha: Journal of the Armagh Diocesan Historical Society*, 20:2, 2005, pp 245–92.

Walsh, J. J., *Recollections of a Rebel* (Tralee: The Kerryman, Ltd, 1944).
Ward, Margaret, *Unmanageable Revolutionaries: Women and Irish Nationalism* (London: Pluto Press, 1989, 1995 edn).
Whelan, Yvonne, 'The construction and destruction of a colonial landscape: Monuments to British monarchs in Dublin before and after independence', in *Journal of Historical Geography*, 28:4, 2002, pp 508–33.
White, Gerry and O'Shea, Brendan, *The Burning of Cork* (Cork: Mercier Press, 2006).
Wilson, Trevor, *The Myriad of Faces of War: Britain and the Great War, 1914–1918* (Cambridge: Polity Press, 1986).
Winstanley, Michael J., *Ireland and the Land Question 1800–1922* (New York: Routledge, 1984).
Winters, Harold et. al., *Battling the Elements: Weather and Terrain in the Conduct of War* (Baltimore: The Johns Hopkins University Press, 1998).
Woodward, Rachel, *Military Geographies* (Malden, MA: Blackwell Publishing Ltd, 2004).
Yeates, Pádraig, *A City in Turmoil: Dublin 1919–1921* (Dublin: Gill & MacMillan, 2012).

Index

Abbey Street, Dublin 5, 10, 19
Abbeydorney, County Kerry 102
Action Française 125
Æ (George Russell) 98–9
aeroplanes 58
afforestation 61
Agnew, Arthur 8
agrarian damage xvii–xviii, 135–42, 152
agrarianism 136
Aherne, Sergeant 1
Allen, Abraham 32
Allied Loyalty League 125–7
Alsace-Lorraine 112, 115, 118
American Association for the Recognition of the Irish Republic 127
American Commission on Conditions in Ireland 88, 90, 93, 101, 116, 120, 126, 128
American Commission on Relief in Ireland 98–9
American Committee for Relief in Ireland (ACRI) 120–1
American Society of Friends 116
Amiens Street Station (Connolly Station), Dublin 7–8, 37
Amritsar massacre 89
An t-Oglach 39, 41, 54, 59
Ancient Order of Hibernians 120
Anglo-American Oil Company 65
Anglo-Celt 3
Anglo-Irish 'Big House' 135, 140–2, 147
Anglo-Irish Treaty xiii, 143
Anglo-Irish War *see* War of Independence
Annesgrove House, County Cork 140
Antient Concert Rooms, Dublin 6
Anti-Reprisals Association 89–90
Antrim, County 64, 120
Arklow, County Wicklow 117
Armagh, County 64, 71
Armagh town 119
armoured cars 57–9, 96, 119
arms, acquisition of 54
arms caches 35–44, 152
arms raids 37–8, 55, 62
Army Pensions Board 93
Arnotts department store, Dublin 19

arson 10–11, 35, 41–2, 70, 87, 91–2, 103–4, 140–2
arson campaign *see* Irish Republican Army
artillery xvi, 7–8, 10–13, 53, 61, 143–4
Ashtown, Lord (Frederick Oliver Trench) 141
assassination xvii, 70, 85–8, 92, 117, 143
Association of Municipal Authorities in Ireland 85
Athea, County Limerick 31
Athlone 7, 72
Aud 4
Augusteijn, Joost 59, 70–1
Auxiliaries xvii, 34, 75, 85, 89, 97, 103, 115, 118, 141

Babington, Seamus 39
Balbriggan, County Dublin 100–1, 104, 115, 121–2
Balbriggan Relief Committee 100
Ballaghaderreen, County Roscommon 92
Ballinatone, County Wicklow 34
Ballinger, W.A. 55–6
Ballybunion RIC barracks 32
Ballyduff, County Kerry 102
Ballyshannon, County Donegal 66
Ballytrain, County Monaghan 69
Baltimore Sun 117
Banc na Talmhan (National Land Bank) 140
Bandon, County Cork 35, 60, 69
Barlow, John Henry 120
Barrett, Annie 62
barricades xiv, xvi, 4–8, 10, 13, 18, 20, 54–5, 59–61, 68, 119, 143–4, 146
Barry's Hotel, Dublin 144
Bealen, Patrick 16
Bean Uí Luasa, Maighread (Margaret Lucey) 93
Beasley family 69
Beck, James M. 125–6
Beggar's Bush Barracks 142
Begley, John 61
Belfast 36–7, 56, 122
Belfast Newsletter 18, 68, 99
Belgium 112–18, 122–5, 127–8
Benedict XV, Pope 124
Bennett, Richard 86

167

Bentinck, Lord Henry 123
Béraud, Henri 122
Bew, Paul 136
Bianconi, Carlo 'Charles' 56
'Big House' *see* Anglo-Irish 'Big House'
Birrell, Augustine 8
Birrell Act (1909) 136
Black and Tans 89, 93, 96–7, 100–1, 112, 115, 118, 141
Blackwell, John 146
Blythe, Ernest 147
Bodyke, County Clare 60
Bohcrash Cross, County Cork 60
Boland's Mill, Dublin 6, 11, 15, 17
bomb factories 2–3, 39–40, 44
bombs 15, 34, 36, 38–9, 56, 69, 71, 90–2 *see also* explosives
Bonar Law, Andrew 31
Borgonovo, John 92
Borough Surveyor, Dublin 18
Bouladuff, County Tipperary 90
boycotting xv, 40, 43, 136–7
Bracken, Peadar 1, 8
Brazil, John 141
Breathnach, Proinnsias 99
Breen, Dan 144–5
Brennan, Maurice 32
Brennan, Michael 72
Brennan, Robert 15, 96
Brereton Barry, Ralph 34
Brickell, Katherine 94
bridges, destruction of xvii, 4, 6, 18, 36, 40, 53, 55, 58–61, 68, 145–7
British Army xv, xvii, 2, 8, 11, 62–3, 75, 143 *see also* Crown Forces
Browne, Bishop Robert 91
Bruen, Willie 17
Bruff, County Limerick 44, 64
Buckley, Joseph 31
built environment, damage to xv–xvi, 53, 63–74, 88, 92, 100, 143–4
Bureau of Military History Witness Statements 15, 59, 70, 94, 144
burials, unofficial 15–17
Burke, Peter 100
Burke, Thomas 36
Burke, William Peter 100
businesses xiv–xvi, 2, 5–6, 9, 18–19, 35, 39, 43, 54, 63, 67, 85–8, 90–2, 97–101, 103–4, 121, 144
by-elections 30, 32, 136
Byrne, Joseph 55, 86
Byrne, Catherine 3
Byrne, Sir Joseph 33
Byrne, William 30

Caddan, John Joseph 91
Callaghan, Leo 62
Callaghan, Michael 37
Cameron Highlanders 91
Campbell, Fergus 137–8
Capel Street, Dublin 9
Carey, Patrick 44, 91
Carlow, County 60, 71
Carrigabrick, County Cork 62
Carrol, Hughie 68
Casement, Sir Roger 4, 114, 121
Cashel, County Tipperary 44, 67, 138
Castletownbere, County Cork 55
Catholic Church 30, 34, 112, 124–5
Catholic Herald 115
cattle driving 35, 67, 136–8, 140, 146
cattle maiming xviii, 35, 135, 138
Causeway, County Kerry 102
Cavan, County 71–2
Cavan town 6
Cavell, Edith 113
Ceannt, Áine 31
Central News 7
Centre for Motor Transport, Phoenix Park 57
Chalmers, Sir Robert 19
Chamberlain, Austen 85
Chamberlain, Inspector General Neville 4
Chesterton, G.K. 123
Chicago Tribune 38
Childers, Erskine 95–6, 124
Church Street, Dublin 5
Churchill, Winston 87
Clan na Gael 120
Clancy, George 35, 95
Clancy, Mary 95–6
Clanricarde, Marquis of (Hubert de Burgh-Canning) 34
Clanwilliam House, Ballsbridge 10
Clare, County 41, 71, 98, 120, 136–7
Clare County Council 61
Clark, Gemma 141
Clark, Roger 120
Clarke, Charles 44
Cleeve's creameries 101–2
Clerihan, County Tipperary 61
Clery's department store, Dublin 9–10, 103
Clogher, County Sligo 64
Clontarf, Dublin 3, 14
Cloyne, County Cork 66
coast guard stations 41, 66–7, 141
Cobh (Queenstown), County Cork 91
Cohalan, Bishop 30
Colbert, Con 31
Colby, Bainbridge 126
Coleman, David 146
Coleman, Marie 70

College Green, Dublin 8
Collins, Joseph 74
Collinstown Aerodrome 36
Collooney, County Sligo 34
communications 6–7, 55–6, 67–8, 104, 145
Congested Districts Board 136
Connacht 35, 57, 61, 72, 88, 138
Connolly, James 7–8, 12
Connolly, Linda 93
Connolly, Nora 15
Connolly Station, *see* Amiens Street Station
conscription 4, 30–4, 44, 54, 68, 137
Constabulary Gazette 41
co-operatives xvii, 75, 86, 97–9, 136 *see also* creameries
Cooper-Key, A. 66
Corcoran, William 100
Cork, County 68, 71–2, 102, 136–7, 140–1
Cork City 31–2, 34, 66, 90, 93, 102–4, 115, 117, 121–2
Cork City Gaol 32
Cork Corporation 103
Cork Distress Relief Committee 103
Cork Examiner 35, 103, 145–6
'Cork Explosion' 40
Cork Incorporated Chamber of Commerce and Shipping 103
Corofin, County Clare 41
corpses xvi, 15–17, 20, 122
    of animals 15
Cosgrave, W.T. 142, 146–7
counter-insurgency xiii, xvii, 58, 87, 104, 123, 135
courthouses 32, 63, 66–7, 94, 141
courts 87, 138
    land 140
    military 87
Coyle, Albert 128
Crane, County Inspector 1
creameries xv, xvii, 75, 86, 98–9, 101–2, 104, 120, 146
Crewe, Marquis of 119
Criminal Law and Procedure (Ireland) Act 33
Criminal and Malicious Injuries (Ireland) Act 101
Crofts, Thomas 93
Croix, La 125
Crown forces xiv–xv, xvii, 35, 53, 55, 59, 70, 117–18, 141
    interrogations 94–5, 119
    reprisals by: 85–104, 112, 115, 135, 152; economic targets 97–104; effects on civilians 92–7
Cullybackey, County Antrim 43
Cumann na mBan 1–2, 12, 16, 31–4, 59, 74, 95

Curragh military camp 6–7
Curraghboola House, County Longford 140

Dáil Éireann 38, 41, 85, 88, 114, 124, 140
Daily Chronicle 14, 103
Daily Express offices, Dublin 16
Daily News 95, 115
Daily Telegraph 115
Dalton, William 6
Daly, Daniel 39
Daly, Edward 'Ned' 5
Daly, Francis 3
Daly, Seamus 3, 10
Damage to Property (Compensation) Act 61
Danchin, Emmannuelle xiii
Darcy, John 32
Dawson Street, Dublin 7–8
de Brún, Seosamh 13
de Burgh-Canning, Hubert (Marquis of Clanricarde) 34
de Valera, Éamon 32, 64, 137
Deede's, Templar & Co., Balbriggan 101
Defence of the Realm Act 3, 32–3, 87
Defence of the Realm Regulations (DRR) 1
demonstrations 29–35, 117
Dempsey, Frank 101
Department of Agriculture and Technical Instruction (DATI) 98
Department of Public Works 57
Derreen, County Cork 142
Derry (Londonderry) City 36, 119
Derry (Londonderry), County 64, 71, 121
DeSelby Quarries 37
Desmond, Shaw 89
Devine & Sons, Dublin 6
Dickson, Thomas 16
Dillon, John 37, 39
Dingle Peninsula, County Kerry 64, 102
Dobbs, Colonel 63
Doherty, Gabriel 92
domicide 94 *see also* homes
Donegal, County 71
Donnelly, Simon 60
Donovan, Con 32
Donovan, T. 93
Dooley, Terence 140
Doon, County Limerick 91
Douglas, James 121
Down, County 64, 71
Downey, Jeremiah 40
Doyle, James 44
Doyle, Michael Francis 116
Drislane, John 36
Drogheda Independent 72, 115
Dublin, County 71
Dublin Castle 7–8, 16–17, 30, 64, 67

Dublin City 122
Dublin City Council 18
Dublin Corporation 18–20
Dublin Distillers' Company 20
Dublin Fire Brigade 10, 18
Dublin Fire and Property Losses Association 19
Dublin Jewish Board of Guarding 20
Dublin Metropolitan Police (DMP) 9, 37–8, 118
Dublin and South Eastern Railway 6
Duffy, Patrick 96
Duke, Henry 30, 33
Dún Laoghaire *see* Kingstown
Dunboy House, County Cork 141
Dunkellin, Lord 34
Dwyer, James 98

Earl Street, Dublin 9–10, 19
Easter Rising xiii, xvi, 1–18, 30, 53, 75, 112, 121
   aftermath 18–21, 29–31, 53
   cost of 19–20
   sensory experiences of 12–18
Echo de la Loire 115
Echo de Paris 125
Eden Quay 19, 31
Egan, Maurice 125
Ehrlich, Cyril 99
elections *see* by-elections; general elections
Elton, County Limerick 64
emergency legislation 117
Enniscorthy, County Wexford 6
Ennistymon, County Clare 101, 120
environmental damage xiv–xv, xvii–xviii, 20–1, 35, 44, 59, 62, 68–75, 90, 92–3, 103, 113, 152–3 *see also* agrarian damage; built environment; landscape damage; landscape manipulation
Essex Regiment 90
Evening Herald 115
explosives xvi, 3, 5, 11, 34, 36–41, 44, 64–6, 69, 143 *see also* bombs; gelignite
   training in 39
Eyre Square, Galway 34

Falaize, Urbain 115
Fanning, John 62
Farrelly, Sean 65–6
Farrington, Annie 144
Fenianism 4, 30, 136
Fennelly, John 20
Fermanagh, County 71–2
Fermoy, County Cork 62–3, 90–1, 117
Ferriter, Diarmaid 63, 86–7, 98, 124
Fianna Éireann 3, 5

Figgis, Darrell 124
Finlay, T.F. 99
Finnegan, Luke 90
Firearms Act (1920) 66
fires 10, 12, 14, 18–19, 65 *see also* arson
First World War (Great War) xiii–xiv, xvii, 1, 4, 13–14, 35, 37, 53, 61, 85–6, 89, 112–18, 121–2, 124, 127–8, 136–7
   Armistice 54, 121
   peace conference 121, 127
Fitzgerald, District-Inspector 1
Fitzgerald, Desmond 9
Fitzgerald, George 16
Fitzpatrick, David 35, 54, 59, 70, 92, 100, 123, 137
Fitzwilliam Place, Dublin 14
flags
   Sinn Féin 34
   tri-colour xiv, xvi, 31, 35, 44, 136
   Union Jack 126
Fleming, Mrs R. Lester 126
Fletcher, George 57
flooding 53, 55, 138, 145–6
Floreal 122–3
Folks, Homer 114
Forrest, M.D. 101
Forrest's, Cork 103
Fortnightly Review 118
Four Courts 5, 119, 142–4
Fox, Jim 7
France 112–15, 117, 121–2, 125, 127–8
Freeman's Journal xiii, 15, 60, 66, 69, 98, 103, 118–19, 144
French, Lord 58
French, Sir John 38, 115
Frenchpark, County Roscommon 92
Friends of Irish Freedom (FOIF) 120, 123–4
Frith, William 17
Frongoch camp, Wales 29
Fullerton, Edward 68
Furnas, Paul 120

G Division 118
Gaelic Athletic Association (GAA) xvi, 32
Gaelic League xvi, 30, 32–3, 39
Gallagher, James 20
Galway, County 64, 67, 71, 88
Galway City 6, 34, 66, 99, 122
Galway Express 99
Garbett, Bishop Cyril 123
Garvin, Tom 70, 72
Gaulstown Mansion, County Westmeath 140
Gavan Duffy, George 124
Geary, James 17
gelignite 3, 36–9, 66, 69

general elections
    1918: 55, 114
    1922: 143
General Post Office (GPO) xvi, 4–5, 12, 15, 19, 29, 31
German Plot 33, 121
Gibbs, Philip 89
Gilmartin, Archbishop Thomas 91
Ginnell, Laurence 30, 137
Gladwin, Derek 64
Glashakeenleen, County Cork 61
Glasnevin Cemetery, Dublin 31
Glenahiery House, County Waterford 141
Glencullen House, County Dublin 39
Good, Joe 8
Gormanston, County Meath 57
Gough, Lord 36
Goulding, Sir William 19
Goulding Committee (Property Losses (Ireland) Committee) 9, 19
Government of Ireland Act (1920) 87
Granard, County Longford 121
Grand Canal, Dublin 6
Grant's, Cork 103
Grantstown Hall, County Tipperary 39
graziers 136, 147
Great Brunswick Street (Pearse Street) 143
Great Southern and Western Railway 31–2
Great War *see* First World War
Greenwood, Sir Hamar 85–9, 122
Gregg, Kathleen 6
grenades 3, 10, 13, 36, 38
Grenville Peek, Roger 62
Grievances from Ireland 141
Griffith, Arthur 115
guerrilla warfare xiii, 41, 44, 55–68, 119, 135, 144, 147, 152
gun running 29
Gwynn, Stephen 124

Hall, David 60
Harbour Court, Dublin 19
Harding, Warren 126
Harker, Christopher 94
Harnett, Mossie 65
Hart, Peter 54, 59, 70, 72, 87
Haugh, Liam 120
Hawes, Major General L.A. 56
Hayes, Michael 95
Healy, James 16, 19
Hegarty, George 93
Hegarty, Timothy 40
Helga 11–12
Henderson, Arthur 121
Henderson, Frank 37
Hennessy, Patrick 35

Henry Street, Dublin 12, 15, 19
Herberton Lane, Dublin 20
Herbertstown, County Limerick 64
Heron & Lawless, Messrs, Dublin 39
Heuston Station *see* Kingsbridge Station
Hickey, Thomas 146
Higgins, Dave 39
Hobson, Bulmer 9
Hodkinson, Louis 44
Holycross, County Tipperary 69
Home Office 66
Home Rule 32–3, 85, 87, 121, 136, 152
homes
    damage to/destruction of xiv, xvi, 5, 18, 35, 40, 63, 67, 75, 85–6, 88, 90–2, 100–3, 120–1
    raids on xv, xvii, 92–7, 117, 120
Hopkinson, Michael 103–4, 145, 147
Horan, Agnes 93
Horan, Christine 93
Horne, John 114
horses 15, 32, 43–4, 58
Hospital, County Limerick 91
hotels 5, 7–8, 14–15, 44, 67, 90, 104, 144
housing 85 *see also* homes
Housing (Ireland) Act (1919) 85
Howlett, Thomas 38
Howth, County Dublin 29
Hughes, Brian 43
Hunter, Thomas 32
Hurley, Charles 55
Hylan, John Francis 126

illness 74, 144
Illustrated Sunday Herald 14
industrial action xvi, 17, 33, 57
infrastructure 56–7 *see also* communications; railways; roads
international views of Ireland 121–8
internment 29–30, 117
Irish Agricultural Organisation Society (IAOS) 98–9
Irish Anti-Conscription Committee 34
Irish Bulletin xvii, 88, 94, 99–100, 114–15, 118, 124
Irish Citizen Army 2, 8
Irish Civil War xiii, xviii, 121, 135, 142–7, 152
    cost of 147
Irish Convention 32
Irish diaspora 123, 125
Irish Executive 20, 33, 55, 57
Irish Exile 123
Irish Free State xiii, 60–2, 152
    Constitution 143
    National Forces 146
Irish Homestead 98–9

Irish Independent 40, 43, 65, 96, 101–3, 115, 119, 147
'Irish Louvain' 113, 115, 123–4
Irish National Volunteers 1, 36
Irish question 30, 32, 124
Irish Parliamentary Party (IPP) 1, 29, 37
Irish Republican Army (IRA) xiii, xv, xvii, 33, 36–41, 54, 58–75, 85–96, 99–100, 102–4, 117, 138, 140–7 *see also* guerrilla warfare
    ambushes xv, xvii, 38, 41, 53, 55–6, 58–60, 62–3, 69–72, 85–9, 91–2, 96, 98, 101, 103, 117, 120, 135, 143, 145, 152
    arson campaign (1920) xv, 66–7, 90
    Brigade Activity Reports (BAR) 54, 59
    in Britain 67–8
    flying columns 55, 65, 74, 88
    General Headquarters (GHQ) 39, 55
    intimidation by 41–4
    split 142
    tactics 53–5, 63, 117
    targets 63
    training 55
Irish Republican Brotherhood (IRB) 1–4, 37
Irish Self-Determination League of Great Britain 112, 123
Irish Statesman 98, 147
Irish Times 11, 65
    offices 5, 10
Irish Volunteers 1–6, 10, 30, 32–4, 36, 38 *see also* Irish Republican Army
Irish White Cross xvii, 121, 125
Irregulars xiii, 146–7

Jacob's Biscuit Factory 5, 7, 13–14
Jeudwine, Lieutenant General Hugh 87
Johnson, Nuala 34
Jones, Norbert 112
Jones, William 63
Jordison, Ernest 14

Kautt, William 58
Kavanagh, Seamus 7
Keash, County Sligo 64
Keely, Thomas 36
Kelly, Major Henry 118
'Kelly's Fort', Dublin 11
Kenneally, Ian 114–15
Kennedy, Ray 38–9
Kent, David 32
Kent, Susan Kingsley 89
Kerry, County 71, 102, 136
Kerry Weekly Reporter 5
Kessel, Joseph 122
kidnapping 91

Kilbride, Bernard 40
Kilbrittain, County Cork 61
Kilcommon, County Tipperary 90
Kildare, County 3, 71
Kildare town 6
Kilkenny, County 64, 71
Killaloe, County Clare 60
Killester House, County Dublin 140
Killorglin, County Kerry 102
Kilmovee, County Mayo 41
King's County (Offaly) 71
King's Shropshire Light Infantry 62–3, 90
Kingsbridge (Heuston) Station, Dublin 6, 8
Kingstown (Dún Laoghaire) 6–7
Kinsale, County Cork 90
Knocklong, County Limerick 64
Kramer, Alan 114
Kynoch's factory, Arklow 38

Labour Commission to Ireland 90, 97, 121
Labour Party, British 121
Labour Party, Irish 33
Lahinch, County Clare 101, 120
Land Acts 136–7
land agitation 136–8, 140, 142, 146
Land Commission 140
land purchase 136
land question 135–7
land seizures 140, 147
land wars 138, 142
landlordism 34, 136, 138, 141
landscape 56–9
    vernacular 96
landscape damage 112–14, 152 *see also* environmental damage
landscape manipulation 59–75, 145
Landsdowne, Lord 142
Lanterne, Le 122
Laois, County (Queen's County) 71
Larkin, Jim 34
Larne, County Antrim 29
Lawless, Joseph V. 14–15, 39
Lawton, Sergeant 69
Leeson, David 88–9, 102
Leinster 72
Leinster (ship) 113
Leitrim, County 71–2, 88
Lendrum, Captain Alan 120
Leopold II, King 114
Liberté, Le 122
Liberty Hall, Dublin 11–12, 29
lighthouses 38, 94
Limerick, County 31, 71, 102, 145–6
Limerick City 90–1, 145
Limerick City Hall 35
Linenhall barracks, Dublin 10, 19

Lisburn, County Antrim 120–1
Lissycasey, County Clare 41
Listowel, County Kerry 92
Liverpool 67
Lloyd, Demarest 127
Lloyd George, David 86, 119
London Times 63
Londonderry *see* Derry
Longfield, R.E. 104
Longford, County 71–2
Longford, Joseph Henry 118
Longford County Council 40
Longford town 6
looting xvi, 8–9, 11, 19, 32, 63, 87, 91, 101, 142
Lord Mayor's Fund (Mansion House Fund) 20
Louth, County 71
Louvain 114, 116–17, 124
Lowe, Major-General 7–8
Loyal Coalition 125–7
Lucas, General Cuthbert 91
Lucey, Margaret (Maighread Bean Uí Luasa) 93
Lusitania 113
Lynch, Diarmuid 32
Lynch, Liam 62
Lynd, Robert 96
Lyons, F.S.L. 86, 141

Maam, County Galway 64
Macardle, Dorothy 86, 117–18
McCabe, Alex 3
McCarthy, Ellen 90
McCarthy, Michael (Cork) 44
McCarthy, Michael (Thurles) 90
McCormack, John 68
McCormack, Count John 20
McDermott, Sergeant and Mrs Terence 43
MacDonagh, John 7, 14
MacDonagh, Thomas 7, 14
McDonnell, Andrew 3, 39
McDonnell, James 38
McGarry, Fearghal 8
McGill, John 60
McGinley, Bernard 43
MacIntyre, Patrick 16
McMahon, Mrs 40
McMahon, Timothy 30
MacNeill, Eoin 1, 4, 64
MacPherson, Ian 98
Macready, General Sir Nevil 57–8, 87, 91, 119
MacSwiney, Muriel 126
MacSwiney, Terence 95, 126–7
machine guns 8, 11, 13, 53, 113, 118–19, 144
Mahon, Lieutenant General Sir Bryan 30, 33

Malicious Injuries Act 19
Mallow, County Cork 62, 96, 101, 104, 121, 145
Manchester 67
Manchester Guardian 117
Manchester Guardian News Bulletin 89
Mannix, Archbishop Daniel 126
Mansion House Fund (Lord Mayor's Fund) 20
Markiewicz, Constance 3
Marlborough Street, Dublin 9
martial law 11, 33, 88, 97–8, 102–3, 115, 117
Maryborough *see* Portlaoise
Massy, Lord 39
Mauri, Angelo 124
Maurice, Major-General Sir F. 104
Maxwell, General Sir John 8, 11–12
Mayo, County 67, 71, 88, 136
Meath, County 60, 71
Meeting of Suffering 120
Mercier, Cardinal 124
Metropole Hotel, Dublin 7, 15
militarisation xiv, xvi–xvii, 36–44, 55, 57, 87, 96–7, 115–22, 127, 152
Miltown Malbay, County Clare 35, 101, 120
mines, explosive 36, 39, 54, 69, 143–5
mining 38
Monaghan, County 64, 71
Monroe Chapel, Tipperary 41
monuments 34–5, 44
moonlighting 137
Moore, Cissie 40
Moore Street, Dublin 6
Morehampton Road, Dublin 16
Morgan, Denis 90
Morris, Leslie 69
Mosely, Oswald 119
Moulton, Mo 123
Mount Street Bridge, Dublin 7, 18
Mulcahy, Richard 32
Munster 36, 61, 64, 70–2, 98, 103
murder 35, 53, 55, 63, 67, 87, 90–2, 95, 100, 115, 123
Murphy, Dick 40
Murphy, Fintan 15
Murphy, William 32
Murphy, William Martin 7, 19

Nathan, Matthew 8
National Land Bank (Banc na Talmhan) 140
National Relief Fund 20
nationalism xvi–xvii, 1–2, 4, 12, 18, 29–35, 44, 55, 59, 70, 92–3, 101, 104, 113–14, 117, 119, 122, 124–8, 135–7, 140–1
nationalist symbols 117 *see also* flags; tricolours

Navan, County Meath 138
Nelson's Pillar, Dublin 31
Neville, Reginald 16
Nevin, Anastasia 74
Nevin, Fr Eugene 33
New York Times 126
New York World 115–16
Newport, County Tipperary 41
Newry, 32
Newtownards, County Down 57
noise 69, 96
Noonan, Gerard 68
North Brunswick Street, Dublin 16
North Dublin Union 16
North King Street, Dublin 5
North Wall, Dublin 8
Northumberland Road 16, 18

O'Brien, Marie 124
O'Brien, William 136
Observer 124
O'Byrne, Joseph 17
O'Byrne, Peter 17
O'Callaghan, Cáit 94–5
O'Callaghan, Donal 116, 126
O'Callaghan, Michael 35, 91, 94–5
O'Casey, Seán 97
O'Connell, Christopher 141
O'Connell, J.J. 143
O'Connell, Patrick 38
O'Connell, Seán 40
O'Connell Bridge, Dublin 9
O'Connell Street *see* Sackville Street
O'Connor, Fergus 32
O'Connor, Frank 113
O'Connor, Sir James 33
O'Connor, Jeremiah 141
O'Connor, Joseph 6, 10, 13
O'Connor, Rory 39
O'Doherty, Bishop 117
O'Donoghue, Michael V. 39
O'Donovan, James 38
O'Duffy, Eimar 13, 18
O'Dwyer, Liam 141
L'Oeuvre 122
O'Faoláin, Seán 54
O'Farrell, Elizabeth 12
Offaly, County (King's County) 71
O'Flanagan, Michael 3
O'Hare, Dan 68
O'Keeffe, Seán 6
O'Kelly, Seán T. 124
Oldcastle, County Meath 66
O'Leary, Jeremiah 9–10
O'Leary, Thomas 35
O'Loughlin, John 35

O'Mahony, Ross 100
O'Malley, Ernie 9, 12–13, 73, 142–3
O'Mullane, Brighid 73–4
O'Neill, Fr Peter 34
Orange Order 119
Oranmore, County Galway 65
Oranmore Urban Council 91
O'Regan, Con 31
Oriel Street, Dublin 37
O'Shea, James 7
O'Shea, Seán 9
O'Shiel, Kevin 140
O'Sullivan, Micheal Og 141

Pallasgreen, County Limerick 60
Palmer, Mitchell 126
paraffin xiv, 65–7
Parnell Square (Rutland Square), Dublin 8, 37, 143
Parnell Street, Dublin 9
Patrick Street, Cork 32
Peace with Ireland Council 123
Pearse, Patrick 1–2, 7, 9, 12
Pearse Street (Great Brunswick Street) 143
Pearson, Chris 41
Petit Parisien 122
petrol xv, 5, 42, 54–5, 63, 65–7, 92
Phillips, Percival 15
Phoenix Park, Dublin 5
pigeons 58, 68, 104
Pile, Steve 70
Pinkman, John 67
Pius X, Pope 112
Plunkett, Count George Noble 30, 125, 136–7
Plunkett, Horace 98–9, 125
Plunkett, Joseph 7
Poe, Lieutenant Colonel Hutchinson 20
police xvi, 1–3, 19, 31–44, 55, 60, 63–8, 86–7, 89, 91–2, 94–104, 116–19, 122, 140–1
  see also Auxiliaries; Dublin Metropolitan Police; Royal Irish Constabulary
attacks on 1, 102
pollution xvi, 2, 10, 15, 18, 65
Portlaoise, County Laois 6
Portobello barracks, Dublin 16
Portumna, County Galway 67
Prendergast, Sean 143
Prescott-Decie, Brigadier-General Cyril 92
press, foreign 121–8
prisoners, release of 29–31, 35, 87
Pro-Cathedral, Dublin 10
propaganda 54, 85, 88–9, 96, 113–15, 119, 123, 125–7, 135, 146
Property Losses (Ireland) Committee (Goulding Committee) 9, 19
Provisional Government xiii, 103, 142–7

Prussia 114, 117–18, 127
Public Health Department 17
Punchestown racecourse, County Kildare 29
Purcell, Fire Captain 10
Purcell's shop, Dublin 9

Quakers (Society of Friends) 116, 120
Quane, James 146
quarries 38
Queen's County (Laois) 71
Queenstown (Cobh), County Cork 91

Raemaekers, Louis 114
railways 56
    destruction/damage 4, 6, 18, 54–5, 58–9, 71, 145–6
Ranch War 136
Reader, John 122–3
Reader, Seamus 3
Red Cross 114
Redmond, John 1, 137
refugees 100, 102
    Belgian 112
Regan, John 144
Register of Crime 88
Reiska, County Tipperary 90
reprisals 63, 93 *see also* Crown forces
republicanism xiii, xv–xvii, 2–3, 7, 20, 29–35, 40–4, 54–5, 57–60, 62–70, 74, 85–9, 92, 97–8, 104, 114, 117, 123, 125, 127, 140–7
Restoration of Order in Ireland Act (1920) (ROIA) 87, 92, 104
Restoration of Order in Ireland Regulations (ROIR) 33
Richmond Hospital, Dublin 16
rifles 4, 10, 13, 29, 36, 62, 65, 118
Rineen, County Clare 101
roads 56–8, 64, 72–3 *see also* trenches
    blocking 54, 59–61, 69–70, 145–7
    destruction/damage xv, xvii, 18, 36, 53–5, 59, 61, 71, 146
Robinson, Annot Erskine 93, 120
Robinson, Seamus 38
Roche, David 146
Rochesfordtown House, County Cork 140–1
Rock, Michael 100
Roscommon, County 62–3, 67, 71–2, 88
Roscrea, County Tipperary 6, 98
Ross, County Sligo 64
Royal Air Force 65
Royal College of Surgeons, Dublin 7, 16
Royal Irish Constabulary (RIC) xv–xvi, 1–2, 41–2, 55, 63–4, 75, 138, 140, 147 *see also* police
    barracks/stations: 32, 41–4, 57, 63–4, 70, 87, 141, 143; closures 64–5
    depot 57
    reports 3
Rumpf, Erhard 70, 136
Russell, George (Æ) 98–9
Russell, Seán 5
Rutland Square *see* Parnell Square
Ryan, Desmond 9
Ryan, Michael 40

St Enda's School 2
St Patrick's Day parades 30
St Stephen's Green, Dublin 7–8, 15–16, 18
St Vitus' dance (Sydenham's chorea) 97
sabotage xv–xviii, 4, 53, 55, 58, 65, 87, 91–2, 99–101, 135, 137, 144, 146–7
    see also agrarian damage; bridges; communications; railways; roads
Sackville Street (O'Connell Street), Dublin xvi, 5, 8–10, 12, 14–15, 18–19, 29, 31, 143–4
Santry, Dublin 14
Scramogue, County Roscommon 62–3
sexual violence 93
Shannon, Bishop 115–16
Sheehy-Skeffington, Francis 10, 16
Shelbourne Hotel, Dublin 8
Sherwood Foresters 7
shops 2, 5, 8, 10–11, 29, 37, 39–40 *see also* looting
    attacks on xv, 31, 86, 89–91, 97, 100, 102–3, 120–1
Shortt, Edward 37
Simon, Sir John 125
Sims, Rear Admiral William 126–7
Sinn Féin 3–4, 30, 32–3, 40, 55, 64, 85, 88, 114, 119, 124–7, 136–8, 140, 147
Sinn Féin hall, Tullamore 1–2
Sinn Féin Rebellion Handbook 11
Skerries, County Dublin 121
Skibbereen, County Cork 44
Skibbereen Eagle 62
Slaugher, Captain 20
Sligo, County 64, 71–2, 88
Sligo Corporation 58
Smyth, Lieutenant-Colonel Gerald 92
Smyth & Co., Balbriggan 101
Society of Friends 116, 120–1
Soloheadbeg, County Tipperary 38
South Dublin Union 7
special juries 33
Spectator 104
Sperling's Journal 99
Spillane, Tim 141
Stanley, Joseph 137

175

statues *see* monuments
Stephens, James 11, 13, 113
Store Street Police Station, Dublin 17
Strabane Chronicle 16
Strickland, Major-General Peter 63, 104
strikes *see* industrial action
Stuard, Head-Constable 1
Sunday Independent 29
Svět 127
Swindlehurst, J.P. 118–19
Sydenham's chorea (St Vitus' dance) 97

tanks 58–9, 96, 118–19
Tara Street, Dublin 11
tax offices 65–7, 70
Taylor, John 92
Teeling, Bartholomew 34
Templehouse, County Sligo 64
Templemore, County Tipperary 121
Temps, Le 125
Tennant, John Harold 62
Tèry, Simone 122
Thurles, County Tipperary 90, 117, 121
Tierney, Timothy 61–2
tillage 136, 146–7
Tilly, Charles 137
Tipperary, County 38, 60, 71, 102
Tipperary town 98
Tobin, Michael 40
Tobin, William 32
Tounafulla, County Limerick 65
Townshend, Charles 3–4, 70, 87
trade unions 33
Tralee, County Kerry 34, 68, 91, 102
trauma 92–7
Traynor, Oscar 5, 10, 15
Treasury 60–1
Treaty of Rapallo 124
tree-felling xiv–xv, xvii, 53–5, 58–63, 68–71, 135, 141, 145–6
Trench, Frederick Oliver (Lord Ashtown) 141
trenches xiv–xv, xvii, 6–7, 36, 53–4, 58–62, 68, 70–1, 74, 119, 135, 145–6
tri-colours *see also* flags 30–1
Trim, County Meath 60, 121
Trinity College, Dublin 8, 12
Truth 147
Tuam, County Galway 44, 91, 99, 115, 117

Tubbercurry, County Sligo 102, 121
Tullamore, County Offaly 1–2
Tullow, County Carlow 99
Tyrone, County 31, 64, 71, 136

Ulster 36, 70, 72
unemployment 20, 34, 85, 100–1, 103
United Irish League 136
University College Dublin 38
University College Cork (UCC) 38–9

vandalism 9, 29–31, 34–5, 70, 92, 144
victim narrative xvii, 94, 112–28, 152
von Bissing, General Moritz 115, 118

Wallace, Nora 74
Walsh, Dr (Oranmore) 91
Walsh, J.J. 32
War of Independence xvii, 35–44, 53–75, 113
Truce 97
War Office 57, 61, 87
Ward, Margaret 95
Waterford, County 71
Waterford City 32
weather 72–4
Weekly Summary 87
'Wesleyan raid' 62–3
Westmeath, County 71
Westmeath Independent 144
Wexford, County 64, 71, 136
Whelan, Paddy 17
Whelan, Yvonne 34
Wicklow, County 71
Wilkinson, Ellen 93, 120
Wilkinson, Ellen C. 101
Willis, G. de L. 98
Wilson, Sir Henry 143
Wilson, Woodrow 127
Wimbourne, Lord 8, 11, 33
Women's International League 93, 120
Women's National Health Association of Ireland 18
Wood-Renton Commission 101
Wrafter, Joe 1
Wyndham Land Act (1903) 136, 141

Youghal, County Cork 34, 41
Young, Arthur 56